AGENCY AND PARTNERSHIP

Examples and Explanations

AGENCY AND PARTNERSHIP

Examples and Explanations

Daniel S. Kleinberger

Professor of Law
William Mitchell College of Law

Library of Congress Catalog Card No. 94-77904

ISBN 0-316-49854-8

Fourth Printing

MV-NY

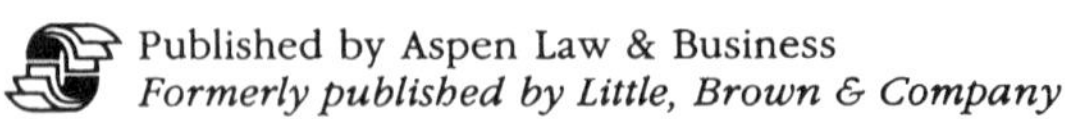

Published by Aspen Law & Business
Formerly published by Little, Brown & Company

Printed in the United States of America

to Carrie, without whom there would be no book
nor anything else worthwhile
and
to Rachael and Sammy, who are my wealth

Summary of Contents

Contents

Preface

Nine years ago, when I left the full-time practice of law to teach and write, I knew little of agency and partnership law. My practice had centered on commercial law. My law school "Business Units" course dealt primarily with corporate and securities law, with agency and partnership law receiving fleeting, if any, mention.

As I have taught and re-taught agency and partnership law, I have developed an affection for both subjects. The affection has two sources: the practical import of each topic and the analytic lessons inherent in their conceptual structure. As a practical matter, agency law questions are everywhere in the law. Personal injury lawyers cannot do without the doctrine of respondeat superior. Commercial lawyers must understand concepts of agency authority and the power to bind. Employment lawyers owe some of their fundamental constructs to the notion of the servant.

Partnership law issues are perhaps less ubiquitous but nonetheless important. Thousands of businesses are organized as partnerships, and the newest forms of business organization — limited liability companies and limited liability partnerships — owe much or most of their structure to the law of partnerships.

The conceptual lure of agency and partnership law involves their ability to teach part of what is loosely called "thinking like a lawyer." I cannot define that phrase completely, but I know that it includes a process I call "categories and consequences" — that is, analyzing situations by defining categories of behavior and then attaching consequences to those categories. This is not the only way in which lawyers understand the world, but it is certainly a fundamental one. Agency law is a superb way to learn about categories and consequences. Indeed, the analytic training that comes with understanding agency law's approach to issues rivals the analytic training available in confronting the Rule Against Perpetuities. Fortunately, mastering agency law is far less traumatic.

The analytic benefits of studying partnership law come both from the categories and consequences approach and from developing familiarity with the concept and role of "default rules." Studying partnership law also helps one distinguish between issues within an organization and issues between an organization and third parties.

I believe you will find this book useful whether you are taking a course that provides substantial coverage of agency and partnership law or one that gives — as mine did — only cursory treatment to these topics. Depending on your circumstances, you can use this book to confirm your understanding of the fundamental concepts discussed in class and to clarify some of the more difficult issues raised by class discussion and your other readings, or to help you walk through both the basic concepts and the sophisticated aspects on your own. In any event, you will find here a plethora of examples — some simple, some complex — to illustrate both elementary and esoteric points of law. The more than 100 Problems will develop and test your ability to use legal principles the way lawyers do: to answer practical questions and solve clients' problems.

I solicit your help in preparing the next edition. If you have suggestions for improvements (including different solutions to the Problems or additional topics to be covered), I invite you to contact me.

For her help in researching this edition, I am grateful to Carolyn C. Sachs, Esq. Materials obtained from the *Uniform Laws Annotated* are reprinted with the permission of West Publishing Company. Materials from the Restatement (Second) of Agency are copyright © 1958 by The American Law Institute, and reprinted with the permission of The American Law Institute.

December 1994 *Daniel S. Kleinberger*

Introduction

The structure of legal rules. Agency law, like many other areas of law, does much of its analysis by applying labels to facts.

> ***Example:*** A multinational corporation lends millions of dollars to a local grain and seed company and tells that company how to run its business. The local company becomes insolvent, owing substantial debts to local farmers. The farmers try to recover from the multinational corporation. Whether they can do so depends on whether they can label the local company as the "agent" of the corporation.

> ***Example:*** A national franchisor requires its local franchisees to follow a thick volume of operating regulations. A customer slips and falls while on the franchise's premises and attempts to recover from the national franchisor. Whether the customer can do so depends on whether the customer can label the franchisee as the "servant" of the franchisor.

The link between categories and consequences controls the structure of legal rules. Every legal rule can be stated as an IF/THEN proposition, with the IF component stating the elements and the THEN component stating the consequences.

IF: the facts of situation meet specified elements (i.e, if the situation fits a particular category)

THEN: specified consequences result

For example:

IF:
- a party makes an assertion of fact concerning a proposed transaction,
- another party justifiably relies on that assertion and is thereby induced to make a contract with the asserting party, and
- the assertion is:
  - — inaccurate
  - — material, and
  - — fraudulent

THEN: the misled party may rescind the contract

Those who are more graphically inclined can think of each legal rule as a box. On top, the box has a name of a legal category, for example, "fraudulent inducement." The front panel of the box contains the "entrance criteria" — the elements that must be satisfied to qualify a situation to fit into the box. The right side panel contains the legal consequences created by the rule. If a situation fits "in the box," the consequences follow.[1] Figure 1 illustrates this approach.

In all events, you should keep in mind the link between labeling (categorization) and consequences. By doing so, you will synchronize your way of thinking with the way the law of agency approaches its subject matter.

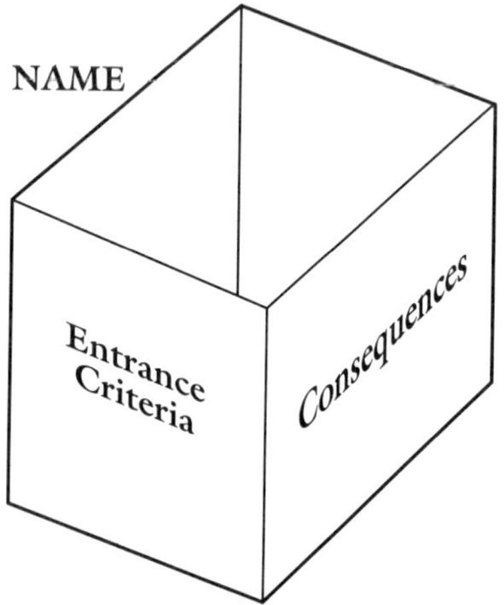

Name of the box (i.e., the legal category)
- fraud in the inducement

Entrance criteria (i.e., elements of the rule)
- a party makes an assertion of fact concerning a proposed transaction
- another party justifiably relies on that assertion and is thereby induced to make a contract with the asserting party
- the assertion is inaccurate, material, and fraudulent

Consequences
- defrauded party may rescind contract

1. Perhaps this metaphor helps explain why lawyers are often accused of trying to pigeonhole everything and everybody.

Legal analysis for preventative lawyering. Some of the questions in this book ask you to think proactively — that is, to consider a client's situation and goals, to identify potential legal problems, and to suggest a course of conduct that will prevent the problems from materializing. You may initially find these questions disconcerting, since law school analysis often operates from a post hoc, litigation perspective. That is, you consider a dispute that has already materialized, analyze each party's prospects, and predict the outcome of the dispute.

You may find the following protocol helpful in thinking preventatively:

1. Review the facts (e.g., the client's current situation and proposed conduct) and identify legal rules whose application might produce unpleasant consequences for the client.
2. For each such rule, identify the facts that are key to:
   a. making the rule applicable, and
   b. causing the rule to produce an unpleasant outcome for the client.
3. For each such fact, try to imagine a change that will make the problematic rule inapplicable or avoid the problematic outcome, but will not frustrate the client's goals.

Special Notice

Unless otherwise indicated, all references to the Restatement are to the Restatement (Second) of Agency (1958), promulgated by the American Law Institute.[2]

Unless otherwise indicated, "person" means "legal person" and includes not only human beings but also organizations, such as corporations and partnerships.

2. The American Law Institute is a private, nonprofit organization whose members are distinguished lawyers, judges, and law professors. The Institute has published a number of Restatements, each of which attempts to state and explain the law in a particular field. Each Restatement contains a large number of "black letter" propositions, accompanied by explanatory comments and illustrations. Adopted in 1958, the Restatement (Second) of Agency has been and continues to be very influential in courts throughout the United States.

AGENCY AND PARTNERSHIP

Examples and Explanations

PART ONE

Agency

1

Introductory Concepts in the Law of Agency

§1.1 The Agency Relationship Defined and Exemplified; Its Players Identified

Agency is the label the law applies to a relationship in which:

- by mutual consent (formal or informal, express or implied)
- one person or entity (called the "agent")
- undertakes to act on behalf of another person or entity (called the "principal"),
- subject to the principal's control.

Agency relationships are everywhere in the commercial world and in noncommercial realms as well. Whenever a person or organization seeks to act through the efforts of others, the legal concept of agency likely applies. For example:

- A law student, rushing to prepare for graduation and the fabulous buffet party to follow, gives a friend a list of last-minute additions to the menu and asks her to "make sure the caterer includes these on the buffet." The friend agrees and becomes the student's agent.
- Miles Standish, seeking to court "the damsel Priscilla," entreats his friend, John Alden, to communicate to Priscilla the depth and direc-

tion of Standish's feelings toward her. Alden agrees and becomes Standish's agent.[1]

- A corporate shareholder, who is unable to attend the corporation's annual meeting, signs a "proxy" that authorizes another individual to cast the shareholder's votes at the meeting. By accepting the appointment, the proxy holder becomes the shareholder's agent.
- A landowner, preparing to leave for an around-the-world tour and wishing to sell Greenacres as soon as possible, gives a real estate broker a "power of attorney." This credential authorizes the broker to sell Greenacres on the owner's behalf and to sign all documents necessary to form a binding contract and to close the deal. The broker is the owner's agent.
- A supermarket chain that is about to purchase fancy new computerized cash registers retains a consultant to advise on what type of registers to buy and to arrange the purchase of the new machines on the chain's behalf. The consultant will act as the chain's agent.
- A bank, understanding that not all customers like dealing with ATM machines, hires tellers to handle customer deposits, withdrawals, and similar transactions. The tellers are agents of the bank.

In each of these situations someone (the *principal*) has asked someone else (the *agent*) to provide services or accomplish some task on behalf of the principal and subject to the principal's control. In each situation the agent has agreed to do so. To each situation, the label of "agency" applies.[2]

The agency relationship may at first appear to involve only the principal and the agent. But principals often use agents to deal with others, so third parties figure prominently in the law of agency. Each of these players can be individual human beings or organizations, such as corporations, not-for-profit corporations, and partnerships.[3]

---

1. Henry Wadsworth Longfellow, "The Courtship of Miles Standish," in Hiawatha, the Courtship of Miles Standish, and Other Poems (Oxford U. Press 1925).

2. The law of agency also applies when a party merely appears to be authorized to act for another. Chapter Two discusses the law of "apparent authority."

3. Agency law also subdivides the categories of principal and agent. In some circumstances, consequences vary depending on whether a principal is *disclosed*, *partially disclosed*, or *undisclosed*. See sections 2.2.2 (defining these terms), 2.2.4 (discussing contract claims and undisclosed principals), 2.3.3 (explaining why apparent authority is generally inapplicable to undisclosed and partially disclosed principals). Likewise, in some circumstances it matters whether an agent is a *general* or *special* agent. See section 2.5.2. In other circumstances it matters whether an agent is a *servant* agent or an *independent contractor*. See section 3.2.4.

§1.2 Creation of the Agency Relationship

§1.2.1 *The Restatement's View of Creation*

The first section of the Restatement describes the creation of an agency relationship as follows:

> Agency is the fiduciary relation which results from the manifestation of consent by one person [the principal] to another [the agent] that the other [the agent] shall act on his[4] [the principal's] behalf and subject to his [the principal's] control, and consent by the other [the agent] so to act.[5]

Several aspects of this description warrant special attention. Some relate to elements necessary to create an agency relationship. Others relate to the consequences that follow from the creation.

§1.2.2 *Manifestation of Consent*

The creation of an agency relationship necessarily involves two steps: manifestation by the principal and consent by the agent. The manifestation by or attributable to the principal[6] must somehow reach the agent; otherwise the agent has nothing to consent to. When the agent then manifests consent, an agency exists — even though the principal may initially be unaware of the manifestation.

> ***Example:*** Rushing to meet a publishing deadline, a law professor says to her student research assistant, "Please go to the corner and buy me an extra large coffee." The student says, "Sure," and an agency relationship comes into being. The principal has made a manifestation directly to the agent, and the agent has consented directly to the principal.

> ***Example:*** As the research assistant is leaving the law professor adds, "Do you know anyone who is good at authority checking?" The assistant answers, "Martha's great at that stuff." The professor says, "If you see her, ask her if she will authority check this chapter within the next

---

4. Like most legal writing of its era, the Restatement uses the masculine pronoun to include males and females, as well as genderless entities. This book strives for a gender-neutral or gender-balanced approach to pronouns but preserves the original usage in all quoted materials.

5. Restatement §1.

6. A manifestation can be "attributable to the principal" under the doctrines of agency law. See Chapter Two.

couple of days." Later the assistant sees Martha and communicates the message. Martha then telephones the professor and says "Yes." An agency relationship exists. Even though the principal did not communicate the manifestation directly, the manifestation reached the agent. The agent directly communicated consent.

Example: For a long time Martha has wanted to help the professor. In class one day a question arises, and the professor says, "I'll have to look into that." After class Martha decides to research the question for the professor. Unbeknownst to Martha, the professor has decided to ask Martha's help and has left a message to that effect on Martha's answering machine. No agency relationship exists. The professor has made a manifestation, but Martha is unaware of it. Martha's conduct, therefore, cannot be seen as consent.

§1.2.3 Objective Standard for Determining Consent

To determine whether a would-be principal and would-be agent have consented, the law looks not to their inner, subjective thoughts but rather to their outward manifestations.[7] Has the would-be principal done or said something that the would-be agent reasonably interpreted as consent that the would-be agent act for the would-be principal? Has the would-be agent done or said something that, reasonably interpreted, indicates agreement to act?

Typically it is the parties' words that evidence their reciprocal consents. However, given the law's objective standard, a party's conduct can also evidence consent. For example, an agent can manifest consent by beginning the requested task:

Example: Rachael, the owner of Blackacre, writes to Sammy: "Please act as my broker to sell Blackacre." Sammy puts a "For Sale" sign on Blackacre. By beginning the requested task Sammy has given the necessary manifestation of consent. An agency relationship exists.

The objective standard also means that, in the eyes of the law, two parties can be agent and principal even though one of them had no subjective desire to create the legal relationship. If, for instance, a person says something that someone else reasonably *mis*interprets as a request for services, an agency relationship may result.

Example: Frustrated by the recalcitrance of Thomas Becket, the Archbishop of Canterbury, Henry II of England exclaims, "Will nobody rid me of this troublesome cleric?" Four of Henry's barons overhear the

7. In this respect, agency law follows the modern approach to contract formation.

remark and proceed to kill Becket. Although Henry later protests that he never intended for anyone to kill the Archbishop, the barons nonetheless acted as his agents. In these circumstances Henry's outward manifestation, reasonably interpreted, indicated consent. Even assuming that Henry's protest is genuine, his subjective intent is irrelevant.

§1.2.4 *Consent to the Business or Interpersonal Relationship, Not to the Legal Label*

Agency is a legal concept — a label the law attaches to a category of business and interpersonal relationships. If two parties manifest consent to the type of business or interpersonal relationship the law labels "agency," then an agency relationship exists. The legal concept applies and the label attaches *regardless of whether the parties had the legal concept in mind and regardless of whether the parties contemplated the consequences of having the label apply.*

Sometimes when parties form a relationship they expressly claim or disclaim the agency label. For instance, franchise agreements[8] often include a statement to the effect that "This agreement does not create an agency relationship" or that "The franchisee is not for any purposes the agent of the franchisor." Courts do consider such statements when trying to determine just what relationship the parties actually established. However, the parties' self-selected label is never dispositive and is relevant only as a window on the underlying reality. For example, a disclaimer of agency status may help show that neither party consented to act on the other's behalf and subject to the other's control. However, if the actual relationship between two parties evidences the elements necessary to establish agency, then all the disclaimers in the world will not deflect the agency label. To a paraphrase a former President of the United States, "You can hang a sign on a pig and call it a horse, but it's still a pig."[9]

§1.2.5 *Agency Consensual, But Not Contractual; Gratuitous Agents*

Agency is not a subcategory of contract law; not all consensual relationships belong to the law of contracts. Although agents and principals often super-

8. In a franchise agreement, one business ("the franchisor") authorizes another business ("the franchisee") to use the franchisor's name and trademark and to sell either a product produced by the franchisor or an array of services developed by the franchisor. In return, the franchisee typically pays an initial franchise fee plus an ongoing royalty, commission, or service fee. Franchise agreements typically obligate franchisees to operate their business in compliance with requirements set by the franchisor. These requirements can be quite detailed and comprehensive.

9. Bush Urges Racial Harmony, Attacks "Quota Bill," N.Y. Times, June 2, 1991, at A32 (George Bush objecting to certain aspects of the 1991 Civil Rights bill) ("You can't put a sign on a pig and say it's a horse.")

impose contracts on their agency relationship,[10] the agency relationship itself is not a contract.

Therefore, since the doctrine of consideration belongs exclusively to the law of contracts, an agency relationship can exist even though the principal provides no consideration to the agent. Agents who act without receiving any consideration are *gratuitous agents*. In most respects the rights and powers of gratuitous agents are identical to those of paid agents. The major exceptions concern the right of the parties to terminate the agency[11] and the standard of care applicable to the agent.[12]

§1.2.6 Formalities Not Ordinarily Necessary to Create an Agency

An agency relationship can exist even though the parties never express their reciprocal consents in any formal fashion. There is ordinarily no requirement that the parties consent in writing. Indeed, as section 1.2.3 indicates, conduct alone can suffice; words themselves are not necessary.

There are some limitations on the informality. In some jurisdictions the "equal dignities" rule applies. Under that rule, if a transaction must be in writing in order to be enforceable, then an agent can bind a principal to that transaction only if the agency relationship is documented in a writing signed by the principal. For example, Cal. Civ. Code §2309 states: "An oral authorization is sufficient for any purpose, except that an authority to enter into a contract required by law to be in writing can only be given by an instrument in writing." Similarly, Ga. Code Ann. §10-6-2 states: "Where the exercise or performance of an agency is by written instrument, the agency shall also be created by written instrument."

§1.2.7 Consent and Control

To create an agency, the reciprocal consents of principal and agent must include an understanding that the principal is in control of the relationship. "Since the whole purpose of the relation of agency is that the agent shall carry out the will of the principal,"[13] agency cannot exist unless the "acting for" party (the agent) consents to be subject to the will of the "acted for" party (the principal). The control need not be total or continuous and need not extend to the way the agent physically performs, but there must be some sense that the principal is "in charge." At minimum, the principal must have the right to control the goal of the relationship.

---

10. See sections 1.3, 4.1.6, and 4.3.3.
11. See section 5.2.3.
12. See section 4.1.4.
13. Restatement, chapter 5, topic 1, Introductory Note.

Often the manifestations creating a relationship do not expressly address the issue of control. If the issue is in question, courts will examine how the relationship actually operated in order to decide whether the "acting for" party consented to be controlled. The facts of the relationship may imply consent.

> ***Example:*** A hospital patient caught hepatitis from contaminated blood and sought to sue the blood supplier for breach of warranty. To succeed, the patient had to show that he was in privity with the blood supplier, but it appeared that the hospital, not the patient, had made the purchase from the supplier. The patient claimed he was nonetheless in privity, asserting that the hospital was acting as his agent when it obtained the blood. The court rejected the patient's claim, noting that there was no indication that the hospital was in any way subject to the patient's control.[14]

While this section treats "consent to control" as an element necessary to establish an agency relationship, issues of control also play major roles in at least three other parts of agency law. It is important to keep all four roles distinct from each other. The other three roles are:

1) *Control as a substitute method for establishing agency status.* When a creditor exercises extensive control over its debtor's business, that control can by itself establish an agency relationship. The law treats the debtor as the agent and the creditor as the principal. As a consequence, the creditor becomes liable for the debtor's debts to other creditors.[15]
2) *Control as an element of "servant" status.* Whether the principal has a right to control the physical performance of the agent's tasks determines whether the agent is a "servant" or "nonservant" agent. As discussed in Chapter Four, this distinction is crucial to determining the principal's liability for certain torts committed by the agent.
3) *Control as a consequence.* As a consequence of agency status (rather than as an element necessary to create that status), the principal has the power to control the agent. Even though the agent may have consented to give the principal only limited control, once the agency relationship comes into existence the principal has the power (though not necessarily the right) to control every detail of the agent's performance.[16]

---

14. *Krom v. Sharp and Dohme, Inc.,* 180 N.Y.S.2d 99 (1958).

15. See section 6.3 for an extensive discussion.

16. An understanding between the principal and the agent may limit the principal's *right* to exercise control. If a principal violates that understanding when exercising the *power* of control, the agent may sue for damages and may also terminate the agency relationship. See sections 4.1.3 and 4.1.6.

§1.2.8 *Consent to Serve the Principal's Interests.*

To create an agency relationship the agent must manifest consent to act *for* the principal; that is, the agent must manifest a recognition that serving the *principal's* interests is the primary purpose of the relationship. The facts of the relationship can and often do imply that recognition.

> ***Example:*** A law student, rushing to prepare for graduation and the fabulous buffet party to follow, gives a friend a list of last-minute additions to the menu and asks her or him to "do me a favor and make sure the caterer includes these on the buffet." The friend agrees. The friend has impliedly recognized that the endeavor's primary purpose is to meet the law student's needs, not to serve any separate agenda the friend may have.

§1.3 The Relationship of Agency and Contract

Although agency itself is not a contractual relationship, the parties to an agency can make contracts regarding their agency relationship. To take the most common example, the parties can agree that the principal will pay the agent for the agent's services. For further example, the parties can by agreement set a definite term to the relationship or limit the principal's right to control the agent with regard to matters connected with the agency.

> ***Example:*** A manufacturing company plans to build a large plant and retains a "construction management" firm to manage the project on behalf of the manufacturing company. The contract between the manufacturing company and the construction management firm states: "Using reasonable care, FIRM will select the various contractors to build the plant."

Contracts between agent and principal have limited impact. They can change the rights and duties that exist between agent and principal, but they cannot abrogate the powers that agency status confers on each party to the relationship. Thus, for example, despite any contract provisions to the contrary:

- the principal always has the power to control every detail of the agent's performance[17]
- the agent may have certain powers to bind the principal[18]

---

17. See sections 4.1.3 and 4.1.6.

18. For example, if the principal allows the agent to run the principal's business and to appear as the owner, the agent has the power to bind the principal "through transactions usual in such businesses . . . although contrary to the directions of the principal." Restatement §195. For further discussion, see section 2.5.2.

- both the principal and the agent have the power to end the agency at any time[19]

When an agent or principal exercises a power in breach of the other's contract right, the injured party can bring an action for damages. But the exercise of power cannot be undone or enjoined.

§1.4 Major Issues in the Law of Agency

By way of an overview, the major issues in the law of agency can be organized according to the relationship among agency's three players: principals, agents, and third parties.

§1.4.1 Between the Principal and the Agent

Under what circumstances does an agency relationship exist? As the Restatement explains, "agency is a legal concept which depends upon the existence of required factual elements."[20] Agency law is therefore fundamentally concerned with whether particular kinds of relationships qualify as agency relationships. For example, must both parties subjectively consent to the relationship? Must they intend to create the legal relationship? Must they even be aware that they are creating the legal relationship? Must the agent be promised contract-like consideration by the principal?[21]

What duties does the agent owe the principal? The principal relies on the agent to get things done. How perfect must the agent's performance be? In dealing with the principal, may the agent follow the rules for "arm's-length" transactions, such as might apply to the parties to an ordinary contract? In carrying out the tasks of the agency, must the agent think only of the principal's interests, or may the agent also consider its own interests as well?[22]

What duties does the principal owe the agent? Must the principal compensate the agent for the agent's efforts? If the agent somehow gets into trouble, must the principal help out the agent? Must the principal alert the agent to risks involved in the agent's task?[23]

---

19. See section 5.1.1.

20. Restatement §1, comment *b*.

21. See section 1.2.

22. See section 4.1.

23. See section 4.3.

§1.4.2 Between the Principal and Third Parties

If a third party has made a commitment to an agent, under what circumstances can the principal enforce that commitment? People and organizations use agents to get things done, and often the agent's task involves making arrangements with third parties on the principal's behalf. For example, you might use a friend to make last-minute arrangements with the caterer you have hired for your graduation party. A bank might use its tellers to accept deposits from customers and give in return a paper evidencing the bank's resulting indebtedness (i.e., a deposit slip).

When an agency relationship involves this "arrangement making" function, it is essential that the principal be able to enforce commitments that third parties have made to the agent. Otherwise, the agent could not accomplish much for the principal. For example, it would do you little good to send a friend to deal with the caterer for your graduation party if the caterer could later ignore those dealings and say, "But that doesn't count. We weren't dealing with you directly." The ability to bind third parties to the principal is thus an essential attribute of the agent's role, and questions about that attribute are therefore very important in the law of agency.[24]

If an agent makes a commitment to a third party, under what circumstances may the third party enforce that commitment against the principal? When an agency relationship involves the "arrangement making" function, it is essential that third parties be able to enforce against the principal commitments made by the agent. Otherwise agents could not accomplish much for principals; third parties would generally insist on "dealing direct."

Imagine, for example, that you go to Alice's Service Station to have your car repaired. You leave the car with Bob, a mechanic who works for Alice. Bob works on your car but the work turns out to be defective. When you complain to Alice, she says, "It's not my problem. You didn't deal directly with me." Would you ever again be willing to deal with one of Alice's agents? Or would you insist on dealing only with Alice? The ability to bind the principal to third parties is thus an essential attribute of the agent's role, and questions about that attribute are therefore very important in the law of agency.[25]

If the agent possesses certain information, under what circumstances will the law treat the principal as if the principal possessed that information? In many situations the law cares whether and when a party has particular kinds of information. Since principals often act through agents,

---

24. Chapter Two deals with such questions.

25. For a discussion of such questions, see Chapter Two.

the law of agency must decide when to hold the principal responsible for information possessed by the agent.

For example, Sammy sells Blackacre to Rachael, innocently assuring her that Blackacre contains no toxic waste. Sammy uses an agent to consummate the sale, and Sammy's agent knows that a former owner of Blackacre buried loads of noxious chemicals on the land. The agent does not disclose this information either to Sammy or to Rachael. In Rachael's subsequent fraud suit against Sammy, will the law attribute to Sammy the knowledge possessed by his agent?[26]

If the agent conveys certain information, under what circumstances will the law treat the principal as if the principal had conveyed that information? In many situations the law cares whether and when a party communicates particular kinds of information. As with information *possessed* by an agent, the law of agency must decide when to hold the principal responsible for information *conveyed* by the agent.

For example, Sammy uses an agent to sell Blackacre to Rachael. Without Sammy's knowledge or consent the agent tells Rachael that Blackacre contains a lake "full of delicious trout." In fact, the lake contains nothing larger than minnows and the agent knows it. Will the law attribute the agent's intentional misrepresentation to Sammy?[27]

If an agent's act or omissions cause tort injuries to a third party, under what circumstances can the third party proceed directly against the principal? When an agent commits a tort, the injured party can of course proceed against the agent. The third party may, however, wish to pursue the principal. (For instance, the principal may have a deeper pocket or may make a less sympathetic defendant.) The law of agency must therefore determine under what circumstances a principal is liable for the tortious acts of its agent. For example, suppose the law student's friend, rushing to make last-minute arrangements with the caterer, drives negligently and runs over a dog. May the dog's owner recover damages from the law student? Or suppose the consultant who is being used by the supermarket chain to recommend new cash registers disparages a particular brand of register. May the company that sells the disparaged brand sue the supermarket chain?[28]

26. See sections 2.2.4 and 2.3.8.

27. Id.

28. For a discussion of these questions, see Chapter Three.

§1.4.3 Between the Agent and Third Parties

When an agent arranges a commitment between the principal and a third party, under what circumstances may the third party hold the agent responsible for the commitment? This question is of great importance to both the agent and the third party. From the agent's perspective, the risks differ greatly as between merely arranging a contract for the principal and being personally liable for that contract's performance. From the perspective of the third party, it may well have been the reputation of the agent, not the principal, that induced the third party to make the commitment in the first place.[29]

29. See section 4.2.

2

Binding Principals to Third Parties in Contract and Through Communications

§2.1 "Binding the Principal"

§2.1.1 *The Importance and Meaning of "Binding the Principal"*

Perhaps the most important consequence of the agency label is the agent's power to bind the principal to third parties and to bind third parties to the principal. The Restatement defines *power* as "the ability . . . to produce a change in a given legal relation (between the principal and third parties) by doing or not doing a given act,"[1] and, as explained previously, an agent's power to bind is central to an agent's ability to accomplish tasks on the principal's behalf.[2]

The concept of agency power is essentially a concept of attribution. To

1. Restatement §6.
2. See section 1.4.2.

the extent an agent has the power to bind, the agent's conduct is attributed to the principal. In the words of a venerable agency law maxim, *Qui facit per alium facit per se.*[3] Thus, when a third party asserts that an agent's act or omission has "bound the principal," the third party wants the principal treated legally as if the principal itself had acted or failed to act. Although the attribution rules differ depending on whether the underlying matter sounds in contract, sounds in tort, or concerns the communication of information, the concept of attribution is ubiquitous.

> ***Example:*** George, acting as agent for the Bronx Zoo, contracts with Martha, a "bring 'em back alive" hunter of wildlife, to procure a hippopotamus for exhibition at the Zoo. Later, Martha seeks to hold the Zoo to the contract, asserting that in making the contract George bound the Zoo. Martha wants the Zoo treated as if the Zoo itself had made the contract.

> ***Example:*** A discount warehouse in Iowa contracts with a railroad to transport 150 tractors from Newark, New Jersey to the railroad's terminal in Iowa City. The contract between the warehouse and the railroad specifies that the warehouse must pick up the tractors "within three days after receiving notice of their arrival at the Iowa City terminal, and WAREHOUSE shall pay storage fees at a rate of $500 per day for any delay in pick up." The railroad sends notice of arrival by telephoning the loading dock at the warehouse after normal business hours and speaking to a janitor. The janitor fails to inform the warehouse, the warehouse fails to make a timely pick up, and the railroad claims storage fees. In assessing the storage fees, the railroad wants the warehouse treated as if the warehouse itself had received the notice.

> ***Example:*** Sammy sells Blackacre to Rachael, innocently assuring her that Blackacre contains no toxic waste. Sammy uses an agent to consummate the sale, and Sammy's agent knows that a former owner of Blackacre buried loads of noxious chemicals on the land. The agent does not disclose this information either to Sammy or to Rachael. In Rachael's subsequent fraud suit against Sammy, Rachael wants Sammy treated as if he directly possessed and suppressed the information about the noxious chemicals.

> ***Example:*** Walking into class, a law student slips, falls, and injures herself. The law school's maintenance crew had negligently overwaxed

3. This maxim translates as "Who acts through another acts himself." Black's Law Dictionary 1249 (1990).

the floor. In her suit against the law school, the student seeks to legally attribute the crew's negligence to the school, that is, to have the school treated as if the school itself had been negligent.

Attribution can also work in favor of the principal, as when a principal seeks to hold a third party to a contract entered into by an agent or to information received or communicated by an agent.

Example: An art dealer's employee attends an auction on the dealer's behalf and makes the winning bid on a painting. Later the dealer tenders payment and seeks to compel the auction house to deliver the painting. The dealer seeks to be treated as if it itself had made the winning bid.

Example: A residential lease allows either party to terminate on 60 days' notice. The landlord's resident manager gives the proper 60-day notice to a tenant, but the tenant fails to vacate the apartment. In the subsequent eviction action, the landlord wishes to be treated as if it itself had given the requisite notice.

§2.1.2 "Binding the Principal" and Questions of Agency Power

Agency law uses its concept of power to analyze "binding the principal" questions. The question of "Under the law of agency did *X*'s act or omission bind *Y*?" thus becomes "Under the law of agency, did *X* have the power to bind *Y* through that act or omission?" Agency law approaches questions of power through five subcategories. An agent can have the power to bind a principal through:

(i) actual authority (including express and implied actual authority),
(ii) apparent authority,
(iii) estoppel,
(iv) inherent power, and
(v) ratification.

More than one subcategory of agency power may apply in any particular situation. If at least one subcategory applies, then the agent's conduct will bind the principal.

Given appropriate facts, each of the subcategories of power can apply to bind a principal in contract. We will consider each subcategory in turn. Most of the subcategories are also relevant with regard to information possessed or communicated by an agent, such as representations made by an agent on behalf of a principal and notices received by an agent on behalf of a principal. This chapter also considers those matters. With regard to a principal's liability for an agent's torts,[4] the chief subcategory is *inherent power*. *Apparent authority* is also relevant occasionally. Chapter Three considers the attribution rules relevant to tort claims.

§2.1.3 *Distinguishing the* Power *to Bind from the* Right *to Bind*

As will be discussed throughout this chapter and the next, various circumstances can *empower* an agent to bind the principal. An agent has the *right* to bind the principal only to the extent that the principal has authorized the agent to do so. A principal gives this authorization in the same way (and often at the same time) that the principal initiates the agency relationship — namely, by making a manifestation that reaches the agent.[5]

To the extent an agent has the right to bind a principal, the agent automatically has the power to do so. It is possible, however, for an agent to have the *power* to bind while lacking the *right*. In such circumstances, if the agent exercises the power and binds the principal, the agent wrongs the principal. Then, consistent with the right/power distinction:

- the agent is liable to the principal for the wrongful conduct, but
- the principal is nonetheless bound to the third party.

> ***Example:*** Alice, the owner of Alice's Service Station, promotes Bob to the position of general manager and puts him in charge of the Station's day-to-day operations. Although service station managers ordinarily place orders for batteries, tires, and other accessories, Alice instructs Bob to leave that ordering to her. Nonetheless, Bob orders batteries. Under the doctrine of inherent agency power,[6] Alice is bound, even though Bob had no right (vis-à-vis Alice, his principal) to place the order.

§2.2 Actual Authority

§2.2.1 *Actual Authority and the Agent's Authorized Power to Bind*

For an agency relationship to come into existence, the principal must manifest consent to have the agent act on the principal's behalf with respect to some

4. This subcategory overlaps information the agent has conveyed to others.

5. The Restatement and many cases call this *authorized* power "actual authority." For a detailed discussion of actual authority, see section 2.2.

6. See section 2.5.2.

task or goal. Therefore, at the core of any agency relationship is a zone of endeavor as to which the principal has authorized the agent to act. The principal's authorization creates "actual authority" in the agent; an agent has the power to bind the principal through any act or omission within the agent's actual authority. Authorized acts can include not only the making of agreements and the doing of tasks but also the receipt, possession, and communication of information.

§2.2.2 *Creation of Actual Authority*

Mechanics. Paralleling the creation of the agency relationship itself, creation of actual authority involves:

- an objective manifestation by the principal
- followed by the agent's reasonable interpretation of that manifestation
- which leads the agent to believe that it is authorized to act for the principal.

In the words of §26 of the Restatement:

> authority to do an act can be created by written or spoken words or other conduct of the principal which, reasonably interpreted, causes the agent to believe that the principal desires him so to act on the principal's account.

Example: Two traveling salespeople, Bernice and Joe, are in the hotel bar. As Joe gets up to get another bowl of pretzels, Bernice says, "It's Happy Hour. While you're up, order another round of drinks for us and charge them to me." Joe orders the round and charges the price to Bernice's room. In doing so, Joe has acted within his actual authority. Bernice's statement constituted the necessary manifestation and Joe's action reflects his interpretation of that manifestation — that is, that Bernice (the principal) "desires him so to act on the principal's account." In the circumstances, Joe's interpretation is certainly reasonable.

Example: Same situation as above, except that when Joe gets to the bar he discovers that "Happy Hour" has ended and that prices have gone up. From the bar he conveys that information back to Bernice, who responds by waving her hand in a forward motion. When Joe charges the drinks to Bernice's room, he is again acting within his actual authority. By checking he has reinforced the reasonableness of his interpretation.

Source and nature of principal's manifestation. A principal's manifestation can reach the agent directly or indirectly and, in some circumstances, can consist of inaction. Most often the principal will communicate directly with the agent, but a manifestation that reaches the agent through intermediaries can still give rise to actual authority. The principal's inaction can constitute a manifestation when silence, reasonably interpreted, indicates consent. For example, when an agent takes particular action, the action comes to attention of the principal, and the principal makes no objection, the agent may well have actual authority to repeat the action in similar circumstances.

> ***Example:*** For years the mechanics at Sally's Service Station have, on an ad hoc basis, offered a 10 percent discount to regular customers on major service jobs. Sally, the owner, never explicitly authorized the practice, but she has been aware of it and has not previously objected to it. As a result of Sally's silent acquiescence, the mechanics have actual authority to offer the discount. The acquiescence satisfies the "manifestation" requirement.

Necessity, source, and nature of agent's belief. For an agent to have authority to do a particular act, the agent must believe that authority exists, that belief must be based on some manifestation from the principal, and that belief must be reasonable. In the words of the Restatement, §33:

> An agent is authorized to do, and to do only, what it is reasonable for him to infer that the principal desires him to do in the light of the principal's manifestations and the facts as he [i.e., the agent] knows or should know them at the time he acts.

Agency law determines the reasonableness of the agent's interpretation by considering the same sorts of information that figure into determinations of reasonableness in other areas of law. "All other matters throwing light upon what a reasonable person in the position of the agent at the time of acting would consider are to be given due weight."[7]

---

7. Restatement §34, comment *a*. The text of §34 provides the following non-exhaustive list of factors that figure into determining the reasonableness of the agent's interpretation:

> (a) the situation of the parties, their relations to one another, and the business in which they are engaged;
> (b) the general usages of business, the usages of trades or employments of the kind to which the authorization [i.e., the principal's manifestation] relates, and the business methods of the principal;
> (c) facts of which the agent has notice respecting the objects which the principal desires to accomplish;
> (d) the nature of the subject matter, the circumstances under which the act is to be performed and the legality or illegality of the act; and
> (e) the formality or informality, and the care, or lack of it, with which an instrument evidencing the authority is drawn.

The Restatement's reference to "reasonable person" reflects an objective standard. In determining the scope of an agent's actual authority what matters is the principal's objective manifestation and the agent's reasonable interpretation of that manifestation. Any secret, subjective intent of the principal is irrelevant.[8]

Principal's control of agent's interpretation. A principal can always cut back or countermand previously granted authority simply by making a manifestation to the agent and seeing that the manifestation reaches the agent. If it comes to the agent's attention that the principal desires to take away some or all of the agent's authority, the agent can no longer reasonably believe that it has the authority the principal desires to take away.

> ***Example:*** Sally, the owner of Sally's Service Station, decides that she can no longer afford the 10 percent discount. She calls the mechanics together and says, "Effective right now, no more 10 percent discounts." The next day, one of the mechanics, momentarily forgetting Sally's instruction, offers the discount to a customer. In doing so, the mechanic has acted without actual authority. After Sally's instruction, the mechanic cannot *reasonably* believe himself authorized to give 10 percent discounts.

In cutting back or countermanding previously granted authority the principal may be breaching a contract between the principal or agent.[9] The principal may also be leaving intact the agent's inherent power to bind the principal or an enforceable appearance of authority, or both.[10]

Irrelevance of third party knowledge. The mechanics for creating actual authority involve the principal and the agent and have nothing to do with what third parties may or may not happen to know. As a result, in determining the existence and extent of an agent's actual authority, the law focuses on the relationship between the principal and the agent (the inter se relationship). An agent can have actual authority (and therefore power to bind the principal to third parties) even though at the time of the relevant occurrence the third party neither knows nor has reason to know the extent of the agent's authority. Indeed, an agent can have actual authority even though at the time of the "binding" act or omission the principal is:

---

8. See section 1.2.3.
9. See sections 1.3, 4.1.3, and 4.1.6.
10. See sections 2.5.2 (inherent power) and 2.3 (apparent authority).

- only *partially disclosed* (i.e., the third party knows or has reason to know that the agent is acting for another, but not who that other is);[11] or even
- totally *undisclosed* (i.e., the third party does not know or have reason to know that the agent is acting as an agent).[12]

When a principal is undisclosed or partially disclosed, the third party will acquire evidence of the agent's actual authority only after the agent's exercise of that authority. Nonetheless, if the authority existed at the time of the transaction, the principal will be bound.

> ***Example:*** A power company authorizes a coal broker to buy coal for it. The broker contracts to buy the coal in its own name. When the coal seller later prepares to deliver the coal to the broker, the seller discovers that the broker has gone out of business. Then the seller discovers that the broker was making the purchase on the power company's behalf and had actual authority to do so. By asserting actual authority, the seller can hold the *undisclosed principal* (the power company) to the contract. Because actual authority is at issue, it is irrelevant that at the time of contracting the seller was ignorant of the agency relationship.

> ***Example:*** An attorney contacts an art dealer and contracts to buy a famous Picasso print. The attorney explains that she is acting for a client but declines to identify the client. (The client dislikes notoriety.) If the art dealer later learns the identity of the *partially disclosed* principal (the client) and can prove that the attorney acted with actual authority, then the art dealer can enforce the contract against the client.[13]

§2.2.3 Actual Authority: Express and Implied

In addition to the authority expressly indicated by the principal's words and other conduct, an agent may also have *implied* authority. Restatement §35

11. In such situations, the fact that there is a principal is disclosed (or at least reasonably knowable) but the identity of the principal is not. Disclosure is partial. Contrast a *fully disclosed* principal. For example, you bring your car into Alice's Service Station and talk to Alice's Manager, Bob, to arrange for an engine tune-up. You know that Bob is acting for another, and you know who that other is. The principal, Alice, is *fully disclosed*.

12. The third party cannot know or have reason to know who the principal is, since the third party does not even know or have reason to know that a principal exists. In limited circumstances a third party can escape claims made *by* an undisclosed principal. See section 2.2.4.

13. Whether a principal is disclosed, partially disclosed, or undisclosed matters substantially as to the agent's liability on a contract. See section 4.2.1.

states: "Unless otherwise agreed, authority to conduct a transaction includes authority to do acts which are incidental to it, usually accompany it, or are reasonably necessary to accomplish it." Comment *b* to §35 states the very simple rationale for this concept of implied authority. "In most cases the principal does not think of, far less specifically direct, the series of acts necessary to accomplish his objects." Implied actual authority fills in the gaps.

> ***Example:*** A company gave its plant manager express authority to purchase materials and supervise production of a product. Although the company expressed no instructions whatsoever concerning the handling of surplus raw materials, the manager had implied authority to act on the company's behalf and sell the surplus to a third party.

> ***Example:*** An insurance broker acted as local agent for an insurance company, with express authority to conduct business for the company in the locality. Although the insurance company had given no express instructions to the broker on how to handle cancellation notices received from policy holders, the broker had implied authority to receive such notices. Accordingly, notice to the broker was notice to the insurance company.

The express manifestations of the principal can always negate implied authority.

§2.2.4 *Consequences of Actual Authority*

Contracts. If an agent acting with actual authority makes a contract on behalf of a principal, then the principal is bound to the contract as if the principal had directly entered into the contract. In most circumstances, the third party is likewise bound on the contract to the principal.

Enforcing contract claims of undisclosed principals. The general rule's sole exception relates to contracts made by an agent on behalf of a totally undisclosed principal.

A third party can escape liability to an undisclosed principal only if either:

- the contract between the third party and the agent provides that it is inoperative if the agent is representing someone, or
- the agent fraudulently represents that the agent is not acting for the principal, the third party would not have entered into the contract

knowing the principal was a party, and the agent or undisclosed principal knows or should know that the third party would not have made the contract with the principal.

Active misrepresentation of the principal's role is insufficient. The third party must also show (i) that had the third party known of the principal's role, there would have been no contract and (ii) that the agent or principal had reason to know of the third party's aversion. Mere failure to disclose the principal's existence is always insufficient.

Example: A musician is selling his guitar. A fellow musician wishes to buy, but knows that on account of a longstanding feud the seller will refuse to sell the guitar to him. The would-be buyer therefore asks a friend to make the purchase. The seller asks the friend, "What are you going to do with this if I sell it to you? You're not going to give it to someone else are you?" The friend says, "No way. This is for me." The seller agrees to a deal, but learns the truth before turning over the guitar. The seller is not obligated to go through with the sale. The agent affirmatively misrepresented the principal's role, that misrepresentation induced the seller to make the contract, and both the agent and the principal knew that the seller would not have made a contract with the principal.

Example: A gay man, well-known as a gay rights advocate, seeks to buy a house for sale in a fashionable neighborhood, but fears that the owner, a well-known opponent of gay rights, will refuse to sell to him. The would-be buyer therefore secretly authorizes a friend to negotiate and consummate the purchase, ostensibly in the friend's name. It never occurs to the seller that the ostensible purchaser might be a front, and the seller asks no questions to that effect. The friend of course makes no comment on the subject. At closing the seller learns that the gay man is the undisclosed principal. The seller is nonetheless obligated to go through with the transaction. Although both the agent and the undisclosed principal had reason to know that the third party would have refused to deal with the principal, there was no affirmative misrepresentation.[14]

Example: A railroad company wishes to acquire three parcels of land for a new line. The company fears that the landowners will ask too much money if they learn that the railroad needs the land. It also fears

14. This Example assumes the locale in question does not have a law prohibiting discrimination in real estate sales on account of sexual orientation.

the same result if the landowners are contacted by someone representing an unnamed principal. The company therefore uses three different "straw men." Each of these agents individually approaches one of the landowners. Each of the agents affirmatively states that they are acting on their own account. Each negotiates for and signs a land purchase contract in his or her own name. Even though the agents have actively misrepresented the role of the undisclosed principal, the landowners cannot escape the contracts. Neither the agents nor their undisclosed principal had reason to know that the third parties would refuse to contract with the principal. To the contrary, both the agents and principal thought the third parties would be delighted to contract with the railroad — but at a substantially higher price.

Even though an undisclosed principal may have the right to enforce the contract, the third party can insist upon rendering performance to the agent if the contract requires the third party to perform personal services or if in some other way rendering performance to the undisclosed principal would significantly increase or change the third party's burden. This rule makes sense, since when the third party entered into the contract it expected to render performance to the agent, not the principal. Deviating from that expectation is justified only if the deviation does not significantly alter the third party's burdens.

Information possessed or conveyed by the agent. With one exception, information held by an agent with actual authority is imputed to the principal.

As to information the agent knows because a third party has notified the agent. If the agent has actual authority to receive the notice, then notice to the agent has same effect as notice made directly to the principal — regardless of whether the agent actually communicates the notice to the principal.[15]

As to information the agent knows for some other reason. If the agent's information concerns a matter within the agent's actual authority, the agent's information is attributed to the principal, regardless of whether the agent communicates the knowledge to the principal.

As to information the agent should know but does not. According to the Restatement and most courts, the unknown information is not attributable to the principal. However, even under the Restatement, if the principal has an independent duty to use reasonable care to discover the information, the agent's failure to use such care is attributable to the principal.[16]

---

15. The consequence does not attach if the party giving notice has itself received notice that the agent is acting contrary to the principal's interests.

16. See Restatement §277.

As to information the agent has communicated to others. If an agent acting with actual authority

- gives notice to a third party, or
- makes a statement or promise to a third party,[17]
- makes a misrepresentation to a third party,[18]

the information conveyed has the same legal effect under contract law as if the principal had conveyed the information directly.[19]

§2.3 Apparent Authority

§2.3.1 The Misnomer of "Apparent Authority"

"Apparent authority" is a misnomer. The term refers to the power to bind, not the right. The power derives from the *appearance* of legitimate authority; the doctrine exists to protect third parties who are misled by appearances.[20]

§2.3.2 Creation

Mechanics. Creation of apparent authority involves:

- an objective manifestation from one party ("apparent principal"),
- which somehow reaches a third party, and
- which causes the third party to reasonably believe that another party ("apparent agent") is indeed authorized to act for the first party (i.e., for the apparent principal).

---

17. Not all promises are enforceable, even if made directly by a principal. Agency law only attributes the agent's promise to the principal; contract law determines whether the promise is enforceable.

18. How can an agent have actual authority to make misrepresentations? Having actual authority to make accurate statements, that agent might make a misstatement innocently — reasonably believing the misstatement to be true. According to Restatement §162, comment *b*, that misstatement would come within the agent's actual authority. Other instances are also possible. A nefarious principal might indeed authorize fraud, and an innocent principal might authorize statements that turn out to be misrepresentations. In any event, where actual authority leaves off, inherent agency power takes over. An agent of a disclosed or partially disclosed principal has inherent power to make an inaccurate statement which, if accurate, would have been within the agent's actual authority. See section 2.5.3.

19. The impact under tort law is subtly different. See section 3.4.2.

20. For a more extensive explanation of the doctrine's rationale, see section 2.3.7.

In the words of the Restatement, §27:

> apparent authority to do an act is created as to a third person by written or spoken words or any other conduct of the principal which, reasonably interpreted, causes the third person to believe that the principal consents to have the act done on his behalf by the person purporting to act for him.

Relationship to actual authority. Apparent authority can coexist and be coextensive with actual authority.

Example: Two travelling salespeople, Bernice and Joe, are in the hotel bar. As Joe gets up to get another bowl of pretzels, Bernice says, "While you're up, order another round of drinks for us and charge them to me." Joe orders the round and charges the price to Bernice's room. If the bartender overheard Bernice's instructions, Joe had apparent as well as actual authority to charge the drinks.

Apparent authority can also extend an actual agent's power to bind the principal beyond the scope of the agent's actual authority.

Example: An Art Collector arranges for Broker to attend a forthcoming art auction and bid on certain items on Collector's behalf. Collector sends a letter to the Auction House, stating, "At your upcoming auction, Broker will represent me." In the past Broker has often placed bids for Collector in excess of $50,000. This time Collector tells the Broker, "Don't bid more than $25,000 on any item." Collector does not, however, communicate this limit to the Auction House. Although the Broker's actual authority to bid is limited to $25,000 per item, the limit does not apply to the Broker's apparent authority.

Apparent authority can also exist where no actual agency exists.

Example: The Art Collector arranges for Broker to attend a forthcoming art auction and bid on certain items on the Collector's behalf. Collector sends a letter to the Auction House, stating, "At your upcoming auction, Broker will represent me." Subsequently Collector changes his mind and instructs Broker not to bid for him. Collector neglects, however, to inform Auction House of this change. Although Broker has no actual authority to bind for Collector, Broker does have apparent authority.

The question of reliance. When a third party seeks to bind an apparent principal by claiming apparent authority, must the claimant show that it relied to its detriment on the appearance of authority? The Restatement

Figure 2-1. The Role of Reliance in Creating Apparent Authority

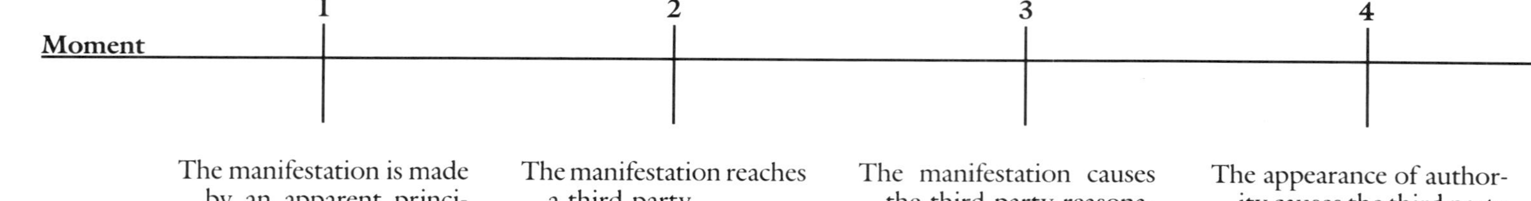

Moment	1	2	3	4
	The manifestation is made by an apparent principal.	The manifestation reaches a third party.	The manifestation causes the third party reasonably to believe that the apparent agent is authorized to act for the apparent principal. That is, the third party has *relied* on the manifestation in inferring that the apparent agent is authorized. (The Restatement uses reliance in this sense.)	The appearance of authority causes the third party to act or omit to act to its detriment. That is, the third party has *detrimentally relied* on the appearance of authority. (Many jurisdictions require reliance in this sense.)

requires that the claimant's inference of authority rely on the principal's manifestation, but does not require the claimant then rely to its detriment on the appearance of authority.[21] Many jurisdictions, however, do require the second, detrimental reliance. Indeed, some jurisdictions refer to apparent authority as *agency by estoppel*.[22] Figure 2-1 illustrates the two different occasions for reliance.

This doctrinal difference may have little practical significance. If a false appearance of authority does not cause a third party to act or omit to act to its detriment, then probably no claim will arise.

§2.3.3 *The Necessary Peppercorn of Manifestation*

For apparent authority to exist, the third party must be able to point to at least some peppercorn of manifestation attributable to the apparent principal. This peppercorn must form the basis of the third party's reasonable belief that the apparent agent is actually authorized. Conduct by the apparent agent may bear on the reasonableness of that belief, but the belief must ultimately rest on some manifestation attributable to the apparent principal.

This requirement means that, with one rarely important exception (discussed below), the statements of the apparent agent cannot give rise to apparent authority.[23]

> ***Example:*** A silver-tongued salesman, nattily dressed and appearing for all the world to be precisely who he claims to be, rings your doorbell and introduces himself as a representative of the Acme Burial Insurance Company. He shows you an impressive, glossy brochure and a printed contract form. You sign on the dotted line and give the man a $100 down payment. You later discover that the silver-tongued fellow had no connection whatsoever with Acme and that he had created the phoney brochures and contract forms as props. Unfortunately, you have no recourse against Acme. Although your belief that the salesman was acting for Acme may have been reasonable, you cannot point to any manifestation by or attributable to Acme, the apparent principal. Consequently, there is no apparent authority.

21. Restatement §8, comment *d*.

22. The Restatement also has a rubric of agency by estoppel, but the Restatement's concept of estoppel is subtly different from the doctrine of apparent authority. See section 2.4 (authority by estoppel).

23. A manifestation by one agent of a principal can, in contrast, give rise to apparent authority for another agent of the principal — if the first agent's manifestation is legally attributable to the principal. For a simple illustration of this phenomenon, see the first Example in section 2.3.4. See also section 2.7.

An apparent agent can supply the necessary peppercorn of manifestation only if the apparent agent (i) is actually authorized to act for the principal, and (ii) while actually authorized, accurately describes the extent of its authority. Every agent has the implied actual authority to accurately describe the agent's own actual authority,[24] and such accurate descriptions are therefore attributable to the principal.

> ***Example:*** You operate a horse ranch. One day a woman approaches you and informs you that she buys horses on behalf of Acme Rodeo Company and that she has the authority to pay up to $2,500 per horse. At that time, her statements are accurate. Two weeks later she returns and purports to commit Acme to purchase a quarter horse for $2,200. Unbeknownst to you, however, three days earlier Acme had expressly restricted her authority to purchases of $1,700 or less. You should be able to hold Acme to the contract through an apparent authority claim. You can certainly show a manifestation attributable to the apparent principal. When the buying agent earlier described her buying authority, she acted within her implied actual authority. That description is therefore a manifestation attributable to Acme.

The manifestation requirement also means that apparent authority never applies to undisclosed principals and rarely to partially disclosed principals. To establish apparent authority the third party must show that, at the moment of the event in question, some manifestation attributable to the apparent principal caused the third party to believe that the apparent agent had authority to act for that particular apparent principal. How can the third party make such a showing when at the moment of the event the third party did not know who the principal was, or even that the principal existed?[25]

§2.3.4 *Noteworthy Modes of Manifestation*

Through intermediaries. A manifestation that reaches the third party through intermediaries can still give rise to apparent authority. It is not necessary that the intermediary be an agent of the apparent principal.

---

24. Restatement §27, comment *c*. The principal can remove this authority by directing the agent not to represent her authority.

25. According to some authorities, apparent authority can apply to partially disclosed principals. As their chief examples, however, these authorities refer to partnership law, noting that one partner can bind fellow partners even though the third party does not know the identities of those other partners. See section 10.2.4 (actual authority). The Restatement gives only one nonpartnership example: "giving an agent possession of a horse, with a note stating 'the possessor has been authorized by the owner of the horse to sell the horse,' creates apparent authority to give a customary warranty." Restatement §159, comment *e*.

Example: Acting on instructions from the Art Collector, the Art Collector's personal secretary sends a letter to the Auction House stating: "On behalf of Art Collector, I am writing to inform you that, at your upcoming auction, Broker will be representing and bidding for Art Collector." Broker has apparent authority to bid for the Art Collector, even though the Art Collector herself (the apparent principal) never personally made the relevant manifestation. The secretary's letter constitutes a manifestation *attributable* to the Art Collector because the secretary's communication, made within the zone of actual authority, binds (i.e., is attributable to) the secretary's principal.[26]

Example: A local radio station tells its listeners, "Look for our roving 'You Win a Pizza a Week for a Year' Van. The van carries our station's call letters and logo. If the driver asks you, 'What's happening?' and you say 'Pizza a Week for a Year' and dance a jig, you win a pizza a week for a year." You never listen to that radio station, but a friend tells you of the promotion. Later an imposter, driving a van with the station's call letters and logo, approaches you. Believing the imposter to be a genuine representative of the station, you say the words and dance a jig. The imposter videotapes your performance. You may well be able to hold the radio station to its promise by asserting apparent authority. You can certainly establish that the station's announcement was a manifestation of the apparent principal. The manifestation reached you through an intermediary (your friend), albeit one who was not acting as an agent of the station. Whether the imposter had apparent authority to bind the radio station thus depends only on whether your inference of authority was reasonable.

By position. Sometimes the principal's sole manifestation to the third party may be to put an agent in a particular position. In light of local custom and standard business practices, that placement by itself may cause a third party to reasonably believe that the agent has certain authority. This type of apparent authority is sometimes called *authority by position.*

Example: The owner of a dry cleaning store hires Ralph to work at the counter and expressly authorizes him to accept clothes for cleaning, give receipts, return cleaned clothes to customers, and accept payment from customers. Although the owner expressly forbids Ralph to promise to have any garment cleaned in less than two working days, Ralph promises a law student to have her "interview suit" cleaned "by tomorrow." The doctrine of apparent authority may hold the dry cleaning

26. For a more detailed discussion of this type of attribution, see section 2.7.

store to Ralph's promise. Ralph's position (as counter clerk) constitutes the necessary manifestation. The question is whether, based on that bare manifestation, the customer reasonably believed that Ralph had the authority to make the promise. Since it is customary for counter clerks to tell customers when clothes will be ready, and since 24-hour service is not unusual in the dry cleaning business, the answer is probably "yes."[27]

Example: After lengthy negotiations with a claims adjuster, an attorney purports to settle her client's insurance claim for $25,000. Unless the client has given the attorney actual authority to settle for that amount, the client is not bound. The mere position of an attorney does not create apparent authority to bind a client to a settlement.

By acquiescence. Sometimes the principal makes the necessary manifestation by acquiescing in an agent's conduct.

Example: On several occasions the caretaker of an apartment complex contracts with a roof repair service to fix a leaking roof. Each time the repair service sends an invoice to the owner of the complex, and each time the owner pays. The repair service has no other contact with the owner. On the next service call, all goes as usual except that the owner refuses to pay. The owner claims "the caretaker has no authority to order repairs." Even if the owner is correct, the repair service can still collect. Regardless of whether the caretaker has actual authority to contract for repairs, the caretaker has apparent authority to order repairs from that particular repair company. By paying the previous invoices without comment, the owner of the complex has made the predicate manifestation.

Example: After the first two days of trial, attorneys for the two sides negotiate a settlement. With the parties present in open court, the two attorneys read the settlement into the record. Neither party objects. Both parties are bound to the settlement, regardless of whether either attorney had actual authority to settle. The clients' acquiescence imparted apparent authority to their respective counsel.

By inaction. In limited circumstances, an apparent principal's inaction may constitute a manifestation. For an apparent principal's inaction to give rise to apparent authority, the following criteria must be met:

---

27. As a "general agent," Ralph may also have bound the owner through inherent agency power. See section 2.5.2.

- Someone (including the apparent agent) must assert that the apparent agent has actual authority.
- The apparent principal must be aware of those assertions and fail to do anything to contradict them.
- The third party claimant must be aware of:
  — the assertions themselves,
  — the apparent principal's knowledge of the assertions, and
  — the apparent principal's failure to contradict the assertions.
- It must be the apparent principal's failure to contradict the assertions that causes the third party to believe that the apparent agent is authorized.[28]

In these circumstances, the apparent principal's silence amounts to acquiescence and is a manifestation that is known to the third party.

> ***Example:*** Charlie goes to a trade show and approaches a booth displaying the products of Acme Widget Company. At the booth he meets Alice, the owner of Acme. Charlie asks, "Who shall I call to get a quote on prices on special orders?" Another customer, who has done business with Acme for years, interjects, "Oh, you want to call Brenda, their national sales manager. She's the one who gives those quotes." Brenda has been demoted and no longer has that authority, but Alice does not want to embarrass Brenda in front of customers. Alice therefore says nothing. As to Charlie, Brenda has apparent authority to quote prices. The manifestation is not the customer's assertion but rather Alice's inaction in the face of that assertion.[29]

§2.3.5 The Third Party's Interpretation — The Reasonableness Requirement

Mere belief insufficient. For apparent authority to exist, a manifestation by the apparent principal must cause the third party to believe that the apparent agent has authority. Mere belief, however, is not enough. Apparent authority will exist only to the extent that the third party's belief is reasonable.

In determining whether a third party has reasonably interpreted the apparent principal's manifestations, the law of apparent authority considers the same kinds of information that are relevant to determining whether an agent

28. If this element is missing, the closely related doctrine of "estoppel" may help the third party. See section 3.4.

29. The same analysis applies to the other customer, who in addition can point to past experience as a manifestation attributable to the principal.

has reasonably interpreted the manifestation of its principal.[30] Apparent authority analysis thus parallels actual authority analysis, except that apparent authority focuses on the interpretations of the third party, not the agent. We can therefore adapt Comment *a* to Restatement §34 to read: "All matters throwing light upon what a reasonable person in the position of the [third party] at the time of acting would consider are to be given due weight."

The third party's duty of inquiry. In some circumstances, an apparent principal's manifestations may create an appearance of authority, yet it remains unreasonable for a third party to act upon that appearance without knowing more. The reasonable interpretation requirement thus imposes a duty of inquiry on the third party claimant. For instance, the manifestation itself may be ambiguous. Or, the apparent agent's conduct may be sufficiently unusual as to raise doubts. In such circumstances, the third party cannot reasonably interpret the manifestation as an indication of authority without first making some inquiry of the apparent principal.

> ***Example:*** A supplier of construction services and a general contractor dispute whether the general contracting company is liable to the supplier for services furnished to a subcontractor. The president of the general contracting company writes a letter denying liability. The supplier subsequently telephones the general contracting company and talks with a vice president. Without consulting the president and without actual authority, the vice president acknowledges the liability and signs an agreement guaranteeing the subcontractor's payment. When the general contracting company repudiates the vice president's action, the supplier claims that the vice president had apparent authority to make the acknowledgement and sign the guarantee. A court holds otherwise, stating that "The fact that the [supplier] had been notified in writing by [the contracting company's] president that [the contracting company] denied liability for these services put the [supplier] on inquiry as to the authority of any other [contracting company] employee to countermand such a position."[31]

The role of the apparent agent's conduct. With the one exception discussed in section 2.3.3 (the Example about the horse buyer), the apparent agent's conduct cannot satisfy the manifestation requirement. That conduct can, however, enter into the reasonableness determination.

> ***Example:*** Recall the Example of the radio station, the "Pizza a Week for a Year" promotion, and the imposter. If the imposter's van carries

30. See section 2.2.2.

31. *Truck Crane Service Co. v. Barr-Nelson*, 329 N.W.2d 824, 827 (Minn. 1983).

a well-painted and accurate logo and the imposter has the radio station's patter down right, then those facts might support your claim that your belief in the imposter was reasonable. If, in contrast, the van was poorly painted and the imposter did a lousy job of imitating a radio personality, your reasonableness claim would be weakened.

§2.3.6 *The Necessity of Situation-by-Situation Analysis*

Although an apparent agent may have apparent authority as to a wide range of acts and as to a wide range of third parties, each claim of apparent authority must be analyzed separately — even different claims from the same claimant. The reasons for this approach inhere in the elements necessary to create apparent authority. For any given claim of apparent authority, the third party must show:

(1) a manifestation occurred that was attributable to the apparent principal
(2) the manifestation reached the third party
(3) the manifestation caused the third party to believe that the apparent agent was authorized
(4) the third party's belief was reasonable

If the apparent principal has made more than one manifestation, Element 1 may vary from claimant to claimant. Elements 2, 3, and 4 may vary depending on the identity of the third party claimant and on the specific act claimed to be authorized. For example, two different third parties may draw different conclusions from the same manifestations. Or, two different third parties may draw the same conclusion, but for one — possessing knowledge or expertise lacked by the other — the conclusion may not be reasonable. Similarly, even with regard to the same third party, one act may reasonably appear authorized while another act may not.

One implication of this situation-by-situation approach is that efforts to counteract an impression of apparent authority will be effective only to the extent that the counteracting manifestations reach the third party.

Example: Sally, the owner of Sally's Service Station, decides that she can no longer afford the 10 percent discount she has long offered to regular customers. She calls her mechanics together and says, "Effective right now, no more 10 percent discounts." The next day, one of the mechanics, momentarily forgetting Sally's instruction, offers the discount to a customer. The customer accepts and leaves the car for servicing. When the customer returns to pick up the car, the mechanic says, "Hey, I'm sorry. I forgot. We don't give 10 percent discounts anymore."

The customer is nonetheless entitled to the discount. Based on past dealings, the mechanic had apparent authority by acquiescence. Although the mechanic now lacks actual authority, the apparent authority remains intact because Sally's counteracting manifestation has not reached the third party.

§2.3.7 *Rationale of the Apparent Authority Doctrine*

When an appearance of authority has confused a third party to its detriment, the apparent authority doctrine decides which of two relatively blameless parties (the apparent principal and the third party) will bear any resulting loss.[32] The doctrine puts the loss on the apparent principal. Two different policies underlie the doctrine:

(1) So long as the third party has not been careless or silly, any loss from the confusion should be imposed on the party who could have prevented the confusion in the first place.
(2) Any loss should be imposed so as not to disrupt normal commercial operations.

Both policies point in the same direction. Under the first policy, so long as the third party's misunderstanding is reasonable the loss rests with the party who is responsible for the manifestations that lead to the confusion. Under the second policy, commercial entities can rely on appearances of authority so long as the appearances trace back to the apparent principal and so long as the commercial entities are reasonable in construing the appearances.

§2.3.8 *Consequences of Apparent Authority*

Contracts. As to contracts, apparent authority creates essentially the same results as does actual authority.[33] If an apparent agent, acting with apparent authority, makes a contract on behalf of an apparent principal, then the principal is bound just as if the principal had itself entered into the contract. The third party is likewise bound to the contract.

32. In a perfect world this question would perhaps be moot, because the apparent agent would "make good" any harm done. For the relevant legal theories, see sections 4.2.2 (warranty of authority) and 4.1.2 (duty to act within authority). In the real world, however, holding the apparent agent accountable costs time, effort, and money. Moreover, the apparent agent may be judgment-proof, beyond the jurisdiction of the court, or simply nowhere to be found.

33. The exception for undisclosed principals, discussed at section 2.2.4, does not apply, because apparent authority cannot apply to an undisclosed principal.

Information possessed or conveyed by the apparent agent. Information held or communicated by an agent with apparent authority may or may not be inputed to the apparent principal according to the following rules:

As to information the apparent agent knows because a third party has notified the apparent agent. Apparent authority to receive a notice has the same effect as actual authority. Notice to the apparent agent has same effect as notice made directly to the principal, regardless of whether the apparent agent actually communicates the notice to the apparent principal.

As to information the apparent agent knows for some other reason. This information is not attributed to the apparent principal.[34]

As to information the apparent agent should know but does not. This "should know" information is not attributable to the apparent principal.

As to information the apparent agent has communicated to others. If acting with apparent authority an apparent agent gives notice to a third party, makes a statement or promise to a third party,[35] or makes a misrepresentation to a third party,[36] the information conveyed has the same legal effect under contract law as if the apparent agent had actual authority. That is, the principal is bound just as if the principal had directly and intentionally conveyed the information.

§2.4 Estoppel

To establish apparent authority, a third party must show some manifestation of authority attributable to the principal. But what if an asserted principal has made no such manifestation and has merely sat by while someone else has claimed an agency relationship? What if these claims of authority have lead third parties to extend credit, incur costs, or otherwise change their position? What if the asserted principal knew of the claims and of the danger to third parties and yet still did nothing?

In such situations, apparent authority is rarely applicable, because only in very narrow circumstances can the asserted principal's inaction serve as a manifestation.[37] To prevent injustice beyond those narrow circumstances, the

34. This rule contrasts with the corresponding rule for actual authority. See section 2.2.4. Perhaps the explanation for the difference relates to a difference in duty. A true agent has a duty to communicate information to its principal. See section 4.1.5. An apparent agent has no such duty toward its apparent principal.

35. Not all promises are enforceable, even if made directly by a principal. Agency law only attributes the apparent agent's promise to the principal. Contract law determines whether the promise is enforceable.

36. Restatement §265 requires that the third party show reliance on or belief in the misstatement, but that requirement is implicit in the formulation stated in the text. Absent reliance or belief, no action is available even if the principal directly made the statement.

37. See section 2.3.4 (manifestation by inaction).

Restatement and some courts use the concept of *estoppel*. In the words of the Restatement, estoppel imposes liability on a person for:

> a transaction purported to be done on his account . . . to persons who have changed their positions because of their belief that the transaction was entered into by or for him, if
> (a) he intentionally or carelessly caused such belief,
> or
> (b) knowing of such belief and that others might change their positions because of it, he did not take reasonable steps to notify them of the facts.[38]

In concept, the distinction between apparent authority and estoppel is clear enough. Unlike apparent authority, estoppel can apply even though the claimant can show no manifestation attributable to the asserted principal.[39] Estoppel liability can arise from the asserted principal's mere negligent failure to protect against a misapprehension.

Unfortunately, the case law often blurs this distinction. Many jurisdictions make detrimental reliance an element of apparent authority and even refer to apparent authority as "agency by estoppel." Moreover, most situations that give rise to apparent authority also give rise to estoppel. If an asserted principal makes a manifestation sufficient to support a reasonable inference of authority (i.e., to create apparent authority), the asserted principal can probably be said to have "intentionally or carelessly caused such belief" (i.e., estoppel).[40]

The distinction between apparent authority and estoppel is probably best illustrated by an example.

> ***Example:*** Emma Posster arrives with great fanfare in the mid-sized city of Regionville. She purports to be the personal representative of Mo Gull, a millionaire tycoon who lives in Metropolis, a large city some 250 miles away from Regionville. Posster claims that Gull is interested in developing Regionville's riverfront property and is looking to her to make the preliminary "go/no go" recommendation. Posster is wined and dined by Regionville's political leaders. On the strength of her purported relationship to Gull, she takes the most expensive suite at Regionville's most expensive hotel and opens and uses charge accounts

---

38. Restatement §8B(1).

39. For jurisdictions that follow the pure Restatement view of apparent authority there is another distinction: apparent authority can exist without a showing of detrimental reliance. See section 2.3.2 for a discussion of the Restatement's view of apparent authority. As noted in that section, many jurisdictions differ with the Restatement on this point.

40. The quoted language is from Restatement §8B(1)(a).

at several of the city's most exclusive restaurants and shops. In fact, Posster has no relationship whatsoever with Gull, and Gull has no interest in Regionville's riverfront.

Posster's style is flamboyant, and a wire service runs a story about her, her work for Gull, and the contemplated riverfront project. The story runs in the Metropolis paper, and Gull reads it. Rather than doing anything to alert people in Regionville, Gull merely chuckles, sits back, and says to himself, "What a bunch of chumps." Shortly after the story runs, Posster (still on credit) throws an extravagant party for Regionville notables, buys a new mink coat from a Regionville furrier, and disappears without paying any of the bills. The irate merchants seek payment from Gull. They will not succeed with a claim of apparent authority, because they cannot point to any manifestation legally attributable to Gull. However, for amounts charged *after* Gull read the story in the Metropolis paper, the merchants can succeed with a claim of estoppel. After reading that story, Gull knew that Regionville merchants believed Posster to be acting on his behalf. Yet "knowing of such belief and that others might change their positions because of it, he did not take reasonable steps to notify them of the facts."[41] Since the merchants did in fact change their positions "because of their belief,"[42] Gull is estopped from denying Posster's authority to bind him.

§2.5 Inherent Agency Power

§2.5.1 *A "Catch-All" Doctrine Based on Fairness*

In some situations, an agent has neither actual nor apparent authority, estoppel does not apply, and yet the agent has the power to bind the principal.

Example: Paul, the owner of Paul's Dry Cleaning, hires Eli to manage the dry cleaning store. Although dry cleaning stores customarily order cleaning solvent in large quantities, Paul instructs Eli never to buy more than $50 worth of solvent at a time. Disregarding these instructions, Eli places a phone order for solvent costing $450. The seller knows only that Eli is calling "for Paul's Dry Cleaning" and has no idea that Eli is the manager. Eli has acted without actual authority; his principal's manifestations expressly prohibit the order Eli made. Eli has also acted without apparent authority; there can be no apparent au-

41. Restatement §8B(1)(b).
42. Restatement §8B(1).

thority by position when the third party is unaware of the agent's position.[43] Nonetheless, agency law will bind Paul on the order.

Example: An agent, acting within her authority, negotiates a contract with a third party under which the agent's principal will sell widgets to the third party. During the negotiations the agent falsely describes the widgets. The principal has not authorized the agent to make misstatements, and nothing in the principal's manifestations to the third party created an appearance of such authority. Nonetheless, agency law will attribute the misstatements to the principal.

In neither of these situations is the principal responsible on account of its own culpable conduct. To the contrary, in each situation the agent has caused mischief while acting counter to the principal's wishes. Yet the third party is also without blame, and so a legal and policy issue arises: As between the principal and the third party, who should bear the risk of the agent's misconduct? Who should have the burden of pressing claims against the agent or absorbing the harm the agent has caused?[44]

To deal with this issue, the Restatement and some courts use a catch-all agency doctrine labelled *inherent agency power*.[45] In a wide range of situations, the doctrine imposes *enterprise liability*, that is, it places the loss on the enterprise that stands to benefit from the agency relationship. As explained by the Restatement:

> It is inevitable that in doing their work, either through negligence or excess of zeal, agents will harm third persons or will deal with them in unauthorized ways. It would be unfair for an enterprise to have the benefit of the work of its agents without making it responsible to some extent for their excesses and failures to act carefully. The answer of the common law has been the creation of special agency powers or, to phrase it otherwise, the imposition of liability upon the principal because of the unauthorized or negligent acts of its servants and other agents.[46]

Inherent agency power plays a major role in attributing tort liability to principals, and those attribution rules are discussed in Chapter Three. With

---

43. For an explanation of this point, see section 2.3.4.

44. In a perfect world, free of transaction costs, both parties could look to the agent. The world, however, is not perfect. See supra note 32. If the principal is not relatively blameless (e.g., it has negligently hired an agent with a background of misbehavior), other doctrines will place the loss on the principal. For a discussion of a principal's liability for direct negligence, see sections 4.4.1 and 4.4.2.

45. Some courts call the doctrine "inherent agency authority."

46. Restatement §8A, comment *a*.

regard to topics covered in this chapter, inherent power performs two important functions: It holds a principal responsible for (1) certain unauthorized acts of an agent whom the principal has entrusted with ongoing responsibilities, and for (2) certain false representations of an agent or apparent agent.

§2.5.2 *A Rule of Inherent Power: Unauthorized Acts by a General Agent*

When a principal entrusts an agent with ongoing responsibilities, the notion of an enterprise fairly applies. As a result, the agent has the inherent power to take certain actions even though the principal may have forbidden those actions. Agency law uses the category of "general agent" as the entrance criterion to this type of inherent power.

General and special agents defined. If a principal authorizes an agent "to conduct a series of transactions involving a continuity of service,"[47] the law calls the agent a *general agent*. If, in contrast, a principal authorizes the agent only to conduct a single transaction, or to conduct a series of transactions that do not involve "continuity of service," then the law calls the agent a *special agent*. Perhaps the simplest example of a general agent is an employee in charge of a store, a factory, or other place of business. It is not necessary, however, to have wide-ranging or important responsibilities in order to be a general agent. A fulltime photocopy clerk is a general agent with regard to photocopying duties.

> ***Example:*** Acting as an agent for a law student who is preparing for a party, a friend of the law student arranges for the delivery of a dozen helium-filled balloons, each saying "Congratulations . . . and you thought you'd never survive the first year!!!" In this single transaction, the friend is a special agent.

> ***Example:*** A wealthy first-year law student, believing that life without recreation is no life at all, hires a friend to arrange weekly parties, throughout the first semester, for the members of the student's study group. Through this series of transactions (i.e., the parties) involving a continuity of service (i.e., throughout the semester), the friend is a general agent.

> ***Example:*** The law student who is throwing a graduation party asks a friend to (a) make last-minute arrangements with the caterer, (b) order helium-filled balloons, and (c) pick up flowers from the florist. The

47. Restatement §3(1).

friend consents and becomes a special agent. Although the principal has authorized a series of transactions, the agency involves no continuity of service.

In theory, the "special vs. general" distinction is an "either/or" matter. That is, with regard to any particular responsibility, an agent must be either a general agent or a special agent. In practice, however, this either/or categorization encounters many grey situations.

It is possible for an agent to be a general agent with regard to some matters and a special agent with regard to others. The key factor separating general agency status from special agent status is whether the agent has an ongoing responsibility.

Example: A bank employs Larry as a teller. One day the bank asks Larry to deal with a caterer and arrange refreshments for a retirement party. With regard to his teller duties, Larry is a general agent. With regard to the party arrangement, Larry is a special agent.

Inherent agency power of general agents. Under the doctrine of inherent agency power, if:

- the agent is a general agent with actual authority to conduct certain transactions,
- the agent is acting in the interests of the principal, and
- the agent does an act usual or necessary with regard to the authorized transactions,

then the act binds the principal regardless of whether the agent had actual authority and even if the principal has expressly forbidden the act.

Although this rule applies in slightly different forms to all principals, it makes the most difference for undisclosed and partially disclosed principals. With a disclosed principal, apparent authority by position will often produce the same result as inherent power. With an undisclosed or partially disclosed principal, however, apparent authority is of no help.

Example: Sylvia decides to enter the silk importing business. The trade is notoriously biased against women, and she fears that her company will suffer if her interest in it is known. She therefore hires Phil as her general manager, but sets up the company so that Phil appears to the outside world as the owner. It is common in this trade for silk importers to sell to large customers on credit, but Sylvia instructs Phil never to extend more than $50,000 of credit to any customer without Sylvia's approval. One day, in order to close an important deal, Phil agrees without consulting Sylvia to extend $150,000 of credit to one customer.

> Although Phil acted without actual or apparent authority, Sylvia, the company's true owner and Phil's undisclosed principal, is bound. "An undisclosed principal who entrusts an agent with the management of his business is subject to liability to third persons with whom the agent enters into transactions usual in such businesses and on the principal's account, although contrary to the directions of the principal."[48]

This rule of inherent agency power has two policy-based limitations. It does not apply if either (i) the third party knows that the agent is acting without authority or (ii) the agent is not acting in the principal's interest. If the third party knows of the lack of authority, then the third party is not innocent and the rule's rationale does not apply.[49] If the agent acts on its own behalf, the conduct is not part of the enterprise from which the principal stands to benefit and again the rule's rationale does not apply.

§2.5.3 *A Rule of Inherent Power: False Statement by the Agent*

Under the doctrine of inherent power, an agent's false statements are attributable to the principal if:

- the principal is disclosed or partially disclosed, and
- a true statement concerning the same subject would have been within the agent's actual or apparent authority.

Once the doctrine of inherent power attributes the agent's misstatements to the principal, the principal faces the same contract law consequences that would result from the principal making the misstatement directly — namely, breach of contract claims and, in appropriate circumstances, rescission.[50]

This rule does not apply to false statements about the scope of the agent's authority. That is, although an agent ordinarily has actual authority to *truthfully* describe its authority, an agent has no inherent power to *falsely* describe that authority. Without this exception, inherent power would give every agent unlimited ability to create apparent authority.[51]

---

48. Restatement §195 (acts of manager appearing to be owner). See also Restatement §161 (unauthorized acts of general agents) and §194 (acts of general agents).

49. Recall from section 2.5.1 that inherent agency power functions to allocate the risk between two relatively blameless parties.

50. For the subtly different implications under tort law, see section 3.4.2.

51. See section 2.3.3 (explaining how an agent's actual authority to truthfully describe the agent's authority can create apparent authority).

§2.6 Ratification

§2.6.1 *The Role, Meaning, and Effect of Ratification*

All the attribution rules considered so far apply as of the time of the relevant event. For example, if what's at issue is the actual authority of an agent to make a contract, then the question is whether the agent had that authority *at the time of contract formation*. Likewise, if a third party seeks to bind a purported principal to a contract by apparent authority, inherent power, or estoppel, the question is whether the necessary conditions existed when the contract was formed.

Agency law also contains another attribution rule — one with a different sense of timing. When a party "ratifies" an act done on the party's behalf, the party approves the act *retroactively*. For ratification to be relevant, someone must have purported to act for another ("the purported principal") while lacking the power to do so. Ratification occurs if the purported principal subsequently affirms the earlier act.

> ***Example:*** Ralph is a janitor in a large residential apartment complex. He has neither actual nor apparent authority to act for the owner of the complex in renting apartments. He also lacks inherent agency power. Nonetheless, he shows apartment 101B to Alice and agrees to rent the apartment to her. Later, when Alice telephones the rental office to check on her move-in date, she speaks to the actual owner. The owner says, "Well, you know Ralph had no business renting that apartment to you. He's just the janitor. But your application looks okay, so go ahead." The owner has ratified Ralph's previously unauthorized actions.

Ratification validates the original unauthorized act and produces the same legal consequences as if the original act had been authorized. If, for instance, a party ratifies a contract, the ratification binds both that party and the other party to the contract. Ratification also releases the purported agent from any liability for having made an unauthorized contract.[52]

Ratification typically concerns "the making or breaking of a contract"[53]

---

52. See section 4.1.2 (agent's duty to act within authority) and 4.2.2 (agent's warranty of authority).

53. Restatement, §84, comment *a*. The Restatement also contemplates the ratification of tortious acts, and there are indeed a *few* cases that cite ratification as the reason for holding one party liable for another's tort. Most of those cases seem to involve the ratification of a course of conduct that happened to include a tort, rather than a purposeful embracing of the tort and its attendant liability.

For example, suppose the friend of the owner of a coal delivery service takes the friend's delivery van and makes a coal delivery. While delivering the coal, the friend

and in theory is relevant only when no other attribution rule applies. If an actor has actual or apparent authority, or inherent agency power, or if estoppel applies, there is no need to retroactively validate the act. In practice, however, parties often argue ratification in the alternative. For example, "When *X* made this contract on behalf of *Y*, *X* had actual authority to do so. *Y* is therefore bound. And, even if *X* lacked actual authority, *X* had apparent authority and so *Y* is bound. And, even if *X* lacked both actual and apparent authority, *X* had the inherent power to bind *Y*, and so *Y* is bound. And if even *X* lacked both the authority and power to bind *Y*, estoppel applies and so *Y* is bound. And, even if *X* lacked both the authority and power to bind *Y* and estoppel does not apply, *Y* subsequently ratified *X*'s act and so *Y* is bound."

§2.6.2 *Mechanics of Ratification*

For ratification to occur, two requirements must be met. Certain preconditions must exist, and the purported principal must purposely embrace the previously unauthorized act ("affirmance").

Preconditions. Ratification can occur only in the context of certain preconditions:

- Someone ("the purported agent") must have purported — either expressly or impliedly — to act on behalf of another (the "purported principal") in some transaction with a third party;
- the purported agent must have acted without either agency authority or agency power and estoppel must not apply;
- at the time of the act the purported principal must have existed and must have had capacity to originally authorize the act;[54] and
- at the time of the attempted ratification, the third party must not have indicated — either to the purported agent or to the purported prin-

carelessly breaks a window. The owner does not ordinarily employ the friend, and in fact when delivering the coal (and breaking the window) the friend acts without the consent or knowledge of the owner. The owner does, however, bill the customer for the delivered coal and in due course receives payment. The owner has ratified into existence a master-servant relationship and is consequently liable for the broken window.

For the rules of master-servant liability, see Chapter Three. For the case that served as the model for this example, see *Dempsey v. Chambers*, 28 N.E. 279 (Mass. 1891) (Holmes, J.).

54. This precondition explains why a corporation cannot ratify a contract made on the corporation's behalf before the corporation came into existence. See section 2.6.5, which contrasts ratification with novation and assumption.

cipal — an intention to withdraw from the transaction (i.e., the transaction must still be available to ratify).[55]

Affirmance — the act (or inaction) of ratification. If the necessary preconditions exist, a purported principal affirms by either:

- making a manifestation that, viewed objectively, indicates a choice to treat the unauthorized act as if it had been authorized, or
- engaging in conduct that is justifiable only if the purported principal had made such a choice.

In the simplest of situations, a purported principal affirms just by stating a choice.

> ***Example:*** Having read that car dealers generally make better deals for male customers than for female customers, Sally hires Ralph to purchase a used car on her behalf. She specifically instructs him, however, not to buy any foreign-made car. Purporting to act on Sally's behalf, Ralph makes a great deal on a used BMW. When Sally hears of the deal, she says, "Okay, for a deal like that I don't have to 'Buy American.' I'll take the car." Sally has ratified the deal.

Affirmance occurs when the manifestation occurs. The manifestation need not reach the third party to be effective.[56]

A purported principal can also affirm through inaction, that is, by failing to repudiate the act "under such circumstances that, according to the ordinary experience and habits of men, one would naturally be expected to speak if he did not consent."[57] Such failure to repudiate creates a situation resembling agency by estoppel.

---

55. The Restatement analogizes a transaction subject to ratification to an offer awaiting acceptance. An offeror can terminate an offeree's power to accept by withdrawing the offer. Likewise, a third party can preclude ratification by withdrawing from the underlying transaction. Restatement §88, comment *a*. The third party's withdrawal precludes ratification even if the third party is unaware that the transaction needs to be ratified. Thus, the third party can withdraw from a transaction while it appears to the third party that the withdrawal constitutes breach and yet escape without liability because, in fact, the transaction was unauthorized, the purported principal was not bound, there was no contract to breach, and the third party's timely withdrawal prevents the purported principal from ratifying a contract into existence. Even if the transaction is still available to ratify, in certain circumstances the third party may avoid the attempted ratification. See section 2.6.4.

56. This rule parallels the rule governing an agent's consent to act on behalf of a principal. See sections 1.2.2-1.2.3. In that case also, the manifestation is viewed objectively and need not reach the other relevant party to be effective.

57. Restatement, §94, comment *a*.

> ***Example:*** Acting without either authority or power to bind the owner of an apartment complex, Ralph, the janitor, offers a resident manager job to Felix. The landlord learns of the offer and also hears that Felix is planning to quit his current job so he can become resident manager. The landlord says nothing to Felix, and Felix quits his current job. By this inaction, the landlord has ratified Ralph's offer.

A purported principal can also ratify by accepting or retaining benefits while knowing that the benefits result from an unauthorized act. If the purported principal accepts benefits *without* the requisite knowledge, the third party may have an action in restitution or quantum meruit. Ratification is usually preferable for the third party, however, because ratification entitles the third party to the full benefit of the bargain. Restitution or quantum meruit, in contrast, entitles the third party only to the value of the benefit actually conferred.

> ***Example:*** Ralph, the self-aggrandizing janitor, offers to rent an apartment to Mike for a year at $50 per month off the regular monthly rent if Mike agrees to keep the grass well mowed. During his first month as a tenant, Mike mows the grass four times. If the landlord knew of the unauthorized offer, the landlord has ratified the agreement by accepting the services. Mike may therefore hold the landlord to the full bargain (i.e., to a lease and a rent reduction for a year). If, however, the landlord did not know of the offer, Mike has a right only to restitution or quantum meruit (i.e., only to be paid for the fair value of the mowing work he has already done).[58]

Ratification occurs on an "all or nothing" basis. If a purported principal attempts to ratify only part of a single transaction, then either the entire transaction is ratified or there is no ratification at all.

> ***Example:*** Acting without authority, Alice purports to sell Linda's car to Michael for $500. Alice also purports to extend a 90-day warranty on the car. Linda cannot ratify the sale without also ratifying the warranty.

Whether ratification has occurred is a question of fact, depending essentially on whether the purported principal:

---

58. If a third party has fully performed an unauthorized contract, the difference may well be immaterial. In theory, the measure of recovery will be different — benefit of the bargain versus value of services conferred — but in practice courts often use the contract price to measure the benefit.

- has manifested an intent to ratify and sought to impose some exclusions or qualifications (in which case the entire transaction has been ratified and the sought-after exclusions and qualifications are ineffective), or
- has manifested an intent to be bound only if the exclusions or qualifications are part of the transaction (in which case there is no ratification and neither the purported principal nor the third party are bound, unless the third party manifests consent to the conditions).

This fact determination resembles the determination made under §2-207(1) of the Uniform Commercial Code. That "battle of the forms" provision distinguishes between "a definite . . . expression of acceptance . . . which . . . states terms additional to or different from those offered" and an expression in which "acceptance is . . . made conditional on assent to the additional or different terms."

The role of consideration. An affirmance almost never needs consideration to be effective, because the contract being ratified provides consideration to the purported principal. In the BMW Example on page 46, for instance, Sally's consideration is the car dealer's promise to deliver her a BMW.[59]

When, however, an allegedly ratified transaction provides no benefit to the principal, the third party must indeed establish some independent consideration.

Example: An employee of Caliban Coal Company is injured on the job and sues to obtain workers compensation benefits. Caliban has workers compensation insurance, so the employee's dispute is with the insurance company. An adjuster for the insurance company offers to settle the dispute with a package of benefits plus the assurance that the employee can have "employment for life" at Caliban. The employee wishes in any event to return to work at Caliban once the injuries heal. Believing that the adjuster has authority to bind not only the insurance company but also Caliban, the employee accepts the settlement offer. The employee makes no reciprocal promise to stay permanently with Caliban.

A few years later Caliban discharges the employee, who then sues on the promise of permanent employment. Since the insurance adjuster had neither authority nor power to bind Caliban, the employee asserts that Caliban affirmed the promise by continuing to employ the employee. Even if the employee is correct on that point, no ratification has occurred. The workers comp settlement conferred no benefit on Cali-

---

59. Even when a purported principal affirms by accepting benefits, the ratified contract still provides the essential consideration. Conceptually, the role of the benefits is to estop the purported principal from denying that it has made an affirmance.

ban; it was the insurance company that was released from liability. The employee must therefore establish that Caliban received some independent consideration. The employee's continued work for Caliban is insufficient, because there is no evidence that the employee would have refused to return to work absent the promise of permanency.[60]

"Independent consideration" cases are interesting in the abstract, and several authorities refer to the concept. However, actual reported cases are extremely rare.

§2.6.3 Principal's Escape from Ratification: Rescission on Account of Ignorance of Material Facts

A principal can avoid the effects of ratification by establishing ignorance of material facts. According to the Restatement, "If, at the time of affirmance, the purported principal is ignorant of material facts involved in the original transaction, and is unaware of his ignorance, he can thereafter avoid the effect of the affirmance."[61] In the Restatement's view, the purported principal's lack of knowledge allows the rescission of the ratification. Many courts, however, treat the purported principal's knowledge of material information as a precondition to ratification. That is, the purported principal cannot effectively ratify if ignorant of material facts. This difference in view matters only with regard to the burden of proof. If knowledge is a precondition, then the party claiming ratification (typically the third party) has the burden of proving the purported principal's knowledge. If lack of knowledge allows an escape from liability, then the party claiming that escape route (i.e., the purported principal, seeking rescission) has the burden of proving that lack. For simplicity's sake, the following discussion will use the rescission approach.

Materiality defined. The Restatement defines *material facts* as those that "so affect the existence and extent of the obligations involved in the transaction that knowledge of them is essential to an intelligent election to become a party to the transaction."[62] The Restatement then confines this rather broad category by specifically excluding knowledge:

- of the legal effect of ratification
- about the value of the transaction or the transaction's desirability, other than knowledge of important representations made by the agent or third party as they entered into the transaction.

60. *Texas Pacific Coal & Oil Co. v. Smith*, 130 S.W.2d 425 (Tex. Civ. App. 1939).

61. Restatement §91(1).

62. Restatement §91, comment *d*.

> ***Example:*** When considering whether to affirm Ralph's purchase of the BMW, Sally is unaware (a) that the resale value of a used BMW is not as good as the resale value of a used Mercedes, and (b) that the car dealer has represented to Ralph that this particular BMW was once involved in a major traffic accident. The first fact is not material, since it concerns the value of the deal. The second fact is material, since it concerns a representation made by one of the dealmakers as they entered into the deal.

> ***Example:*** Same situation (including the accident), except that the dealer makes no representation about the accident. Sally's ignorance of the accident does not entitle her to rescind her ratification. The fact of the accident relates to the value and desirability of the transaction and not to any important representations made by either Ralph or the dealer.[63]

The ignorance requirement muddied. At first glance, the ignorance requirement seems straightforward. Ignorance is a state of mind. What should matter, therefore, is whether the purported principal lacks subjective knowledge of material facts, not whether the purported principal has reason to know those facts.

Unfortunately, however, both the Restatement and case law muddy this seemingly clear rule with two important exceptions:

- If the principal knows information that would cause a reasonable person to infer the missing information, then the trier of fact can conclude that the principal did indeed "know" the missing information.
- If the principal faces a situation in which a reasonable person would first inquire, and the principal affirms without inquiry, then the principal has assumed the risk of any lack of knowledge. That is, the principal cannot assert lack of knowledge as a basis for rescinding the ratification.[64]

Taken together, these exceptions come exceedingly close to a "reason to know" standard.

> ***Example:*** After Ralph makes the unauthorized commitment to have Sally buy the BMW, the salesperson calls Sally and says, "We're delighted to have you as a customer. I'm sure that Ralph has filled you in on the

---

63. Under applicable fraud and contract law, however, Sally may be able to rescind the contract itself.

64. See, e.g., Restatement §91, comments *c* and *e*.

history of this particular vehicle." The salesperson's comment would prompt a reasonable person to at least inquire, "What history?" Sally, however, affirms the purchase without asking any questions. Later she learns that the car dealer had represented to Ralph that this particular BMW was once involved in a major traffic accident. She cannot rescind her ratification. By failing to inquire when a reasonable person would have inquired, Sally assumed the risk of her own ignorance. She cannot assert that ignorance as grounds for rescission.[65]

The principal's escape blocked by the third party's reliance on the purported ratification. A principal's right to rescind gives way if:

- the third party has learned of the principal's affirmance, and
- in reliance on that affirmance the third party:
  - — has done something it would not otherwise have done, and
  - — that something will disadvantage the third party if the ratified transaction does not go through.[66]

Example: Sally affirms Ralph's commitment to purchase the BMW, unaware of the car dealer's representations to Ralph concerning the accident. The deal as made by Ralph obliges the car dealer to do a custom repainting job on the car. After Sally tells the salesperson, "I'm looking forward to having that car," the dealership does the paint job. When Sally later learns about the representation about the accident, she cannot rescind the ratification. The custom painting job, done in reliance on Sally's affirmance, precludes rescission.

§2.6.4 *The Third Party's Escape: Avoiding the Effect of Ratification*

Ordinarily, a purported principal's affirmance binds not only the purported principal but also the third party. As explained previously, a third party can *preclude* ratification by giving notice of withdrawal from the transaction *before* the purported principal affirms.[67] In two situations, the third party can also *avoid* an otherwise binding ratification by acting *after* the affirmance.

Changed circumstances. The third party may avoid a ratification if (a) after the purported agent and the third party make some arrangement but before the purported principal ratifies, (b) circumstances change so materially

65. Modelled on §91, illustration 17.

66. Restatement §91, comment *b*.

67. See section 2.6.2.

that holding the third party to the arrangement would be unfair. Obviously, at some point the third party will have to inform the purported principal of the changed circumstances. The third party need not, however, give notice before the affirmance.

The Restatement gives the classic example:

> Purporting to act for *P* but without power to bind him, *A* contracts to sell Blackacre with a house thereon to *T*. The next day the house burns. A later affirmance by *P* does not bind *T*.[68]

Conflicting arrangements. A third party can also avoid ratification if the third party:

- learns that the purported agent acted without authority,
- relies on the apparent lack of authority, and
- makes substitute, conflicting arrangements or takes some other action which will cause prejudice to the third party if the original transaction is enforced.[69]

For the necessary reliance to exist, the third party must act before learning of the purported principal's affirmance.

> ***Example:*** The car dealership learns that Ralph had no authority to commit Sally to buying the BMW. The dealership promptly sells the car to another customer, but does not inform either Sally or Ralph. Subsequently, Sally telephones the dealership and says, "I'm very pleased with Ralph, and I'm looking forward to taking delivery." Sally's affirmance does not bind the dealership to the original contract. After learning of the lack of authority and before learning of the affirmance, the dealership made conflicting arrangements. Since the dealership made the second contract in reliance on the apparent lack of authority, and since the dealership is in any event bound to the second contract, the ratification is avoided.[70]

§2.6.5 *Ratification Contrasted with Adoption and Novation*

Cases often confuse and interchange the terms *ratification*, *adoption*, and *novation*. Many of those cases involve contracts made by corporate promoters

---

68. Restatement §89, Illustration 1.

69. Restatement §95, comment *b*.

70. The dealership could have produced the same practical result by acting to preclude rather than avoid ratification. If *before Sally's affirmance* the dealership had notified either Sally or Ralph of the resale, that notice would have eliminated one of the preconditions of ratification. See section 2.6.2.

on behalf of corporations not in existence when the contract is made. To the extent the three terms have separate meanings, those meanings are as follows:

Ratification. As described in this section, *ratification* is the retroactive approval of a previously unauthorized act. Ratification binds both the purported principal and the third party to the original undertaking and discharges the purported agent from any liability on that undertaking.

Adoption. *Adoption* occurs when:

- a purported agent has purported to bind a purported principal to an agreement while lacking the power to do so;
- the purported principal cannot ratify the purported agent's unauthorized act, typically because at the time of the act the purported principal either did not exist or lacked capacity to authorize the act;
- the original agreement made by the purported agent and the third party expressly or impliedly empowers the purported principal to choose to receive the benefits and assume the obligations of the agreement; and
- the purported principal manifests — either expressly or through a course of conduct — its desire to receive the benefits and assume the obligations of the agreement

Like ratification, adoption binds both the principal and the third party to the original agreement. *Unlike* ratification, adoption does not relate back in time to the unauthorized act. So, if for any reason the starting date of the relationship between the adopting principal and the third party is important, that date is the date of the adoption, not the date of the unauthorized act. Moreover, adoption does not release the purported agent from any liability it may have to the third party on account of the original agreement, unless the original agreement contemplates that the principal's adoption will indeed release the agent.

Novation. A *novation* is a new, independent agreement between the principal and the third party. Novations arise from the same circumstances that give rise to adoptions, and it is often the original, unauthorized contract that causes the purported principal and the third party to consider doing business with each other. The terms of the novation may be and often are identical to the terms of the prior, unauthorized agreement.

Nonetheless, a novation reflects an entirely separate process of contract formation. Once formed, the novation contract completely displaces the original, unauthorized contract and relieves the purported agent from any liability it may have had to the third party on account of that prior contract.

Whether the new arrangement is an adoption (which does not release the purported agent) or a novation (which does) is a question of the parties' intent.

> ***Example:*** Rachael decides to go into business with a 1950s-style hamburger joint. She plans to incorporate the business under the name of "Sammy's, Inc." She signs a lease for the restaurant, however, before actually forming the corporation. In signing the lease she purports to act as "President of Sammy's, Inc." and neglects to inform the lessor that Sammy's Inc. has not yet come into existence.
>
> Since a nonexistent corporation cannot authorize anyone to do anything, Rachael's act in signing the lease is unauthorized and does not bind the corporation. As of that moment, Rachael, not the corporation, is liable to the lessor on the lease.[71]
>
> When Rachael does form the corporation, the corporation may decide to take responsibility for the lease. However, the corporation cannot by itself take Rachael off the hook. Ratification would release Rachael, but ratification is not possible: At the time of the lease signing the corporation did not exist, so one of the necessary preconditions to ratification is absent. The corporation can adopt the lease, but that adoption will not release Rachael. If the corporation later defaults, she will still be liable.
>
> If the lessor agrees, the corporation and the lessor can make a novation. A new contractual relationship between the lessor and the corporation will replace the original lease, the corporation will be bound, and Rachael will no longer be liable.

§2.7 Chains of Authority

§2.7.1 Multilevel Relationships

The examples used so far is this chapter are in a sense "flat." The principals act through a single agent. Agents draw their authority directly from manifestations made by the principal him or herself. Third parties claim apparent authority from manifestations made personally by a principal.

Real life relationships tend to be more intricate.

> ***Example:*** Marcia is the manager of an airport office of a rental car company. As part of her job, she hires, supervises, and when necessary, fires the people who staff that office. Those people are agents of the rental car company, not of Marcia, even though (1) it was Marcia who told each of them, "You're hired", and (2) the company itself has never made any direct manifestation to any of them.

71. See section 4.2.2.

Example: Seeking to increase business, Marcia retains the services of Abitatruth, Inc., an advertising agency. Acting on behalf of the rental car company, Marcia authorizes the agency to spend $10,000 to rent advertising space around the airport on the company's behalf. The agency assigns the work of renting the advertising space to Alan, one its employees. Alan has the power to bind the rental car company, even though (1) Marcia has never made any manifestation to Alan, and (2) Marcia does not even know that Alan exists.

Each of these examples involves a "concatenation" of responsibility. That is, in each situation a *chain* of relationships or events makes the rental car company the principal and gives the person at the bottom of the chain the power to bind. Thus, a person can be an agent without ever having met or communicated directly with the principal.

For instance, in the first example (Marcia hires the staff), the employees are agents of the rental car company because another agent of the company (Marcia), acting within her actual authority, has made manifestations (attributable to the company) that the company (as principal) desires the employees to act on the company's behalf and subject to the company's control. See Figure 2-2 and 2-3.

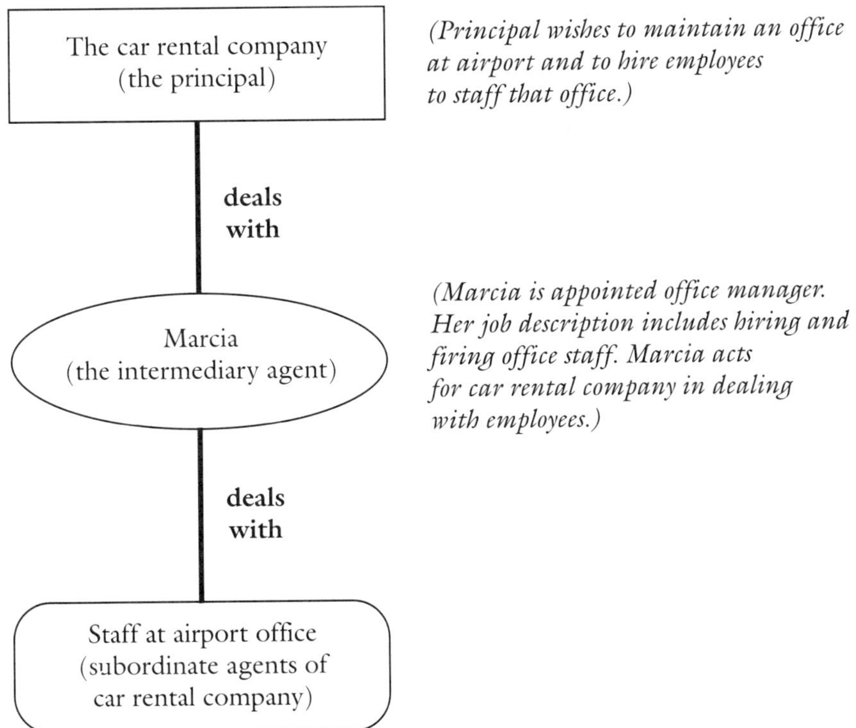

Figure 2-2. Concatenating Authority — The Practical Structure

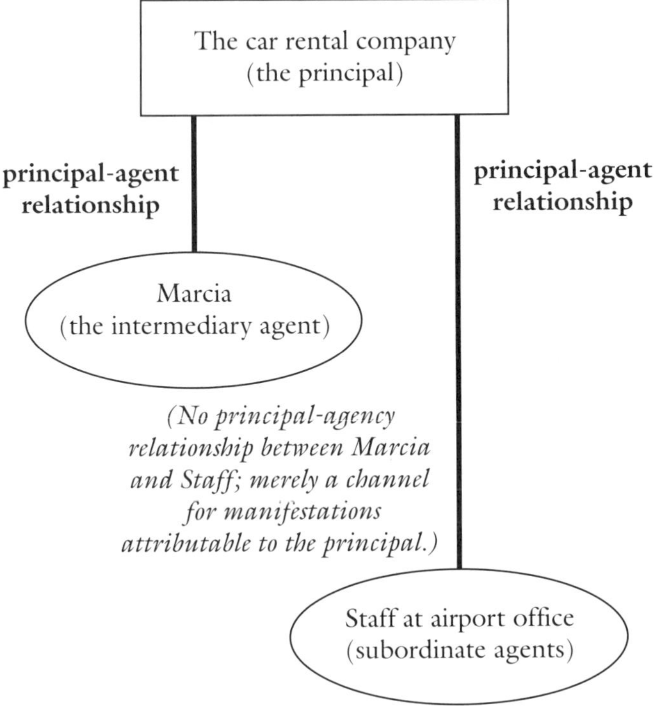

Figure 2-3. Concatenating Authority — The Agency Structure

Agency law handles such complexity in characteristic fashion. It establishes categories, labels the categories, and attaches consequences to the categories. In matters of contract and communication, the key labels are *intermediary agents*, *subordinate agents*,[72] and *subagents*.

§2.7.2 *Intermediary and Subordinate Agents*

The categories. As section 2.7.1 illustrates, a principal can use one of its agents to appoint, direct, and discharge other agents of the principal. Using "intermediary agents" to deal with "subordinate agents" is merely a specific instance of a principal acting through its agents. The principal uses one (or more) of its agents to manifest its desires to the principal's other agents.

This concatenated, hierarchal structure is commonplace. Only the smallest of organizations can operate without the "top dog" delegating some re-

72. Neither the Restatement nor the case law provide any names for these important links in the chain of agency authority. The terms "intermediary" and "subordinate" are the author's.

sponsibility to intermediary agents. Moreover, the delegation often works through several levels (in military terms, the "chain of command"), with agents being simultaneously intermediary agents vis-à-vis those "below" them, and subordinate agents vis-à-vis those "above" them.

> ***Example:*** Marcia's actual authority to run the airport office might derive as follows: The car company's regional manager appointed her to the position and generally described to her the duties and authority of the position. The regional manager obtained the actual authority to make such manifestations on behalf of the company when the Vice President for Leasing Operations appointed him to the regional manager position. The Vice President, in turn, obtained her actual authority to manifest the company's choice of regional managers (and to manifest the company's wishes as to the duties and authority of those managers) when the Chief Executive Officer appointed her as Vice President and outlined the duties and authority of that position. The company made the necessary manifestations to appoint and authorize the CEO when the company's Board of Directors elected the CEO.[73] See Figure 2-4.

A principal can also authorize an intermediary agent to formulate the principal's desires for it, and then to manifest those desires as necessary to the principal's other agents and to would-be agents.

> ***Example:*** The board of directors of Rollerskating, Inc. adopts a resolution instructing its CEO to "develop and implement a plan for aggressively marketing the company's new generation of in-line skates." Acting within the resulting actual authority, the CEO decides on a marketing approach, interviews various advertising agencies that wish to provide services to implement the concept, selects an agency for the project, and delegates numerous tasks to various Rollerskating employees.

No matter how much authority and discretion the intermediary agent has, however, the intermediary acts on behalf of the principal and not on the intermediary's own account. So long as the intermediary agent acts with actual authority, apparent authority, or inherent agency power, the intermediary's manifestations — whether to the subordinate agents themselves or to third parties — are attributable to the principal. The subordinate agents remain in all respects agents of the principal, not of the intermediary.

---

73. As to the conduct of a corporation's day-to-day affairs, the board of directors has the ultimate authority and power. See, e.g., Revised Model Business Corporation Act §8.01(b) ("All corporate powers shall be exercised by or under the authority of, and the business and affairs of the corporation managed under the direction of, its board of directors. . . .")

Figure 2-4. The Rental Car Company's Chain of Command

Board of Directors

manifests the Company's consent and establishes actual authority in

the Chief Executive Officer [an intermediary agent]

who, acting within his actual authority as an agent of the Company, did an act attributable to the Company, namely—appointing

the Vice President for Leasing [a subordinate agent and simultaneously an intermediary agent]

who, acting within her actual authority as an agent of the Company, did an act attributable to the Company, namely—appointing

the Regional Manager [a subordinate agent and simultaneously an intermediary agent]

who, acting within his actual authority as an agent of the Company, did an act attributable to the Company, namely—appointing

Marcia, the manager of the airport office [a subordinate agent and simultaneously an intermediary agent]

The subordinate agent's power to bind the principal. A subordinate agent binds its principal under the same rules applicable to "plain" agents. The key questions are therefore the same, namely, did the subordinate agent act with actual authority? apparent authority? inherent agency power? under circumstances giving rise to estoppel? Answering these questions involves looking at the conduct attributable to the principal, including any manifestations made by intermediary agents within the scope of their actual authority, apparent authority, or inherent agency power.

> ***Example:*** Marcia, the manager of the rental car company's airport office, has engaged Abitatruth, an ad agency, to develop advertising for the rental car company. Marcia brings along Sara, one of her assistants, to a series of conferences with Abitatruth. During these conferences Marcia repeatedly seeks Sara's opinion as to choices posed by the ad agency and occasionally defers to Sara's judgment. Later, when the ad agency cannot get in touch with Marcia, it asks Sara to approve the content of several advertising posters. Although Marcia has stated pri-

vately to Sara that Marcia plans to approve all posters, Sara tells the ad agency, "Go ahead."

This approval binds the rental car company. Although Marcia's private statements to Sara preclude a claim based on actual authority, Sara did have apparent authority. Apparent authority presupposes a manifestation *of the rental car company*, which Marcia's conduct supplies. Consulting with and relying on subordinates — even in the presence of others — was certainly within Marcia's actual authority. That conduct is therefore, by attribution, the conduct of the rental car company. Coupled with the ad agency's resulting, reasonable belief in Sara's authority, this attributed manifestation gave Sara apparent authority to approve the posters on the rental car company's behalf.

Intermediary agent's limited responsibility for the misconduct of subordinate agents. All agents owe a duty of care to their principal,[74] and intermediary agents must exercise care in selecting, directing, and discharging subordinate agents. If an intermediary agent fails to do so and that breach of duty proximately causes injury to the principal, the intermediary agent is liable to the principal for resulting damages.

Example: Marcia hires Henry to drive the courtesy van that takes passengers between the airport and the car rental office. Marcia carelessly fails to check Henry's references and driving record. The references are false, and the record includes several drunk driving convictions. One day Henry drives the van while drunk and causes an accident. Under the doctrine of respondeat superior, the car rental company is liable for any damage Henry caused to others.[75] Marcia is liable to the car rental company for its obligations to others, plus any damage to the company's courtesy van. She breached her duty of care in selecting and supervising a subordinate agent.

Except in such circumstances the intermediary agent is not responsible if the subordinate agent messes up. The intermediary agent is not the guarantor of the subordinate agent's performance.

Example: Same situation, except Henry's references are okay, his driving record is clean and Marcia uses reasonable care in hiring and supervising Henry. The car rental company remains liable to others for harm caused by Henry's drunken driving, but Marcia is not liable to the car rental company.

---

74. See section 4.1.4 (agent's duty of care).

75. See section 3.2.4.

§2.7.3 Subagents

The category. When a principal entrusts a task to its agent, the principal has in effect delegated that task to the agent. If that agent, acting with authority, in turn redelegates part or all of that task to an agent of its own, then the second agent becomes a subagent of the original principal.

> ***Example:*** Veronica wishes to sell her home and engages Allen, a real estate broker, as her selling agent. The "listing agreement" authorizes Allen to use the services of other brokers as he sees fit. Acting as Veronica's agent, Allen advertises the house. Bernice, another real estate broker, approaches Allen and tells him that she might be able to find a buyer for the house. Allen says, "Bring me any potential buyers you know of, and if the deal goes through, I'll split my commission with you." Bernice becomes simultaneously Allen's agent and Veronica's subagent.

> ***Example:*** Marcia hires Abitatruth Inc. to prepare and place radio advertisements for the rental car company. Abitatruth becomes the car company's agent. Abitatruth, however, cannot perform the tasks of its agency directly. As a corporation, it may be "real" as a legal concept, but it has neither a voice with which to speak, nor fingers with which to type. So Abitatruth in turn delegates its agency tasks to its employees. Those employees, agents of Abitatruth, are subagents of the rental car company.[76]

The agent's authority to redelegate. As a general rule an agent has no authority to delegate its tasks to another. However, a principal can authorize its agent to delegate, and the general rules for creating actual authority apply to determine whether the principal has done so.

Consistent with those rules, implied actual authority to delegate exists when: (i) the delegation relates merely to the mechanical aspects of the agent's tasks; (ii) the agent is a corporation, partnership, or other organization; or (iii) it is customary for agents in similar situations to delegate. As with all instances of implied actual authority, a manifestation of the principal can restrict or even completely negate the implied authority. However, when the agent is a corporation or other legal entity, some authority to delegate must remain. Legal "persons" can act only through the endeavors of natural persons.

---

76. As indicated supra note 73, the delegation begins with decisions made by the corporation's board of directors.

> ***Example:*** Sylvia brings a garment to David, a tailor, for mending. David employs several assistants, and they do most of the repair work. Sylvia, however, says, "This one requires your skill. Don't let anyone else work on it." David has no authority to delegate the work.

> ***Example:*** David telephones Pauline's Cartage Service ("Pauline's") and arranges to have a large sewing machine taken from his shop and delivered across town. Pauline's is a corporation, with the necessary right to delegate the task. David, however, imposes a condition, saying, "Make sure whoever comes has been with you for at least five years."

A subagent's power to bind the principal. Assuming that an agent has the authority to delegate tasks to a subagent, determining the scope of a subagent's power to bind the principal involves a two-stage analysis:

1. What is the scope of the agent's power to bind the principal?
2. Of that scope, what has the agent authorized the subagent to perform?[77]

A Restatement comment reflects this two-stage approach: "A subagent performing acts which the appointing agent has authorized him to perform [stage 2] in accordance with an authorization from the principal [i.e., an authorization in which the principal authorizes the agent to delegate tasks] is an agent of the principal and affects the relations of the principal to third persons as fully as if the appointing agent had done such acts [stage 1]."

> ***Example:*** The car rental company (acting via Marcia) gives Abitatruth actual authority to spend up to $10,000 in renting advertising space [stage 1]. Moe is a junior vice president of Abitatruth, with actual authority (from Abitatruth) to make leasing commitments of $1,000 or less [stage 2]. Moe has neither apparent authority nor inherent agency power to exceed the $1,000 limit while acting for Abitatruth [stage 2]. Moe purports to commit the car rental company to space Alpha for $800 and to space Beta for $1,250.
>
> In each instance Moe has acted as an agent for Abitatruth and subagent for the car rental company. The commitment on space Alpha binds the car rental company, because the commitment was within Abitatruth's authority vis-à-vis the company [stage 1] and within Moe's authority vis-à-vis Abitatruth [stage 2]. The commitment on space Beta

77. Restatement §5, comment *d.*

does not bind the car rental company, because that commitment exceeded Moe's authority vis-à-vis Abitatruth [stage 2].

To bind the principal, a subagent's act must be both within the subagent's power to bind the agent and within the agent's power to bind the principal.

Subagent acts that do not bind the principal may nonetheless bind the agent.

Example: The car rental company (acting via Marcia) gives Abitatruth actual authority to spend up to $10,000 in renting advertising space [stage 1]. Abitatruth's executive vice president has actual authority to make all rental decisions on behalf of Abitatruth [stage 2]. The executive VP purports to commit the car rental company to leasing a billboard for 12 months for a total of $15,000. This commitment comes within the authority granted the VP by Abitatruth [stage 2], but exceeds the authority granted Abitatruth by the car rental company [stage 1]. Therefore, the VP's act does not bind the car rental company.

Abitatruth, however, may be bound. The VP's act was within the actual authority granted by Abitatruth, so that act is attributable to Abitatruth. Through that act Abitatruth has, in effect, inaccurately represented itself as having authority to bind the car rental company. That representation turns out to be false, and as a result Abitatruth may be liable for breaching the "warranty of authority."[78]

Agent the guarantor of the subagent's performance. When the agent delegates all or part of its responsibilities to a subagent, that delegation does not relieve the agent of its responsibilities. To the contrary, the agent remains "on the hook." If the subagent's performance satisfies the obligations the agent owes to the principal, then the agent, acting through the subagent, has performed its responsibilities as agent. If, however, the subagent's performance fails to satisfy the agent's obligations, then the agent is directly responsible to the principal.[79]

PROBLEM 1

Captain Miles Standish loved the fair damsel Priscilla, but Standish's intense shyness prevented him from speaking to her. One day Standish lamented the situation to his friend John Alden, and Alden offered to speak to Priscilla and on Standish's behalf invite her to an upcoming community dance. Standish

78. See section 4.2.2.

79. The rule stated here closely parallels a rule of contract law: When an obligor delegates its performance obligations to another, that delegation does not by itself discharge the obligor's duties to the obligee.

responded, stroking his beard reflectively, "I dunno. That might be a good idea." Alden took that comment as assent and rode off to see Priscilla. Actually, however, Standish did not intend to consent. Right after Alden rode off, Standish wrote in his diary, "Told Alden that I would think about his offer. Have done so and will reject it as soon as I next see him."

Before Standish saw Alden again, however, Alden saw Priscilla. Alden explained Standish's great love, and — purporting to act on Standish's behalf — invited Priscilla to accompany Standish to the dance. Priscilla accepted. Later, Standish saw Alden and told him not to talk to Priscilla. Alden told Standish, "Too late, fellow; you're going to the dance."

Assume that, as a matter of contract law, contracts to attend dances are valid and enforceable. Is Standish bound?

EXPLANATION

Standish is bound only if Alden had actual authority to extend the invitation.[80] The creation of actual authority requires (i) a manifestation by the principal, (ii) the agent's reasonable interpretation of that manifestation as a request that the agent acts for the principal, and (iii) the agent's manifestation of consent to act. The first and last certainly occurred. Standish's comment ("That might be a good idea") suffices as a manifestation. Alden's action reflects his consent. The question of the agent's interpretation, however, is more difficult. Although Standish's subjective intent is irrelevant, Standish's response was objectively ambiguous. Especially given what Alden knew of Standish's shyness, it was probably unreasonable for Alden to consider himself authorized without having first sought clarification. Therefore, no actual authority existed and Standish is not bound on the contract.

PROBLEM 2

A tenant rents her apartment on a month-to-month tenancy, with each term beginning on the first of the month. Under local law, the tenant can terminate the tenancy by giving a full calendar month's notice. For example, for the tenancy to end on March 31, the tenant must give notice before March 1. The building is managed by a resident manager, whom the landlord has authorized to receive notices from tenants. On December 28, the tenant gives proper notice to the resident manager, stating that the tenant will vacate by January 31. Unfortunately, the resident manager fails to pass the notice on to the landlord until January 3. Will the tenancy end on January 31?

80. Since there is no indication of Priscilla's being aware of any manifestation by Standish, there can be no apparent authority. Since Alden is not a general agent, there can be no inherent power. Since Priscilla has not changed position to her detriment, there can be no estoppel (the facts do not indicate that she has bought a new dress or rejected other invitations).

Explanation

Yes. When an agent has actual authority to receive a notice, receipt of that notice is attributable to the principal. The agent's failure to communicate the information to the principal may be a breach of the agent's duty to the principal[81] but has no effect on the attribution rule.

PROBLEM 3

Jessica and Sally attend an art auction together. Jessica is well known and does not want to appear to be bidding. The following whispered conversation occurs and is not overheard by anyone.

Jessica: I'd like you to bid for me on the next picture being auctioned. You can bid up to $10,000. If you win, of course I'll pay the price. Win or lose, I'll give you $100 for your trouble.

Sally: Sounds good to me. Let's do it.

Just after the conversation, the auctioneer happens by. He asks Jessica, whom he knows, whether she plans on buying anything at the auction. Jessica responds, "Not today. I'm just here to watch." Sally tells the auctioneer that she is excited because she is "looking for something impressive to hang on my living room wall." Sally makes the winning bid at $9,200. Is Jessica bound on the contract? Is the auction house? (Assume that on this particular sale the auction house was acting on its own account, that is, it owned the painting being sold.)

Explanation

Both Jessica and the auction house are bound. The conversation between Jessica and Sally established Sally's actual authority, with Jessica as the undisclosed principal. The fact that the auction house was unaware that Sally was acting for Jessica is irrelevant. Actual authority results from dealing inter se the principal and agent. A third party can escape a contract with an undisclosed principal only if (i) there has been an affirmative misrepresentation as to the undisclosed principal's status, and (ii) either the undisclosed principal or the agent had reason to know that the third party would refuse to deal with the principal. The first factor is present, but the second is not.

---

81. See section 4.1.5.

PROBLEM 4

Mr. and Ms. Yup, high-powered corporate lawyers, mesh their schedules and arrange a week's vacation hiking in the Andes Mountains. To babysit their offspring ("Little Yup") and to housesit their house, the Yups hire a babysitter ("Babysitter"). The Yups provide the babysitter, among other information, the name, office phone number, and office address of Little Yup's pediatrician. They also leave a health insurance card that indicates a health insurance account number for Little Yup. Unfortunately, while the Yups are away, Little Yup becomes seriously ill. The babysitter takes Little Yup to the hospital, where expensive medical procedures enable Little Yup to recover. In order to have the hospital provide the services, Babysitter shows the health insurance card and signs a contract with the hospital. Queried about the child's parents, Babysitter responds, "They're backpacking in the Andes. I am babysitting for their child for this week." Babysitter signs the hospitalization contract: "I.M. Babysitter, for Mr. and Ms. Yup." Are Mr. and Ms. Yup bound on that contract?

EXPLANATION

The Yups are bound, certainly on actual authority and perhaps on apparent authority as well. Merely by entrusting the child to Babysitter for a week and leaving the country, the Yups manifested consent to have Babysitter arrange for necessary medical care. Providing the name of the pediatrician and the health insurance card reinforced that basic manifestation. The Yups did not specifically mention hospitalization and did not specifically authorize Babysitter to sign hospital contracts on their behalf, but Babysitter certainly had implied actual authority to arrange hospitalization in an emergency and to sign all reasonably necessary documents for that purpose.

The argument for apparent authority is also strong. The hospital must be able to point to some manifestation of the Yups which, reasonably interpreted, led the hospital to believe that Babysitter was authorized to bind the Yups. The hospital can identify three manifestations: the Yups' entrusting of their child to Babysitter; the Babysitter's possession of the insurance card; the Babysitter's statement about her responsibilities. The first manifestation arguably establishes apparent authority by position, although babysitters do not customarily commit parents to large hospital bills. The possession of the insurance card made it more reasonable for the hospital to believe that the parents had given Babysitter authority to arrange for medical services. It is the third manifestation — Babysitter's statement — which is perhaps the strongest point. Had that statement been made directly by the Yups, there would have been no question of Babysitter's apparent authority. When Babysitter accurately described her authority, she was acting within her actual authority. As a consequence, her statement had the same effect as if the Yups had made it themselves.

PROBLEM 5

Jean Valjean breaks into a bakery to steal a loaf of bread. A police officer who is passing by sees a light in the bakery and enters to investigate. Hearing the officer enter, Valjean quickly dons a baker's hat and apron. Valjean greets the officer with a smile, explaining that he is the new night baker. The officer believes Valjean. Flushed with his success, Valjean continues the conversation and tells the officer that the bakery has adopted a new program available only to "those who protect our safety." For a one-time payment of $50, the officer can come in for breakfast at the bakery each morning for a year and have "all you can eat." The officer pays Valjean $50 and leaves.

The next morning the owner of the bakery refuses to honor the supposed commitment. The officer responds, "He was in your shop, behind your counter. I took him for what he appeared to be, and I paid him $50." Is the bakery bound to make good on Valjean's promise?

EXPLANATION

The bakery is not bound. Valjean had neither actual nor apparent authority. Actual authority requires, among other things, a manifestation by the principal that the principal wishes the agent to act on the principal's behalf. Valjean is a burglar. The bakery has made no manifestation of any type to him.

For apparent authority to exist, again there must be a manifestation by the principal — this time to the third party claimant. Again, the bakery has made no manifestation. The actions of Valjean, the apparent agent, cannot create apparent authority. (The bakery was unaware of Valjean's actions, so there can be no question of a principal's manifestation by acquiescence.) The doctrine of *authority by position* is likewise of no help to the police officer. That doctrine requires some action by the principal in placing the agent in the position. It was Valjean, not the bakery, who put Valjean in the bakery in hat and apron.

PROBLEM 6

Henry comes to town one day looking for some land to purchase. He learns that Eleanor has a parcel of lakefront property that she wishes to sell. Henry meets Eleanor, explains that he is "in town acting for a group of investors who are looking for lakefront in this area" and goes with Eleanor to inspect the property. Henry appears impressed, but says to Eleanor, "I'm just the gofer. I'll have to check with the folks in charge." The next day Henry comes back and tells Eleanor that he is authorized to pay her $30,000 for the prop-

erty. Eleanor thinks the price is a fair one, and together they go to a local stationery store and buy a legal form entitled "Contract for the Sale of Land." They fill in all the blanks, Eleanor signs as seller and Henry signs as "agent for the Aquitaine Corporation, Buyer." As completed and signed, the contract indicates that on behalf of Aquitaine Corporation Henry has put $100 down and that the corporation will deliver the rest of purchase price within 30 days.

Two weeks after the contract is signed, Eleanor sees Henry walking down a street in town. Walking with Henry is a man whom Henry introduces as Richard, President of the Aquitaine Corporation. (This man is indeed Richard, and Richard is indeed President of Aquitaine.) After casual remarks about the weather, Eleanor asks, "Does Henry do a lot of work for your corporation, Richard?" Richard responds, "We've used him on a number of occasions. He's quite a go-getter."

Thirty days pass after the signing of the contract, and Eleanor receives no payment. When she contacts the Aquitaine Corporation, it denies that Henry was authorized to act on its behalf. It truthfully states that it never made any manifestation to Henry regarding Eleanor's parcel. It truthfully states that Henry never had any ongoing responsibilities with Aquitaine but instead occasionally received specific assignments. Aquitaine denies any responsibility for the Eleanor-Henry transaction and flatly refuses to pay.

Henry being nowhere to be found, Eleanor brings suit on the contract against Aquitaine Corporation. Assume that the "equal dignities" rule does *not* apply in the jurisdiction. Assume also that Richard's comments to Eleanor are attributable to Aquitaine. What result in Eleanor's suit?

EXPLANATION

Eleanor will lose. She will be unable to attribute Henry's actions to Aquitaine.

Since Aquitaine never made any manifestation to Henry regarding Eleanor's parcel, actual authority did not exist. Since Henry's role with Aquitaine never involved any "continuity of service," he was never a general agent. Consequently, he had no inherent agency power to enter into contracts on Aquitaine's behalf. The doctrines of apparent authority and estoppel are Eleanor's only hope, and that hope is forlorn.

The problem with apparent authority is one of timing: The apparent principal's manifestation came too late. To establish apparent authority, Eleanor must show some conduct attributable to Aquitaine that — *as of the moment of contract formation* — caused her to reasonably believe that Henry had authority. Until just prior to the execution of the form contract, Eleanor did not even know who the supposed principal was. Even when Henry disclosed Aquitaine's identity, Eleanor's inference that Henry had authority was based solely on Henry's remarks, not on any conduct of Aquitaine.

In some circumstances, an apparent principal's silence in the face of an apparent agent's known conduct will suffice as a manifestation. However, in this case there is no indication whatsoever that at the time of contract formation Aquitaine Corporation was aware of Henry's claim of agency status.

The conversation between Eleanor and Richard cannot salvage the situation for Eleanor. Even if Eleanor reasonably interpreted Richard's comments to mean that Henry had authority, there remains the problem of timing.  Even under the Restatement view, the claimant must link the manifestation to a reasonable belief that existed *as of the moment of the relevant act*. A post hoc manifestation cannot justify an ante hoc belief. By the time Eleanor spoke with Richard, Eleanor had already executed the contract.

The Eleanor-Richard conversation will be likewise unavailing for a claim of estoppel. Even assuming that Richard's casual remark "intentionally or carelessly" caused Eleanor to believe that Henry had acted with authority,[82] that belief did not cause any relevant harm. Eleanor had already signed the contract. Unless she can show that she suffered some additional prejudice subsequent to her conversation with Richard (e.g., turning down another potential buyer), she cannot establish estoppel.[83]

PROBLEM 7

At a party Joyce meets Al, who informs her that he is a stockbroker. Joyce tells Al that she has just inherited $10,000 from an aunt and is looking for a place to invest that money. One thing follows another, and after a few subsequent conversations Joyce agrees to invest the money with Al in a discretionary account. (In a discretionary account, the broker makes all investment decisions.) Al gives Joyce his card, which identifies him as a broker of the local brokerage firm of Take a Chance, Inc., and tells her to call him at his office so they can make arrangements for the deposit of her funds into the discretionary account.

On the following Tuesday Joyce calls the brokerage firm to talk to Al. The receptionist answers the phone, "Take a Chance Brokerage. May I help you?" When Joyce asks for Al, the receptionist says, "One moment, please," and then connects the call. During that call, Joyce and Al make final arrangements about the account. The next day Joyce sends Al a check made out, at his instructions, to his order. (Al had explained to Joyce that since the account was a discretionary account the check should be made out to his order, rather than to the order of the brokerage firm.) On Friday of that week Joyce again telephones Al at the brokerage firm. She again reaches the receptionist, who again puts her on hold and then connects her to Al. During this phone conversation, Joyce confirms that Al has indeed received the check.

82. Restatement §8B(1)(a), discussed at section 2.4.

83. To assert that Richard's comments caused a ratification is too much of a stretch. Ratification requires a manifestation of affirmance, and the purported principal's manifestation must relate specifically to the unauthorized act being ratified.

When Al and Joyce were first discussing investments, Al told Joyce, "The best thing to do with this kind of account as a customer is just forget it for about six months. Just let me do my work and get back to me in half a year and you'll see how much your investment has grown." Joyce follows this advice. Six months after the date she sent the check she again calls Al at the brokerage office. The receptionist tells Joyce that Al is not there. When Joyce asks to leave a message, the receptionist says, "I don't think that's possible. After all, he doesn't work here." When Joyce asks when he left, the receptionist responds, "Well, he never worked here." Concerned (as well she ought to be), Joyce does some checking and discovers the following:

(i) Al never worked for the brokerage firm.
(ii) Al was never a licensed broker.
(iii) The brokerage firm never gave or authorized Al to have a business card with the firm's name. Al had the card made up on his own, to facilitate his scams.
(iv) During a period of approximately a month, Al was quite friendly with the office manager of the brokerage firm and was discussing a possible consulting relationship between Al and the firm. During that month-long period, as a matter of convenience, Al spent a good deal of time working in a conference room in the brokerage's office. During that period, as a courtesy and convenience to Al, the brokerage firm allowed Al to receive calls and also took messages for him.
(v) The brokerage firm never received any of Joyce's money, Joyce's money is gone, and Al is nowhere to be found.
(vi) The brokerage firm was unaware of Al's scam until Joyce brought the problem to the firm's attention.

Joyce brings suit against the brokerage firm, claiming that the brokerage is liable for Al's conduct under the doctrines of apparent authority and agency by estoppel. What result?

Explanation

Apparent Authority. The question is a close one. The brokerage firm made two mundane but significant manifestations. By allowing Al to receive phone calls and mail at the brokerage office for an extended period of time and never explaining Al's true status, the brokerage company gave Joyce the impression that Al was an employee.[84] In reliance on that appearance of authority, Joyce entrusted her money to Al.

84. This causal link probably satisfies the Restatement's reliance requirement — that is, reliance on the principal's manifestation when inferring that the apparent agent is authorized. See section 2.3.2.

But given such arguably meager manifestation, was it reasonable for Joyce to believe that Al was authorized to receive a large check on the firm's behalf — especially a check made out to him personally?

Two points support Joyce's claim of reasonableness. First, it is reasonable to expect that a brokerage firm, which regularly handles other people's money, will take some care in selecting and supervising its employees. Therefore, when it reasonably appeared to Joyce that Al worked for the firm, it reasonably appeared to her that Al was trustworthy. Second, Al had prepared his scheme well. He even had a phoney business card. Although the card is not a manifestation attributable to the firm, it does suggest that Joyce's being deceived resulted not from her carelessness but rather from Al's deviousness.

Two other points argue forcefully against Joyce. Foremost is Al's instruction to make the check out to him personally. Such an unusual instruction should raise a question in the mind of any reasonably careful investor. The suggestion to stay out of touch for six months is likewise suspicious. In the circumstances, Joyce had a duty to inquire before acting. On balance, Joyce's apparent authority claim will probably fail.

Estoppel. For her estoppel claim, Joyce must prove either that the firm knew of Joyce's mistaken belief and failed to take reasonable steps to notify her, or that the firm intentionally or carelessly caused her belief. The firm was unaware of Joyce's mistaken belief and did nothing to intentionally cause it. As for a claim that the firm carelessly caused her belief, the carelessness seems as much Joyce's as the firm's. She is unlikely to prevail.[85]

PROBLEM 8

A small real estate company is planning to rent office space to an entrepreneur who needs "a place to hang my hat, pick up my mail, and get telephone calls." The real estate company's premises are small and its phone very basic. The entrepreneur's calls will come through the main switchboard without a dedicated line, and her desk will be located in the same open space used by employees of the company. How can the real estate company minimize its exposure to the kind of risks that faced the brokerage firm in Problem 7?

85. This Example is drawn from *Foley v. Allard*. The state appeals court and supreme court came to opposite conclusions. See 405 N.W.2d 503 (Minn. App. 1987) (reversing summary judgment for the defendant and holding that an issue of material fact existed as to apparent authority), *rev'd*, 427 N.W.2d 647 (Minn. 1988) (reinstating summary judgment and holding that there was no apparent authority because the plaintiff had failed its duty of inquiry).

EXPLANATION

Perhaps the most important safeguard is to expend the time and effort necessary to check into the *bona fides* of the would-be tenant. Problems will arise only if the entrepreneur cheats her customers or suppliers.

As for the agency law analysis, the brokerage case shows that the main risks would come from (i) ambiguous manifestations by the real estate company, and (ii) reasonable misinterpretations by third parties. Due to the limitations of the phone system and the office setup, certain manifestations are inherent in the proposed arrangement. The key, therefore, is to preclude reasonable confusion. The safest approach is to make sure that an appropriate clarification accompanies each potentially confusing manifestation. For example, when the receptionist receives a call for the entrepreneur, the receptionist should use a greeting that indicates that the entrepreneur is not employed by the real estate company. As for the office setup, a sign on the office entrance should indicate the entrepreneur's independent, unassociated status.

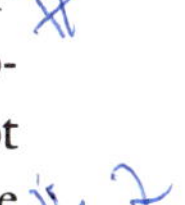

PROBLEM 9

The resident building manager in an apartment building serves regularly as the information "go-between" between the tenants and the landlord. On January 25 the landlord fires the manager, effective immediately, and gives the manager until the end of the next month to vacate his apartment. The next day a month-to-month tenant gives notice to the resident manager, stating that the tenant will vacate her apartment by the end of February. Angry and embarrassed about the firing, the fired manager accepts the notice, says nothing to the tenant about being fired and purposely does not pass the notice on to the landlord. Is the notice effective against the landlord? If so, what could the landlord have done to avoid being bound by a notice the landlord never actually received?

EXPLANATION

The notice is effective. Although the firing terminated the manager's actual authority to receive notices, the apparent authority continued. The landlord's past use of the resident manager as a channel of communication satisfies the manifestation requirement. So long as the former manager remained in the same apartment and no one told any of the tenants of the firing, it remained reasonable for the tenant to believe the former manager was authorized to receive notices for the landlord.

The landlord had available a simple preventive measure — promptly notifying the tenants of the change and directing them not to give notices to the former manager. No tenant who received this message could have reasonably believed that the former manager remained authorized.

PROBLEM 10

A television star wants to sell his yacht but wishes to avoid publicity. He therefore places the yacht with a yacht dealer, commissions her to sell the yacht, but instructs her not to disclose his identity. He does permit her to disclose that she is selling the yacht for an unnamed owner. The dealer succeeds in selling the yacht but in doing so inaccurately represents the yacht's sailing range. Can the purchaser hold that inaccuracy against the TV star in a breach of warranty action? If so, how might the star have avoided or minimized this risk?

EXPLANATION

The misstatement is attributable to the TV star. The dealer had express actual authority to sell the yacht on the star's behalf, and that authority carried with it the implied actual authority to accurately describe the yacht. When an agent of a disclosed or partially disclosed principal has actual authority to make a true statement on a particular subject, the agent has inherent agency power to make a false statement on that subject.

As for prevention, the TV star could not have avoided the dealer's inherent agency power without giving up the disclosed agency relationship, but could have decreased the likelihood of a false statement making that power relevant. For example, he might have briefed the dealer in detail about the yacht's characteristics. Or, he could have prepared a detailed description of the yacht and required the dealer to (i) furnish a copy to any prospect, and (ii) use a sales contract that expressly incorporated the description and conspicuously disclaimed any contrary representations. These precautions would not have absolutely prevented misstatements, but they would have undercut any assertion that a misstatement was material, induced reliance, or became part of the basis of the bargain.[86]

PROBLEM 11

Jeffrey is a buyer's broker in the recycled newspaper business. On behalf of various newsprint manufacturers, he locates and purchases recycled newspapers. Each time Jeffrey makes a purchase, he is acting on behalf of a particular customer. He nonetheless makes each purchase in his own name.

For the past five years, one of Jeffrey's customers has been Amalgamated Newsprint. During that time Jeffrey has made about four purchases per year for Amalgamated. On each occasion Jeffrey and Amalgamated have followed the same procedure: Amalgamated places an order with Jeffrey, stating a quan-

86. Under fraud, contract, and UCC law, to undercut these assertions is to significantly undercut the buyer's claim for relief.

tity and a maximum price. When Jeffrey finds the necessary newspapers, he purchases them in his own name and informs Amalgamated of the delivery date and price. Amalgamated then wires funds to Jeffrey, and Jeffrey pays the vendor. A commission structure rewards Jeffrey for bringing in an order below the maximum allowed price. Jeffrey understands that he is not authorized to make any purchases for Amalgamated without first having an order in hand.

Nonetheless, after five years Jeffrey has begun to anticipate Amalgamated's needs. Last week he saw a great purchase opportunity and, expecting an order from Amalgamated, he agreed to make the purchase. Although as always Jeffrey made the purchase in his own name, he noted the purchase on his books as "for Amalgamated." If Jeffrey is unable to pay for the purchase, can the vendor enforce the contract against Amalgamated?

Explanation

Probably not. Since Jeffrey lacked authority to purchase for Amalgamated without first having an order and since Amalgamated was an undisclosed principal, neither actual nor apparent authority apply. Also, since the vendor and Amalgamated were unaware of each other, there can be no estoppel.

The vendor's only hope is inherent agency power. The vendor must (i) label Jeffrey as Amalgamated's general agent, (ii) delineate Jeffrey's agency function as acquiring newspaper for Amalgamated on an ongoing basis, and (iii) characterize the purchase contract as "usual or necessary" to Jeffrey's authorized activities.[87]

The vendor will likely fail in all three respects, because it will fail in the first. Jeffrey is not a general agent. He is not "authorized to conduct a series of transactions involving a continuity of service."[88] To the contrary, he receives and needs separate authorization for each individual transaction. As a result, Jeffrey has no "ongoing" authorized responsibilities and the unauthorized purchase was not "usual or necessary" to any authorized activity.

PROBLEM 12

Jeffrey makes the unauthorized purchase described in Problem 11, but in doing so tells the vendor that the purchase is being made on behalf of Amalgamated. Jeffrey then calls Amalgamated and reports his "great find." Amalgamated shocks Jeffrey by saying, "Nothing doing. No order with us, no deal from us."

Jeffrey immediately contacts the vendor, seeking a brief delay on delivery.

---

87. Restatement §194 (inherent agency power of general agent of undisclosed principal), discussed at section 2.5.2.

88. Restatement §3(1) (general agent defined), discussed at section 2.5.2.

"I bought this for a customer," he explains, "and I didn't exactly have their OK in advance. They're balking a bit. I've got to make nice with them." Jeffrey then calls Amalgamated again, apologizes profusely and extols the benefits of this bargain. After a 45-minute conversation, Amalgamated relents and says "Alright. We'll take it."

Jeffrey immediately calls the vendor back and says, "No problem. We're fine." The vendor responds, "I'm fine anyhow. As soon as I learned that you were a go-between and had no authority, I went looking for another buyer. Just two minutes ago I sold the goods to somebody else."

Can Amalgamated enforce the original agreement against the vendor?

Explanation

No. Amalgamated did eventually affirm Jeffrey's unauthorized act, and ordinarily that affirmance would bind both the vendor and Amalgamated to the contract. In this instance, however, the vendor can avoid the ratification. In reliance on Jeffrey's lack of authority, the vendor changed its position and bound itself to another buyer. The fact that Amalgamated ratified before that change in position took place is irrelevant. What matters is that the vendor changed position before learning of the ratification.

PROBLEM 13

Assume that Amalgamated ratified the newspaper contract before the vendor found another buyer. Subsequently, Amalgamated learns that the newspaper contains an unacceptably high percentage of glossy advertising inserts. As a result the newspaper is unsuitable for Amalgamated's recycling process. Is Amalgamated nonetheless obliged to accept delivery?

Explanation

Probably. Although Amalgamated ratified while ignorant of an important fact, that fact may be legally immaterial. The percentage of glossy paper could be seen as relating to the value of the transaction or the transaction's desirability.

PROBLEM 14

The board of directors of Rollerskating, Inc. adopts a resolution authorizing the CEO "to appoint such officers, managers, and employees of the corporation as the CEO deems appropriate and to prescribe their respective duties, subject only to the numerical limits established by the board of directors from time to time." Aware of the resolution, Rollerskating's CEO appoints Rachael to be its purchasing agent. The CEO provides Rachael with a four-page memo, outlining the internal approvals necessary before Rachael may place an order. For instance, orders costing less than $50,000 can be approved by the CEO; orders costing less than $25,000 may be approved by any vice president; orders costing less than $5,000 may be approved by any department manager. Rachael receives a request from a vice president to order a Model 5400 Wodget from Samuel Equipment Corporation ("Samuel Equipment") at a price of $15,000, and she places the order. Does the order bind Rollerskating?

Explanation

Yes. In placing the order, she is acting with the reasonable belief that she is authorized to do so. Her belief is based on manifestations from an intermediary agent (her appointment to the position of purchasing; the memo of internal procedures). Those manifestations are within the intermediary agent's actual authority and are therefore attributable to the principal. In short, Rachael has actual authority.

PROBLEM 15

Over the next three months, Rachael places several more orders with Samuel Equipment Company, each properly requested by a Rollerskating vice president and each costing between $10,000 and $24,000. In due course Samuel Equipment delivers the equipment and bills Rollerskating. The bills come to the Rollerskating comptroller, whom the CEO has made responsible for reviewing and approving for payment all invoices over $1,000. The comptroller reviews the invoices, notes that each order was properly authorized and has been fulfilled, okays the payment, and signs and sends to Samuel Equipment a payment for the invoiced amount.

Subsequently, Rachael is promoted out of the purchasing department and is replaced by Herman. Rachael's last responsibility as purchasing agent is to brief Herman on his new responsibilities. Rachael does so, directing Herman's attention to the CEO's memo on internal approvals. Herman reads the memo but promptly forgets its provisions.

The next day Herman receives a rush request to order another Model 5400 Wodget from Samuel Equipment Company at a price of $15,000. The request comes from a department manager, not a vice president, but Herman places the order anyway. Does Herman's order bind Rollerskating?

Explanation

After having read the CEO's memo, Herman lacked actual authority to place the order. He could not *reasonably* have believed himself authorized. He did, however, have apparent authority. Rollerskating is therefore bound.

The apparent authority arises from manifestations attributable to Rollerskating, Herman's principal. Those manifestations were (i) Herman's position as Rollerskating's purchasing agent, and (ii) Rollerskating's conduct on past orders placed with Samuel Equipment. On each prior occasion, Rollerskating's comptroller approved and sent payments. The comptroller was acting within her actual authority, so her actions are attributable to Rollerskating. The sequence of events — order from a purchasing agent followed by payment without protest — presumably led Samuel Equipment to believe that Rollerskating purchasing agents have authority to place such orders. In light of the past events, that belief was certainly reasonable.

Herman may also have had inherent agency power. He was a general agent, acting in his principal's interest. Ordering the Model 5400 could be seen as an act usual or necessary to serving Herman's authorized purpose.[89]

PROBLEM 16

In an effort to establish a women's professional baseball league, Albert Gum hires the Ajax Baseball Scout Corporation to locate prospective players and bring them to Chicago for a tryout. Ajax has been in the scouting business for many years and provides scouting services to many ballclubs through a network of individual scouts located throughout the United States.

Gum agrees to pay Ajax a flat fee for each player who actually makes it through the tryouts and to reimburse Ajax for the reasonable expenses of food, lodging, and transportation in getting the prospects to the tryouts. Ajax informs its scouts of the project and in a telegram exhorts them to "get the good ones on the train, because Gum reimburses for travel expenses on all of them but we only make money on the ones who get through."

"Lefty" Glen, one of Ajax's scouts, spots an astounding prospect playing catcher in a charity softball game. He invites her to the tryouts, and she very much wishes to go. However, she has a regular job managing a dairy and still has four months left on her employment contract. Glen approaches the dairy owner and explains the situation, but the dairy owner refuses to release the

89. In one respect, this Explanation is unrealistically "flat." The third party, Samuel Equipment, has no mind in which to form or harbor beliefs and therefore cannot *directly* believe anything about Herman's authority. The relevant beliefs are those of Samuel Equipment's agents, which are attributable to their principal according to agency law. Whether those attributed beliefs are reasonable depends in part on what Samuel Equipment knows or has reason to know. Since Samuel Equipment cannot *directly* know anything, what it knows or has reason to know likewise depends on the attribution rules of agency law.

catcher. In the past Glen has sometimes put a few dollars into the pocket of a parent who did not want to lose a son's help on the family farm or in the family business. On those occasions, Ajax has always reimbursed Glen. Glen thinks, "Girl, boy — what's the difference? It's all baseball." He says to the dairy owner, "Tell you what. Let her come to Chicago. She's makes the team, you'll let her out of her contract and Mr. Gum will pay you $500." The dairy owner agrees.

The catcher excels at the tryouts and makes the team. Does Gum owe the dairy owner $500?

Explanation

No. Glen is Gum's subagent. For a subagent's act to bind the principal, the act must be within the subagent's power vis-à-vis the agent and within the agent's power vis-à-vis the principal. It is possible that Ajax gave Glen actual authority to pay or commit to pay money in order to "extract" top prospects. The past incidents constitute a manifestation from which Glen could have reasonably inferred authority to make the arrangement with the dairy owner. There is no indication, however, that Gum gave any such authorization to Ajax. To the contrary, Gum was quite specific in identifying covered expenses: food, lodging, and transportation.

Apparent authority will not help the dairy owner. There is no manifestation attributable to Gum sufficient to justify a belief that Gum had authorized Ajax to buy people out of contracts. The dairy owner can point to only one manifestation at all — the fact that Gum had engaged Ajax. Perhaps that manifestation caused the dairy owner to believe that Ajax's scout could bind Gum. Even so, the surrounding circumstances were sufficiently unusual as to oblige the dairy owner to inquire further before acting on that belief. As for inherent agency power, Ajax was arguably a general agent, since the search for female ballplayers involved a continuity of service. However, buying prospects out of contracts seems sufficiently peculiar as to fall outside a general agent's inherent power to do things "which usually accompany or are incidental to [authorized] transactions."[90]

PROBLEM 17

The ____________ Law School Exam Conflict and Make-Up Policy, printed in the Student Handbook, states in part:

> Students will take exams at the time and place announced in the exam schedule unless:

90. Restatement §161 (Unauthorized Acts of General Agent).

> (1) A student is prevented from taking the exams because of his or her illness or illness or death in the student's immediate family;
> (2) A student has two exams scheduled on the same day;
> (3) A student has three exams scheduled within a period of three calendar days. . . .
> (4) A student has two exams scheduled to begin within 23 hours of each other;
> (5) A student has exceptional circumstances that, in the discretion of the Dean of Students, justify a rescheduling. Exceptional circumstances must relate to personal situations, not to a burdensome examination schedule.
>
> No make-up exam will be given more than one week after the end of the regular exam period, except when such a delay is necessitated by illness or other exceptional circumstances.
>
> No student shall take any exam before the regularly scheduled time for the exam.

On account of a serious illness in the immediate family, a student requests permission to reschedule an exam. Due to long-standing and significant employment responsibilities, the only practical time for the make-up exam is three days before the regularly scheduled time. The Dean of Students grants the request, and the student buys two nonrefundable airline tickets. The Dean is aware that the student will be purchasing airline tickets but not that the tickets will be nonrefundable.

Subsequently, the professor whose exam is involved learns that an unidentified student will take a make-up in advance of the rest of the class. The professor objects and asserts that an advance make-up violates the Policy quoted above. Has the action of the Dean of Students bound the College to allow the advance make-up?

Explanation

The Dean can bind the College through some form of agency power (actual authority, apparent authority, inherent agency power) or through estoppel. In this matter, none of these attribution rules apply and the College is not bound.

For actual authority to exist, some manifestation of the principal must cause the agent to reasonably believe the agent has the right to bind the principal. The most salient manifestation given by the facts is the Student Handbook. That Handbook expressly precludes the scheduling of advance make-ups. The Dean's discretion, mentioned in item (5), relates to adequate cause for a make-up and does not override the subsequent, express prohibition on advance make-ups. The Dean could not reasonably believe that he or she has the right to schedule advance make-ups.

For similar reasons, apparent authority will not help the student. For apparent authority to exist, some manifestation of the principal must cause the third party (here, the student) to reasonably believe the agent has the right to bind the principal. Arguably, at least, the Dean's position constitutes a manifestation, as does the Handbook's reference to the Dean as the person who authorizes make-ups. However, those who rely on the appearance of authority have a duty of reasonable diligence. For a law student, that duty encompasses knowing the contents of the Student Handbook. Therefore, the student could not *reasonably* believe that the Dean has the authority to violate the Policy.

Inherent authority also will not help the student, even though the Dean is a general agent (i.e., authorized "to conduct a series of transactions involving a continuity of service"). In some circumstances a general agent has the inherent power to bind its principal even through an unauthorized act. However, the power does not exist when the third party has reason to know that the act is unauthorized.[91]

Estoppel is likewise unavailing. The student may have believed the Dean authorized to permit an advance make-up, but — given the clear statement in the Student Handbook — the College cannot be said to have "intentionally or carelessly caused such belief."[92] Moreover, through the Student Handbook, the College had taken "reasonable steps to notify [the student] of the facts."[93]

91. It would be a mistake to argue that the Dean's approval of an advance makeup constituted a misrepresentation about the scope of the Dean's actual authority and thereby bound the College through inherent agency power. Inherent agency power extends to misstatements concerning the subject matter of the transaction (e.g., quality of goods being sold) and not to the scope of the agent's authority. To argue otherwise means that an agent would always have the power to expand the scope of its power to bind. See section 2.5.3.

92. Restatement §8B(1)(a), discussed section 2.4.

93. Restatement §8B(1)(b), discussed section 2.4.

3

Binding the Principal in Tort

§3.1 Overview

In a modern economy, most principals work through agents and most tortious conduct is committed by agents.

> ***Example:*** A delivery company uses appropriate care in selecting, training, and scheduling its drivers. On the way to make a delivery, one of the company's drivers drives negligently and injures a third party. The driver's conduct is directly tortious, but the company's is not.

> ***Example:*** The owner of an office building hires a real estate broker to sell the building. The broker finds a prospect and, in extolling the building's virtues, purposely misrepresents several material matters. The owner is unaware of the misrepresentations and certainly has not authorized them. The broker's conduct is fraudulent, but the building owner's is not.

In the two circumstances just described, and in many others, the principal will be responsible for the agent's tort. Agency law contains rules for attributing an agent's tort to its principal, even though the principal has not itself engaged in any wrongful conduct.[1]

---

1. If a principal does engage in wrongful conduct, *direct* liability results. For a discussion of the direct duties of principals to third parties, see section 4.4.

These attribution rules divide roughly into two categories, according to the nature of the agent's conduct and the nature of the third party's injury. If an agent's physical conduct causes physical harm to a third party's person or property, then the concepts discussed in Chapter Two are largely irrelevant and the applicable doctrine is *respondeat superior*. This rule of inherent agency power applies only to a subcategory of agents known as "servants." A principal is generally not responsible for the physical torts of its nonservant agents.[2]

In contrast, if the agent's misconduct consists solely of words and the third party suffers harm only to its emotions, reputation, or pocketbook, the servant/nonservant distinction is rarely relevant. Respondeat superior is largely inapposite,[3] and attribution occurs according to the same rules of actual authority, apparent authority, and inherent agency power that apply to contractual matters.

§3.2 Respondeat Superior

§3.2.1 The Rule Defined

When an agent's tort causes physical injury to person or property, the principal's indirect liability exists, if at all, on the basis of respondeat superior.[4] When triggered, respondeat superior automatically attributes the agent's misconduct to the principal and imposes responsibility regardless of whether the principal (i) authorized the misconduct, (ii) forbade the misconduct, or (iii) even used all reasonable means to prevent the misconduct. The doctrine is one of strict, albeit vicarious liability. Most respondeat superior cases involve claims that an agent has been negligent, but the doctrine also applies to intentional torts involving physical harm.

The doctrine does not apply, however, to all agents. To the contrary, it applies only to a subcategory of agents labelled "servants." Under Restatement §220(1), an agent is a servant if the principal controls or has the right to control the agent's "physical conduct in the performance of the [agency] services." When the agent is a servant, the principal is called a *master*.

> ***Example:*** Dennis works as a baker's assistant in Suzanne's bakery. Suzanne provides all the necessary equipment, sets Dennis's hours, assigns his particular tasks, and supervises his performance. Dennis is Suzanne's servant agent, and Suzanne is the master.

---

2. Liability may exist when the work involved is inherently dangerous.

3. Respondeat superior is relevant in certain borderline areas, such as malicious prosecution and intentional interference with business relations. See section 3.4.4.

4. The injured party may also assert claims of direct responsibility. See section 4.4. In any event, the tortfeasor agent will be directly liable. See section 4.2.3.

Example: Dennis decides to quit work and hires Eli, an attorney, to work out a "severance package" with Suzanne. Dennis tells Eli what kind of package he wants, but the details of the negotiations are up to Eli. Eli is Dennis's nonservant agent.

In the agency law sense, the term *servant* has nothing to do with servile status or menial tasks. Servants are everywhere in modern society: A maid may be a servant, but so too are the top executives in any large corporation. Neither the exercise of responsibility nor the possession of professional skills negate servant status.[5] A carpenter employed by a general contractor is likely a servant, as is the skilled staff physician employed by a hospital. The typical modern employee is, in agency parlance, a servant.

Not all servant misconduct triggers respondeat superior liability. The servant must have been acting "within the scope of employment." According to the Restatement, a servant's conduct is within the scope of employment only if:

(a) it is of the kind he is employed[6] to perform;
(b) it occurs substantially within the authorized time and space limits;
(c) it is actuated, at least in part, by a purpose to serve the master, and
(d) if force is intentionally used by the servant against another, the use of force is not unexpectable by the master.[7]

Example: Early one morning, Dennis, the baker's assistant, is at his job kneading dough in the bakery. He notices that a stray cat has wandered in and is about to jump on a counter that is covered with freshly baked cookies. Dennis scoops the cat up and gently tosses it out the door into the alley. Unfortunately, the cat lands atop a crate packed with cut glass that belongs to the china shop next door. The crate falls over and the glass breaks. Dennis has acted within the scope of his employment. He was doing the kind of work he was employed to perform, in his usual (and therefore authorized) place and during the usual (and therefore authorized) time. He acted to serve his master's

---

5. However, in some circumstances an alleged servant's skills can argue against servant status, especially when the alleged master lacks the necessary expertise to effectively exercise control. See section 3.2.4.

6. In ordinary parlance, the word "employment" describes a business relationship that agency law classifies as master-servant. In contrast, the Restatement uses "employment" as a term of art, to mean a principal's engagement of an agent to accomplish some task or provide some service. Thus, in Restatement terms, a principal can "employ" a nonservant agent.

7. Restatement §228(1).

interests. Using force against a cat is not, in Restatement terms, using force "against another."[8]

Example: After work one day Dennis stops by a bookstore, looking for a book on baking techniques. He wishes to improve his own skills so that he can do a better job at the bakery. While browsing through the aisles he trips over a step-stool and bumps another customer. This accident was not within the scope of his employment. Although he was "actuated, at least in part, by a purpose to serve the master," he was not doing the type of work for which he was hired. Moreover, he was outside the authorized time and far from his authorized place of work.

In sum, a master is strictly and vicariously liable for the physical torts of a servant acting within the scope of the servant's employment.

§3.2.2 *The Rule's Rationale*

The doctrine of respondeat superior rests on three rationales: enterprise liability, risk avoidance, and risk spreading. It sometimes seems, however, that the doctrine's real purpose is to "find the deep pocket."

Enterprise liability. As explained in more detail in Chapter Two, according to this rationale risks should follow benefits.[9] Respondeat superior reflects that viewpoint by placing the risk of agent misconduct on the enterprise that stands to profit from the agent's services.

Risk avoidance. According to this rationale, respondeat superior serves to protect society from dangerous occurrences. Since the existence of servant status means that the master has the right to control the servant's physical performance, the master is well positioned to prevent the servant from engaging in careless or otherwise improper conduct. Imposing strict liability creates a strong incentive for the master to use its position of control to achieve "risk avoidance."

Viewed from this perspective, the rule may seem overbroad. If we are looking to encourage "safety-producing" conduct by masters, why impose liability even if the master has taken reasonable care in selecting, training, and supervising its servants? Why, that is, have strict liability? Why not impose

8. Although respondeat superior applies, the china shop will prevail against Suzanne only if it can demonstrate that Dennis's act was negligent.

9. See section 2.5.1 (discussing enterprise liability as a rationale for inherent agency power).

liability only when the master has failed to properly select, train, or supervise?[10]

The answer is one of expediency. A narrowly tailored rule would present significant problems of proof, and those problems of proof would make a narrowly tailored rule ineffective. The difficulty of proving direct negligence on the part of the master warrants a rule of vicarious, strict liability.[11]

Risk spreading. According to this theory the master should strictly and vicariously bear the risk of its servants' misconduct because the master can (i) anticipate the risks inherent in its enterprise, (ii) spread the risk through insurance, (iii) take into account the cost of insurance in setting the price for its goods or services, and (iv) thereby spread the risk among those who benefit from the goods or services.

The deep pocket theory. In modern society, the typical master-servant relationship is that of employer and employee. The overwhelming majority of servants therefore have fewer resources than do their masters. It may be tempting to look to this economic reality and characterize the doctrine of respondeat superior as a mere guise for reaching non-negligent defendants with convenient deep pockets.

Indeed, a few cases have expressly sought to justify respondeat superior as a mechanism for assuring victim compensation, and the rule does owe its practical importance to the deep pockets of masters. However, as discussed above, the doctrine has independent theoretical justification.

§3.2.3 The Reach of Respondeat Superior: *Servant Status and Scope of Employment*

The power of respondeat superior depends on the definition and application of two key concepts: *servant status* and *scope of employment*. The more expansively each is defined, the broader the scope of the rule. As a result, disputes between an injured third party and an alleged master typically involve battles over characterization. Was the tortfeasor a servant? Was the tortious conduct within the scope of employment?

10. A master (or other principal) can be directly liable on this basis. See section 4.4.1.

11. In this regard this rationale for respondeat superior parallels one of the rationales for strict product liability. See, e.g., *Phipps v. General Motors Corp.*, 363 A.2d 955, 958 (Md. 1976) (strict liability warranted in part due to the difficulty of proving producer negligence).

§3.2.4 *Servant Status*

Servant contrasted with independent contractor. Agency law applies the label "independent contractor" to a nonservant who provides services or undertakes tasks for others. As a result, respondeat superior disputes often begin with a struggle over labels — servant versus independent contractor.[12] As stated previously, the ultimate determining factor is whether the principal controls or has the right to control the agent's "physical conduct in the performance of the [agency] services."[13] The Restatement provides ten factors to aid in making that determination:

> (a) the extent of control which, by the agreement, the master may exercise over the details of the work;
> (b) whether or not the one employed is engaged in a distinct occupation or business;
> (c) the kind of occupation, with reference to whether, in the locality, the work is usually done under the direction of the employer or by a specialist without supervision;
> (d) the skill required in the particular occupation;
> (e) whether the employer or the workman supplies the instrumentalities, tools, and the place of work for the person doing the work;
> (f) the length of time for which the person is employed;
> (g) the method of payment, whether by the time or by the job;
> (h) whether or not the work is a part of the regular business of the employer;
> (i) whether or not the parties believe they are creating the relation of master and servant; and
> (j) whether the principal is or is not in business.[14]

No single factor is determinative, and the language of an agreement will not prevail over the reality of the relationship. Formal independence will be discounted if the master's right to fire results in practical control.

---

12. In theory, there should be a preliminary question. At least according to the Restatement, a servant is a type of agent. Yet cases determining servant status rarely, if ever, consider the threshold question of whether the party in question actually qualifies as an *agent*. Instead, the decisions typically skip directly to the issue of servant versus independent contractor. History may explain the omission. The notions of servant status and respondeat superior predate the modern law of agency, and perhaps, given that history, the doctrine of respondeat superior should be seen as an autonomous area of law. Within that autonomous area, a servant is a servant — pure and simple. The notion that servant status is a subcategory of agent status may be disregarded as a modern and distracting gloss.

13. Restatement §220(1).

14. Restatement §220(2).

> ***Example:*** A pizza shop contracts with a driver to provide home delivery. A written agreement between the shop and the driver has the following terms: It labels the driver an "independent contractor"; it permits the pizza shop to terminate the contract at any time without cause; it requires the driver to provide his own car, car insurance, and uniform; it requires the driver to know the streets of the delivery area and to choose his own route on each delivery; it provides for payment by delivery, not by the hour. The contract also permits the driver to have other jobs, even for other pizza shops, so long as the driver is available at times scheduled by the pizza shop. The driver, however, has no other employment. While making a delivery the driver has an auto accident. The other driver sues the pizza shop, successfully invoking respondeat superior. Despite the driver's formal freedom of action and the contract's label of "independent contractor," the pizza shop's right to terminate at any time gave the shop effective control of the driver's performance. Given the driver's dependence on the job, the driver was likely to obey any "suggestions" the shop happened to make. Moreover, given the unskilled nature of the work, the shop had whatever expertise was necessary to actually make suggestions or give orders.

The right to terminate is not by itself dispositive, however. It carries weight only to the extent that it creates the practical ability to control the agent's performance.

> ***Example:*** Suzanne, the baker, hires Paul, a carpenter, to remodel the front of the bakery. Suzanne provides a detailed plan for the remodelling and agrees that Paul will work on a "time and materials" basis. That is, Paul will charge her for the materials he uses, plus an hourly fee for the time he spends working. Paul agrees that Suzanne can end the job at any time for any reason. Despite Suzanne's right to terminate, Paul is an independent contractor, not Suzanne's servant. Carpentry is a skilled occupation, and Suzanne lacks the expertise to control the details of the work.

> ***Example:*** Paul wants to speed up the remodelling, so he hires Dorothy to work on the project. Like Paul, Dorothy is a skilled carpenter. Paul agrees to pay Dorothy an hourly wage, and Dorothy understands that Paul can fire her at any time. Despite Dorothy's skill, she is Paul's servant. His right to fire her gives him effective control over her performance. His expertise will allow him to exercise that control. (The hourly wage also argues in favor of servant status.)

The impact of servant status on other areas of law. The servant concept helps set the scope for a wide range of statutes designed to regulate or tax the modern employment relationship. In areas ranging from civil rights to payroll taxes, these statutes typically cover "employees" but neglect to define the term. Courts must therefore develop a definition, and many have turned to the agency notion of servant. Some decisions make explicit reference to the law of agency; others use its concepts without attribution.

Servant concepts have influenced the reach of statutes in the following areas, among others:

- discrimination in employment
- unemployment compensation
- workers' compensation
- social security
- payroll taxes

§3.2.5 *Scope of Employment*

The rationale and reach of the concept. *Scope of employment* is the other main respondeat superior battleground. Even if the tortfeasor is a servant, vicarious liability results only if the tort occurred within the scope of employment.[15] This restriction arises from the rationale of the rule. Respondeat superior is a doctrine of inherent authority, and the "scope of employment" element seeks to confine the master's liability to risks that inhere in the servant's assigned tasks.

The Restatement lists ten factors to be considered in determining whether a servant's conduct is within the scope of employment:

(a) whether or not the act is one commonly done by such servants;
(b) the time, place, and purpose of the act:
(c) the previous relations between the master and the servant;
(d) the extent to which the business of the master is apportioned between different servants;
(e) whether or not the act is outside the enterprise of the master or, if within the enterprise, has not been entrusted to any servant;
(f) whether or not the master has reason to expect that such an act will be done;
(g) the similarity in quality of the act done to the act authorized;

15. A master may nonetheless face direct liability. For example, if a resident manager rapes an apartment tenant, that conduct is probably outside the scope of employment. See section 3.2.6 (discussing respondeat superior and intentional torts). However, if the manager had an extensive criminal record involving violence toward women and the landlord overlooked that record, the landlord may be directly liable on a claim of negligent hiring or for failure to provide safe premises. See sections 4.4.1-4.4.2.

(h) whether or not the instrumentality by which the harm is done has been furnished by the master to the servant;
(i) the extent of departure from the normal method of accomplishing an authorized result; and
(j) whether or not the act is seriously criminal.[16]

As these factors indicate, scope of employment is not limited to the servant's proper or authorized conduct. To be within the scope of employment, "conduct must be of the same general nature as that [actually] authorized, or incidental to the conduct authorized."[17] However, the notion of "incidental" goes a long way. It is foreseeable that servants will on occasion transgress and that some of the misconduct will occur on the periphery of the servant's authorized work. An act can therefore be within the scope of employment even though (i) the master has expressly forbidden the act, (ii) the act is tortious,[18] or (iii) the act constitutes a minor crime.

Example: A bar owner instructs a bouncer never to use a certain chokehold in restraining obstreperous customers. One night the bouncer overreacts to an especially troublesome patron and uses the hold. The patron subsequently files a civil suit against the bar owner and seeks to press criminal charges against the bouncer. Nonetheless, the bouncer acted within the scope of employment; the relevant conduct fits within the general guidelines of Restatement §228(1).[19] The alleged tort does not change the outcome. Respondeat superior exists to attribute the torts of servants. The use of a forbidden tactic also is immaterial here. Unauthorized conduct can be within the scope of employment. Likewise, the alleged simple assault does not matter. "The master can reasonably anticipate that servants may commit minor crimes in the prosecution of the business."[20]

A servant's failure to act can also come within the scope of employment, but only if: (i) the omitted act is within the servant's duties, and (ii) the servant's failure to act causes the master to breach a duty to the injured third party.

---

16. Restatement §229(2).

17. Restatement §229(1).

18. If tortious acts were necessarily outside the scope of employment, respondeat superior would never impose vicarious liability. The doctrine operates to attribute the servant's tort to the master.

19. Quoted at section 3.2.1. Restraining patrons is the kind of work a bouncer is "employed to perform." The bouncer's purpose was to serve the bar owner (by quieting a disruption), and the actions occurred when and where they were supposed to. A bouncer's use of force should come as no surprise to a bar owner.

20. Restatement §231, comment *a*.

Example: A grocery store employee is supposed to check the produce aisles regularly to make sure that small, littered pieces of produce do not cause a hazard. The employee neglects to do so, and a customer slips and falls on a lettuce leaf. The employee's failure to act was within the scope of employment because (i) the employee had a duty to the principal (the grocery store) to act, and (ii) on account of the employee's failure the principal breached its duty to its customers to maintain the premises in a reasonably safe condition.[21]

The relationship of the master's control to the scope of employment. The principal's right to control determines whether a party is a servant but as a general matter does not influence the servant's scope of employment. A principal must have a certain amount of control over the agent's physical performance in order for servant status to exist, but that control will not necessarily extend to every aspect of the servant's tasks. It is therefore possible for a servant's scope of employment to include areas in which the master does not exercise control.

Example: Suzanne, the baker, employs Sarah, an expert wedding cake designer. Suzanne pays Sarah a weekly salary and provides the location and all necessary equipment and materials for Sarah's efforts. Suzanne determines Sarah's working hours and working conditions and assigns Sarah particular cake orders to fill. In short, Sarah is Suzanne's servant. Nonetheless, Suzanne and Sarah both expect Sarah to use her own judgment, discretion, and expertise in designing, baking, and constructing wedding cakes. On one occasion, Sarah leaves a small metal wire inside an apparently edible portion of a cake, and a customer is injured. Sarah's negligence is within the scope of her employment. Even though the negligence occurred outside the master's zone of control, the conduct was nonetheless "of the same general nature as that [actually] authorized, or incidental to the conduct authorized."[22]

---

21. There might appear to be another way to analyze this type of situation. A principal does not discharge its duty to a third party merely by delegating that duty to an agent. See section 4.4.2. Therefore, if the agent fails to perform the duty, the duty remains undischarged and unperformed. As a consequence, the principal is directly liable. This analysis works if the principal's duty involves strict or absolute liability. If, however, the principal's duty is a duty of care, the analysis contains an unstated assumption — namely, that the delegation itself does not satisfy the principal's duty. Assume, for example, that (i) the principal owes business invitees a duty to use reasonable care in maintaining the principal's premises, (ii) the principal delegates maintenance of the premises to a servant, and (iii) in selecting and supervising the servant the principal uses due care. But for the rule stated in the text, the principal's nonnegligent delegation would satisfy the principal's duty to use reasonable care.

22. Restatement §229(1).

Some older cases have reached the opposite conclusion. These cases generally involved automobile accidents, and the servants were often sales representatives whose jobs required them to move from place to place. The servants used automobiles as transportation, but in contrast to, say, delivery van drivers, the servants' driving did not *directly* benefit the master and the master did not supply the vehicle. Noting that the master did not control the driving, these cases held the driving to be outside the scope of employment.

Although this approach confuses the test for servant status with the test for scope of employment, the reasoning may seem to reflect respondeat superior's risk avoidance rationale. If the master lacks detailed control over some aspect of the servant's endeavors, how can the master be expected to alleviate risks outside its control?

The answer is simple enough and grounded in practicality. If a principal indeed has enough control to be a master, the principal very likely has the practical power to extend its control to all the details of performance. For example, a company that hires travelling sales representatives could require those representatives to take driving safety courses and to drive defensively. Moreover, the car accident cases ignore the other two rationales for respondeat superior — risk spreading and enterprise liability. Neither of these rationales have anything to do with the zone of control; they relate to the zone of endeavor.

Tangential acts — frolic and detour. An act can come within the scope of employment even though it is merely tangential to the authorized work, so long as there is some connection. The servant must be "actuated, at least in part, by a purpose to serve the master."[23] When a servant does something purely for its own reasons, that conduct is outside the scope of employment.[24]

> ***Example:*** Nick and Nora drive a delivery van for Acme Delivery Company. During their lunch break, they take the company truck and drive to the Opera House to buy tickets to "La Boheme" for their own use. During this trip they are not acting within the scope of their employment. To use a term first introduced in an 1834 English case, they are on a *frolic* of their own.[25]

Scope of employment can, however, cover situations in which the servant has temporarily detoured for some personal reason while still essentially serving the master's purposes.

---

23. Restatement §228(1)(c).

24. In the context of intentional torts, recent cases have somewhat attenuated this rule. See section 3.2.6 (respondeat superior and intentional torts).

25. *Joel v. Morrison, England, Nisi Prius (Exchequer)*, 6 Car. & P. 501, 172 Eng. Rep. 1338 (1834).

Example: On their way to make a delivery for Acme, Nick and Nora realize that they are hungry and that the city's best deli is just two blocks off their direct route. They are entitled to a full lunch break but know that the customer is anxiously awaiting delivery. They decide just to get something "to go" at the deli. On their brief trip to the deli, they remain within the scope of their employment. Although they are temporarily on business of their own, they remain "actuated, at least in part, by a purpose to serve the master." In traditional terms, they are merely on a "detour."

Frolic and *detour* are powerful labels. They determine whether respondeat superior applies. Unfortunately, neither the cases nor the commentators provide coherent, specific guidance for determining when which label applies. One famous case requires the conduct to be at least "incidental" to the servant's duties.[26] But how to determine whether a detour is incidental enough to avoid being a frolic? One prominent commentator has suggested, "A temporary deviation from one's work can be incidental to one's task; a temporary abandonment cannot be."[27] But how to distinguish between a deviation and a temporary abandonment?

There are no simple answers to these questions. The cases sometimes refer to the distinction being "a matter of degree" or to the determination necessarily being made on a "case-by-case basis." Such expressions are really a code for "we know the difference when we see it (maybe), but we cannot articulate any rule to allow lawyers (or law students) to easily predict outcomes."

In the face of this uncertainty, those seeking to predict outcomes should read a range of scope of employment cases, try to develop a sense of their "flavor," and keep in mind the following themes:

- Servants predictably engage in small-scale deviations from single-minded concentration on the master's interests. Ordinary, expectable deviations are likely to be considered mere detours.
- Deviations that pose risks of harm of a type significantly different than the types inherent in the servant's task are more likely to be considered frolics.[28]
- If the servant's deviating conduct occurs far outside the "time and space" authorized by the master, the deviation is more likely to be a frolic.

---

26. *Fiocco v. Carver*, 137 N.E. 309, 311 (N.Y. 1922).

27. J. Hynes, Teacher's Manual to Agency and Partnership: Cases, Materials, Problems 41 (3d ed. 1989).

28. Respondeat superior is a doctrine of inherent agency power, and this theme is consistent with that doctrine's rationale, i.e., imposing liability on the principal only for risks inherent in the enterprise. See section 3.2.2.

- If the master instructs or controls a servant as to matters that would otherwise be the servant's purely personal concern (e.g., personal hygiene, off-duty recreational activities), the servant's conduct in those matters is neither a detour nor a frolic. The master's instructions bring the matters directly within the scope of employment.

Frolics rarely last forever. At some point, the servant will be, in Restatement terms, "re-entering employment"[29] and respondeat superior will again apply. Re-entry has certainly occurred once the servant is fully back in the master's service, that is, once the servant is

- again actuated at least in part by a desire to serve the master's interest,
- again within the authorized space and time limits, and
- actually is taking (or has taken) some action in the master's interests not necessitated by the frolic itself.

Example: After purchasing their opera tickets, Nick and Nora get back into the Acme delivery van, drive to their next delivery stop, and begin unloading packages. One of the packages falls and lands on the toe of a passerby. Assuming that Nick and Nora have been negligent, respondeat superior will apply. Nick and Nora's frolic has ended, and they have re-entered employment.

The analysis is murkier, however, if a servant negligently causes harm while merely "on the way back" to employment. Indeed, the law here is as difficult to pin down as the law distinguishing frolic from detour. The following themes provide some guidance:

- A servant has not re-entered the scope of employment merely by deciding to return to serving the master's interest.
- In most jurisdictions the servant must be at least "reasonably near the authorized space and time limits" for re-entry to occur.[30] In some jurisdictions, merely starting back toward a place where servant duties are to be performed suffices to re-enter the scope of employment. In other jurisdictions, the servant must have actually returned to the authorized "time and space."
- A servant does not necessarily have to return to the point the frolic began in order to re-enter the scope of employment.

Example: Nick and Nora's trip to the opera house has taken them a half-hour off their regular delivery route. After purchasing their tickets,

29. Restatement §237, comment *a*.
30. Restatement §237.

they get back into the Acme delivery van and head for their next stop. As they are pulling away from the curb, they negligently hit another car. In some jurisdictions, respondeat superior will apply, since the servants have started back to their authorized work location (i.e., the next delivery stop). In other jurisdictions, the distance between that location and the accident site will preclude a finding of re-entry into employment.

§3.2.6 *Intentional Torts*

Although most respondeat superior cases involve torts of negligence, the doctrine's rationale and reach also extend to intentional torts. When a servant, acting within the scope of employment, commits an intentional tort causing physical harm, the master is vicariously liable. Overly aggressive barroom employees provide prime examples.

> ***Example:*** Seeking to remove an unruly patron, a bar's bouncer applies an overly aggressive wrist lock. The bar's owner is vicariously liable for the intentional tort of battery.

> ***Example:*** A customer in a bar refuses to pay for a drink. Outraged, and seeking to collect on the debt owed the bar's owner, the bartender strikes the customer. The bar's owner is vicariously liable for the intentional tort of battery.

As with any respondeat superior claim, the third party in an intentional tort case must show that the servant acted within the scope of employment. For many years the key question in this respect was whether the servant was motivated at least in part by a desire to serve the master.[31]

> ***Example:*** During a horse race, two horses are struggling for the lead. One of the jockeys strikes the other and thereby gains a competitive advantage. The striking jockey's employer is vicariously liable for the intentional tort. The servant was seeking, albeit wrongfully, to advance the master's interests.

> ***Example:*** Throughout a lengthy bus ride a passenger is noisy and disruptive. After the bus arrives at the terminal and the passenger has disembarked, the bus driver grabs the passenger and punches him. The

31. Restatement §228(1)(c), discussed section 3.2.1, makes this an entrance criterion to scope of employment.

bus company is not vicariously liable.[32] Since the trip is over and the passenger's misbehavior no longer affects the master's interest, the servant could not be actuated by a desire to serve the master.

The "purpose rule" has always been pliable. "Judge Learned Hand concluded that a drunken boatswain who routed the plaintiff out of his bunk with a blow, saying 'Get up, you big son of a bitch, and turn to,' and then continued to fight, might have thought he was acting in the interest of the ship."[33] One court has even found the necessary "purpose to serve the master" when a police trainee, practicing his quick draw inside the police station, accidentally shot a fellow officer. The court held that the trainee was trying to improve his firearms techniques, to the benefit of his employer.[34]

Some recent cases have gone beyond manipulating the purpose test and have looked instead to foreseeability, that is, "whether such conduct should fairly have been foreseen from the nature of the employment and the duties relating to it,"[35] or "whether the risk was one that may fairly be regarded as typical of or broadly incidental to the enterprise undertaken by the employer."[36]

Example: A psychologist employed by a clinic engages in sexual relations with a patient. The patient later asserts that the psychologist's emotional control over her vitiated any apparent consent and that the psychologist's conduct constituted an intentional tort. She sues both the psychologist and the clinic. The clinic may well be liable vicariously, because the psychologist's conduct was both foreseeable and incidental to his job. "[S]exual relations between a psychologist and a patient is a well-known hazard and thus, to a degree, foreseeable and a risk of employment. In addition, the . . . situation would not have occurred but for [the psychologist's] employment; it was only through his relation to [the patient] as a therapist that [the psychologist] was able to commit the acts in question."[37]

---

32. If the bus company owns the terminal, it may be directly liable for failing to provide safe premises to business invitees.

33. *Ira S. Bushey & Sons v. United States*, 398 F.2d 167, 170 (2d Cir. 1968), *citing Nelson v. American-West African Line*, 86 F.2d 730 (2d Cir. 1936), *cert. denied*, 300 U.S. 665 (1937).

34. *Thompson v. United States*, 504 F. Supp. 1087 (D.S.D. 1980).

35. *Marston v. Minneapolis Clinic of Psychiatry and Neurology, Ltd.*, 329 N.W.2d 306, 311 (Minn. 1983).

36. *Whitson v. Oakland Unified School District*, 123 Cal. App. 3d 133, 142 (1981) (citations and internal quotations omitted).

37. Marston, supra note 35, at 311.

§3.3 Liability for Physical Harm Beyond Respondeat Superior

In general, a principal is not vicariously liable for physical harm caused by the torts of a nonservant agent. Respondeat superior controls most such cases, and it applies only to servants. In a few situations, however, other rules apply, and these rules impose liability for the torts of nonservants.

§3.3.1 *Principal's Direct Duty to a Third Party*

If a principal owes a direct duty of care to a third party and relies on an agent for the necessary performance, the agent's negligence may result in liability for the principal.

> ***Example:*** An amusement park hires a lawn service company to maintain the park grounds. The contract requires the lawn service company to do its work when the park is not open to the public, but otherwise the amusement park has no right to control the manner in which the company performs its services. One day, the company negligently leaves a mower blade attachment in the grass. A day later a patron of the park steps on the attachment and injures a foot. Since the lawn service company is an independent contractor, respondeat superior will not apply. However, since the park owes a duty to exercise reasonable care for the protection of its customers, the park may face liability as a result of the lawn service company's negligence.[38]

§3.3.2 *Intentional Torts of Nonservant Agents*

When a nonservant agent commits an intentional tort and causes physical injury, the relevant law is muddy. According to some authorities, the principal is not liable unless (i) the principal intended or authorized the result or the manner of performance,[39] or (ii) the principal owed a duty to the injured party to have the agent's task performed with due care. Notable exceptions exist to

---

38. For a more extensive discussion of this point, see section 4.4. A comparable rule exists under the doctrine of respondeat superior. See section 3.2.5 (servant's failure to act is within scope of employment if the omitted action is within the servant's duties and the omission causes the master to breach a duty to a third party).

39. In such circumstances, a master would also be liable for the intentional tort of its servant. The master's intent would bring the servant's act within the scope of employment.

this rule. For example, store owners often face liability when their hired guard service falsely arrests or imprisons a customer of the store. The liability comes despite the store owner's protestation that the guard service acted as an independent contractor. Some of the cases that impose liability rest on a finding of control. Others assert that the principal ratified the guard service's wrongful act (e.g., by not terminating services of the independent tortfeasor). Other cases hold the store liable for breaching its duty to protect its customers from unwarranted attack.[40] Still other cases simply hold that independent contractor status does not bar vicarious liability for an agent's *intentional* (as distinguished from negligent) torts.

§3.3.3 *Misrepresentation by an Agent or Apparent Agent*

If (i) a person has actual or apparent authority to make statements within a particular subject, (ii) the person makes a misstatement of fact within that subject, (iii) a third party relies on that misstatement, and (iv) the third party suffers physical harm as a result, then the actual or apparent principal is liable to the third party.[41]

> ***Example:*** Office Realty Inc. ("Realty") is substantially remodelling an office building that it owns and wishes to allow prospective tenants to see the work in progress. Realty has hired a construction manager to supervise the remodelling work and instructs that manager to tell prospective tenants which sites within the building are safe to view. One day the construction manager makes a mistake and sends Irv, a prospective tenant, into an unsafe stairwell. Irv is injured. Realty is vicariously liable, regardless of whether the construction manager is a servant or independent contractor. Realty's agent had actual authority to identify the safe locations, and the agent's misstatement on that subject caused Irv physical harm.[42]

40. Under this theory, the store is not vicariously liable for the guard service's intentional tort. Rather, the store is directly liable for having breached its duty to provide safe premises for its business invitee. See section 4.4.2.

41. Restatement §251(b) contains the rule for statements made with actual authority. Restatement §266 contains the rule for statements made with apparent authority and also refers to statements made within the apparent scope of employment. The latter notion seems to add little, if anything, beyond apparent authority. That is, any statement within a person's apparent scope of employment will likely be within the scope of that person's apparent authority as well.

42. Irv may also have two other theories of recovery: (i) Realty's direct liability for failure to use reasonable care to protect business invitees, see section 4.4.2, and (ii) Realty's liability for the construction manager's negligence in supervising the worksite, see section 3.3.1.

Example: Realty tells Selma, another prospective tenant, "If you want to see how the place will look, go over to the building. It's under construction, but one of our people will tell you where it's okay to go." Selma goes over to the building and meets a security guard, who is employed by a guard service hired by Realty. Neither the guard service nor its employees have actual authority to direct prospective tenants. However, when Selma asks, "How do I get to look at some redone offices?" the guard responds by directing Selma into the unsafe stairwell. If Selma is injured as a result, she can hold Realty vicariously liable. The guard's statement was made with apparent authority.[43]

§3.3.4 Negligence of Apparent Servants

In one area, the doctrine of respondeat superior meshes with the law of apparent authority and produces vicarious liability for those who merely appear to be masters. In the words of the Restatement:

> One who represents that another is his servant or other agent and thereby causes a third person justifiably to rely upon the care or skill of such apparent agent is subject to liability to the third person for harm caused by the lack of care or skill of the one appearing to be a servant or other agent as if he were such.[44]

Example: An oil company conducts a national advertising campaign, encouraging customers to have their cars serviced at service stations carrying the company's logo. In the words of the ad campaign: "You can trust your car to the man who wears the star." Some of the service stations are, in fact, independently owned and operated. In agency parlance, they are independent contractors, not servants. One such independent contractor negligently repairs a car, and the customer suffers injury as a result. The injured customer may well have a claim against the oil company. The ad campaign may have created an appearance of servant status and the customer may indeed have "trusted" to that relationship in choosing the service station. If so, the oil company will be vicariously liable.[45]

---

43. For the rules for establishing apparent authority, see section 2.3.

44. Restatement §267.

45. *Gizzi v. Texaco, Inc.*, 437 F.2d 308 (3d Cir. 1971) (directed verdict for defendant reversed; jury question as to whether ad campaign induced reasonable reliance).

§3.4 Torts Not Involving Physical Harm

§3.4.1 *The Basic Paradigm: Closer to Contracts Than to Physical Torts*

If an agent's misconduct consists solely of words and the third party suffers harm only to its emotions, reputation, or pocketbook, the agency analysis resembles the approach used for contractual matters. The key rules are those of actual authority, apparent authority, and inherent agency power.[46] Except for the borderline areas of malicious prosecution and intentional interference with business relations, respondeat superior is largely irrelevant.

§3.4.2 *Misrepresentation*

The attribution rule. A principal is vicariously liable for an agent's tort of misrepresentation if:

- the agent makes a misstatement that is tortious under the law of the relevant jurisdiction,
- the misstatement comes within the agent's actual authority, apparent authority, or inherent agency power, and
- a third party relies on the misstatement and suffers harm as a result.[47]

For an agent's misstatement to be tortious, the statement must be material and the agent must act with the required, culpable state of mind (e.g., intent to deceive, reckless disregard of the truth or falsity of the statement, negligence).[48]

> ***Example:*** Rebecca retains Michael to sell a plot of land she owns near the river. She gives him the authority to truthfully describe the land and its vicinity. Michael shows the land to Samantha, who seems quite interested. She asks, "Has there ever been any trouble with flooding from the river?" Michael knows that, in fact, almost every spring the river floods at least a little and that often the water temporarily covers a quarter of Rebecca's plot. However, fearful of losing the sale, he responds, "Oh no. Not at all." Samantha agrees to buy the land and

---

46. For a detailed discussion of these rules, see Chapter Two.

47. Restatement §257.

48. The state of mind requirements vary from jurisdiction. In particular, not all jurisdictions recognize a claim for negligent misrepresentation.

signs a purchase agreement. Planning to build a house near the river, she hires and pays an architect to do preliminary plans. She then learns the truth about the flooding and, pursuant to contract law, rescinds the purchase agreement.[49] The architect's plan are now worthless to Samantha, and she may recover their cost from Rebecca. Michael, Rebecca's agent, made a material misstatement with intent to deceive and thereby committed the tort of intentional misrepresentation.[50] Since Michael had the actual authority to truthfully describe the flooding situation, he had the inherent agency power to give a false description.[51] Samantha relied on the false statement and as a consequence suffered injury. Rebecca is therefore vicariously liable in tort.

In one type of situation, an agent's innocent misrepresentation may produce tort liability for the principal. If:

- a *principal* (i) has information relevant to a transaction, (ii) authorizes an agent to conduct the transaction, and (iii) does not provide that information to the agent;
- the *agent,* lacking that information, innocently makes a material misstatement; and
- a *third party* relies on the misstatement and suffers injury as a result,

then the principal may be liable for misrepresentation. If the principal believed that the agent would make the misstatement, the principal is liable for intentional misrepresentation. If the principal merely had reason to know that the agent would make the misstatement, then principal is liable for negligent misrepresentation.[52]

Example: Carolyn owns a vacation cabin near a lake. She wishes to sell the cabin and asks Rachael, a local resident, to show the cabin to prospective purchasers and to arrange a sale. Like all lake cabins in the area, this cabin is not connected to city sewer lines. Instead, the cabin flushes wastes into a septic system. Carolyn therefore believes that a serious prospective purchaser will ask about the septic system. Rachael has visited Carolyn's cabin many times, and the septic system has always been in working order. Carolyn consequently believes that Rachael will represent to prospective purchasers that the septic system is trouble free. In fact, last summer Carolyn had the septic system inspected and learned that the system is on the brink of failure and within a year or

49. Michael's misstatement as to the flooding is attributed to Rebecca, so Samantha can rescind for fraud in the inducement. See section 2.5.3.

50. Michael is also liable. See section 4.2.3.

51. See section 2.5.3.

52. Restatement §256.

two will require very costly repairs. She withholds this information from Rachael. Rachael eventually sells the vacation home, having in fact innocently represented that the septic system in good condition. When the buyer learns the truth, the buyer rescinds, but not before having incurred significant expenses in reliance on the deal. Carolyn is liable to the buyer for those expenses, on the grounds of intentional misrepresentation.[53]

In this sort of situation, the liability is more direct than vicarious. In essence, the principal is liable for having intentionally or negligently caused an agent to make a misrepresentation.

Tort attribution contrasted with contract attribution. Besides saddling a principal with tort liability, an agent's misstatements can also give rise to contractual claims against the principal, particularly claims for breach of warranty and rescission.[54] The tort attribution rules differ from the contract rules, however, with regard to what is being attributed and, consequently, with regard to the role of innocent misstatements.

For tort law purposes, the principal's liability is vicarious, and the attribution involves a complete tort: a material misstatement made by an agent with the requisite state of mind (e.g., intent, negligence), followed by a third party's injurious reliance. Establishing the principal's liability involves two steps: tort law recognizes a tort as committed by the agent; agency law attributes that completed tort to the principal. Therefore, since innocent misstatements do not constitute torts, an agent's innocent misstatements do not trigger the tort attribution rules.[55]

The process works differently with contractual claims. Unless the principal is undisclosed, no contractual claim is complete at the agent's level and no complete claim exists to be attributed.[56] Instead, agency law attributes the agent's statement, and contract law then imposes liability as if the principal had itself made the statement. The principal's liability is direct ("on the contract"), even though one of the elements creating liability (the misstatement) is satisfied only by attribution. For contract law purposes, therefore, an agent's misstatement is attributed regardless of whether the misstatement was innocent,

53. Whether Carolyn is liable for more — expectation damages, punitive damages — depends on the tort law of the jurisdiction.

54. See section 2.5.3 (for contract law purposes, misstatement attributable to principal if made within agent's actual authority, apparent authority, or inherent agency power; if agent has actual authority to make true statement on a subject, agent has inherent power to make false statements on that subject).

55. As previously discussed, a principal can be directly liable for intentionally or negligently causing an agent to make an innocent misrepresentation.

56. If the principal is undisclosed, the agent is a party to the contract and the third party's claim will be valid against the agent as well as the undisclosed principal. See section 4.2.1.

negligent, reckless, or intentional. Indeed, the attribution occurs essentially as if the statement were accurate.[57] For a graphic explanation, see Figure 3-1.

§3.4.3 *Defamation*

A principal is liable for an agent's defamation if the agent acted with actual or apparent authority in making the defamatory statement. It is not necessary that the agent be actually or apparently authorized to commit defamation, but rather that the agent be actually or apparently authorized to make the statement. For apparent authority to be relevant, the agent must have appeared authorized to "those hearing or reading the statement."[58]

> ***Example:*** A credit bureau authorizes its employees to report to subscribers information contained in the bureau's data base. A bureau employee receives a call from a subscriber who is seeking information

Figure 3-1. Comparison of Tort and Contract Attribution Paradigms

	Agent's Level	*What Is Being Attributed*	*Principal's Level*
Tort	Agent commits a tort of misrepresentation (which necessarily involves a non-innocent misstatement).	Agent's tort	Vicarious Liability for the attributed tort of Agent
Contract	Agent makes a statement, which may be a misstatement, which in turn may be innocent.	Agent's (mis)statement	Direct Liability, in part due to the attributed statement of Agent

57. Assume, for example, that a principal authorizes an agent to sell the principal's car and to describe the car's characteristics to prospective purchasers. The agent says to a third party, "This car will get at least 25 miles per gallon on the highway," and in reliance the third party agrees to buy the car. Agency law attributes the mph statement to the principal, and under contract law the statement creates a warranty that binds the principal. If the statement happens to be true, contract law gives the buyer no claim against the principal. If the statement happens to be false, contract law will provide the buyer several remedies (e.g., rejection, revocation of acceptance, action for damages for breach of warranty). The distinction drawn in the text parallels a distinction between contract law and tort law. Under contract law, innocent misstatements by a party can be actionable. Under tort law, they are not.

58. Restatement §247.

about James Hobbs. The employee consults the data base and reports, "Two convictions for larceny, and 12 bounced checks." In fact, the data base is completely wrong, and, up to this moment, Mr. Hobbs's reputation has been unblemished. The credit bureau is liable for defamation. The employee had actual authority to make the report which turned out to be defamatory.

Example: A newspaper columnist has written a series of columns harshly criticizing the city parking commissioner. The newspaper's publisher becomes concerned that the columns are getting perilously close to the "actual malice" necessary to allow a public figure to recover for defamation. The publisher therefore orders the columnist to cease writing about the commissioner. Assuming that the columnist will obey, the publisher neglects to mention the order to the paper's managing editor. The columnist disobeys the publisher's order, and another column appears that contains scurrilous statements that are clearly defamatory. The newspaper is liable to the commissioner for defamation. Although the columnist lacked actual authority to write on the subject, to the newspaper's readers the columnist appeared to be authorized.[59]

The example of the columnist highlights the policy behind using apparent authority as an attribution rule for defamation. In the words of the Restatement:

> [D]efamation is effective, in part at least, because of the personality of the one publishing it. Thus, one who appears to have authority to make statements for the employer gives to his statements the weight of the employer's reputation.[60]

Servant agents. According to the Restatement, the scope of a master's vicarious liability may be broader than that of a nonmaster principal, encompassing not only actual and apparent authority but also the servant's scope of employment. Thus, if a servant's defamatory statement is neither actually nor apparently authorized, the master may still be bound if the statement comes within the servant's scope of employment.

In most instances, however, this theoretical increase in exposure will have little practical consequence. Most, though not all, activities within a servant's scope of employment are either expressly or impliedly authorized.[61] As for the rest, if the scope of employment is relevant, it is likely that (i) the relevant

59. The newspaper's manifestation was, of course, the running of the column.

60. Restatement §247, comment *c*.

61. See section 3.2.5 (acts forbidden by the principal come within the scope of employment).

third party listeners or readers will be aware of the employment, and (ii) apparent authority by position will exist and suffice to bind the principal. Consider, for instance, an illustration offered by the Restatement to demonstrate how the scope of employment can inculpate a master for its servant's defamation:

> *P* employs *A* as general manager of an electric lighting company. Unreasonably believing that *T*, a customer, has been stealing electric current, *A* calls *T* to the office and charges him with this before a number of people. This conduct is within the scope of *A*'s employment.[62]

Unless the "number of people" were ignorant of the manager's position, the scope of employment analysis is redundant. Apparent authority by position binds the electric company in any event.

§3.4.4 Malicious Prosecution and Interference with Business Relations

These torts often involve both words and actions, and in this borderline area respondeat superior is the chief rule.

> ***Example:*** Todd is a salaried sales rep for the Nickel Surgical Products Company ("Nickel"). Nickel trains its sales reps to pursue business aggressively. Todd persuades Ace Hospital to stop buying its surgical drapes from Amalgamated Hospital Supply ("Amalgamated") and buy instead from Nickel. Ace's decision and subsequent purchases from Nickel breach a contract with Amalgamated. Todd has tortiously induced that breach of contract, and Nickel is vicariously liable.[63]

§3.5 Attributing Torts in Complex or Multilevel Relationships

Respondeat superior attributes a servant's tort to the master, that is, the principal with a right to control the servant's performance. In some situations, however, it may be difficult to identify the responsible master. For example, one master's servant may come under the temporary control of another party, as when an equipment leasing company lends an equipment operator to a construction company or when a surgeon conducts an operation with the

---

62. Restatement §247, Illustration 5.

63. For a discussion of the factors used to determine scope of employment see section 3.2.5.

assistance of nurses employed by a hospital. Agency law analyzes such situations using the *borrowed servant* doctrine. Another type of problem arises when the servant of one master commits a tort, that master itself is subject to substantial control by another party, and the tort victim seeks to recover from that other party. These *chain of masters* situations arise most often in franchise relationships, although they also occur frequently in the construction industry. Agency case law and the Restatement offer several different views on the subject.

Borrowed servant. This concept is best introduced by example.

> ***Example:*** Hoister Crane Company ("Hoister") owns and leases out large cranes used in major construction projects. Operating such a crane requires considerable skill, so Hoister employs a staff of trained, full-time operators and assigns an operator to run each leased crane. Hoister charges its customer a single fee that includes both the use of the crane and the services of the operator.
>
> Hoister rents a crane to General Contractor, Inc. ("General Contractor"), a construction company building a large office building. At the worksite, Hoister's operator runs the crane, but General Contractor's site supervisor tells the operator what tasks to do and when to do them. When the crane is in operation, the site supervisor uses hand signals to direct the operator. While lifting a load of steel bars, the operator negligently allows three bars to fall. They injure a passerby. Whether respondeat superior implicates Hoister or General Contractor depends on whether, at the time of the accident, the crane operator was General Contractor's borrowed servant.

> ***Example:*** Jeff Couteau, a surgeon, has operating privileges at Morgan Hospital ("the hospital") but is not a hospital employee. When he performs surgery at the hospital, he is assisted by operating room nurses who are hospital employees. During the course of an operation these nurses take orders from whatever physician is in charge.
>
> At the end of one of Couteau's operations, a nurse neglects to make a proper sponge count and the patient is closed with one sponge still inside. In the subsequent malpractice action, the patient asserts that respondeat superior makes Couteau liable for the nurse's negligence. Whether this claim succeeds depends on whether, during the operation (and more particularly, at the time of the negligent sponge count), the nurse was Couteau's borrowed servant.

The precise contours of the borrowed servant doctrine vary from jurisdiction to jurisdiction, and application of the rule is always very fact-intense. In most jurisdictions a party invoking the rule must show that:

- the regular master (sometimes called "the general employer") assigned or allowed its servant to work for and under the supervision of another party (sometimes called "the special employer");
- at the time of the servant's tortious conduct
  - — the special employer had the right to control in detail the performance of the servant's work, and
  - — the general employer retained no significant right of control over the servant, including the right to reassign the servant to other tasks.[64]

The doctrine is relevant only when a servant is alleged to have committed a tort, so "the important question is not whether or not [the servant] remains the servant of the general employer as to matters generally, but whether or not, as to the act in question, [the servant] is acting in the business of and under the direction of [the general employer] or [the special employer.]"[65]

Although the borrowed servant doctrine can be described as an exception to respondeat superior, the doctrine is better understood as an application of respondeat superior principles. Respondeat superior attributes a servant's negligence to the servant's master, and the borrowed servant doctrine redirects that attribution away from the regular master ("the general employer") to a temporary master ("the special employer"). The redirection is appropriate because the special employer has a transitory but complete right to control the servant. Since respondeat superior rests on the master's right to control, vicarious liability should follow the control. When the general employer allows the special employer to control the servant's performance, the "borrowed" servant's torts should be attributed to the special employer.

As for the case of the crane operator, courts have gone both ways.[66] Some have looked to the general contractor's detailed control over the operator

---

64. Sometimes the injured party asserts the theory, seeking to impose vicarious liability on the more solvent defendant. Sometimes the general and special employer contest the issue, each seeking to place vicarious liability on the other. Sometimes an allegedly borrowed servant will itself invoke the doctrine, seeking to escape the constraints of the workers compensation statute so as to assert tort claims against the servant's regular employer. (Ordinarily an employee cannot sue its employer in tort and must instead pursue the less remunerative remedies of the workers compensation system. However, if at the time of the accident the employee is the borrowed servant of the special employer, the workers compensation statute applies not to the general employer but rather to the special employer. The employee therefore receives workers compensation benefits from the special employer and is free to pursue tort remedies against the general employer.)

65. Restatement §227, comment *a*.

66. Compare *DePratt v. Sergio*, 306 N.W.2d 62 (Wis. 1981) (holding crane operator who obeyed hand signals to be a borrowed servant) and *Gulf, Colorado & Santa Fe Co. v. Harry Newton, Inc.*, 430 S.W.2d 223 (Tex. Civ. App. 1968) (holding crane operator not to be a borrowed servant even though operator was following instructions of the special employer).

(e.g., the hand signals) and have found the operator to be the general contractor's borrowed servant. Other courts have held to the contrary, following a Restatement comment that "a continuation of general employment is indicated by the fact that the general employer can properly substitute another servant at any time, that the time of the new employment is short, and that the lent servant has the skill of a specialist."[67]

As for the medical malpractice case, if the hospital lacked the right to reassign the nurse during the operation, the borrowed servant doctrine probably applies.

Chain of masters.[68] In this area too the issues are best introduced with examples.

> ***Example:*** A franchisor licenses a local company to run a hotel using the franchisor's name, logo, business practices, and national reservation system. The franchise agreement requires the franchisee to abide by a thick book of regulations on topics ranging from style of linen to lawncare. One winter a custodial employee of the *franchisee* carelessly shovels a sidewalk and leaves behind a thin sheet of ice. A customer of the franchisee slips and falls. The customer sues not only the franchisee but also the franchisor.

> ***Example:*** A construction company ("the general contractor") wins a bid to build a new apartment building. It subcontracts the electrical work to an electrical subcontractor and the plumbing work to a plumbing subcontractor.[69] Concerned about workplace safety, the general contractor has its own site supervisor regularly check on the work of all the subcontractors. An electrician, employed by the electrical subcontractor, negligently leaves some equipment lying around, and an employee of the plumbing subcontractor trips and suffers injury. The injured employee sues not only the electrical subcontractor but also the general contractor.

---

67. Restatement §227, comment *c*. Presumably the operator's skill makes it less practical for the special employer to assert effective control. See section 3.2.4 (when agent possesses special skills that principal lacks, principal is less able to exert control and less likely to be a master).

68. Unlike "borrowed servant," this phrase does not appear in the Restatement or in case law. It is instead the author's shorthand.

69. Sometimes a business that is providing services or producing a product will delegate or "subcontract" part of the work to another business. The reasons for this practice vary: The delegating party may lack the necessary in-house expertise; it may have the expertise, but its own employees may be busy on other projects; it may be able to save money by delegating work to a company that is more efficient or that pays its employees lower wages. Subcontracting is characteristic of the construction industry and increasingly prevalent in the manufacturing sector.

The outcome of each of these situations depends on whether the plaintiff can find a chain of attribution that links the tortfeasor (i.e., the custodian and the electrician) to the distant party (i.e., the franchisor and the general contractor). Unfortunately, many of the cases in this area fail to articulate a complete analysis. For example, courts in franchise cases often (i) note that the tortfeasor is the servant of the franchisee, (ii) determine that the franchisee is the servant of the franchisor, and (iii) on that basis alone hold the franchisor liable for the tortfeasor's misconduct. These courts neglect to explain why the franchisor is responsible for the torts of its servant's servant.

At least three different theories could apply. First, the tortfeasor could be deemed the subservant of the distant party. According to the Restatement, if a master's servant engages servants of its own to conduct the master's business, then the servant's servants are subservants of the master.[70] In that event, respondeat superior attributes the subservant's torts (if within the scope of employment) directly to the master.[71] Under this approach, the franchisor and the general contractor would be masters, the franchisee and the electrical contractor would be servants, and the custodian and the electrician would be subservants. See Figure 3-2.

The problem with this analysis is that, for a subservant to exist, the master must have expressly or impliedly authorized the servant to engage servants of

Figure 3-2. Subservant Analysis

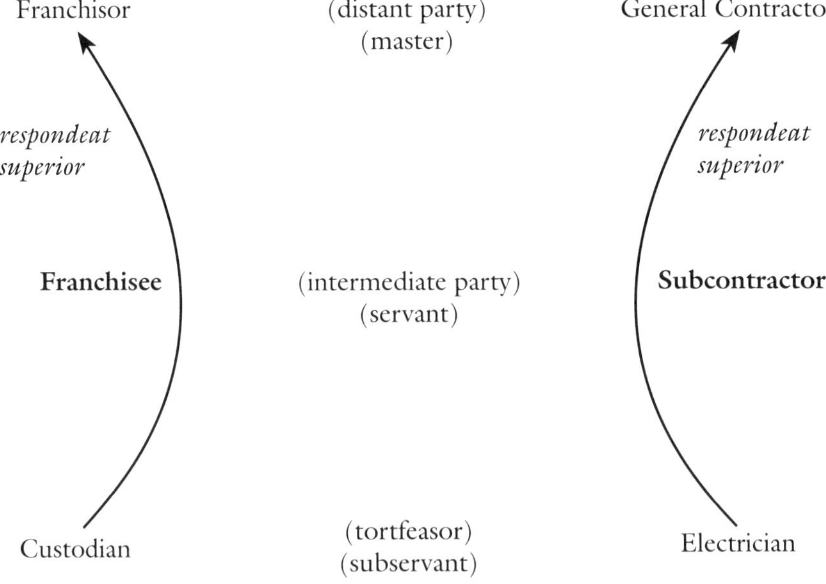

70. Restatement §5(2).

71. Restatement §5(2), comment *e*.

its own to do the master's business. Moreover, the master will have the "prerogative of overriding his servant in giving directions [to] the subservant."[72] In the situations under discussion, neither of these elements is present. The distant party (i.e., the franchisor and the general contractor) does not consider the intermediate party (i.e., the franchisee and the electrical contractor) to be its servant. To the contrary, the typical franchise agreement and the typical construction subcontract expressly disclaim any agency status whatsoever. It is therefore unlikely that the distant party has consented to having the intermediate party engage *sub*servants. Likewise, the intermediate parties see themselves as independent contractors, especially when it comes to control of their employees. They would hardly view the distant party as having the "prerogative" to directly control their employees.

The second approach follows more closely the actual business relationships and involves two steps of attribution. Under this approach the tortfeasor (i.e., the custodian and the electrician) is seen simply as the servant of the intermediate party (i.e., the franchisee and the electrical contractor), and the intermediate party is seen as the servant of the distant party (i.e., the franchisor and the general contractor). Respondeat superior then operates twice: The tortfeasor's negligence is attributed to the intermediate party, and the intermediate party's (attributed) negligence is attributed to the distant party. See Figure 3-3.

Figure 3-3. Master of Master Analysis

Franchisor	(distant party) (master)	General Contractor
↑ *respondeat superior*		↑ *respondeat superior*
Franchisee	(intermediate party) (servant of distant party; master of tortfeasor)	**Subcontractor**
↑ *respondeat superior*		↑ *respondeat superior*
Custodian	(tortfeasor) (servant of intermediate party)	Electrician

72. Id.

Figure 3-4. Direct Control Analysis

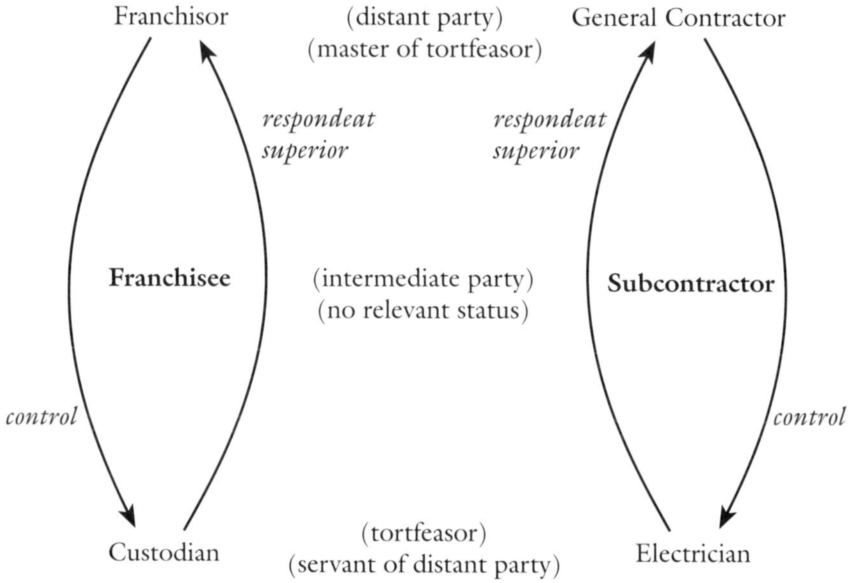

The third approach is the most direct, holding that the distant party has retained or exercised a direct right to control the intermediate party's employees and is accordingly the tortfeasor's master. Respondeat superior therefore applies directly. See Figure 3-4. In most circumstances, there will be no express evidence of the distant party's right of control. Indeed, the typical franchise agreement and the typical construction subcontract will state to the contrary. However, the parties' conduct may belie their formal manifestations. If, for example, the general contractor's site supervisor regularly issues orders to the employees of the electrical subcontractor and those employees obey, then the right to control is present and respondeat superior may well apply. Similarly, if the franchisor regularly sends out inspectors, these inspectors give orders directly to the franchisee's employees, and the employees obey, then the franchisor may well find itself at the receiving end of respondeat superior liability.

PROBLEM 18

Rachael hires Joe, an experienced attorney, to represent her in a commercial dispute. Driving to a settlement conference, Joe negligently hits a pedestrian. The pedestrian sues Rachael, asserting respondeat superior. What result?

Explanation

The pedestrian's claim will fail. For respondeat superior to apply, the tortfeasor must be a servant. For servant status to exist, the principal must have the right to exercise detailed control of the agent's manner of performance. A lawyer's client does not have that right. The client sets the goal and may make major strategy decisions. Tactics, however, are the lawyer's domain.

PROBLEM 19

Samuel buys new vinyl tile for his kitchen floor from Athos Floor Coverings Unlimited ("Athos"), a discount retailer of carpet, linoleum, tile, and other floor coverings. Athos does not have any installers on staff, but tells Samuel that it will arrange to have the tile installed by one of the "licensed, bonded contractors who do this sort of work for us." Athos arranges for Michael Planchet to install Samuel's tile. Planchet runs his own small contractor business and does jobs for various retailers and directly for homeowners. Athos does not guarantee him any regular work and pays him a flat fee per square yard on each installation. (The fee does vary depending on the floor covering being installed.)

In due course, Planchet arrives at Samuel's kitchen with the tile and the installment materials. Those materials include an effective but highly volatile adhesive for securing the tiles to the subfloor. Unfortunately, Planchet fails to read or follow the instructions on the adhesive can, and a fire breaks out. Samuel sues Athos, asserting respondeat superior. What result?

Explanation

Samuel will lose. Planchet is an independent contractor, not Athos's servant.

Virtually all the factors listed in Restatement §220(2) indicate Planchet's independence. Athos, the alleged master, has no control "over the details of the work." Planchet, the alleged servant, is skilled, "is engaged in a distinct occupation or business," and supplies his own tools. The employment is episodic, not sustained, and payment is by the job. Moreover, Athos and Planchet do not consider themselves master and servant.[73]

PROBLEM 20

A newspaper provides its customers home delivery through a network of "independent delivery agents." A written contract between the newspaper and each agent (i) assigns each agent a particular route, (ii) provides the agent a percentage commission based on the subscription price of papers delivered,

73. Restatement §§220(2)(a), (b), (d), (e), (f), (g) & (i), respectively.

(iii) allows the newspaper to terminate the relationship at any time without cause, and (iv) expressly disclaims any master-servant relationship. The newspaper conducts training programs on how to make deliveries and increase sales. Although the contract does not mention these programs, the newspaper considers regular attendance to be mandatory. Each delivery agent supplies his or her own car or van to make the deliveries. Many of the routes are quite large, and many of the agents have no other gainful employment. The newspaper does not withhold social security taxes from the commission checks and does not pay the employer's portion of social security on the commission amounts.

While delivering papers one morning, one of the agents loses control of the car and crashes into a building. The building owner sues the newspaper, asserting respondeat superior. What result?

Explanation

The building owner may well prevail, although several Restatement factors point the other way.

The parties apparently did not consider themselves master and servant. The contract expressly disclaimed that relationship, and the principal did not withhold or pay social security taxes on account of the commissions.[74] The newspaper did not pay a set wage or salary,[75] and the delivery agent supplied the key instrumentality (i.e., the car).[76]

The key question, however, is the right to exercise control. The newspaper's right to terminate without cause and without advance notice suggests that, practically speaking, the newspaper had considerable control over the agents' performance. The fact that few of the agents were "engaged in a distinct occupation or business"[77] made each especially susceptible to the threat of termination. That the threat carried weight is evidenced by the required attendance policy.

Although the Restatement factors may thus point in opposite directions, the policies underlying respondeat superior clearly favor a finding of servant status. Home delivery is an integral part of the newspaper's enterprise, and that enterprise should bear the costs of accidents foreseeable in that phase of the business. As for risk avoidance, the training sessions demonstrate that the newspaper can and already does influence the agents' manner of performance. Moreover, as for risk spreading, the newspaper is far better able to anticipate, calculate, and spread the cost than are the individual agents.

---

74. Restatement §220(2)(i).
75. Id. §220(2)(g).
76. Id. §220(2)(e).
77. Id. §220(2)(b).

PROBLEM 21

A manufacturing company employs a staff of full-time research scientists. Each scientist receives a salary, a well-equipped laboratory, and necessary materials. Each scientist reports to the company's Director of Research, who assigns research projects and keeps tabs on research progress. According to company policy, however, all scientists are to spend at least 20 percent of their time on projects they have conceived. The company believes that this "bootleg research" will spur creativity and innovation. The Director of Research does not review the bootleg projects in any detail, but instead merely inquires on occasion as to their subject matter.

One afternoon, a company research scientist leaves the lab and goes to a city park. As part of a bootleg project, the scientist wishes to test a new waterproofing substance in the brook that runs through the park. (It's also a nice day for a walk.)

Although the scientist is certain that the substance is stable and nontoxic, the substance disintegrates in and pollutes the brook. Clean-up costs total $35,000. The city sues the manufacturing company, alleging respondeat superior. What result?

EXPLANATION

The city will prevail. The scientist is the company's servant and was acting within the scope of employment.

Servant status is evident. The only possible contrary factor is Restatement §220(2)(c) — the great degree of "skill required in the particular occupation." That skill does not, however, undercut either the master's right or ability to control. The Director of Research, who acts for the master,[78] has ample expertise to supervise the scientist.

The scope of employment issue is almost as clear. Although the scientist was away from the authorized workplace,[79] the work was (i) within the authorized time,[80] "of the kind [the scientist was] employed to perform,"[81] and "actuated at least in part by a purpose to serve the master."[82] The bootleg nature of the project is immaterial. Although the master did not exert active control over the project, the master certainly retained the right to do so. Nothing prevented the company from changing or eliminating the bootleg

78. Under the terminology developed in Chapter Two, the Director of Research is the master's intermediate agent. See section 2.7.2.

79. Restatement §228(1)(b).

80. Id.

81. Id., §228(1)(a).

82. Id. §228(1)(c). The scientist was also actuated in part by a personal desire to take a walk in the park.

policy. Moreover, in determining the scope of employment, what matters is the zone of the servant's endeavors, not the zone of active control.

PROBLEM 22

Sandpit Gravel Company ("Sandpit") is excavating a deposit of gravel from a large open pit. Among the Sandpit servants working in the pit are a group of dump truck drivers. There are two ways to drive out of the pit: one safe but very time-consuming, the other quick and quite dangerous. Sandpit has repeatedly instructed the drivers to take the safe route and has repeatedly forbidden them to use the dangerous one. The drivers are generally happy to comply, since the company pays them by the hour. At closing time, however, the drivers have a different attitude. When the closing whistle blows, the drivers are "off the clock" and want to get themselves home as soon as possible. Nonetheless, they obey the rules and take the slow way out, until one day, when a driver in a big rush tries the fast route. The truck slid off and rolled over, crushing the leg of an OSHA inspector. The OSHA inspector sues Sandpit, alleging respondeat superior. What result?

EXPLANATION

Sandpit is liable. A servant's act can come within the scope of employment even though forbidden by the master. In this case, the driver was conducting the master's business, with an "instrumentality . . . furnished by the master;"[83] the act was quite similar "in quality . . . to the act authorized;"[84] "the departure from the normal method of accomplishing an authorized result"[85] was moderate; and "the master [had] reason to expect that such an act [would] be done."[86]

PROBLEM 23

A shopping mall employs its own staff of private security guards. These guards receive regular wages, wear uniforms supplied by the mall, report to the mall's Director of Security, and work shifts assigned by the Director. The mall, through the Director, has forbidden the security guards to carry guns.

One day a guard disobeys that policy and brings an unlicensed gun to work. While at work the guard has a scuffle with an unruly patron, and the

83. Restatement §229(2)(h).

84. Id. §229(2)(g).

85. Id. §229(2)(j).

86. Id. §229(f). The master saw a need to repeat the prohibition, suggesting that the master considered the prohibited conduct to be at least somewhat attractive to the drivers.

gun inadvertently discharges and wounds a patron in the leg. The patron sues the mall, alleging respondeat superior.[87] What result?

Explanation

Assuming that the patron can establish the guard's underlying tort, vicarious liability will probably exist. Dealing with unruly patrons is central to the guard's responsibilities, and as shown in Problem 22, a forbidden act can be within the scope of employment. The servant's illegal act — carrying an unlicensed weapon — will undercut the patron's claim only if that act is considered "seriously criminal" and even then only if the act is considered unforeseeable.

PROBLEM 24

An amusement park has a staff of employees to maintain the park's rides. The park assigns one of the employees, Rudy, to check out the Ferris wheel each morning before the wheel begins to operate. Rudy has always been an exemplary employee, well-trained, diligent, and careful.

One night, however, Rudy has his first experience over-indulging in alcohol. The next morning he suffers from a colossal hangover, barely gets to work, and forgets to check out the Ferris wheel. Unfortunately, the safety device on one of the gondolas is loose, and later that day a rider falls out and is injured. A proper inspection would have spotted and remedied the problem.

The rider sues the amusement park, asserting respondeat superior.[88] What result?

Explanation

The rider will prevail. A servant's omission is within the scope of employment if (i) the omitted act is within the servant's duties and (ii) the servant's omission causes the master to breach a duty. Both elements are present here. Rudy's job included checking the Ferris wheel, and his failure to check caused the park to breach its duty to provide reasonably safe rides.

PROBLEM 25

Domestic Safari, Inc. ("Safari") takes teenagers on summer camping treks throughout the country. For each trek Safari employs a trek leader and a group

87. The patron would probably also assert direct claims, such as failure to provide reasonably safe premises to customers and negligent hiring. See section 4.4.2.

88. The rider would probably also assert direct claims, such as failure to provide reasonably safe premises to business customers and negligent supervision. See section 4.4.2.

of counselors. During one trek, the leader sends a counselor into town to buy food for the next week's camping. The counselor takes a Safari jeep and drives to a shopping mall. While at the mall the counselor also buys a few items for her personal needs. Returning to the campsite, the jeep runs into another car. That car's driver sues Safari, asserting respondeat superior. What result?

Explanation

If the driver can prove the counselor negligent, then the driver will win. Even assuming that the counselor's purchase of personal items constituted a frolic, she had reentered the scope of employment by the time of the accident. Since Safari had authorized the trip to and from the mall, the return trip was well within "the authorized space and time limits."[89] Moreover, since the counselor was transporting the sought-after food, she was again "acting with the intention of serving [her] master's business."[90]

PROBLEM 26

A major league pitcher is having a bad day on the mound. Not only are the opposing batters doing well, but a heckler in the stands is increasingly obnoxious. Finally, distracted beyond endurance, the pitcher whirls and fires the ball straight at the heckler. This pitch is right on target, hitting the heckler on the head. The heckler sues the pitcher's employer, the ballclub. What result?

Explanation

This intentional tort may be one instance in which the incidental/foreseeable test is worse for the plaintiff than the more traditional purpose test. Beaning a spectator is hardly incidental to pitching a ball game, and the foreseeable reactions of heckled ballplayers do not include assaulting patrons from a distance. It might be established, however, that the pitcher's purpose was in part to serve the master. The heckling was distracting the pitcher and interfering with his ability to perform well for his employer. To silence the heckler therefore was to advance the master's interests. The result will thus depend on whether the court uses the purpose test and, if so, how malleable the court considers that test to be.[91]

---

89. Restatement §237.

90. Id.

91. In any event, the heckler may have a direct claim against the owner of the ballpark for failing to provide reasonably safe premises to a customer, see section 4.4.2, and can certainly sue the pitcher for battery. See section 4.2.3.

PROBLEM 27

A large school district, serving tens of thousands of students and with thousands of employees, assigns a custodian to work at a high school. Subsequently, the custodian sexually assaults a student at the high school. The student sues the school district, asserting respondeat superior.[92] What result?

EXPLANATION

If the jurisdiction uses the purpose test, the student will inevitably lose. By no stretch of the imagination can a sexual assault be said to serve the school district's interests.

Even if the jurisdiction uses some form of the incidental/foreseeable test, the student's chances are slim. Abstractly, it may be foreseeable that an organization that has a large enough number of employees will inevitably employ some "bad apples." However, for an intentional tort to be foreseeable in the sense of respondeat superior, there must be something about the nature of the servant's job or the master's enterprise that facilitates or occasions the harm. Unlike the psychologist-patient relationship discussed previously,[93] a custodian's role does not make the victim especially vulnerable to sexual assault. Sexual assault is not incidental to custodial work.

PROBLEM 28

A cable TV company ("the cable company") arranges with an independent contractor ("Acme Installers") to install decoder boxes and cables at the homes of the cable company's subscribers. For PR purposes, the cable company permits Acme Installers' vans to carry the cable company's name and logo. An Acme Installers employee gains access to a home to do an installation. The homeowner allows the employee to work without observation, and the employee's negligence causes a fire. May the homeowner recover from the cable company?

EXPLANATION

Perhaps. Since Acme Installers is an independent contractor and since there is no indication that the cable company had any control over Acme's employees, ordinary respondeat superior will not work. The cable company may be liable, however, on an apparent servant theory. The homeowner must show that (i) the cable company held out the employee as its employee and (ii) as

---

92. The student would probably assert direct claims as well, such as failure to provide safe premises and negligent hiring and supervision. See sections 4.4.1-4.4.2.

93. Supra section 3.2.6.

a result the homeowner relied on the employee's competence. Upon these showings, respondeat superior will apply as if the cable company was in fact the employee's master.

The van logo supports the first showing. Reliance, the second showing, is evidenced by the homeowner's willingness to allow the employee to enter the home, undertake the installation, and work unobserved. The cable company can escape vicarious liability if either (a) the homeowner knew, despite the logo, that the employee worked for someone else, or (b) the homeowner would still have allowed the employee to enter and perform the work, even if the homeowner had known that the employee did not work for the cable company.

PROBLEM 29

A hotel franchisor is concerned about apparent servant liability, but still wants its franchisees to make abundant use of the franchise name, logo, and trademarks. Consistent with that business purpose, how can the franchisor reduce its exposure to apparent servant liability?

Explanation

The core of apparent servant liability is the appearance of servant status. Therefore, the simplest solution, at least in concept, would be to eliminate the appearance at its source. The legal problem would disappear if the franchisees were to remove all insignia that make their hotels appear to belong to the franchisor and that make their employees appear to be the franchisor's servants. This would be legally perfect treatment — after which the patient (i.e., the business) would unfortunately die. A less pure but more practical solution would be to leave the insignia in place but act affirmatively to avoid the misapprehension. For example, the franchisor could require all its franchisees to prominently indicate that their hotel, although part of the national chain, is "independently owned and operated." The proclamation might appear on all significant signage, the hotel's stationery, and on all check-in and check-out documents.

PROBLEM 30

An air conditioning manufacturer is about to ship a valuable load of equipment to a developer that is constructing a new office building. The manufacturer is, however, concerned about the developer's ability to pay for the equipment. The developer assures the manufacturer, "No problem. We've got a loan commitment from First National Bank that will cover the entire cost of construction. Why don't you call the Bank's Vice President for Commercial Loans and get that confirmed?"

The manufacturer takes the suggestion and calls the Vice President. The Vice President confirms that the Bank has committed to a loan up to $10 million and that current cost projections total only $8.5 million. Satisfied, the manufacturer ships the equipment.

Unfortunately for the manufacturer, the Bank had made no loan commitment. The Vice President lied in return for a $5,000 bribe from the developer. The office building project eventually folds, the manufacturer's equipment is nowhere to be found, and the developer is bankrupt. Can the manufacturer recover from the Bank?

Explanation

Yes. The Bank's agent, its Vice President for Commercial Loans, committed the tort of intentional misrepresentation. That tort will be attributed to the Bank if the agent had actual authority, apparent authority, or inherent agency power to make the statement in question. The Vice President had apparent authority by position. It is customary for Bank officers to provide the type of information the Vice President provided, so it was reasonable for the manufacturer to believe the Vice President was speaking for the Bank. The Vice President's ulterior motive is immaterial. Apparent authority can exist even though the apparent agent does not intend to serve the interests of the apparent principal.[94]

PROBLEM 31

You are planning on selling your house through a real estate agent. You know that your agent will put the house on the local multiple-listing service, which means that literally hundreds of other agents may be showing your house and making representations about it. You fear that, carelessly or otherwise, one of these agents may make a misrepresentation about the house which may come back to haunt you. Keeping the house off the multiple-listing service is impractical. What else might you do?

Explanation

As explained in Chapter Two, your listing agreement will expressly or impliedly authorize your broker to enlist the services of other brokers. Those other brokers will be your subagents, and their torts of misrepresentation, if made within their authority or power, will be attributed to you.[95]

---

94. See Problem 7 in Chapter Two (apparent agent can bind apparent principal even though apparent agent intends to take for itself the benefits of the transaction).

95. See section 2.7.3 for a discussion of subagents and their authority and power to bind the principal.

It is not practical to check the *bona fides* of hundreds of brokers whom you have never met. Your preventative actions must therefore go toward (i) reducing their authority and power to make inaccurate statements and (ii) making sure that inaccurate statements do not become tortious. You can accomplish both by having the purchase agreement conspicuously state that: (a) the purchase agreement contains the parties' entire understanding; (b) no broker has any authority to make any representations different from or additional to the purchase agreement; and (c) the buyer is not relying on any statements, descriptions, or other representations outside of the purchase agreement. Against the background made by point "a," point "b" undercuts any claim of agency authority or power, and point "c" may prevent a misrepresentation from becoming tortious. (A representation is tortious only if it induces reliance.)[96]

PROBLEM 32

Morgan Hospital has an in-patient psychiatric ward that is run under the direction of Dr. Stanley, a board-certified psychiatrist who is a full-time employee of the hospital. Dr. Stanley has become increasingly frustrated with Medical Indemnity Company, an insurance company that provides health insurance coverage to many people in Morgan's vicinity. Medical Indemnity has been disallowing a large number of claims made by patients treated in Morgan's in-patient psychiatric ward. Dr. Stanley believes that most of these disallowances are unjustified, and he faults two psychologists who review patient claims for Medical Indemnity. Dr. Stanley's job has never involved public relations, but he decides that "enough is enough." In a fit of frustration and without discussing the matter with any of Morgan's higher-ups, he fires off a letter to the local medical association, the local association of clinical psychologists, and the President of Medical Indemnity. The letter, written on Morgan Hospital letterhead and signed by Stanley as "Director, In-Patient Psychiatry Unit, Morgan Hospital," scathingly criticizes the two psychologists. Embarrassed and humiliated, the two psychologists sue both Dr. Stanley and Morgan Hospital for defamation. Should Morgan Hospital be worried about the psychologists' claim?

EXPLANATION

Yes. If the letter was indeed defamatory, the hospital is probably liable. An agent's defamatory statement is attributable to the principal if the agent had actual or apparent authority to make the statement. Dr. Stanley probably lacked actual authority. Nothing in his job implied the authority to speak for

96. This Problem may seem familiar. Recall Problem 10 in Chapter Two (the television star and the boat dealer). Although the trappings differ, the legal issues are quite similar. As a result the preventative measures are similar as well.

Morgan Hospital on matters of public concern, and Dr. Stanley did not receive any specific authorization before sending the letter. To those who received the letter, however, Dr. Stanley may have appeared to be speaking on Morgan Hospital's behalf. Morgan arguably manifested as much when it clothed Dr. Stanley with an impressive title. Certainly, Dr. Stanley's use of the title added weight to the comments and power to the defamation.

PROBLEM 33

Ziegler Limo Leasing and Sales, Inc. ("Ziegler") sells and leases limousines and also provides limousine service on an hourly, daily, and weekly basis. Newly wealthy, Irv is considering buying a limousine from Ziegler. Selma, Ziegler's owner, says, "Tell you what, I'll let you use a limo and a driver for a week for free. It's kinda slow for us right now, and you'll get a feel for what it's like to have a limo at your beck and call. Then you can decide. Just one thing, though — if business heats up I'll have to take the limo back."

Irv happily agrees to the arrangement, and Selma assigns Jeffrey, one of her best drivers, to drive a stretch limo for Irv. Selma tells Jeffrey, "Listen. Show him our best red carpet service. That way, if he decides not to buy, he'll know we're the only place to rent from. But also — you know how new millionaires sometimes get aggressive. Remember our safe driving policy."

Two days later Jeffrey is driving Irv to a party, when a sports car cuts them off. Enraged, Irv yells to Jeffrey, "That [expletive deleted] can't do that to us. Catch him and pass him." Ziegler's operating rules require all Ziegler drivers to obey speed limits and strictly prohibit "aggressive driving." Irv is insistent, however, and Jeffrey gives in. In the rush to catch the sports car, the limo sideswipes another car. Assuming that Jeffrey has been negligent, can the driver of the other car successfully invoke respondeat superior against Irv?

EXPLANATION

Probably not. At the time of the accident, Jeffrey probably was not Irv's borrowed servant. Although Jeffrey's general employer (Ziegler) had assigned Jeffrey to work for Irv, Ziegler retained considerable control over Jeffrey's conduct. Selma had reminded Jeffrey that Ziegler's safe driving rules still applied. Moreover, Ziegler had retained the right to reassign Jeffrey at any time. When Irv successfully urged Jeffrey to speed up, Irv was merely persuading Jeffrey to violate the general employer's rules. Irv was not establishing the type of total, temporary control that establishes a special employer.

PROBLEM 34

A city hires an electrical contractor to remove above-ground electrical lines that had once served a trolley system. The contract gives the contractor total control and responsibility for the work, provided only that the contractor minimizes interference with traffic. However, the city's manager of public works worries incessantly about safety on the job. The manager repeatedly makes surprise visits to the worksites and often speaks directly to the contractor's employees. The employees report these contacts to the contractor. The contractor is fearful of losing the contract by offending the public works manager and instructs its employees to take the manager's suggestions "unless they're dangerous, expensive, or off the wall."

Midway through the project, a live line falls on a passing car. Fortunately, no one is injured, but the car is severely damaged. Assuming the conduct of the public works manager binds the city[97] and that the accident resulted from the negligence of an employee of the contractor, does the car owner have a claim against the city?

Explanation

Yes. The city's interference in the performance of the work demonstrates a right to control the employees of the contractor. Those employees are therefore servants of the city, and respondeat superior accordingly applies.

PROBLEM 35

When a business contracts out work, for quality control and safety reasons the business may wish to closely supervise the contracted work. If an accident occurs, however, the injured party will point to the close supervision and seek to invoke respondeat superior. By acting on its concern for quality and safety, the delegating party will have risked vicarious liability. Propose a solution to this conundrum.

Explanation

The problem cannot be totally resolved, because a tension will always exist between the amount of control and the amount of risk. The key is to find ways to influence performance that stop short of actionable control. The first step, whenever possible, is to reduce the risk by avoiding mishaps. The delegating party should therefore find contractors that have good safety records and justified reputations for quality work. Second, the delegating party should limit its review of the work to inspection and suggestion. This step will, perhaps, prevent the delegating party from being deemed the master of the contractor. Third, the delegating party should avoid any direct instructions to the contractor's employees. This step will, perhaps, prevent those employees from being deemed servants of the delegating party.

---

97. For a discussion of this type of question, see Chapter Two.

4

Duties and Obligations of Agents and Principals to Each Other and to Third Parties

§4.1 Duties and Obligations of the Agent to the Principal

§4.1.1 Duty of Loyalty: Hallmark of Agency Status

Agency is emphatically not an arm's length relationship. The Restatement, in its very first blackletter line, labels agency a "fiduciary relation,"[1] and the duty of loyalty is a hallmark characteristic of agency status. The agent's role is a selfless one, and the principal's objectives and wishes are dominant. The agent is important merely as a means to accomplish the principal's ends.[2] Except

1. Restatement §1(1).

2. This legal characteristic does not always comport with the practical reality. In the lay sense, the agent may be the "star" and the principal merely the supporting context. Consider, for example, Beverly Sills singing for the Metropolitan Opera or Willie Mays playing baseball for the San Francisco Giants.

when the principal has knowingly agreed to the contrary or when extraordinary circumstances exist,[3] the agent is obliged to prefer the principal's interests over its own and to act "solely for the benefit of the principal in all matters connected with [the] agency."[4]

The duty of loyalty is so deeply ingrained into agency law that few cases address the rationale underlying the duty. Some modern commentators speak in terms of economic efficiency. It would certainly be woefully inefficient if each agent and principal had to negotiate their expectations in detail prior to each formation of an agency relationship. Having a standard set of loyalty rules thus reduces transaction costs. In addition, a strict regime of selflessness probably reduces the principal's monitoring costs.[5]

This perspective finds little voice in the case law, however. When judges explain the duty of loyalty, they do so with a decidedly moralistic tone. When a principal engages an agent, the principal reposes trust and confidence in that agent and the agent accepts a position of trust and confidence. To allow an agent to violate that confidence, betray that trust, and then profit from the abuse is simply unacceptable.[6]

Whatever the underlying rationale, an agent's duty of loyalty includes a number of specific duties of selflessness, all serving to protect the principal's economic interests.

Unapproved benefits. Unless otherwise agreed, an agent may not profit from its efforts on behalf of the principal. This rule applies regardless of whether the value is received from the principal or from a third party.

Of course, in most agency relationships the principal agrees to compensate the agent for the agent's efforts, so the agent has the right to receive and retain those benefits. An agreement to allow the agent to profit may be express or implied.

Confidential information. An agent has a duty to safeguard the principal's confidential information and not to use that information for the agent's own

---

3. See infra this section for discussion of "Reshaping the Duty of Loyalty By Consent" and "The Agent's Legitimate Disloyalty."

4. Restatement §387.

5. "Monitoring costs" are the principal's costs of keeping guard against misconduct by the agent. The stricter the rules of loyalty, the easier it will be to establish misconduct and obtain a right of recovery. The most important monitoring costs, however, relate not to recovering for misconduct but rather to preventing it. It is not clear how strict loyalty rules reduce those costs.

6. Justice Cardozo's comment in *Meinhard v. Salmon*, 164 N.E. 545, 546 (N.Y. 1928), exemplifies this tone: "Many forms of conduct permissible in a workaday world for those acting at arm's length, are forbidden to those bound by fiduciary ties. A trustee is held to something stricter than the morals of the market place. Not honesty alone, but the punctilio of an honor the most sensitive, is then the standard of behavior." *Meinhard* concerned a joint venture but the case is often cited and Cardozo often quoted in cases concerning an agent's duty of loyalty.

benefit or the benefit of others. Confidential information includes any information that is not generally known and that either carries an economic benefit for the principal, or could, if disclosed, otherwise damage or embarrass the principal. Trade secrets, customer lists, unique business methods, and business plans are examples of confidential information.

The duty of nondisclosure and nonuse applies to any confidential information the agent acquires or develops during the course of the agency relationship. The duty applies even if the confidential information does not relate to the subject matter of the agency. The duty does *not* encompass any special skills that the agent develops while performing agency tasks.

> ***Example:*** Ralph works as a waiter in an upscale restaurant. None of Ralph's duties involve preparing food. One day, while standing in the kitchen waiting for an order, Ralph sees and reads the restaurant's secret recipe for stuffed mushrooms. Ralph may not use the recipe or disclose it to others. Even though his role as an agent does not involve preparing food, Ralph must keep the recipe confidential.

> ***Example:*** Bernice works as an assistant cook in the same restaurant. She learns all of the restaurant's special recipes and also learns how to make pate brisée (a type of pastry that is standard in upscale cooking but very difficult to make well). Bernice may not use the recipes outside her job, because they are confidential information. Bernice's knowledge of how to make pate brisée, however, is an expertise, not confidential information. Subject to her duty not to compete (discussed below), Bernice may make pate brisée wherever she likes.

The duty to respect confidential information continues even after the agency ends. Confidential information belongs to the principal, and the end of the agency relationship does nothing to alter the principal's property rights in the information.[7]

No competition. Unless otherwise agreed, the agent has a duty not to compete with the principal in any matter within the scope of the agency relationship. This noncompetition duty follows from the theme of selflessness and applies regardless of whether:

- the agent uses the principal's facilities, property or confidential information to find or pursue the opportunity
- the agent finds or pursues the opportunity "on its own time."

This aspect of the duty of loyalty runs counter to a strong public policy in favor of open competition. Once the agency relationship ends, that public

7. For further discussion of this point, see section 5.3.4 (use of confidential information following termination of agency).

policy reasserts itself. As a matter of agency law, the noncompetition duty ends. The duty to respect the principal's confidential information remains, but otherwise agency law allows a former agent to compete with its former principal.[8]

No acting for others with conflicting interests. Unless otherwise agreed, an agent may not act for anyone whose interests might conflict with the interests of the principal. The mere existence of a dual agency violates the duty of undivided loyalty. Moreover, the dual agent risks specific conflicts of duty as to a myriad of individual issues. The fact that these individual conflicts may be irreconcilable does not justify the agent ignoring one duty or the other. Rather, if any such specific conflict materializes, the agent is destined to be liable to one principal or the other.

> ***Example:*** A real estate broker agrees to help Sammy locate and purchase a new house. The broker knows that Rachael is interested in selling her house. The broker contacts Rachael and agrees to help sell her house to Sammy. Since Rachael's and Sammy's interests are in some ways conflicting, the broker has breached a duty of loyalty to both Sammy and Rachael merely by acting for both simultaneously.

> ***Example:*** Same situation as above, plus Rachael wishes not to disclose to Sammy certain information which in an arm's length transaction she is privileged to withhold. Rachael mentions the information to the broker but instructs the broker not to tell Sammy. The broker's duty to Rachael compels compliance, while the broker's duty to Sammy requires disclosure.

If an agent arranges a transaction in violation of the dual agency rule:

- if neither principal knows about the dual agency, either principal may rescind;
- if one principal knows, the other principal may either affirm the transaction and seek damages from the agent and the knowing principal or rescind.

Dealing with the principal. When a principal uses an agent to arrange a transaction, the agent may not become the other party to the transaction unless the principal consents. In Restatement terminology, without the prin-

---

8. For further discussion of this point, see section 5.3.4 (post-termination competition).

cipal's consent the agent may not be "the adverse party" and may not "act on his own account."[9]

> ***Example:*** Horace wishes to go into the restaurant business and retains Elizabeth to locate a restaurant that Horace can purchase. Elizabeth happens to own a restaurant and wishes to sell it to Horace. She may do so only if she discloses her ownership to Horace, and he consents. She may not hide her ownership and make the sale through a "straw man."

Even if the principal does consent, the duty of loyalty continues to affect the transaction. In an arm's-length transaction, each party is obliged merely to avoid misstatements. When an agent acts as the adverse party, the agent has an affirmative duty to disclose all facts that the agent knows or should know could affect the principal's decision.

Good conduct. The agent's conduct can reflect on the principal, so the agent must not act in a way that brings disrepute on the principal. This aspect of the duty of loyalty extends not only to the agent's performance of the tasks of agency, but also to other behavior.

> ***Example:*** Charlie works as a manager at a clinic that specializes in teaching people to quit smoking. On the job, Charlie is completely smoke-free. Outside of work, however, he is often seen smoking. Patrons and potential patrons of the clinic begin making remarks like "Some clinic. Its business manager smokes." Since public smoking can reflect adversely on his principal, Charlie's duty of good conduct requires that he refrain at least from smoking where the public can observe him.

Reshaping the duty of loyalty by consent. Agency law allows a principal and agent wide latitude to reshape the duty of loyalty. Agreements can limit or even eliminate each of the specific duties discussed in this section. For instance, a principal can always consent to the agent's disclosure of confidential information or allow the agent to profit from agency efforts.

Two qualifications do exist, however. First, the duty of loyalty applies to the manner in which an agent obtains agreement from the principal. The overall relationship remains a fiduciary one, so arm's length bargaining is inappropriate. When an agent seeks agreement from the principal, the agent must refrain from overreaching and must disclose to the principal all material information.

---

9. Restatement §389, comment *d.*

Example: A real estate broker agrees to help Sammy locate and purchase a new house. The broker already has in mind a house owned by Rachael. Without disclosing that information, the broker asks Sammy, "If I find a house, would you mind if I also worked with the seller to work out a deal you both can live with?" Sammy agrees, but the broker's conflict of interest problem remains. Since the broker breached its duty of disclosure in obtaining Sammy's consent, the consent is ineffective.

The second qualification is both more theoretical and more fundamental. The fiduciary duty of loyalty is at the essence of an agency relationship. If a contract negates all duties of loyalty, that contract may indicate that no agency relationship exists.

The agent's legitimate disloyalty. Even without the principal's consent, the agent may act against the principal's interests "in the protection of [the agent's] own interests or the interests of others."[10] The notion of self-protection seems straightforward. The agent may assert its contract rights against the principal and may defend itself if the principal makes accusations of misconduct. The notion of protecting others is far vaguer. For instance, must the other party's interest be especially substantial in order to warrant the agent being disloyal? If the disloyalty will undermine one of the principal's significant interests, must the other party's interest be even more substantial?

In extreme circumstances, the answers seem clear enough.

Example: Arnold works for a real estate development company in the land acquisition department. He knows that his friend, Alice, is about to give Ralph an option to buy some land she owns. Through his work Arnold knows that (i) the real estate company plans to develop the area in which Alice's land is located, (ii) the value of Alice's land is therefore destined to rise sharply, and (iii) the option Alice plans to grant will allow Ralph, rather than Alice, to profit from the increase in value. Arnold may not disclose his principal's confidential information to Alice.

Example: Through his work in the land acquisition department, Arnold discovers that the real estate company is engaged in a pattern of criminal fraud that, if unchecked, will cost innocent land owners thousands of dollars. Arnold may disclose the information not only to the land owners but also to the police.

---

10. Restatement §387, comment *b*.

Between the extremes, however, the rule is obscure. A court might consider the following factors to determine whether "the protection of . . . the interests of others"[11] justifies an agent's act of disloyalty:

- the legitimacy of the other party's interest and the importance of that interest to that other party;
- the extent to which the other party reasonably expects that the interest will be respected by the world in general and by the principal in particular;
- the legitimacy of the principal's interest and the importance of that interest to the principal; and
- the extent to which the agent might have protected the other party's interests while using means that were either less injurious or less disloyal to the principal.

§4.1.2 *Duty to Act Within Authority*

Although, as discussed in Chapter Two, an agent may have the power to act beyond the scope of actual authority,[12] an agent does not have the *right* to do so. To the contrary, the agent has a duty to act only as authorized.[13] An agent who violates this duty is liable to the principal for any resulting damage. A parallel rule applies to nonagents who purport to be agents and thereby bind the apparent principal.

If an agent has reason to doubt the scope of authority, except in emergency situations the agent has a duty to inquire of the principal.

> ***Example:*** Sally arranges for Ralph to buy a car on her behalf. She specifies, "Buy American." Ralph finds a good deal on a car assembled in the United States from components made almost exclusively overseas. Before buying the car for Sally, Ralph should check with her.

§4.1.3 *Duty to Obey Instructions*

The principal always has the *power* to instruct the agent concerning the subject matter of the agency. Accordingly, an agent has a duty to obey instructions from the principal unless the instructions call for the agent to do something improper.

---

11. Id.

12. See sections 2.3 (apparent authority) and 2.5 (inherent agency power).

13. The scope of that authority is determined objectively, based on the agent's reasonable interpretations of the principal's manifestations. See section 2.2.2.

> ***Example:*** Sammy works for a car dealership in the used car department. He reports to the owner that he cannot sell a particular used car at the desired price because the car has too many miles on it. The owner responds, "Well, just roll back the odometer a bit." Despite being the owner's agent, Sammy has no duty to comply. Rolling back an odometer is illegal, and Sammy has no duty to obey instructions that call for wrongful conduct.

The agent's duty to obey instructions is consistent with the agent's duty to act within authority. Instructions from the principal are manifestations from the principal, and the agent's authority comes from the agent's reasonable interpretation of the principal's manifestations. Therefore, if an agent disregards the principal's instructions, the agent is in effect acting without authority.

The duty to obey instructions exists even if the principal has contracted away the *right* to instruct. The agent may have a claim for breach of contract but nonetheless is obliged either to obey the principal's instructions or resign.[14]

§4.1.4 Duty of Care

An agent has a duty to act with "due care." How much care is due depends on (i) whether the agent is paid or unpaid (gratuitous), and (ii) any relevant agreement between the principal and agent.

For paid agents, due care is usually ordinary care; a standard of ordinary negligence applies. The determination of what constitutes ordinary negligence is quite similar to the determination made under the "negligence" rubric in the law of torts. What would a reasonably careful person in similar circumstances do? As with tort law, a person with special skills or knowledge has a duty to make reasonably careful use of those skills and knowledge. For example, in judging the response of a paid babysitter to a medical emergency, a reasonable care standard will demand more of a trained nurse than of a high school student. Also as with tort law, a person's lack of ordinary skills or knowledge does not relax the due care standard.

For gratuitous agents, the standard of care is the same standard that applies to other gratuitous actors (e.g., gratuitous bailees). That standard is often one of gross negligence.

> ***Example:*** Mark is driving home from college for the holidays. Melinda, who comes from the same home town, is not. She asks Mark, as a favor, to bring home for her the CD player and the amplifier that she had

14. See section 4.1.6.

borrowed from her parents. Mark agrees. On the way home, he stops at a restaurant, leaving the CD player and the amplifier in the back seat, with the car unlocked. When he returns to the car, he discovers that the CD player is missing. Again leaving the car doors unlocked, he goes back into the restaurant and calls the police. By the time he again returns to the car, the amplifier is also gone.

Mark is probably liable to Melinda for the loss of the amplifier but not for the CD player. As a gratuitous agent ("as a favor"), Mark is responsible only for damage caused by his gross negligence. The loss of the CD player probably reflects only ordinary carelessness. But the loss of the amplifier — coming after the first theft gave Mark clear warning — resulted from gross negligence.

An agreement between the principal and agent can heighten or reduce the amount of care owed by the agent. For instance, an agent can contract to produce certain specified results. In that case, the agent is obliged to produce those results and cannot excuse failure by claiming the exercise of due care. Agreements can also reduce the agent's obligations, either by directly choosing a lower standard of care or by prospectively waiving any claims arising from a breach of a higher standard. For instance, a principal might agree (i) that a paid agent was obliged only to avoid gross negligence, or (ii) not to hold the agent responsible for harm caused by ordinary negligence.

Public policy may limit the validity of some "care reducing" agreements. For example, ethical rules prohibit lawyers from making "an agreement prospectively limiting the lawyer's liability to a client for malpractice."[15] In some states, exculpatory provisions relating to negligence are void or subject to very strict construction.

§4.1.5 Duty to Provide Information

If an agent possesses information and has reason to know that the principal may need or desire the information, the agent has a duty to provide the information to the principal. This duty underlies the attribution rule that binds a principal on account of information possessed by its agent.[16] An agent's duty of care may require the agent to acquire information for the principal.

§4.1.6 Contractual Overlay

As this section has discussed, an agent has obligations to its principal as a matter of agency law. Those obligations are only part of the story, however.

15. Model Rules of Professional Conduct Rule 1.8(h) (1983).

16. See section 2.2.4.

A contractual relationship usually overlays the agency relationship, and so an agent typically owes duties in contract as well as under agency law.[17]

Not every agency relationship has a contractual overlay. As explained in Chapter One, an agency relationship is consensual, but not necessarily contractual.[18] Typically, however, the reciprocal consents that create an agency relationship also reflect an exchange of consideration: The agent undertakes to perform some task or achieve some objective for the principal, and the principal undertakes to compensate the agent for the agent's efforts. Thus, a process of contract formation typically accompanies the process of "agency formation."[19]

Rights and duties created by contract often supplement the rights and duties existing under agency law. For example, a contract may set performance standards for the agent, and the agent will then have to satisfy those standards as well as agency law's duty of care.[20] A contract may also define or circumscribe duties arising under agency law. For example, a contract can delineate the scope of an agent's duty of care by specifying the scope of the agent's endeavors. A contract can also waive an agent's agency law duties. For instance, as discussed previously an agent has a duty not to compete with its principal, unless the principal consents.[21] A contract can embody that consent.

There are, however, certain agency law duties that a contract cannot waive. For example, under agency law the principal always has the power to control the goals of the agency relationship and the means by which the agent pursues those goals.[22] A contract may limit a principal's rights in these matters but cannot abrogate the power. Accordingly, when a principal exercises the power of control, the agent has an agency law duty either to comply or to resign. If the principal's exercise of agency law power violates the agent's contractual rights, then the agent may pursue contract law remedies.

> ***Example:*** Ralph hires Sally, a real estate broker, to sell his house. The brokerage agreement gives Sally the right to decide when to show the house. Ralph subsequently decides that he does not want the house shown on weeknights. Sally has a duty to abide by Ralph's decision or to resign. In either case, however, she can sue Ralph, for breach of contract. (To recover, of course, she must prove damages.)

---

17. Likewise the principal may have contractual obligations to the agent. See section 4.3.3.

18. See section 1.2.5.

19. As with most contracts, terms may be implied by custom and usage.

20. Section 4.1.4 discusses the agent's duty of care.

21. See section 4.1.1.

22. If the principal also has the *right* to control the means, then the agent is likely a servant. See section 3.2.4.

In like fashion, the principal always retains the power, if not the right, to terminate the agency relationship.[23]

§4.1.7 *Principal's Remedies for Agent's Breach of Duty*

If an agent's breach of duty causes damage to the principal, the principal can recover those damages from the agent. If an agent's breach of duty renders the principal liable to a third party, the agent must indemnify and hold harmless the principal from that liability.

If the agent breaches a duty of loyalty, the principal's remedies include not only *damages* (if provable) but also *disgorgement* of any profits derived by the agent from the disloyal transaction and *rescission* of any transaction between the principal and agent, if the breach infected that transaction.

> ***Example:*** Mikki is selling her hobby farm to a shopping mall developer and must therefore dispose of five horses. Four of the horses are quite old, but the fifth is quite valuable. Helen approaches Mikki and proposes to sell the four older horses for a five percent commission and then buy the fifth horse for herself at a below-market price. Mikki agrees, on condition that Helen sells to "people who will care about my horses." Helen accepts the condition.
>
> Within a few days Helen reports that she has sold the horses to "some real nice folks." After those horses are shipped, Helen collects her commission and pays for and takes the fifth horse.
>
> Mikki later discovers that Helen sold the four horses to a glue factory. Because Helen gained the commission through dishonesty to her principal, the commission is subject to a constructive trust. Because Helen's disloyalty infected her purchase of the fifth horse, Mikki may rescind that transaction.

Both disgorgement and rescission are considered equitable remedies, and both are available without proof of damage. Courts ordering disgorgement often do so by imposing a "constructive trust" on the agent's ill-gotten gains. A court will order disgorgement even though the remedy leaves the principal better off than the principal would have been had the agent complied with its duty of loyalty.

> ***Example:*** A blockbuster adventure movie creates intense demand for a line of toys based on the movie. Williams Manufacturing, Inc. ("Williams") has the exclusive right to manufacture the toys. Although it raises its prices to take advantage of the demand and increases produc-

23. Chapter Six discusses termination issues.

tion, for several months Williams has more orders than it can fill. During this time, Max, Williams's national sales manager gives order preference to those customers willing to "make it worth my while." The gratuities range from cash to cases of wine to airline tickets. No one else at Williams is aware of what Max is doing. If Williams can prove that Max's conduct damaged Williams's good will, Williams can recover from Max the amount of the damage. Even without proof of damage, Williams can recover from Max the value of the gratuities. By profiting without his principal's consent, Max breached his duty of loyalty. He must disgorge all benefits resulting from that breach.

§4.2 Duties and Obligations of the Agent to Third Parties

§4.2.1 Obligations "On the Contract"

Rules for determining agent's liability. Agents often make contracts on behalf of principals, and agency law provides rules for determining whether the agent is liable on such contracts.[24] The analysis turns on whether the agent's principal is disclosed.[25]

If the principal is disclosed, then the agent is not liable on the contract. The rationale for this rule is straightforward. With a disclosed principal, the third party enters into the contract knowing that the agent is merely a representative and that the principal will be the obligor. The agent is not promising any performance of its own,[26] and the third party may look only to the principal for performance.

This rule applies even if the third party bases a warranty claim on a statement made by the agent.

Example: A patron at a gambling casino approaches the roulette wheel and asks the employee operating the wheel, "Is this game honest?" The employee responds, "As honest as the day is long." The patron places several bets, losing each one. Subsequently the patron discovers that the wheel is rigged and claims breach of warranty against both the

24. Agency law also determines whether the principal is liable. See Chapter Two.

25. Section 2.2.2 (in creation of actual authority, third party knowledge of principal-agent relationship is irrelevant).

26. The agent is, however, implicitly promising that the principal will be obligated. If the principal is not obligated, the agent will be liable. See section 4.2.2 (agent's warranty of authority).

employee and the casino. The claim against the employee will fail.[27] The patron's bets were transactions between the patron and the casino, and the employee's principal was disclosed. The employee is therefore not liable on the contract — even though the employee's statement gave rise to the breach of warranty claim.[28]

If the principal is only partially disclosed, then the agent is liable on the contract. The rationale is again one of expectations. Without knowing the identity of the principal, the third party is presumably relying on the trustworthiness, creditworthiness, and *bona fides* of the agent. When the principal is undisclosed, the agent is liable *a fortiori*. As far as the third party knows, the contract is with the agent and none other.

Example: A power company authorizes a coal broker to buy coal for it. The broker contracts to buy the coal in its own name, without disclosing its status as agent for the power company. The broker is liable on the contract.[29]

Example: An attorney contacts an art dealer and contracts to buy a famous Picasso print. The attorney explains that she is acting for a client but declines to identify the client. (The client dislikes notoriety.) The attorney is liable on the contract.[30]

These rules on contract liability are default rules. They can be overridden by express or implied agreement between the agent and third party.

Example: Return to the roulette wheel scenario (above), adding the following dialogue to the conversation between the patron and the employee:

Patron: Are you sure this wheel is as honest as the day is long?
Employee: I personally guarantee it. I wouldn't work at a crooked wheel.

The conversation reflects an agreement by the employee to guarantee one aspect of the principal's performance — namely, that the wheel will

---

27. The claim against the casino will prevail, however, since the employee's statement is attributed to the casino. See section 2.2.4 (agent's statements attributable to the principal for contract law purposes).

28. If the employee made the misstatement negligently or intentionally, the employee may be liable in tort. See section 4.2.3.

29. The power company is liable too. See sections 2.2.2 and 2.2.4. (in creation of actual authority, third party knowledge of principal-agent relationship is irrelevent). As for the relationship of the broker's liability to the power company's liability, see infra.

30. The client is liable, too. See sections 2.2.2 and 2.2.4.

operate honestly. That agreement overrides the default rule, and the employee is liable, together with the principal.

Example: An attorney hires a doctor to serve as an expert witness in a personal injury lawsuit. Although the expert witness will serve the interests of the attorney's client and the client's identity is fully disclosed, the attorney may nonetheless be responsible to the doctor for the expert witness fees. Custom in the locality may imply a promise by the agent (the attorney) to guarantee payment by the principal (the client).[31]

The agent's liability and available defenses. Unless otherwise agreed, an agent's contractual liability is as a *guarantor*. The agent partakes of any of the principal's defenses that arise from the transaction, plus any personal defenses or setoffs the agent may have vis-à-vis the third party. The agent may not assert defenses or setoffs that are personal to the principal (i.e., defenses arising from other transactions between the principal and the third party).

Example: Acting as Phil's agent, Sylvia negotiates a contract for Phil to sell three horses to Paul. Paul says to agent Sylvia, "I've done business with Phil before and it didn't go so well. How do I know this deal will be any better?" Sylvia responds, "Trust me. I stand by the deals I set up." Paul agrees to the contract.

Paul later sues both Phil and Sylvia, contending that Phil delivered only two horses. Phil defends by claiming that Paul failed to pay for the first two horses. Phil also asserts a setoff of $500 based on a debt he claims Paul has owed for four years.

Sylvia can raise the defense but cannot use the setoff. The defense arises out of the same transaction that gives rise to Paul's claim. The setoff, in contrast, arises from another transaction and is personal to Phil.

§4.2.2 *Warranty of Authority*

When a person purports to bind another person to a contract, the law implies a warranty of authority, that is, a promise that the purported agent actually has authority to act for the purported principal. If the purported principal is

31. This analysis runs counter to some old cases but reflects a modern trend. To avoid uncertainty and unwanted liability, an attorney should have a written understanding with the third party that specifies who is responsible for the third party's fees.

not bound, then the purported agent has breached the warranty of authority and is liable to the third party for expectation damages as well as reliance damages.

The warranty applies:

- both to true agents who act outside their authority and to mere purported agents who have no actual authority at all;
- regardless of whether the purported principal is disclosed or partially disclosed;[32] and
- even though the third party could have discovered the lack of authority by exercising reasonable care.

The warranty does *not* apply if:

- the purported agent disclaims having authority to bind or indicates that it doubts its own authority, or
- the third party knows for some other reason that the purported agent lacks authority.

Example: An employee of Harris, Inc. ("Harris") purports to retain Pauline, a real estate broker, to sell two acres of land that Harris owns. The employee signs an engagement letter, purportedly on Harris's behalf, agreeing that Harris will reimburse Pauline's reasonable expenses and will pay a commission in the event Pauline finds a buyer willing and able to pay the asking price. Pauline finds such a buyer, who signs and delivers an offer letter to her. She takes the letter, making clear that she has no authority to accept the offer on Harris's behalf. When Pauline brings the offer to Harris, she discovers that (i) the Harris employee acted without authority in dealing with Pauline and (ii) Harris does not wish to sell the land. If the deal does not go through, the Harris employee will be liable to Pauline for breach of the warranty of authority. The liability will include not only Pauline's reasonable expenses but also the commission she would have earned on the sale. Pauline, in contrast, will not be liable to the disappointed buyer, since she never represented that she had authority to bind Harris.

If a purported agent acts without actual authority but manages to bind its purported principal through apparent authority, inherent agency power,

32. With a partially disclosed principal, the purported agent will be bound whether or not a contract is formed. If the principal is bound, a contract results and the agent is liable as a guarantor. See section 4.2.1. If the principal is not bound and no contract is formed, then the agent is liable under the warranty of authority. With an undisclosed principal, the warranty does not apply because the agent is not purporting to act on behalf of another. See section 2.2.2 (defining undisclosed principal).

or estoppel,[33] the warranty of authority is not breached. The third party has received just what the purported agent promised — a binding contract with the purported principal.[34] Likewise, no breach occurs if the purported principal ratifies the contract.

> ***Example:*** The counter clerk in a dry cleaner promises to have your interview "power suit" ready by the next day. The clerk has made comparable promises to you before, and the dry cleaner has always fulfilled them. Last week, however, the owner instituted a new policy, depriving employees of the authority to promise next-day service. Although the clerk lacks actual authority to bind the dry cleaner to a contract for next-day service, the clerk's apparent authority binds the principal. Therefore, there is no breach of the warranty of authority.

> ***Example:*** Recall the scenario of Harris, Inc., Pauline the real estate broker, and the land for sale. Assume that Harris initially rejects the deal but then reconsiders. Before the prospective buyer withdraws the offer, Harris — through a duly authorized agent — accepts the offer. Pauline no longer has a claim against the Harris employee for breach of the warranty of authority.

§4.2.3 Obligations in Tort

A tort is a tort is a tort. Being an agent does not immunize a person from tort liability. A tortfeasor is personally liable, regardless of whether the tort was committed on the instructions from or to the benefit of a principal. A tortfeasor cannot defend itself by saying, "Well, I did what I did to serve my principal."[35]

For example, if a supermarket employee negligently drops a carton of cans on a customer's foot, the customer has a negligence claim against the employee.[36] Similarly, an agent who intentionally or negligently misstates a

---

33. For a discussion of these attribution rules, see sections 2.3 (apparent authority), 2.5 (inherent agency power), and 2.4 (estoppel).

34. The purported agent may be liable to the purported principal. See section 4.1.2.

35. The principal may well be liable too. The liability may be vicarious, see Chapter Three, or direct, see section 4.4 (principal's direct duties), or both.

36. For tactical reasons the customer may decide not to assert this claim, instead relying exclusively on claims against the principal (e.g., respondeat superior, failure to provide reasonably safe premises to business invitees). Tactical considerations could include: the small chance of collecting any substantial judgment from the employee; removing the employee as a party to allow the jury to see the matter as a David versus Goliath conflict (i.e., injured "ordinary folk" versus rich, impersonal mercantile establishment); eliminating the employee's financial incentive to justify its own conduct.

material fact while selling its principal's goods is personally liable for misrepresentation,[37] and can also be liable for aiding and abetting the principal's fraud. The agent must know of the fraudulent plan and give substantial assistance. The assistance need not involve directly fraudulent conduct.[38]

> ***Example:*** Al's Used Cars advertises for sale an automobile with interiors of "fine Corinthian leather." In response to that ad, a customer comes in and talks with Emily, a salesperson for Al's. Emily knows that the interiors are not leather and that the ad was a purposeful "come on." However, she closes the deal without mentioning the interiors. She is liable to the buyer for knowingly assisting in her principal's fraud.

Agency-related rights and duties that negate or give rise to torts. Although agency status does not create tort immunity, rights created by agency status can negate the very existence of a tort. For example, an agent acting within the scope of authority may exercise and benefit from its principal's privileges. Those privileges can transform otherwise tortious conduct into lawful behavior.

> ***Example:*** The owner of Sherwood Forest allows none but his guests to enter the Forest. Robin purchases the right to enter the Forest to collect certain examples of local fauna. Acting as Robin's agent, Tuck enters Sherwood Forest to collect specimens. Tuck's conduct is proper. He benefits from Robin's right to enter the land. Were Tuck entering for his own purposes, he would be committing the tort of trespass.

Agency status can also give rise to duties, the breach of which will constitute torts.

> ***Example:*** The owner of Sherwood Forest is leaving the country on an extended sabbatical. She hires John Little to conduct hunting expeditions into the Forest and gives him complete authority to manage the Forest premises. As a matter of tort law, Little has a duty to use care in maintaining the Forest.[39] Little's duty arises from his control of the premises, and that control comes from his authority as an agent.

---

37. If the agent innocently passes on the principal's misrepresentations, the agent is not liable. For the tort of intentional misrepresentation, most jurisdictions require intent to deceive or at least reckless disregard of truthfulness. Some jurisdictions also recognize a claim for negligent misrepresentation.

38. If the agent assists in the fraud by purposely making misstatements, then the agent will be liable for misrepresentation as well as for aiding and abetting.

39. How much care is due depends on the jurisdiction and, in some jurisdictions, on the status of the injured party (e.g., business invitee, trespasser).

§4.2.4 *Breach of Duty to Principal Not by Itself a Breach to Third Party*

When an agent breaches a duty of care or proper performance to its principal and the principal suffers harm, the agent is liable to the principal for damages.[40] The same misconduct may also harm a third party, but an agent's breach of duty to its principal does not automatically create a damage claim for the third party.[41] Rather than simply "borrowing" the principal's breach of duty claim, the third party must transform that duty and breach into a duty and breach running directly to the third party. To do so, the third party must show that:

1. The agent has undertaken to perform tasks for the principal that involve protection of a third party's physical safety or the safety of a third party's tangible property.
2. Either the principal or the third party (or both) have relied on the agent to provide the protection.
3. Without excuse the agent failed to provide the protection, causing injury to the third party or the party's physical property.
4. Either:
   - the agent acted with the intent to harm the third party or the third party's property, or
   - the agent's failure to perform created an unreasonable risk of harm and the agent should have recognized that risk.

The third party may recover only for injury to the person or tangible property (i.e., not for mere "economic" loss).

> ***Example:*** The city hires Sandy to serve as a lifeguard at a small municipal pool. One afternoon, while the sole lifeguard on duty, Sandy takes an unauthorized break, leaving the pool unsupervised. During that break, a child drowns, and Sandy may well be liable to the child's estate. She undertook a duty for her principal (the city) that involved protecting swimmers from physical danger (Element #1). Her principal certainly relied on her. For the time at issue it hired no one else to perform the protective function. The parents of the child may have relied on Sandy as well (Element #2). Through her unauthorized break Sandy failed to provide the expected protection and that failure arguably caused the child to drown (Element #3). Sandy's unauthorized break

---

40. The duty of care arises from the agency relationship. See section 4.1.4. A duty of proper performance may arise from a contract between the principal and agent. See section 4.1.6. Section 4.1.7 discusses the damage remedy.

41. The principal may well be liable to the third party, either vicariously, see section 3.2 (respondeat superior), or directly, see section 4.4.

created an unreasonable risk of harm, and Sandy should have recognized that risk (Element #4).

§4.3 Duties and Obligations of the Principal to the Agent

§4.3.1 *Principal's Duty to Indemnify*

When an agent acts on behalf of its principal, the agent may incur expenses, make payments, suffer injury, and even offend the rights of third parties. As a matter of agency law,[42] a principal has a duty to indemnify its agent for:

- payments made or expenses incurred within the agent's actual authority,
- payments made to the principal's benefit, but without authority, if:
  — the agent acted in good faith, mistakenly believing itself to be authorized, and
  — under the principles of restitution it would be unjust not to require indemnity[43]
- claims made by third parties on contracts entered into by the agent, with authority, and on the principal's behalf
- claims made by third parties for torts allegedly committed by the agent, if:
  — the agent's conduct was within the agent's actual authority, and
  — the agent was unaware that the conduct was tortious.

No duty to indemnify exists for:

- payments made or expenses incurred that are neither within the agent's actual authority nor of benefit to the principal;
- losses resulting from the agent's negligence or from acts outside the agent's actual authority;
- losses resulting from the agent's knowing commission of a tort or illegal act.

---

42. Although the Restatement calls the duty to indemnify "primarily contractual in nature," Restatement §438, comment *a*, that description is confusing. No particular words or circumstances are necessary to obligate the principal. To the contrary, the duty exists because the agency relationship exists. A contract between the principal and agent can, however, modify the duty.

43. Note that a mistaken belief of authority does not by itself qualify the resulting loss or expense for indemnity.

A duty to indemnify is a duty to hold harmless: to reimburse the agent for payments made, to compensate the agent for losses suffered, to protect the agent from third party claims. Protecting against claims means (i) providing or paying for a defense, including reasonable attorney's fees and other costs of litigation ("the duty to defend"), and (ii) paying for any liability, including reasonable settlements.

To invoke the principal's duty to defend, the agent must give the principal reasonable notice of the claim, allow the principal to manage the defense, and cooperate with the principal in the defense. If the agent fails to notify the principal, the principal is not responsible for the costs of defense and will be responsible for the agent's liability only if the agent made a reasonable defense.

> ***Example:*** Alvin, an up-and-coming rock singer, hires Dave as road manager for Alvin's new tour. On Alvin's instructions, Dave uses his credit card to book Alvin into the fanciest suite in the fanciest hotel in each of the tour stops. Alvin has a duty to indemnify Dave for the room charges. Alvin's instructions gave Dave actual authority to incur the expenses.

> ***Example:*** Following a concert, Alvin directs Dave to bring back to the hotel a new amplifier that Alvin used during the concert. The amplifier actually belongs to the owner of the concert hall, and the owner subsequently sues Dave for conversion. Dave promptly notifies Alvin. Although Dave may well be liable for conversion,[44] Dave is entitled to indemnity from Alvin. Dave did not know he was committing a tort, and, as between Dave and Alvin, taking the amplifier was an authorized act. Alvin must therefore (i) defend Dave or pay Dave's reasonable costs of defense, and (ii) cover any liability.

> ***Example:*** Although Dave's responsibilities only relate to the road tour, Dave has visions of getting Alvin a recording contract. Without checking with Alvin, Dave starts wining and dining various record company executives. Dave's efforts are fruitless, but he does manage to run up $2,000 in "entertainment" expenses. Alvin has no duty to indemnify Dave. Dave had no actual authority to incur the expenses, and the expenses were of no benefit to Alvin.

§4.3.2 Principal's Duties in Tort (Physical Harm to the Agent)

Nonservant agents.[45] A principal owes its nonservant agent whatever same tort law duties the principal owes to the rest of the world. In addition, a

---

44. Conversion is a strict liability tort. Therefore, Dave's innocent state of mind is irrelevant to the owner's suit.

45. For the rules that determine whether an agent is a servant, see section 3.2.4.

principal has a duty to warn its nonservant agent of any risk involved in the agent's tasks if the principal knows or should know that (i) the risk exists and (ii) the agent is unlikely to be aware of the risk.

> ***Example:*** Rachael owns and runs her own hauling service, and Samuel hires her to deliver a large load of firewood to Dennis. To pick up the firewood Rachael must come on Samuel's property, and, in most jurisdictions, Samuel will owe her a duty of reasonable care. That duty arises from Rachael's status as nontrespassing entrant on land and not from her status as Samuel's agent.

> ***Example:*** On several occasions Samuel has hired Rachael to haul nontoxic trash to the town dump. He now hires her to haul a load of debris that contains several cans full of highly corrosive material. The cans are not marked. Samuel has reason to know that the cans are dangerous. He also has reason to know that Rachael is unlikely to be aware of the danger. (The cans are not marked and the previous jobs all involved nontoxic waste.) He therefore has a duty to inform Rachael of the risk.

Servant agents. Before the advent of worker's compensation statutes, the common law delineated a master's liability for work-related, physical injuries suffered by its servants. Today, worker's compensation statutes preempt the common law with a no-fault compensation scheme. Although these statutes typically refer to "employers" and "employees" rather than to "masters" and "servants," the statutory concepts are defined and applied so as to effectively overlap the common law concepts.

This historical development simplifies matters for students of agency law, because the common law was complex and confusing. In theory, the master had a duty to provide reasonably safe working conditions for its servants. In reality, three doctrines combined to eviscerate that duty and tilt the law strongly toward the master:

The "fellow servant" rule — This rule prevented servants from holding their masters vicariously liable for the tortious conduct of a "fellow servant." The Restatement defined fellow servants as "servants employed . . . in the same enterprise or household and so related in their labor that, because of proximity or otherwise, there is a special risk of harm to one of them if the other is negligent."[46] The definition (and therefore the rule) swept broadly. For instance, if a master operated several tugboats within a harbor and the negligence of a servant on one boat happened to cause injury to a servant on another, the fellow servant rule barred recovery. Since many workplace injuries resulted, at least in part, from the negligence of fellow employees, this rule left many injured servants without a remedy.

---

46. Restatement §475.

Assumption of risk — At one time this doctrine applied generally within tort law. In the master-servant context, it barred servants from recovering for injuries arising from the ordinary dangers of their work, because servants were said to have assumed the risk of such injuries. The more dangerous the work, therefore, the less likely a servant was to recover.

Contributory negligence — At one time this doctrine also applied generally within tort law. In the master-servant context, it barred recovery whenever an injured servant's own negligence had helped cause the injury.

§4.3.3 Contract-Based Duties

As explained previously, a contract between agent and principal can overlay the agency relationship and impose contractual duties on each party.[47] For principals, the most common contract-based duty is compensation. Indeed, agency law subdivides agents into two categories depending on whether the principal has agreed to pay the agent for the agent's efforts.[48]

Although the rules for construing a principal's contract-based duties are for the most part identical to the rules for construing the duties of any party to any contract, the concept of implied terms does require some special attention. As with contracts generally: (i) circumstances can imply terms; (ii) the parties' conduct can imply terms; and (iii) express terms can imply terms. However, no implication arises from the fact that an agency relationship exists or from the fact that the principal has promised to pay the agent.

> ***Example:*** Dave hires Alvin for a job in a music studio. Dave knows that Alvin lacks the technical knowledge necessary to perform adequately. These circumstances imply a contract-based duty for David to train Alvin.

> ***Example:*** Dave hires Theodore to do the "mixing" work on a new record. Based on this express understanding, Dave has an implied duty not to unreasonably interfere with Theodore's efforts.[49]

> ***Example:*** Dave hires Simon for a low-level job at the music studio, promising to pay Simon $4 per hour. A month later, Dave terminates the agency relationship. Simon complains, contending that Dave: (i) never gave him any on-the-job training, (ii) did not give him enough hours per week to work, and (iii) had no right to fire him without

---

47. See section 4.1.6.

48. See section 1.2.5 (defining gratuitous agents).

49. Dave nonetheless has the power to interfere. See section 4.1.3 (agent's duty to obey instructions even when principal breaches contract by giving the instructions).

"cause." As a matter of agency law, Simon's complaints are unfounded. The mere promise to compensate an agent does not by itself imply a promise to train, a promise to provide any particular amount of work, or a promise to retain the agent for any particular length of time.[50]

§4.4 Duties and Obligations of the Principal to Third Parties

§4.4.1 Agency Law Duties

Duty to properly select and use agents. As discussed in Chapters Two and Three, the acts and omissions of agents often cause principals to be obligated to third parties. In these instances agency law works in tandem with some other area of law, typically contracts or torts. Agency law provides the attribution rules, and the other area of law supplies the rules of obligation. For example, when an agent signs a contract on behalf of its principal, agency law determines whether the signature binds the principal and contract law determines whether that signature has formed a contract. Similarly, when a servant injures a third party, agency law determines whether the servant's conduct is attributable to the master while tort law determines whether the servant's conduct is actionable.

Agency law also imposes some obligations of its own on principals with regard to third parties. A principal has a duty to use reasonable care in choosing, informing, instructing, and supervising its agents. If a principal breaches this duty of care and a third party suffers harm, the principal is liable. This liability results from the principal's direct duty to the third party and exists even though the most proximate cause of the harm was the act or omission of an agent, and regardless of whether the agent's conduct was negligent.

> ***Example:*** The "Speedy Delivery" Company uses college students to deliver messages on bicycles. Speedy does not supply the bicycles, pays per delivery (not by the hour), does not control routes, and requires only that students give at least 48-hour notice of when they plan to work. One day Speedy gives a delivery assignment to a student who is obviously intoxicated. The student rides carelessly and runs into the dean of the law school. The dean drops her portable computer, which breaks. The dean will not succeed with a respondeat superior claim against Speedy, because the student is not a servant. The dean will succeed, however, with a direct claim based on the principal's duty of

50. As a separate matter of statutory law, Simon may have the right to receive unemployment compensation.

care. Speedy breached that duty by selecting an obviously intoxicated person to make a delivery and will therefore be directly liable to the dean. The liability will exist even though it was the student's negligence that most proximately caused the dean's loss.

Example: The servant agent of a lawn care company sprays fertilizer on customers' lawns from a company truck. During one weekend, the company installs a new control device on the truck but neglects to tell the agent. On Monday, at a customer's house, the agent tries to operate the spraying hose using the same procedures that worked well in the past. The hose backfires, sprays a torrent of fertilizer, and kills a large patch of a neighbor's lawn. The company is liable to the neighbor, even though the agent has not been negligent. The relevant negligence is that of the company, which failed to properly instruct and inform its agent.

The fact that an agent has acted negligently does not by itself establish that the principal breached its direct duty of care.

Example: Harris Carpeting sells floor coverings and provides installation services through various nonservant agents. It is customary for Harris to deliver the floor covering to the customer's location and for the installer to arrive separately. Harris uses only skilled installers and follows up with customers to determine their satisfaction both with the carpet and the installation. Harris therefore sees no need to incur the expense of supervising the installers.

One of Harris's regular installers is Albert, who has done installation work for 15 years and has an exemplary record. One day Albert uses a new type of adhesive to install vinyl tile and carelessly fails to read the instructions. He therefore fails to ventilate the room properly, and a fire results. Despite Albert's negligence, Harris has not breached its duty of care. In light of Albert's experience and reputation, it was reasonable to select Albert and to allow him to work without supervision.

Relationship of principal's direct duty to principal's vicarious liability. The principal's liability under the direct duty of care is different from the principal's vicarious liability under the doctrine of respondeat superior. The two liabilities can, however, overlap. If a principal negligently selects, instructs, or supervises a servant agent and that servant agent negligently injures a third party, the principal will be liable to the third party on two counts: directly, for a breach of the duty of care, and vicariously, through the doctrine of respondeat superior.

Besides overlapping, the two liabilities can create a double-bind for principals who hire agents to do potentially dangerous work. If the principal adopts a hands-off attitude and something goes wrong, the principal may be liable for failure to adequately supervise or instruct. If, in contrast, the principal seeks to avoid such a result with a hands-on approach, the law will take the principal's right of control to mean that the agent is a servant. If so, any negligence of the servant will make the principal vicariously liable.

The following table shows how the principal's direct and vicarious liability relate to each other and also how the principal's liability in tort is affected by the negligence of the principal, the negligence of the agent, and the status of the agent as servant or nonservant.

	Principal ***Breached*** *Duty of Care*	*Principal* ***Did Not Breach*** *Duty of Care*
Agent's Conduct ***Negligent***	Principal liable on direct claim. Also liable vicariously *if* agent was a servant and was acting within scope of employment.	Principal not liable on direct claim. Liable vicariouslly if agent was a servant and was acting within scope of employment.
Agent's Conduct ***Not Negligent***	Principal liable on direct claim only, regardless of whether agent is a servant.	Principal not liable.

§4.4.2 "Nondelegable" Duties Imposed by Other Law

Nonagency law sometimes imposes duties on account of a person's status or relationship to others. For example, in most jurisdictions the owner of a business has a duty to use reasonable care to make the premises safe for customers. Although the law sometimes calls such obligations "nondelegable duties," the term is a misnomer. With most such duties a person may indeed delegate the responsibility to others. For example, a store owner may appoint a store manager and leave her in charge of the premises. The mere fact of delegation breaches no duty.

A better, albeit more cumbersome, name for these duties would be "duties that may be delegated but that are not discharged merely by delegation." When a person delegates, its relationship with the person accepting the delegation is a matter of agency law. However, neither the delegation nor the law of agency affect the original duty. Regardless of the care the principal uses in selecting, instructing, and supervising the agent, the principal remains on the hook until and unless the agent properly performs the delegated tasks. If the agent does so, then the principal has satisfied its obligations under nonagency law. If, however, the agent does not perform properly, the principal is liable. The principal may have a claim against the agent, but that claim does not excuse the principal.

> ***Example:*** Under residential landlord-tenant law, a landlord owes a tenant a duty to maintain the premises in "habitable" condition. The landlord hires a resident manager and instructs the manager "to do whatever is necessary to keep this place in good condition." The resident manager neglects the job, and a tenant sues the landlord for breach of the "warranty of habitability." The landlord cannot successfully defend by blaming the resident manager, because delegating the responsibility did not discharge it.[51]

§4.4.3 Duties Assumed Under Contract

In any contract the parties undertake duties to each other, and in most situations a contract obligor may delegate performance of a duty to someone else.[52] When a contract obligor does delegate performance, agency law relates to that delegation in the same way it relates to the delegation of duties imposed by law. The delegation typically creates an agency relationship but does not discharge the duty. The obligor remains strictly responsible to the obligee, even if the obligor uses the greatest care in selecting, supervising, and instructing the agent.

> ***Example:*** Mikki is under contract with Samantha to mow Samantha's lawn by Saturday at noon, in time for a big outdoor party Samantha is hosting. Mikki directs Horace, one of her employees, to do the lawn mowing on Saturday morning. Horace has always been one of Mikki's most responsible employees, and Friday evening Mikki reminds Horace of the job. Unfortunately, at breakfast on Saturday Horace gets food poisoning and is hospitalized before he can warn Mikki to send a replacement worker. The lawn is not mowed, and Mikki has breached her contract with Samantha. Delegating the duty did not discharge it, no matter how reasonable the delegation. Horace's sudden illness is irrelevant.

---

51. The result might be different if landlord-tenant law required only that a landlord use "reasonable efforts" to maintain habitable premises. In that case, the landlord could argue that the delegation to the resident manager constituted reasonable efforts.

52. Sometimes the nature of the obligation (e.g., personal service) precludes delegation. Sometimes the contract validly prohibits delegation. In such circumstances, contract duties are genuinely "nondelegable," and the obligee need not accept the delegated performance.

PROBLEM 36

In his first meeting with Friar Tuck, Robin Hood compels Tuck to carry him across a stream. Hood uses his sword as the instrument of coercion. Tuck undertakes the task, but midway across purposely drops Hood into the stream. Has Tucked breached his duty of loyalty? Would it matter if Tuck's conduct were grossly negligent rather than intentional?

EXPLANATION

Tuck has not breached his duty of loyalty, because none exists. For an agency relationship to exist, inter alia the agent must manifest consent to act on the principal's behalf. Tuck made no such manifestation, but merely yielded temporarily to coercion.

PROBLEM 37

Travelling across country by car after the death of her husband, Alice stops at a roadside diner for lunch. The diner is in chaos. The one waitress has just quit, and Mel, the owner and cook, has a room full of increasingly irate customers. Sensing a job opportunity, Alice says to Mel, "Hey, I can wait tables. Want some help?" Mel responds, "Four dollars an hour. You're hired. Your shift ends at 7 P.M."

Alice works hard and extremely well. By the end of the day, she has collected $80 in tips. She is shocked when Mel says, "The tips belong to me. I didn't saying nothing about you keeping the tips." Is Alice obliged to surrender the tips?

EXPLANATION

No. Although an agent must have the principal's consent to profit from the agency, custom may imply the necessary consent. It is certainly customary for waitresses and waiters to retain their tips.

PROBLEM 38

Victoria commissions Albert to get a contracts casebook for her at the used bookstore. She specifically instructs him that she wants him to buy a book that was previously used, underlined, and annotated by someone who received at least a B-plus in the contracts course. She promises to pay Albert a $5 fee if he succeeds in purchasing for her a book that meets her specifications.

Albert goes to the bookstore and initially attempts to perform his task. However, the bookstore clerk tells Albert that the bookstore has no way of knowing how well the former owner of any particular book did on any particular exam. Not wanting to lose a sale and always on the lookout for a little personal gain, the clerk suggests a little scam. The clerk will telephone Victoria and tell her that the bookstore does indeed have a book which was owned by someone who received an A in contracts. The clerk will also tell Victoria that, since the book has such a good pedigree, the book costs $15 instead of the regular used price of $12. If Albert will back up the story, the clerk will split the extra $3 with him, fifty-fifty. Albert agrees.

The scam works. Victoria gives Albert $20 ($15 for the supposed price of the book and $5 for Albert's commission.) Twelve dollars of Victoria's money goes into the bookstore's cash drawer. The clerk splits the other $3 with Albert. Albert also pockets the $5 commission.

But not for long. The scam unravels when Victoria learns that the former owner of the book flunked out of law school without ever having achieved a grade above C-minus. Threatened with dire consequences, the clerk spills his guts and tells Victoria the whole sordid story. Victoria rescinds her purchase. The clerk returns to Victoria the full $15 purchase price, taking $12 from the bookstore's cash drawer and the other $3 from his own pocket. Victoria then goes after Albert. She sues him not only for the return of the $5 commission, but also to disgorge the $1.50 kickback. Albert concedes the $5 and pays it back to Victoria. Albert contests the $1.50, however. He points out that he has paid the $5 and the clerk has paid the $15, so Victoria is now "whole." According to Albert, Victoria has recovered whatever damages she suffered and is now looking for a windfall. What result?

EXPLANATION

Albert must disgorge the $1.50. When an agent profits by breaching the duty of loyalty, the law imposes a constructive trust in favor of the principal. It is irrelevant that Victoria can prove no damages, and it is immaterial that disgorgement will make Victoria "more than whole" financially. It is better that the principal receive a windfall than the agent profit from a breach of fiduciary duty.

PROBLEM 39

After graduating from law school, Beth goes to work for a law firm. Several months later an uncle contacts Beth and asks her to handle a closing on the sale of some land. Beth says, "I'd be delighted. When would you like to come down to the office?" The uncle responds, "Oh, I don't want to get your office involved. I don't really want to pay downtown lawyer fees. Why don't I just come by your house tonight?"

Beth explains that she is really obligated to work through her firm, but her uncle is insistent. Finally, Beth hits upon a solution. "Listen, uncle," she says, "You're family. Let me do this closing as family, no charge. We'll call it an introductory offer." Her uncle agrees.

Beth spends about six hours preparing for and attending the closing, and all goes well. Two weeks later, she receives at home a beautiful silver necklace, with a note from her uncle: "Dear Beth, With thanks to my favorite niece. Love, Your uncle." The necklace is worth approximately $900. What should Beth do?

Explanation

Beth faces a difficult situation. Presumably, she does not want to hurt her uncle's feelings, and for sentimental, aesthetic, and financial reasons she may well want to keep the necklace for herself. However, as Beth explained to her uncle, she is obliged to do her legal work through her firm. Her duty of loyalty precludes her acting in competition with her principal. No matter how earnest her efforts to avoid a problem and how pure her motives, she cannot retain benefits made through competitive activity unless she has her principal's informed consent.

That analysis dictates Beth's next steps. She must either return the necklace to her uncle or disclose the situation to the firm and seek the firm's permission to retain the necklace.

PROBLEM 40

Samuel obtains from a video game distributor the right to place its video games in bars, restaurants, and video parlors throughout a tri-state area. The right is quite valuable, because this manufacturer has several very popular video games and rations the number of games allowed in any one geographic area. Samuel retains Charlie to represent him in locating the best possible locations for the games and to negotiate with the owners and managers of those locations. Charlie makes a number of recommendations, which Samuel follows. Per their agreement, Samuel pays Charlie a fee of $50 per location selected.

The games do not produce the revenue Samuel expected, and after about six months he looks more carefully into the locations Charlie recommended. Samuel discovers that (i) half of the locations are owned by Entertainment Facilities, Inc. ("EFI"), (ii) during the time that Charlie was advising Samuel he was also on retainer to EFI as a management consultant, (iii) many of the EFI locations are not in high traffic areas, and (iv) Charlie could easily have arranged superior, non-EFI placements that would have produced better revenues for Samuel. What recourse does Samuel have against Charlie?

Explanation

By acting for EFI, a potentially adverse party, without having Samuel's consent, Charlie breached his agent's duty of loyalty. He is liable to Samuel for damages, that is, the present value of the additional revenues that would have been produced by the easily-arranged, superior, non-EFI placements. Charlie may also have to disgorge the compensation he received from Samuel, as well as any compensation Charlie received from EFI for having gotten Samuel's video games into EFI locations.

PROBLEM 41

Sandy agrees to go to an auction for Ralph and bid for a particular picture. Ralph authorizes Sandy to bid up to $20,000. Both Sandy and Ralph expect the auction to end by 6 P.M. The auction runs late and Sandy must leave to pick up a child from day care. The day care center closes at 6:30 P.M. After Sandy leaves, the picture Ralph wanted is sold for $18,000. Ralph later buys the picture from the purchaser for $20,000. He learns that the purchaser would have stopped bidding at the auction when the price hit $19,000. Ralph then sues Sandy for $1,000 — the difference between what would have been a winning bid at the auction and the price Ralph had to pay to get the painting after the auction. What is Ralph's theory of recovery? What will Sandy argue? What will Ralph respond?

EXPLANATION

Ralph will argue that (i) Sandy was his agent, (ii) Sandy owed Ralph an agent's duty of loyalty, which Sandy breached by leaving the auction before the bidding finished (or at least before the $20,000 limit was reached on the picture), and (iii) Sandy is liable for the $1,000 of damages proximately caused by Sandy's breach of fiduciary duty.

Sandy will make two arguments. First, Sandy will argue that, by at least tacit agreement of the parties, the agency (and Sandy's fiduciary duty of loyalty) terminated at 6 P.M., when both the principal and agent expected the auction to be over. Second, Sandy will argue that even assuming the agency continued past 6 P.M., the agent's duty of loyalty yields when necessary to protect important interests of others. Preventing a child from being abandoned at a day care center should qualify as such an interest. Protecting children is certainly a legitimate social value and should outweigh some relatively minor financial harm to the principal.

Ralph will respond that Sandy had available at least two alternatives for protecting the child's interest without sacrificing the principal's. First, by anticipating the problem and disclosing it in advance to Ralph, Sandy would have allowed Ralph to make other arrangements for covering the auction. Second, when the auction appeared to be running long, Sandy could have asked for a brief recess, called the day care center, and tried to arrange for a late pick-up.

PROBLEM 42

Sylvia decides to enter the silk importing business. The trade is notoriously biased against women, and she fears that her company will suffer if her interest in it is known. She therefore hires Phil as her general manager, but sets up the company so that Phil appears to the outside world as the owner. It is common in this trade for silk importers to sell to large customers on credit, but Sylvia instructs Phil never to extend more than $50,000 of credit to any customer without Sylvia's approval. One day, in order to close an important deal, Phil extends $150,000 of credit to one customer without consulting Sylvia. The customer makes only $20,000 of payments and then defaults. Assuming that Phil's judgment about the customer's creditworthiness was reasonable, does Sylvia have any claim against Phil?

EXPLANATION

Yes. Phil owes Sylvia $130,000. He breached his duty to act within his authority, and he is liable to his principal for the resulting harm. The reasonableness of Phil's judgment about the customer's creditworthiness is irrelevant. Sylvia is not claiming breach of the agent's duty of care.

PROBLEM 43

The owner of a car dealership appoints Rachael to manage the used car department. The owner promises that Rachael can have a "free hand" running the department. Rachael decides to open the department on Sundays. Although Sunday openings are not against the law, the owner considers them "inappropriate." The owner instructs Rachael to stay closed on Sunday. Must Rachael comply?

EXPLANATION

Although this instruction breaches the agreement between the owner and Rachael, Rachael has a duty either to obey or to resign. If Rachael can prove damages, she may recover for breach of contract.

PROBLEM 44

Sidney hires Sam, a private detective, to locate and deliver to Sidney a valuable statue of a bird. Sidney agrees to a fee of $100 per day, plus reasonable expenses, with a $5,000 bonus if Sam succeeds in finding and delivering the statue. Sam is on the verge of locating the statue when Sidney learns that Sam is carrying a gun. Sam is properly licensed to do so, but Sidney tells Sam, "I abhor violence. You may not carry that thing when you are working for me." Must Sam obey? Does he have any recourse against Sidney?

Explanation

A principal always has the power to control the agent, so Sam must either obey or resign. Sam may nonetheless have a claim against Sidney for breach of contract. If, for example, the local custom is for detectives to use whatever lawful tactics they choose, that custom may have implied an agreement requiring Sidney to respect Sam's discretion. If so, and if Sam could for instance prove that his lack of a gun cost him the opportunity to retrieve the falcon, Sam could recover the $5,000 bonus from Sidney.

PROBLEM 45

Esther seeks to sell her business and enlists Harry to locate and help evaluate prospective buyers. With Harry's advice, Esther decides on a price of $1.5 million. She is willing to finance the sale (i.e., to receive payments in installments) but only with a down payment of at least 10 percent. Both Esther and Harry believe that buyers are more likely to succeed if they have some of their own money at risk.

Initially Harry has difficulty locating qualified buyers, but after three months he presents an offer from JoDot Enterprises ("JoDot"). JoDot offers to pay $1.5 million, with $150,000 down. Esther accepts the offer, and the sale goes through.

Unfortunately, JoDot cannot operate the business at a profit and defaults on its obligations to Esther. Esther then learns that (i) JoDot did not actually have the $150,000 needed for the down payment and had to borrow $75,000 from a third party, and (ii) Harry was aware of that fact when he presented JoDot's offer to Esther. Does Esther have any recourse against Harry?

Explanation

Yes. Harry breached his duty to provide information to Esther, his principal. Harry understood both the importance of the down payment and Esther's view of the subject. He therefore knew or should have known that Esther would want to know that the prospective buyers lacked a true down payment.[53]

Esther can compel Harry to disgorge any commission he earned on the deal. If she can prove causation, she can also collect damages.

53. It is also possible to view Harry's conduct as a breach of his duty to obey instructions. This view assumes that Esther instructed him to bring her only offers from "qualified" buyers, that is, buyers capable of meeting the 10 percent down payment requirement.

PROBLEM 46

An attorney contacts an art collector, seeking to buy a famous Picasso print on behalf of a client. The attorney explains to the collector that she is acting for a client but declines to identify the client. (The client dislikes notoriety.) The attorney has actual authority to offer up to $450,000 for the print, and she persuades the collector to sell for $415,000. It is late Friday afternoon, and the attorney can have a cashier's check for the contract price by 10 A.M. Monday morning. The attorney wishes, however, to sign a binding sale agreement with the art collector, so that the collector cannot change his mind over the weekend. The attorney has $5,000 of her own money immediately available that she is willing to use as an earnest deposit. The attorney does not, however, wish to be liable on the contract itself. What should she do?

EXPLANATION

The attorney's potential problem comes from a rule of agency law. When an agent makes a contract for a partially disclosed principal, the agent is liable to the third party as a guarantor of the principal's performance — unless the agent and the third party have agreed otherwise. This rule dictates the attorney's strategy. The sale agreement must let her off the hook.

From the attorney's perspective, the ideal solution would be to include in the sale agreement an express statement that the attorney is not liable. It seems possible, however, that the collector would balk at such a term. After all, he would be committing to take the print off the market in return only for a promise to pay from a party whose creditworthiness he is unable to assess. The attorney could respond to this concern by limiting the duration of the collector's risk. The agreement could require payment by cashier's check by Monday at noon and provide that any delay in payment would entitle the collector to rescind the agreement. If the collector required further inducement, the agreement could provide for a nonrefundable "earnest money" payment of $5,000.

PROBLEM 47

Rose's Marina rents berths to various boat owners and also does boat and engine repair. The Marina does not ordinarily sell boats. Phil rents a berth at the Marina for his cabin cruiser. He happens to mention to Rose that he is thinking about selling his boat. Phil then leaves town on a two-week vacation. Three days later Rose meets Irv, who interested in buying a cabin cruiser just like Phil's. Rose shows Phil's cruiser to Irv, and Irv immediately offers to pay $25,000 for the boat. Overcome by her enthusiastic desire to help Phil, Rose says, "OK. He'll take it. Give me $500 earnest money." Irv does so, receiving in return a receipt from Rose: "Received from Irv, nonrefundable down payment on Phil's boat. By Rose, acting for Phil."

When Phil returns to town, he refuses to go through with the sale. Assuming that Phil is not bound,[54] does Irv have any recourse against Rose?

EXPLANATION

Yes. When Rose purported to act on Phil's behalf in selling the boat, she impliedly warranted her authority to bind Phil. In fact, she was not Phil's agent and lacked any power to bind him. She has breached her warranty of authority and is liable to Irv for both reliance and expectation damages.

PROBLEM 48

Jerry, the owner of Jerry's Gas, Service, and Repair Station, instructs Leah, one of his employees, to "pick up the blue Chevy station wagon parked in the driveway of 1346 Lincoln Avenue. Customer called and says it won't start and we should get it and fix it." Leah takes the Station's tow truck and does as instructed. On the way back from the driveway, a semitrailer crosses a median strip and smashes into the station wagon. Fortunately, no one is injured, but the station wagon is totalled. Moreover, it later develops that Jerry made a mistake on the address: The customer who authorized the repair work lives at 1436 Lincoln. Is Leah liable to the owner of the station wagon?

EXPLANATION

Yes. Leah is liable for conversion, a strict liability tort. That she acted on her principal's instructions and without negligence is irrelevant to the question of her liability. Leah certainly has a right to be indemnified by her principal, and her principal is doubtlessly liable to the wagon's owner.[55] Nonetheless, she remains responsible for the tort she committed.

54. According to the rules discussed in Chapter Two, Rose had no power to bind Phil. He made no manifestation that could have *reasonably* caused her to believe that he wanted her to sell his boat. Therefore, she had no actual authority. He made only one manifestation that reached Irv — leaving the boat at the Marina. That manifestation was insufficient to cause Irv to *reasonably* believe that Rose was Phil's authorized agent. Therefore, Rose had no apparent authority. Cf. U.C.C. §2-403(2) (power of merchant who deals in goods of the kind to transfer entrusters title to a buyer in ordinary course). Inherent power is inapplicable, because Rose was not Phil's agent, much less his general agent. Estoppel will not work because Phil neither knew of nor carelessly caused Irv's misapprehension.

55. This liability rests on respondeat superior. See section 3.2.

PROBLEM 49

Tim and May hire Bob, a general contractor, to build them a two-story beach cottage. The contract calls for the cottage to be "fully plumbed, with all plumbing fixtures properly installed and operational." A separate Exhibit to the contract specifies the quality, quantity, and location for various fixtures.

Bob subcontracts the plumbing work to Forrest, an expert plumber. Bob has worked with Forrest before and knows that Forrest takes great pride in his work. Bob does not supervise Forrest's work.

When Tim and May take possession they discover that Forrest plumbed the laundry room incorrectly and that they cannot hook up a washing machine. Correcting the problem will cost $500, and Bob is nowhere to be found. Can Tim and May recover from Forrest?

EXPLANATION

Not under agency law. Forrrest's mistake with the plumbing presumably breached a duty to Bob, but that breach creates no direct liability to Tim and May. An agent's breach of duty to its principal cannot create a claim for a third party when the third party suffers only economic loss.[56]

PROBLEM 50

Seller owned five acres of land on which he had built stables, corrals, fencing, and other improvements useful for raising horses. He retained Broker to sell the land on his behalf. Seller walked the property with Broker, showing Broker the various improvements and the property lines. Together they found most of the boundary markers but could not find some. On the east side of the property, they found the northeast marker but could not find the southeast one. A line of trees seemed to confirm Seller's description of the east boundary. Moreover, Seller assured Broker, "I know where my land is and where I built. All my improvements are on my property." Broker did not independently verify the boundary lines.

When Broker showed the land to the eventual Buyers, Broker represented that all the improvements were within the property. After closing, the Buyers discovered that a corral on the east side of the property encroached several feet into the neighboring parcel. The cost for moving the improvements was $6,000. Was Broker liable for that amount?

---

56. Tim and May could try to recover as third party beneficiaries. They would assert that, when Bob subcontracted his duty of performance to Forrest, they became intended beneficiaries of that subcontract. See Restatement (second) of Contracts §302(1)(b).

Explanation

No. An agent is not liable for an innocent misrepresentation. The third party must show either intentional or negligent misrepresentation. There is no case here for intentional misrepresentation. Broker actually believed its own statements about the boundaries. Nor do the facts support a finding of negligent misrepresentation. Broker had no reason to doubt Seller's assurances, especially when the land's natural features (i.e., the trees) and what markers could be found seemed to support those assurances.

PROBLEM 51

In an attempt to get better booking for his client, Dave (Alvin's road manager), threatens a booking agent with imminent bodily harm. The booking agent sues Dave for assault and for intentional infliction of emotional distress. Is Alvin obliged to indemnify Dave?

Explanation

No. The suit arises from a tort knowingly committed by an agent. The principal therefore has no duty to indemnify.[57]

PROBLEM 52

Emily hires two college students, Peter and Ira, to move her mahogany sideboard out of her second floor apartment. She agrees to pay them $75 to take the sideboard to her sister's house across town. Peter borrows a friend's large pick-up truck, and he and Ira show up to do the moving.

Emily is very concerned that the sideboard not be damaged, and she hovers over Peter and Ira telling them exactly how to move the sideboard. She neglects, however, to mention that the second step down on the stairs is loose. As Ira puts his foot on that step, the step wobbles and Ira loses his grip on the sideboard. Peter then loses his grip, and the sideboard crashes down to the next landing. The sideboard lands on and destroys the first floor tenant's new 20-speed touring bike. Assuming that neither Peter nor Ira was negligent, does that tenant have any claim against Emily?

Explanation

Yes. A principal has a direct duty to use reasonable care in informing its agents of the dangers of their task. When Emily failed to mention the loose step, she breached that duty and became liable for any proximately caused damages.

---

57. Alvin may yet get involved, however, since the booking agent may have a respondeat superior claim. Dave's intentional tort may have been within his scope of employment. See section 3.2.6.

PROBLEM 53

Tim and May hire Bob, a general contractor, to build them a two-story beach cottage. The contract calls for the cottage to be "fully plumbed, with all plumbing fixtures properly installed and operational." A separate Exhibit to the contract specifies the quality, quantity, and location for various fixtures.

Bob subcontracts the plumbing work to Forrest, an expert plumber. Bob has worked with Forrest before and knows that Forrest takes great pride in his work. Bob does not supervise Forrest's work.

On the very first night after taking possession of the beach cottage, Tim takes a bath in the second-floor bathroom. Everything goes well until Tim starts to drain the tub. Then, gallons of water pour through the first floor ceiling into the living room. Later inspection reveals that Forrest had neglected to connect the tub drain to the drain pipe.

Tim and May demand that Bob pay them $2,500: $300 for fixing the plumbing and $2,200 for repairing the damage caused by the cascade of dirty bath water. Bob responds, "I'm real sorry about the trouble, but your complaint is really with Forrest. I trusted him, and I had no reason not to. He's always done excellent work. This time he messed up. You have to go after him, not me." Must they?

EXPLANATION

No. Bob's analysis is coherent, but irrelevant. He is essentially making an independent contractor argument and asserting that he is neither vicariously nor directly liable for Forrest's negligence.[58] But Tim and May are not trying to hold Bob accountable for Forrest's negligence. They are asserting Bob's failure to perform his direct obligations under contract. Bob did not escape those obligations merely by delegating them to Forrest.

58. Rephrased into agency terminology, Bob's argument runs as follows: Bob had no right to control the details of Forrest's performance, so Forrest was not Bob's servant and Forrest's negligence is not attributable to Bob. Moreover, given Forrest's excellent track record, Bob was not negligent in selecting or supervising Forrest and therefore is not directly liable either. For present purposes, it is immaterial whether Bob seeks to characterize Forrest as a complete independent contractor or merely as an independent contractor (i.e., nonservant) agent.

5

Termination of the Agency Relationship

§5.1 Ending the Agency Relationship

An agency relationship may end in numerous ways.

§5.1.1 Through the Express Will of Either the Principal or the Agent

In a true agency situation, both the principal and the agent have the *power* to end the relationship at any time.[1] Either party can exercise this power simply by communicating to the other that the relationship is at an end. The principal's exercise of this power is sometimes called *revocation* (as in revocation of the agent's authority), while the agent's exercise is sometimes called *renunciation*. Like other agency manifestations, communications of revocation and renunciation are judged by an objective standard.

> ***Example:*** The City Opera Company signs soprano Donna Prima to an agreement under which Ms. Prima agrees to perform exclusively on behalf of the Company throughout the upcoming season. Like the opera

1. As discussed previously, power is not the same as right. See sections 1.3, 4.1.3, and 4.1.6. Whether a particular revocation or renunciation is "rightful" depends on the contract overlaying the agency relationship. See section 5.2. If the principal lacks the power to terminate, no true agency exists. See section 6.2 (power [or agency] coupled with an interest; power [or authority] given as security).

star stereotype, Ms. Prima is a mercurial personality and is given to emotional outbursts. During one rehearsal she loudly proclaims, "I am sorry, but I cannot tolerate mediocrity. I resign." On two prior occasions she has made similar announcements during rehearsals only to return a few hours later. Viewed objectively, in light of what the Opera Company knows of Prima's personality and her past conduct, this latest pronouncement does not constitute a renunciation and does not terminate the agency relationship.

> ***Example:*** The sheriff of a Western town is well known as a man slow to make decisions but resolute once a decision is made. Despite receiving no support from the townspeople, the sheriff has just survived a gunfight with several outlaws. As the townspeople come out of hiding and try to congratulate the sheriff, he looks at them with disgust, takes off his badge, and throws it into the dirt. The sheriff has renounced his agency.

§5.1.2 Through the Expiration of a Specified Term

Principal and agent can and often do specify that the relationship will last for a particular period of time. If they do, the relationship automatically terminates at the end of the specified period unless the parties agree to an extension or renewal. That agreement can be inferred from the parties' conduct.

> ***Example:*** Jim retains Susan to find a buyer for Jim's condominium. They agree that Susan will have the exclusive agency for 90 days. They also agree that during those 90 days Susan will have the authority to accept any cash offer of at least $90,000. On the 101st day, Susan purports to accept a cash offer for $92,000. Susan lacks the actual authority to accept the offer on Jim's behalf. That authority, and Susan's role as agent, terminated at the end of 90 days.

> ***Example:*** Same facts, except that following the 90th day, Jim and Susan continue to discuss the condo, and Susan, with Jim's knowledge, continues to show the condo to prospects. The conduct of Jim and Susan implies an agreement to extend the agency.

§5.1.3 Through the Accomplishment of the Agency's Purpose

If the manifestations that create an agency indicate a specific objective, achieving that objective ends the agency. Without further manifestations from the principal, the agent has no basis for believing that either its authority or its agency continues.

Example: Capitalist, Inc. hires Sally to lobby for the passage of a bill in Congress. As part of her lobbying efforts Sally "wines and dines" Congressional staff members. She sends the bills to Capitalist. On October 12th, the bill passes and is sent to the President. The next day, Sally takes three staffers out to a "thank you for all your hard work" lunch. Without some additional manifestation from Capitalist, Sally may not bill this lunch to Capitalist. Her agency relationship with Capitalist ended when the goal of the agency was accomplished.

Sometimes an agent will continue to exert effort for the principal even after accomplishing the agency task. The principal's acceptance or even acknowledgement of those efforts may manifest consent for the agency to continue.

Example: Mark hires Jeff to help arrange a loan to finance Mark's acquisition of a business. Jeff arranges a loan and receives a fee from Mark. Jeff keeps in touch with the lender and some months later learns that Mark is having difficulty meeting his payments. Without first talking to Mark, Jeff contacts the lender to talk about refinancing the loan. At this point, Jeff is not acting as Mark's agent.[2] Subsequently, Jeff talks to Mark and says, "I understand from your lender that the payments are too large. I think I can work something out. Do you want me to try?" Mark replies, "Sure. Why not?" From that point, Jeff is again acting as Mark's agent.

§5.1.4 By the Occurrence of an Event or Condition

Sometimes the manifestations that create an agency indicate that a particular event or condition will end the agency. If so, once the event or condition occurs the agent can no longer reasonably believe itself authorized to act on the principal's behalf. The agency therefore terminates.

Example: Larry hires Howie to sell hot dogs at the beach, "but only until my daughter gets out of summer school." When Larry's daughter arrives, Howie's agency ends.

The same rationale applies if the original manifestations call for the agency to end if a particular event or condition does not occur.

2. Jeff may nonetheless have the apparent authority to bind Mark. See section 5.3.1.

§5.1.5 *By the Destruction of or the End of the Principal's Legal Interest in the Property*

If the agent's role is predicated on some particular property and the property is no longer practically or legally available to the agent, the agency ends.

> ***Example:*** Larry hires Howie to skipper Larry's yacht during the summer. In June the yacht sinks. Howie's agency ends.

> ***Example:*** Larry hires Howie to skipper Larry's yacht during the summer. In June Larry sells the yacht. The yacht still exits, but Larry no longer has a legal interest in it. Howie's agency ends.[3]

§5.1.6 *By the Death, Bankruptcy, or Mental Incapacity of the Agent or Principal*

Any of these events terminate the agency relationship.

§5.1.7 *By the Expiration of a Reasonable Time*

Where the original manifestations set no specific term, the agency relationship expires automatically after a reasonable time has passed. What constitutes a reasonable time depends on a number of factors, including:

- the manifestation of the parties when the agency is created
- the extent and nature of the communications between the parties after the agency is created (including indications by a party that it wishes to end the agency or that it believes the agency has ended)
- the particular objective of the agency
- past dealings, if any, between the principal and agent
- the custom, if any, in the locality with regard to agency relationships of the same or similar type

§5.2 Power versus Right in Termination

As previously indicated,[4] both principal and agent always have the power to end a true agency relationship. Whether either has the right to do so depends

3. If the end of the agency means that Larry has breached an agreement with Howie, Howie may pursue contract remedies. See section 5.2. Nonetheless, the agency ends.

4. Section 5.1.1.

on the content of any contract overlaying the agency relationship as well as on concepts of detrimental reliance and good faith.

§5.2.1 *The Role of Contract*

Contractual terms can, *inter alia*:

- set a specific duration for the agency, during which neither party may end the relationship without having cause
- provide for the agency to continue indefinitely, until ended by either party giving notice
- define "cause" sufficient to allow one party, or the other, or both to end the agency
- provide for the agency to continue so long as the agent meets certain performance requirements

Regardless of its terms, a contract leaves intact the parties' *power* to end the agency relationship. If a principal revokes or an agent renounces in breach of contract, the other party may seek contract damages but cannot avoid the destruction of the agency. In any damage action, ordinary contract rules (e.g., the defense of prior breach, the duty to mitigate) will apply.

Example: Marge enters into a contract calling for her to serve as Mountain Fleece, Inc.'s East Coast Regional Sales Representative for 18 months. Despite the contract, Mountain Fleece terminates the agency a mere six months later. As a matter of agency law, Marge cannot compel Mountain Fleece to continue the relationship.[5] She can, however, sue for damages.

Example: Same situation, except that Marge prematurely renounces. As a matter of agency (and contract) law, Mountain Fleece cannot compel Marge to serve. It can sue her for damages.

§5.2.2 *Implied Terms*

For the most part, the rules on implying terms in an agency contract are identical to the rules for implying terms in any contract. A difference exists,

---

5. Nonagency law may provide for such compulsion. For example, a state statute may protect sales representatives against unfair termination and may allow a court to order Marge's reinstatement.

however, with regard to terms restricting the right of the parties to terminate the relationship.

An express term can certainly restrict either party's right to terminate the agency. For example, most collective bargaining agreements expressly preclude the principal (i.e., the employer) from terminating a servant agent (i.e., an employee) without "just cause." Courts will not, however, easily imply such a restriction. To the contrary, most agents have the right to renounce at will and most serve at the will of the principal.[6]

Courts are most likely to find an implied, contractual limit on termination when:

- the agency relationship is outside the employment context,
- the limitation is asserted against the principal, and
- either
  - — the principal's manifestations are the source of the implication, or
  - — the agent has reasonably incurred costs in undertaking the agency and needs time to earn back those costs.

Example: A manufacturer retains a salesperson as the manufacturer's selling agent and states, "We will supply all the widgets you can sell during the next year." A court may imply a term under which, during that next year, the manufacturer has the right to terminate the agency only for cause.

Example: A manufacturer retains a salesperson as the manufacturer's selling agent. Nothing is said about duration, but the salesperson does buy from the manufacturer demonstration equipment costing $4,200. The manufacturer may be contractually obliged either to buy back the demonstration equipment or to let the agency exist long enough to allow the agent to recoup the $4,200 through commissions.

§5.2.3 Noncontract Limitations on the Right to Terminate

The gratuitous agent. If the agency is gratuitous, then by definition the agent's right to terminate is not limited by contract.[7] However, principles

6. In the employment context, this situation is known as ***employment at will***, and the employment at will doctrine dates back more than a century. Many modern commentators have attacked the doctrine, and some courts have created exceptions relating, for example, to retaliatory firing of whistleblowers and to promissory estoppel. Statutory developments have also made inroads. Statutes prohibiting employment discrimination, for instance, allow "no cause" termination so long as the termination has neither discriminatory purpose nor effect. For the most part, however, the employment at will doctrine remains intact.

7. Although an agency can exist without consideration, a contract generally requires consideration to be enforceable.

akin to promissory estoppel impose some restrictions. If a gratuitous agent (i) makes a promise or engages in other conduct that causes the principal to refrain from making different arrangements, and (ii) the gratuitous agent had reason to know that the principal would so rely, then:

- if alternative arrangements are still possible, the agent has a duty to end the agency only after giving notice so the principal can make alternative arrangements, and
- if alternative arrangements are not possible, the agent has a duty to continue to perform the agency as promised.

Like any other agent, a gratuitous agent always has the power to renounce. However, if a gratuitous agent improperly leaves the principal in the lurch, the agent will be liable for damages.

The principal. Even if a principal has the right to terminate the agency at will, the principal may not exercise that right in bad faith. Most bad faith cases arise when a principal seeks to snatch some benefit away from the agent.

> ***Example:*** Marcia tells Teri, "Find me a bona fide buyer for my restaurant and help put the paperwork together, and I'll pay you a finder's fee of $10,000." Teri finds a prospect. As soon as Marcia learns of the prospect, she tells Teri, "Changed my mind. Think I'll wait awhile." Marcia then contacts the prospect directly and arranges the sale. Even though the agency relationship contained no express limitations on Marcia's right to terminate the relationship, Marcia will be liable to Teri for the finder's fee. Marcia terminated the relationship in bad faith.

§5.3 Effects of Termination

§5.3.1 Effects on Agent's Authority and Power to Bind Principal

At common law, the agent's actual authority to bind the principal terminates when the agency terminates. Any inherent agency power also ends, because that power presupposes the status of general agent.

The fate of the agent's apparent authority depends on the reason the agency terminated. If the principal has died or lacks capacity, the agent's apparent authority terminates immediately. In other circumstances, the agent's apparent authority terminates as to any particular third party only when (i) the third party learns that the agency has ended, or (ii) in light of other information, the third party can no longer reasonably believe that the agent is authorized to act.

Example: Melinda is a rancher. Sammy is a horse breeder. On Monday, Melinda introduces Rebecca to Sammy as "my agent for buying horses." On Tuesday, as Rebecca is negotiating with Sammy, Melinda dies. Unaware of the death, Rebecca and Sammy reach agreement on a horse purchase and Rebecca purports to bind Melinda. Melinda's estate is not bound, however, because Melinda's death terminated Rebecca's apparent as well as actual authority.[8]

Example: Same situation, but Melinda does not die. Instead, Melinda fires Rebecca for insubordination but fails to tell Sammy. The next day, Rebecca purports to buy a horse from Sammy for Melinda. Rebecca's action binds Melinda, although the firing ended Rebecca's actual authority. Because neither death nor incapacity caused the agency relationship to end, Rebecca's apparent authority remained intact.

Example: Percy is a long-time customer of Hunter Brokerage Company and has always done his investing through Jeffrey, one of Hunter's agents. One afternoon, unbeknownst to Percy, Hunter fires Jeffrey. That night Jeffrey calls Percy with a "hot tip" and urges Percy to make a quick investment of $5,000. Jeffrey explains that the opportunity may disappear "overnight" and persuades Percy to bring the $5,000 to Jeffrey's home. Jeffrey has never before tried to rush Percy's decision, and Percy has sent all past investment funds to the offices of Hunter. Percy probably cannot hold Hunter accountable for Jeffrey's actions. The termination of the agency relationship has ended Jeffrey's actual authority to bind Hunter, and Jeffrey probably lacks apparent authority as well. Given Jeffrey's two deviations from standard practice, Percy could no longer reasonably believe that Jeffrey was authorized to act for Hunter.

In some jurisdictions, statutes have changed the common law, providing that upon a principal's death or incapacity the agent's actual authority continues until the agent knows of the death or incapacity and the apparent authority continues until the third party knows.[9] Other statutes allow principals to execute documents creating agency powers that survive the principal's disability or incapacity, even after the disability or incapacity becomes known.[10]

---

8. Rebecca is therefore liable for breach of the warranty of authority. See section 4.2.2.

9. Uniform Durable Power of Attorney Act §4 (1979) (applicable to written powers of attorney).

10. Uniform Durable Power of Attorney Act §2 (1987).

§5.3.2 *Agent's Obligation to Cease Acting for Principal*

Once the agency relationship ends, the former agent has a duty not to act for the principal. If the former agent violates this duty and binds the former principal, the former agent will be liable for damages.[11]

§5.3.3 *Principal's Duty to Indemnify Agent*

The termination of the agency relationship does not eliminate any right of indemnity that the agent may have on account of events that occurred before the termination.

> ***Example:*** As an authorized part of her lobbying for Capitalist, Inc., Sally "wines and dines" important people. She periodically submits her bills to Capitalist for reimbursement. Capitalist one day decides that having lobbyists is not good for its image and therefore terminates its relationship with Sally. At that time, Sally has $500 of reimbursement claims submitted but as yet unpaid and $400 of expenses incurred but not yet submitted for reimbursement. Sally is entitled to both the $500 and the $400. Both amounts relate to events that occurred before the termination of the agency relationship.

§5.3.4 *Agent's Right to Compete with Principal*

While an agency relationship exists, the agent's duty of loyalty precludes competition with the principal. Unless the principal consents, the agent must refrain from engaging in any competitive activity that relates to the scope of the agency relationship.[12]

Once the agency relationship ends, however, so does the absolute barrier to competition. Public policy strongly favors free competition, and the former agent has a right to compete with its former principal. A former agent may even recruit customers from the former principal's clientele.[13]

The right to compete does, however, have three limitations: a prohibition against using the former principal's confidential information; the duty to "get out clean"; and the obligation to abide by any valid "noncompete" agreements.

---

11. This duty is similar to an agent's duty not to act without or beyond its authority. See section 4.1.2.

12. See section 4.1.1.

13. Customer lists can be confidential information, and, if so, a former agent will breach a duty by making use of the lists to compete with the former principal.

Prohibition against using the former principal's confidential information. The agent's duty not to disclose or exploit the principal's confidential information[14] clearly continues after the agency relationship ends. Disputes about the duty center around the question of just what kinds of information are protected from use.

Although in theory the same question exists during the agency relationship, at that juncture the question has far less practical import. Most alleged misuses involve some form of competition, and during the agency relationship competition is itself barred. As a result, during the relationship a claim of misuse of confidential information is often just a "tag along" to a claim of improper competition. The question of whether allegedly misused information is truly confidential (and therefore protected) is unlikely to be dispositive.

Post-termination competition, however, is not by itself improper,[15] and a claim of information misuse can therefore be crucially important in a conflict between former principal and former agent. In that context the question of what constitutes confidential information can be dispositive.

Analyzing that question can involve two different but complementary perspectives:

1. Does the information warrant protection as a trade secret? That is:
   - Has the principal expended effort and incurred expense to obtain or create the information?
   - Does the principal derive economic advantage from the information not being generally known?
   - Has the principal used reasonable efforts to protect the confidentiality of the information?
2. Does the information consist of facts or specialized techniques as distinguished from general expertise that an agent might develop while performing agency tasks?

Duty to "get out clean." During the agency relationship an agent may properly contemplate post-termination competition with the principal. An agent may not, however, disregard its current loyalty obligations to further its post-termination plans. Put colloquially, the agent must "get out clean."

This duty has two major aspects. First, the agent has a duty not to begin actual competition while still an agent. During the agency relationship, discussions with customers or potential customers of the principal violate the duty of loyalty. Also, attempts to enlist other key agents of the principal may

14. See section 4.1.1.

15. A valid "noncompete" agreement can make post-termination competition improper. See below.

violate the duty of loyalty. The agent may, however, have discussions and even make agreements with parties *other than customers, potential customers, and key fellow agents* of the principal. For instance, the agent may properly have stationery printed, rent an office, and apply for a license.

Second, the agent may not actively deceive the principal as to the agent's reasons for terminating the agency relationship. The agent probably has no affirmative duty to provide reasons or even to respond if the principal asks "Why are you quitting?" The agent may not, however, lie to conceal its plan to compete. Moreover, subject to its right not to reveal its plans for the future, the agent must continue to provide agency-related information to the principal[16] right up to the moment that the agency ends.

An agent who fails to "get out clean" may be liable to the former principal both for damages and for disgorgement.[17]

> ***Example:*** May works as the headmaster of a private school. Frustrated by policies set by the board of trustees, she decides to start her own school. Before resigning, she discusses her plans with several of the private school's major donors and obtains commitments from them for start-up funding. She also copies the private school's mailing list of the families of current students. Her actions breach her duty of loyalty. She has the right to compete with the private school for donations, but only after she terminates her agency relationship. She never has the right to purloin her principal's mailing list.

Noncompetition obligations imposed by contract. A contract between the principal and agent can restrain the agent from competing after the relationship ends, although the law's strong pro-competition stance causes courts to scrutinize such agreements carefully. The restraints must be reasonable with respect to the scope of activities foreclosed, the geographic area foreclosed, and the duration of the foreclosure. In some states, overbroad restraints are simply unenforceable. In most states, however, courts will blue-pencil overbroad "noncompetes" — carving the restraints back until they are reasonable.

Despite the judicial skepticism, contractual noncompetes are common and quite important whenever an agent is likely to develop strong relationships with the principal's customers.

> ***Example:*** A wholesale tire company assigns a three-state territory to a sales representative and instructs that representative "to get to know

16. See section 4.1.5.

17. See section 4.1.7 for a discussion of the principal's remedies for an agent's breach of the duty of loyalty.

every potential buyer in the territory. Get them to know us and like us." As the sales rep fulfills those instructions, there will almost necessarily develop a personal relationship between the sale rep and the tire wholesaler's customers. It makes little sense for the tire wholesaler to pay the sales rep to develop all this "good will," if the sales rep can simply resign and take the business to a competing wholesaler.

PROBLEM 54

For the past several years Ventura Company ("Ventura") has been acting as a buying agent for Ilan Enterprises ("Ilan") in the U.S. soybean market. Ventura has had authority to make purchases up to $250,000 without prior approval from Ilan.

Recently, Ilan discovered improprieties in Ventura's conduct. Ilan wishes to terminate the relationship immediately and wants to know how to do so. Ilan is also concerned about its responsibility if Ventura continues to trade on Ilan's account even after Ilan terminates the relationship. Advise Ilan how best to proceed.

EXPLANATION

Ilan can terminate the agency simply by giving notice to Ventura. A principal always has the power to terminate an agency. In this instance Ilan also has the right to do so, since the facts reveal no express or implied agreement as to term. Ilan should make the notice in writing and use some means of transmission that allows proof of delivery. (Agency law does not require written notice. The writing and delivery precautions are to simplify proof.)

As for the possibility that Ventura will bind Ilan through post-termination trading, the termination notice will end Ventura's actual authority and inherent agency power.[18] Ilan should be concerned, however, with Ventura's lingering apparent authority. If Ilan has a list of traders and other parties with whom Ventura has dealt, Ilan should send each a brief notice, stating in effect that "Effective [date of termination] Ventura Company is no longer authorized to sell, buy, make trades, or conduct any other business for Ilan Enterprises."[19] This notice will prevent the recipients from reasonably believing that Ventura remains authorized and will thereby stop them from claiming apparent authority as to any future transactions.

---

18. See section 5.3.1.

19. As a matter of agency law, the notice need not explain why this change has occurred; as a matter of *defamation* law, the notice *should* not explain. (Even if the explanation were accurate and even though truth is a defense to a defamation claim, why invite trouble?)

Ilan must also consider the rest of the marketplace. It is possible that Ventura possesses apparent authority in the soybean market generally — even with parties who have never dealt with Ventura. Ventura may have previously and accurately described itself as having authority, and that description is attributable to Ventura's principal.[20] Moreover, the Ventura-Ilan relationship may be generally known, with that knowledge traceable to the fact that Ilan has followed through on deals made by Ventura.

Because this aspect of the problem relates to a possible public perception, public preventative measures are necessary. Ilan should identify some trade publication or other medium of communication that reaches those who participate in the soybean market and insert in that medium the same "no longer authorized" notice just described.

Besides addressing the apparent authority concerns, Ilan's private and public notices will also block attempts to claim agency by estoppel. Knowing that market participants might believe Ventura still authorized to act for Ilan and that they "might change their position because of it," Ilan will have taken "reasonable steps to notify them of the facts."[21]

PROBLEM 55

Acme Discount Cosmetic Wholesalers ("Acme") is in the business of buying brand-name cosmetics and reselling them to discount retailers. Unable to purchase the Tres Chic cosmetic line directly from the manufacturer, Acme made an agreement with Transhipping, Inc., one of Tres Chic's authorized wholesalers. The agreement had a term of 18 months, and for the first 11 months all went as agreed: (i) Acme placed orders with Transhipping, (ii) Transhipping relayed the orders to Tres Chic under Transhipping's name, (iii) Transhipping received and paid for goods and then reshipped them to Acme at Transhipping's cost plus a percentage commission. During this time Transhipping also sold Tres Chic cosmetics to upscale retailers. After 11 months Tres Chic finally learned of Transhipping's shenanigans with Acme and terminated Transhipping's right to purchase Tres Chic cosmetics. Transhipping subsequently found another source for the cosmetics, declined to deal any further with Acme, and instead started selling Tres Chic cosmetics to Acme's customers. What is Transhipping's best argument for escaping agency law liability for having taken Acme's customers? See Figures 5-1 and 5-2.

---

20. See section 2.3.3 (agent has implied actual authority to accurately describe its authority to act for the principal).

21. Restatement §8B(1)(b). See section 2.4. Note that this Explanation does not mention that Ventura would be breaching a duty if it purported to act for Ilan after receiving a termination notice. Although that assertion is correct, see section 5.3.2, the breach of duty is not relevant to the issue presented.

Figure 5-1. Transhipping Buys for Acme

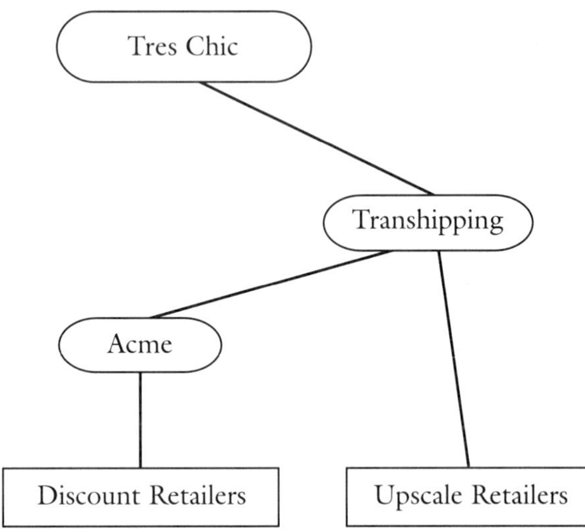

Figure 5-2. Transhipping Sells to Acme's Customers

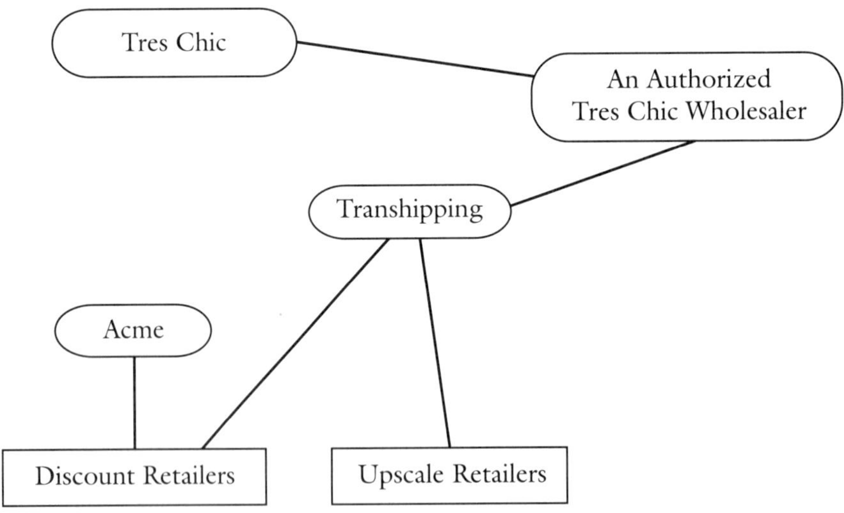

Explanation

Transhipping should argue that — even assuming that it had been functioning as Acme's agent[22] — the agency relationship presupposed Transhipping's continuing ability to buy cosmetics directly from Tres Chic. When that condition failed, the agency ceased. Transhipping then had the right to compete with Acme, its *former* principal.

PROBLEM 56

Roseanne gets a job at a posh new restaurant in an upscale mall where the waitstaff all wear uniforms. Each uniform costs $55 dollars, and the restaurant requires Roseanne to buy four before starting work. Three days after Roseanne starts work the restaurant manager decides that the staff is too large for the current volume of business. He fires the newest employee — Roseanne. Does Roseanne have any recourse?

Explanation

The answer will probably depend on how strongly the relevant jurisdiction adheres to the employment-at-will doctrine. Roseanne will argue that, by requiring her to buy so many uniforms, the restaurant impliedly agreed not to terminate her without cause at least until she had worked long enough to make the uniform purchase an economically rational act. As a fall-back, she will argue that the restaurant must buy the uniforms back from her.

PROBLEM 57

Eli is a regional sales agent for Maurice Ball Bearing, Inc. ("Maurice"). Eli and Maurice have a written agreement that (i) grants Eli an exclusive territory in which to promote and solicit orders for Maurice products, (ii) provides that Eli has no authority to accept any order on behalf of Maurice and that all sales will be made by Maurice directly to customers, (iii) establishes a commission schedule, (iv) requires Eli to follow lawful and ethical business practices but otherwise allows him complete discretion in how he conducts his operations, and (v) allows either party to terminate the relationship without cause on seven days' notice. Under the commission schedule, Eli qualifies for a $25,000 bonus in any calendar year in which he books orders aggregating more than $3 million.

It is October. So far Eli has booked $2.8 million, and he will certainly reach the bonus level by year's end. However, Maurice has decided for its

22. For a discussion of this point, see section 6.1.2 (agent contrasted with supplier).

own reasons to "go direct" in Eli's region. That is, Maurice wishes to use its own employees, rather than Eli, to solicit orders. The CEO of Maurice wishes to terminate Eli immediately and asks you for legal advice. Provide it.

Explanation

Maurice has the power to terminate its agent at any time and appears to have the right to do so simply on seven days' notice. However, with Eli so close to qualifying for the bonus, a precipitous termination could raise suspicions of bad faith. A principal has no right to terminate an agency merely to deprive the agent of benefits that the agent is on the verge of earning.

Even if Maurice succeeds in demonstrating a good faith reason for terminating Eli, Eli might still make trouble by claiming breach of an implied agreement. He could argue that the agreement, which offers a large bonus based on a calendar year's effort, impliedly prohibits Maurice from terminating at year's end any agent who is about to earn the bonus, unless the agent has engaged in misconduct.

If Maurice believes it essential to terminate the agency before year's end, in the long run Maurice may find it less expensive and less stressful to send with the termination notice an offer to pay the $25,000 bonus.

PROBLEM 58

May works as an agent for Broker, Inc., a company that, for a commission, helps U.S. firms sell goods to foreign governments. May's responsibilities include traveling around the United States to try to persuade U.S. companies to use Broker's services. During one trip May decides to go into business for herself. Aware (because Broker has told her) that the government of Argentina is seeking bids for major construction projects, May contacts a number of U.S. companies. She gets "in the door" as a representative of Broker, but once in she tells the companies that she will soon be providing the same services as Broker — and for a lower commission. She does not, however, close any deals for herself. At the end of the trip, May returns to Broker's home office and resigns. She explains her resignation by saying that her brother-in-law has offered her a job in the family upholstery business. May then promptly sets up her own firm, pursues the contacts she made on the last trip, and lands a number of lucrative contracts related to the Argentine project. Does Broker have any recourse against May?

Explanation

Broker has a claim for disgorgement of May's profits. In two and perhaps three ways, May has breached her duty of loyalty. First, by promoting her own services in contrast to Broker's, she began to compete while still an agent.

Second, she lied to her principal about her reasons for leaving. Third, her pursuit of contracts related to the Argentine project *may* have been a misuse of Broker's confidential information. Broker's information about the project certainly was of economic importance to Broker, but Broker would have to show in addition that (a) the existence of the project was not generally known, (b) Broker had expended effort or expense to obtain the information, and (c) Broker used reasonable means to protect the information.

PROBLEM 59

Captain Miles Standish found himself deeply in love with "the damsel Priscilla." Unfortunately, Captain Standish was a shy fellow (except in matters of war) and could not find within himself the strength to approach Priscilla on his own behalf. He turned, instead, to his good friend John Alden. He asked Alden to visit Priscilla and express to her Standish's feelings.

Alden also loved Priscilla, but did not mention that fact to Standish. Instead, "[f]riendship prevailed over love," and Alden agreed to act on Standish's behalf. Alden went to Priscilla's house and explained his mission. Priscilla responded with the immortal words, "Why don't you speak for yourself, John?" Consistent with the principles of agency law, could he? If not, what could he have done to free himself to speak?

Explanation

Alden may not speak for himself right away. He has consented to act on Standish's behalf. He is therefore Standish's agent and has a duty of loyalty that bars selfish conduct. That he is acting gratuitously affects neither his status as agent nor his duty of selflessness. While he remains Standish's agent, Alden simply cannot advance his own cause adverse to his principal's interests.

If Alden wishes to respond to Priscilla's invitation, he must first "get out clean" from his agency. To do so, he must notify Standish that he (Alden) can no longer represent Standish's interests to Priscilla. Although Alden probably has no duty to disclose that he intends to compete for Priscilla's attention, he probably does have a duty to report to Standish what Priscilla has said. That information came to Alden during his agency, and he has reason to know that his principal would consider the information important. He therefore must communicate that information to his principal.

Once has he done so, he may terminate the agency. Then he may indeed speak for himself.[23]

---

23. It might seem at first glance that Alden may not use his knowledge of Priscilla's interest, because he gained that information during the agency. However, the information is not Standish's property; it is not confidential to Standish. Priscilla can rightfully disclose the information as she sees fit.

6

Distinguishing Agency from Other Relationships

§6.1 Agency and Other Beneficial Relationships

§6.1.1 The Existence and Meaning of the Issue

There are a myriad of relationships in which one party benefits another, but not all "beneficial" relationships qualify as agency relationships. Consider, for example, the relationship between you and:

- the dry cleaner that cleans your wool sweater,
- the firefighter who carries you out of a burning building,
- the stationery store that provides you legal pads,
- the law school that provides you a legal education,
- the bank that provides you a student loan,
- the trustee who administers the trust fund established for you by your late, lamented, rich aunt.

In each of these relationships, the other party provides you benefits (goods, services, money), without becoming your agent.

The stakes in determining whether a particular relationship constitutes an agency can be very high, because the agency label carries significant legal consequences. Indeed, disputes about the label are essentially disputes about those consequences. The consequences can follow from agency law itself or from the relevance of agent status to some nonagency rule.

> ***Example:*** A grain elevator goes bankrupt owing money to local farmers and to the multinational company that provided the elevator a line of credit. The farmers try to establish that the elevator acted as the agent of the multinational company. The farmers care about the "agent" label only as a means of establishing that the multinational company is liable for the debts incurred by the elevator.

> ***Example:*** A cattle rancher sells cattle to a cattle company, which resells the cattle to a meat packer. The meat packer pays the cattle company, but the cattle company fails to pay the rancher. The rancher seeks to characterize the cattle company as the meat packer's agent so that agency law attribution rules will make the meat packer liable for the unpaid contract.

> ***Example:*** A manufacturer sells its product through a regional distributor. The distributor decides also to sell a comparable product of its own making. The manufacturer seeks to label the distributor its agent so that the agent's duty of loyalty will bar the distributor from competing with its principal.

> ***Example:*** A manufacturer markets its products by delivering them to intermediaries who then sell them to the ultimate users at a price dictated by the manufacturer. Accused of an antitrust violation known as "resale price maintenance," the manufacturer asserts that the intermediaries are its agents and so the resale price maintenance rule does not apply.

> ***Example:*** A foreign manufacturer ships goods into the United States, for ultimate sale to U.S. customers. The goods are shipped to an intermediary company, which clears the goods through U.S. customs, arranges their transport to the U.S. customers, and follows up on any customer concerns. Paperwork between the foreign manufacturer and the intermediary describes the goods as sold to the intermediary at the manufacturer's suggested list price, minus a discount. The intermediary will sell the goods to customers at the manufacturer's suggested list price, making its money off the discount. The intermediary claims that customs duties should be assessed against the list price minus the discount, because (i) the customs laws apply to the fair market value of the goods as they enter the United States, and (ii) the point-of-entry price

paid by the intermediary best reflects that value. U.S. Customs disagrees, contending that (a) the dealings between the foreign manufacturer and the intermediary constitute an agency relationship, not a sale, (b) the point-of-entry sale is therefore between the foreign manufacturer and the ultimate customers, and (c) customs duties therefore apply against the list price without any discount.

Example: A service station operator obtains gas from an oil company and sells it to customers. The operator fails to pay for the gas and is charged with embezzlement. The prosecution asserts that the operator was the oil company's agent and therefore: (i) the proceeds from the sale belonged to the oil company, minus only the operator's agreed-upon commission, and (ii) the operator had a fiduciary duty to turn the proceeds over to the oil company. The operator defends by denying an agency relationship and asserting that a buyer's failure to pay for goods is not criminal.

§6.1.2 Distinguishing Agency from Other Similar Relationships

Disputes over the existence of an agency relationship usually relate to one of the two elements necessary to establish an agency:

- the understanding that the party receiving the benefits is in control, and
- the understanding that the relationship is fiduciary, i.e., that the primary purpose of the relationship is to meet the needs of the party receiving the benefits.[1]

A beneficial relationship that lacks one or both of these elements is not an agency.

When agency *vel non* is at issue, analysis typically proceeds in an either/or format. One party asserts an agency, while the other seeks to place the relationship into some nonagency category. For example, in the case of the bankrupt grain elevator, the plaintiff farmers contended "agent," while the multinational company asserted "debtor." In the gas station embezzlement case, the prosecution asserted "agent," while the defense contended "independent distributor."

Following are examples of beneficial relationships that resemble agencies closely enough to supply the "or" in the typical either/or analysis. (For graphic representation of the following material, see Figure 6-1.)

1. These elements are introduced in sections 1.2.7 and 1.2.8.

Figure 6-1. The Universe of Those Who Provide Benefits to Others

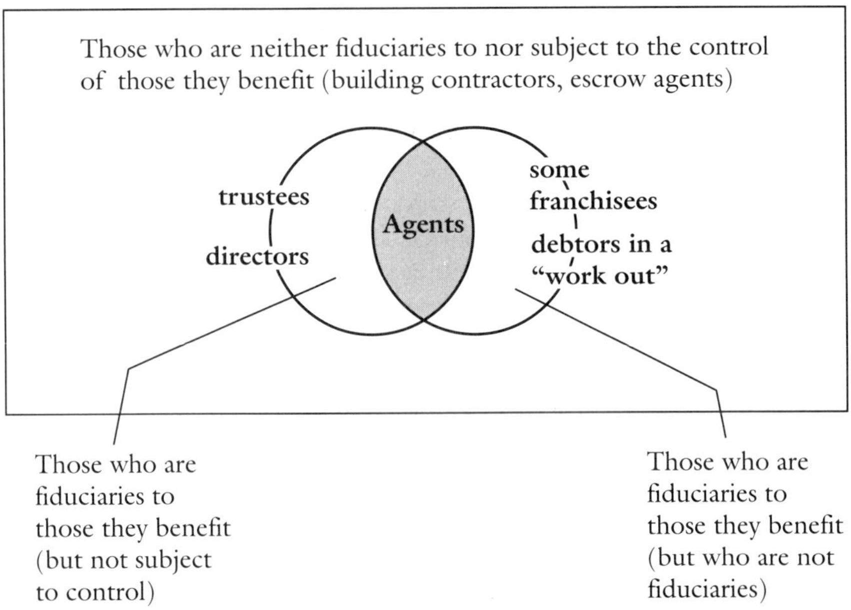

Those who are neither fiduciaries to nor subject to the control of those they benefit (building contractors, escrow agents)

trustees

directors

Agents

some

franchisees

debtors in a "work out"

Those who are fiduciaries to those they benefit (but not subject to control)

Those who are fiduciaries to those they benefit (but who are not fiduciaries)

- **Party Providing the Benefit Is a Fiduciary But Is Not Subject to Control.**
  - — *Trustee of a trust and the trust beneficiary*. The trustee is obliged to act solely for the benefit of the beneficiary, but the beneficiary does not have the right to control the trustee.
  - — *Conservator and conservatee*. Appointed by a court to take care of the financial affairs or personal decisions (or both) of an incompetent person, the conservator is obliged to act in the best interests of the conservatee. The conservatee has neither the right nor power to control the conservator.
  - — *Directors of a corporation and the corporation*. Although the directors do owe duties of loyalty to the corporation, the corporation does not control the directors. To the contrary, the directors control the corporation.[2]
- **Party Providing the Benefits Is Subject to Control But Is Not a Fiduciary.**
  - — *Distributor of goods and its supplier*. Some distribution agreements give the supplier considerable control over the distributor, regarding, for example: (a) where the distributor can resell the goods,

2. Some commentators describe directors as the agents of the shareholders (i.e., of the people and organizations who own stock in the corporation). Although used in this way the agency concept helps analyze certain corporate law issues, the usage does not fit with the legal definition of agency. Shareholders have the right to exercise only limited and intermittent control over the directors.

(b) how the distributor may advertise the goods, (c) what kinds of after-sale service the distributor must provide. The distributor is not the supplier's agent, however, because the relationship's primary purpose is not to benefit the supplier. In this arm's-length transaction, each party's own interest is primary to that party.[3]

— *Supplier of specially designed goods and its customer*. Sometimes a customer may exercise considerable control over its supplier. For example, if the customer is buying components from the supplier to incorporate into the customer's own products, the customer may: (i) design the component, (b) specify the raw materials the supplier is to use, and (c) even insist on the right to approve the supplier's methods for producing the component. The supplier is not the customer's agent, however, because the relationship's primary purpose is not to benefit the customer. In this arm's-length transaction, each party to the relationship seeks its own benefit, and neither party's benefit is primary.[4]

- **Party Providing Benefits Is Not a Fiduciary and Is Not Subject to Control.**

— *Escrow holder and parties to the escrow agreement*. When two parties agree that a third will hold an item of value (e.g., money, stock, a deed) until specified conditions are met and then deliver the item per the agreement, the item is considered in escrow and the third party is the escrow holder. Neither of the escrow parties has a right to control the escrow holder, who is obligated only to perform as the escrow agreement requires. The escrow holder does not act primarily for the benefit of either party to the escrow agreement, but rather acts to fulfill its own obligations. The escrow holder is therefore not an agent.

— *Building contractor and the people for whom the contractor is building a house*. This is an arm's length relationship. The contractor has not consented to serve primarily the interests of the homebuyers, and the homebuyers have no right to control the contractor. The contractor is subject to the obligations of the contract, but that control device is a product of the agreement between the parties.

— *Moving company and its customer*. Again, an arm's-length relationship, in which neither party intends primarily to benefit the other, and neither party is in control.

---

3. Moreover, some arguably crucial aspects of control are lacking, such as the power to set the distributor's resale price.

4. Some courts, seeking the liability consequences that attach to the agency label, will ignore the fiduciary element of the agency relationship and find agency based on control alone. See section 3.2.4 n.12 (for respondeat superior purposes, servant status need not be considered a subcategory of agent status) and section 6.3 (Restatement §140 and *Cargill*).

§6.2 *Ersatz*[5] Agency

In two related circumstances, what may appear to be an agency is in fact a different, irrevocable, nonagency relationship. In each situation:

- one person grants another the right to bind the grantor and lacks the power (not merely the right) to revoke that grant;
- the authority to bind is granted *not* to benefit the grantor (i.e., the party who seems like a principal), but rather to benefit the grantee (i.e., the party who seems like the agent), and
- the grantee (not the grantor) is in charge.[6]

The two circumstances go under the names of "agency (or power) coupled with an interest" and "authority (or power) given as security."

§6.2.1 Power Coupled with an Interest

For a power to be coupled with an interest:

- the grantee's power (i.e., the authority to bind, which appears like agency authority) must relate to some particular right or other property, and
- the same transaction that establishes the grantee's power must also provide the grantee some "interest" in that particular right or other property.

> ***Example:*** Ophelia owns 200 acres of land. To cause Hamlet to sell the land for her, she gives him an undivided one-tenth interest in the land, coupled with an irrevocable power of attorney to sell her interest at any price above $500 per acre. Hamlet's power relates to the land, and he has received that power at the same time he has received an interest in the land. The power is coupled with an interest and is irrevocable. Hamlet is not Ophelia's agent.

For the power to be "coupled with an interest," the power and the interest must relate to the same aspect of the particular property. If the grantee receives an interest not in the underlying property itself but rather in the proceeds that result from the grantee's exercise of the granted power, then a true agency results and the grantee's authority is revocable.

---

5. From the German, meaning "seeming proper but actually not genuine."

6. This description states the default rules. The parties may agree to provide the grantor a right of revocation.

Example: As above, Ophelia owns 200 acres of land and wishes to have Hamlet sell them for her. Instead of giving him an interest in the land, however, she sends him a letter (i) giving him a right to 30 percent of the sale price over $300 per acre and (ii) purporting to grant him irrevocable authority to sell the land for $300 or more per acre. Hamlet's power is not coupled with an interest. His power relates to the land and his interest relates only to the proceeds of the sale of the land. Hamlet is Ophelia's agent, and despite the letter his authority is revocable.[7]

§6.2.2 *Authority (or Power) Given as Security*

If (i) an obligor owes a debt or other obligation to an obligee, and (ii) in order to provide the obligee with security the obligor grants the obligee a power to bind the obligor, then:

- no agency is created,
- the power is "given as security," and
- the power is irrevocable during the life of the obligor.

Example: Ophelia, in Dunsinane, appoints Hamlet as her agent to sell 700 crates of oranges being stored in a warehouse in Elsinore. Hamlet informs Ophelia that $500 of storage fees must be paid or the oranges will be sold by the warehouse. Ophelia has no funds available, and Hamlet agrees to advance the $500. To secure her obligation to repay Hamlet, Ophelia grants him the irrevocable right to collect all payments on the oranges and to repay himself from those proceeds before sending any money to Ophelia. The relationship between Ophelia and Hamlet is no longer an agency. Instead, Hamlet possesses a power given as security, which is irrevocable except through the death of Ophelia.

In this Example, the power given as security is *not* a power coupled with an interest. Hamlet has no interest in the underlying property (i.e., the oranges). Often, however, both concepts apply to the same circumstances. A power given as security is also a power coupled with an interest.

Example: Hamlet borrows money from Ophelia, and as collateral grants Ophelia a security interest[8] in 100 shares of stock in Birnam Forest, Inc. Hamlet also grants Ophelia his proxy to vote the stock. The proxy is

7. The letter probably does obligate Ophelia to refrain from revoking. She nonetheless retains the power to revoke. See section 5.2 (power versus right to terminate).

8. A security interest is like a mortgage on personal rather than real property.

"given as security" for the debt and is therefore irrevocable except by Hamlet's death. Moreover, since the same transaction that granted Ophelia the proxy also gave her a security interest in the underlying property, the proxy is "coupled with an interest." The proxy is therefore irrevocable even if Hamlet dies.[9]

§6.3 Constructive Agency

§6.3.1 *The* Cargill *Case and Restatement §140*

Sometimes a court construes a seemingly arm's-length arrangement into an agency relationship. The case of *A. Gay Jenson Farms v. Cargill, Inc.*[10] provides one of the best known examples of such *constructive agency*.

Cargill arose from the financial collapse of the Warren Grain & Seed Co. ("Warren"), a grain elevator located in rural Minnesota. Warren was in the business of buying grain from farmers and then reselling that grain on the market or directly to grain companies. Cargill, Inc. financed the operations of Warren (i.e., Cargill loaned the elevator money with which to operate) and also bought substantial amounts of grain from Warren. As Warren's debt to Cargill increased, Cargill exercised more and more control over Warren's operations.

Warren's owners diverted large amounts of the company's money to their personal ends, and Warren's business eventually collapsed. At the time of the collapse Warren owed $2 million to farmers who had sold grain to Warren but had not been paid. Warren also owed $3.6 million to Cargill.

The farmers sought to recover their $2 million from Cargill, contending that (i) Warren was Cargill's agent, and (ii) Cargill, as principal, was liable on any grain contracts made by its agent. The jury, the trial judge, and the Minnesota Supreme Court all agreed.

Although *Cargill* also quoted and purported to apply §1 of the Restatement, the decision turns on §140. The comment to the latter section states in part:

> A security holder who . . . takes over the management of the debtor's business . . . and directs what contracts may or may not be made . . . becomes a principal, liable as any principal for the obligations incurred thereafter in the normal course of business by the

---

9. By its terms the proxy will likely be automatically revoked when the underlying debt is paid.

10. 309 N.W.2d 285 (Minn. 1981).

> debtor who has now become his general agent. The point at which the creditor becomes a principal is that at which he assumes de facto control over the conduct of his debtor, whatever the terms of the formal contract with his debtor may be.

The *Cargill* decision held that Cargill had indeed taken over the management of the debtor's business and had consequently become liable as a principal for Warren's debts to the farmer plaintiffs.

§6.3.2 *Conceptual Confusions and Practical Concerns*

The *Cargill* case is troubling both conceptually and practically. The court tries to justify its decision under §1 of the Restatement as well as under §140 and thereby confuses constructive agency with true agency. Practically, the decision is dangerous for any creditor that eschews immediate foreclosure of a problem loan and tries instead to guide its debtor through a workout.[11]

Constructive versus genuine agency. *Cargill* is confusing because it misunderstands the relationship between Restatement §§1 and 140. Although both sections concern agency creation, they apply to quite different situations and state different and even inconsistent rules.

For an agency to exist under §1, the principal must manifest consent for the agent to act on the principal's behalf, and the agent must manifest consent to do so. Section 15 states that "an agency relation can exist *only*" under such circumstances.[12] Yet §140, which also establishes agency status, nowhere mentions consent. Instead, it focuses exclusively on control.

The inconsistency exists because the Restatement is using the same label ("agency") to describe two different kinds of situations:

(1) "garden variety" situations, in which the parties act in a manner that reasonably suggests they intend to establish the consensual and fiduciary relationship of true agency, and
(2) extraordinary situations, in which for policy reasons the law wishes to treat creditors and debtors *as if* they had manifested consent to the garden variety of agency.

---

11. When a debtor has difficulty paying its major lender, the lender can typically demand immediate payment of the full amount due, foreclose on any collateral, and put the debtor out of business. However, with that approach lenders rarely recover the full amount owed. Lenders therefore often try to help the debtor work its way out of its financial difficulties. Hence the term *workout*.

12. Emphasis added.

The situations share a key consequence[13] — the principal's liability on contracts made by the agent — but the criteria that trigger the consequence are fundamentally different: For the garden variety situation, mutual consent; for the extraordinary situation, overbearing control.[14]

The rationales underlying the rules are likewise different. With a true agent, acting within its actual authority, liability arises at least in part from consent. In the extraordinary, §140 situation, liability arises for reasons akin to the rationale for inherent agency power. That is, liability follows control, because those who exercise control have the ability to avoid harm and should therefore be liable when avoidable harm occurs, and because when an undertaking causes harm to others, the cost of that harm should be borne by those who stand to benefit from the undertaking (typically it is those in control who stand to benefit).

The *Cargill* case concerns an extraordinary situation, and the decision becomes confusing when it seeks to apply the garden variety rule (manifestation of consent; fiduciary relationship) as well as the extraordinary rule (exercise of control). Referring, for instance, to the *principal's* manifestation of consent, *Cargill* states, "By directing Warren to implement its recommendations, Cargill manifested consent that Warren would be its agent." This assertion seems to equate control with consent. If party *A* controls party *B*, then through that control *A* manifests consent that *B* act for *A in dealing with third parties*. Although such an inference may often be reasonable, it is not necessarily so. For example, a department store may control in detail the work assignments of a custodian without consenting to the custodian placing orders with dress manufacturers.

Equally troubling is the decision's treatment of the *agent's* manifestation of consent. In this respect the question is whether Warren manifested consent to place Cargill's interests above its own, that is, consented that the primary purpose of the relationship was to serve Cargill, not Warren. The *Cargill* court never mentions any direct evidence on this point. Instead the decision states: "Cargill believed that Warren was not free to become Cargill's competitor, but rather conceded that Warren owed a duty of loyalty to Cargill." The logic here is flawed. An agent's duty of loyalty includes the duty not to compete, but an agreement not to compete does not by itself establish either a full-fledged duty of loyalty or a fiduciary relationship. A party's agreement to defer to another party's interest in one specific area neither constitutes nor implies an agreement to defer to that other party's interest throughout the relationship. To the contrary, noncompete agreements occur in many arm's-length relationships.

---

13. In the extraordinary situation, the agency label does not produce all of the consequences that attend that label in the garden variety situation. No one suggests that under §140 the debtor, as agent, owes a fiduciary duty to its principal, the creditor.

14. The control is "overbearing" in the sense that the creditor "takes over the management of the debtor's business." Restatement §140, comment *a*.

The *Cargill* court would have made matters considerably clearer had it simply stated, "This situation warrants constructive agency analysis. Restatement §14O applies, and therefore §1's garden variety criteria for establishing true agency are irrelevant."

Dangers for workouts. In applying Restatement §14O, the *Cargill* court noted a number of factors that evidenced Cargill's control over Warren. The court acknowledged that many of these same factors appear in ordinary debtor-creditor transactions, but assured the banking community that ordinary delinquent loans were not destined to turn into principal-agent relationships.

To support its assurances, the Court noted the following differences between the Warren-Cargill relationship and an ordinary lending situation: (i) Cargill aggressively financed Warren; (ii) Cargill "was an active participant in Warren's operations rather than simply a financier"; (iii) Cargill's relationship with Warren was "paternalistic"; and (iv) Cargill's purpose in lending money to Warren "was not to make money as a lender but rather to establish a source of market grain for its business."

Of the four distinctions noted by the court, the first three (aggressive financing, involvement in the debtor's operations, a "paternalistic" attitude) occur in most workouts. The fourth purported distinction — that Cargill was really "in it" not for the interest but rather to obtain a supply of grain — is irrelevant under §14O. That provision makes no reference at all to the creditor's purpose in becoming a creditor. Moreover, there are many lending relationships in which the lender seeks more than interest payments. A company like GMAC, for example, lends money to General Motors car dealers in part to allow them to buy cars from GM and lends money to the dealers' customers in order to allow them to buy GM cars from the GM dealers. Is GMAC in it just for the interest, or does GMAC have the ulterior motive of increasing the marketability of GM cars?

In sum, the *Cargill* court's attempt to distinguish the Cargill-Warren situation from normal debtor-creditor relationships is unpersuasive. For lenders considering workouts, the case is a cautionary tale.[15]

---

15. Although any informed lender's attorney will worry about *Cargill*, few other reported cases have taken the *Cargill* approach. Fewer than ten reported decisions have discussed Restatement §14O. Only one affirmed recovery for the plaintiff, and another reversed summary judgment for the defendant. One case, *Buck v. Nash-Finch Co.*, 102 N.W.2d 84 (S.D. 1960), acknowledged that a major creditor had controlled substantial portions of the debtor's operations but denied recovery because the major creditor had not controlled the particular area of operations that gave rise to the plaintiff's claim. Compare section 3.2.5 (respondeat superior liability attaches to servant's scope of employment not to master's zone of control). Another case held that Section 14O imposed liability only when the controlling creditor had engaged in wrongdoing. Mere control was insufficient. *Lubrizol Corp. v. Cardinal Construction Co.*, 868 F.2d 767 (5th Cir. 1989).

PROBLEM 60

A housebuyer ("Would-Be") contacts a real estate broker ("Broker") and solicits her assistance in locating a suitable property. Would-Be seeks a modern, upscale house with enough land to allow the installation of a swimming pool. Over the next two months, Broker calls Would-Be frequently to discuss possible purchases, and occasionally goes with Would-Be to view properties. Eventually she locates a house that Would-Be decides to purchase. As Would-Be contemplates making the purchase, Broker explains that "my fee comes from the seller. It's no big deal. That's the way we do it. So you can figure out the price you're willing to pay without worrying about a commission."

Would-Be makes the purchase and subsequently discovers that his neighbors will raise zoning law objections to any pool. He also learns that the lower portion of his land is subject to flooding during the early spring. He sues Broker for not having informed him of these problems.

Assume that:

- Broker never thought of herself as Would-Be's agent, and never intended to act on Would-Be's behalf. She saw herself as acting at "arm's length" from him.
- Would-Be, in contrast, believed all along that Broker was "on my side, looking out for my interests."
- When Would-Be expressed serious interest in the house he eventually purchased, Broker contacted the seller and arranged to act as the seller's agent in the transaction.
- Other than her comment about the seller paying her fees, Broker never explained to Would-Be her view of her relationship to Would-Be. She never disclosed that she was acting as the seller's agent.
- Broker's view of the relationship is consistent with the way real estate brokers in the locality ordinarily approach similar matters.
- Broker knew that the neighbors would probably object to the building of a pool but never mentioned anything about that problem to Would-Be.
- Broker did not know about the flooding but could have discovered the problem through the exercise of ordinary care.
- Broker never made any representations to Would-Be concerning the pool or the flooding.
- There are no statutes or government regulations relevant to this situation.

Can Would-Be recover from Broker?

EXPLANATION

Since Broker made no representations about the pool or the flooding, Would-Be can recover from Broker only if he can establish that Broker had an affirmative duty to disclose. Moreover, as to the flooding problem, Would-Be will also have to establish that Broker had a duty to inquire.

Both duties existed if Broker was acting as Would-Be's agent.[16] To establish that agency relationship, Would-Be must show (i) some manifestation from him that, reasonably interpreted, indicated his desire to have Broker act on his behalf, and (ii) some manifestation from Broker that, reasonably interpreted, indicated Broker's "consent . . . to so act."[17] The first showing is easy: Would-Be expressly and specifically solicited Broker's assistance. As for Broker's manifestation, her two months of effort provide at least a "peppercorn."

Broker's subjective view of the situation is irrelevant. What matters is the reasonableness of Would-Be's interpretation, and on that point the evidence is mixed. The local custom *as known to brokers* may weigh against reasonableness, but reasonableness is determined from the perspective of an ordinarily prudent person *in the position of the principal*. The facts do not indicate whether the brokers' custom is generally known and understood by ordinary homebuyers.

The payment arrangement may also weigh against reasonableness. If Broker was looking out for Would-Be's interests, why would someone else — especially the adverse party — be paying the fee? Although with the principal's consent an agent may receive compensation from a third party, arguably the circumstances were unusual enough to prompt a reasonable person to inquire.

Despite this negative evidence, Would-Be may still prevail by pointing to Broker's conduct as a whole. Would-Be sought out Broker and asked for her assistance. For two months Broker provided that assistance without once indicating her arm's length attitude. Moreover, when — at the crucial moment — Broker pledged allegiance to the adverse party, she failed to warn or even advise Would-Be. To the contrary, she induced his continuing trust by treating the fee question as "no big deal." Taking all these circumstances together, perhaps it was reasonable for Would-Be to believe that Broker had agreed to act on his behalf.

If so, Broker was acting as Would-Be's agent and was subject to duties of disclosure and due care. Broker would therefore be liable for damages suffered by Would-Be due to Broker's failure to disclose the zoning difficulty and for her failure to discover and disclose the flooding problem.[18]

16. See sections 4.1.5 (agent's duty to disclose information which agent knows or should know is of interest to the principal) and 4.1.4 (agent's duty of care).

17. Restatement §1.

18. Note that if Broker was acting as Would-Be's agent, she has a "dual agency" problem. See section 4.1.1 (no acting for others with conflicting interests).

PROBLEM 61

Tim buys a new truck from a local car dealer. The dealer purchases its truck inventory from the manufacturer under a dealership agreement. That agreement (i) states that the dealer is an independent contractor and not the agent of the manufacturer, (ii) acknowledges that the dealer, not the manufacturer, controls the management of the dealer's business, (iii) describes the three-year warranty that the manufacturer extends to customers who purchase the manufacturer's trucks through the manufacturer's network of dealers, (iv) obligates the dealer to provide service under the manufacturer's warranties at no charge to the customers, and (v) provides that the dealer will bill the manufacturer for this warranty service at specified rates. Each new truck comes with an owner's manual that describes the manufacturer's warranty and directs customers to have warranty service performed at any of the manufacturer's authorized dealers.

Tim is quite happy with his purchase for the first week. Then a problem develops in the truck's steering. Tim immediately notifies the dealer and brings the truck in for repair. Over the next two years, the truck has a series of problems with its steering mechanism. Each time a problem occurs, Tim brings the truck back to the dealer, and the dealer attempts to fix the problem. Each time the dealer assures Tim that "this is under warranty" and there is no charge. After two years, however, Tim has had enough. He decides to sue the dealer for breach of warranty and wishes also to sue the manufacturer.

Under the jurisdiction's version of the Uniform Commercial Code, a remote buyer (such as Tim) can bring a breach of warranty claim against the remote seller (such as the manufacturer) if the remote buyer has given timely notice of the defect to the remote seller or the remote seller has knowledge of the defect.[19] Tim has told the dealer of the problems as they have occurred, so the dealer has known of the defect since one week after the sale. Tim has never informed the manufacturer, however. Under the jurisdiction's case law, it is now too late to first notify the manufacturer. May Tim nonetheless bring a warranty claim against the manufacturer?

EXPLANATION

To safeguard his claim against the manufacturer, Tim must show that his notice to the dealer suffices as notice to the manufacturer. To do that he must use the attribution rules of agency law.

The agreement between the manufacturer and dealership expressly disclaims agency status, but the parties' actual relationship belies their words.

---

19. See Uniform Commercial Code §2-318 (third party beneficiaries of warranties) and §2-607(3)(a) (buyer must give timely notice of breach or be barred from remedy) and comment 5 (requirement of timely notice applies to remote buyer making third party beneficiary claim).

Through its customer warranty, the manufacturer undertook to provide services to Tim. Through its dealership agreement, the manufacturer manifested consent for the dealer to provide those services on the manufacturer's behalf and the dealer manifested consent to do so. For the purposes of providing warranty service, the dealer is indeed the manufacturer's agent.

Under this agency relationship, the dealer may have implied actual authority to receive notices of defects on the manufacturer's behalf. Implied actual authority exists as acts "which are incidental to . . . , usually accompany, . . . or are reasonably necessary to accomplish" expressly authorized acts,[20] and a customer typically invokes the manufacturer's warranty (and triggers the dealer's expressly authorized act) by communicating with the dealer. Notice received within an agent's actual authority (express or implied) binds the principal.

Even if the dealer is not authorized to receive notice on the manufacturer's behalf, the dealer's knowledge of the defect binds the manufacturer. The defect information certainly concerns a matter within the dealer's actual authority and is therefore attributed to the principal.[21]

PROBLEM 62

Fred Hornet ("Hornet") is a mid-level manager at Commerce Bank whose responsibilities include evaluating applicants for business loans. For the past several years, Hornet has been trying to persuade the Loan Committee (i.e., a committee of five senior managers that must approve any business loan) to take a more accommodating attitude toward loan applications from female- and minority-owned start-up businesses. The discussion has proceeded through several stages, with the key points being roughly as follows:

Hornet: Our regular evaluation criteria make it highly unlikely that we will approve loan applications from minority-owned or female-owned businesses. We put a lot of weight on whether the key people in the new business have any significant prior entrepreneurial experience. It's a matter of history that, for women and minorities, access to that type of experience has been far more difficult to obtain. It's important morally,

20. Restatement §35. See section 2.2.3.

21. See section 2.2.4. Tim might also assert that the dealer has apparent authority to receive notices for the manufacturer. This argument seems weaker than the actual authority arguments, because Tim can point to only two relevant manifestations of the principal: the appointment of the dealer as an authorized seller of the manufacturer's trucks and the direction in the owner's manual that customers have warranty work done at the manufacturer's authorized dealers. From these manifestations it is reasonable to believe that the dealer is authorized to act for the manufacturer in providing warranty service, but not necessarily that the dealer is authorized to accept pre-suit notices on the manufacturer's behalf.

and for the social stability of our country, that we increase the access. As a practical matter, that access depends fundamentally on being able to borrow money. The way we're going now, though, it's a vicious circle. Can't borrow the money because not enough experience. Can't get experience running a small business because can't borrow any money to get one started. This bank quite rightfully prides itself on being "a good corporate citizen." To live up to our own ideals we need to relax our emphasis on prior entrepreneurial experience.

Loan Committee: We're with you in spirit, but we also have a responsibility to our stockholders and our depositors not to be careless in lending money. We have found that a lack of "prior entrepreneurial experience" tends to increase the likelihood of a loan going bad. What can you suggest to offset the increased risk?

Hornet: First, more rigorous attention to the application process — the applicant's proposed business plan, for instance. But, more importantly, I suggest an increased commitment at the bank to keeping an eye on these businesses. If we think that trouble is developing, we'll get in and work with the people — provide them advice, make sure they're using sensible business practices. In other words, if we find out that a lack of entrepreneurial experience is beginning to cost them (and threatening their ability to pay us back) we'll temporarily roll up our sleeves and help provide them the expertise that comes with experience. I realize that this approach involves an extra commitment of resources, but I think it's worth it.

Loan Committee: What if the borrowers don't want our help?

Hornet: I think for this program to work we have to be up front with the people, and tell them when they apply what might happen if things go sour later on. Also, we have to choose to lend to people whom we think will be willing to take help. Finally, under our standard loan agreements, if push comes to shove, we have the right to take control.

The Loan Committee is just about convinced to give Hornet's approach a try. Assume that they turn to you, as the Bank's lawyer, and ask, "Are there any legal wrinkles?" Advise them by (i) identifying and explaining any legal risks involved in Hornet's proposal, and (ii) suggesting changes in the proposal that will decrease those risks without sacrificing the business objectives.

Explanation

Cargill and Restatement §140 appear to create a Hobson's choice for the bank. Measures designed to meet the bank's business needs seem destined to increase the bank's legal risk. Moreover, the legal risks will be most substantial just when the business needs are the most intense. The bank is most likely to exert control when a borrower has fallen behind in its loan payments. At that juncture, the borrower is likely also to be falling behind in its obligations to other creditors. Exerting control will create a *Cargill* claim, and the other obligations will constitute the damages.

The solution to this conundrum lies in analyzing Hornet's proposal and separating, as follows, the tactical objective, the tactics proposed to achieve that objective and the rationale that links those tactics to that objective:

- *Tactical objective*: Increase the quality of the borrower's management, especially at times of financial distress.[22]
- *Rationale*: All other things being equal, inexperienced management is likely to be less effective than experienced management. A firm, experienced hand is especially necessary when a business is trying to "workout" from under financial difficulties.
- *Tactics*: Empower the bank to be that firm, experienced hand.

This analysis indicates the source of the legal risks within Hornet's proposal and thereby suggests a way to reduce those risks. Section 140 problems arise from control, and within Hornet's proposal the only flavor of control comes from the proposed tactics. Taking the tactical objective and the rationale as given,[23] the lawyer's challenge is to find substitute tactics that lack that flavor. In other words — to find another firm, experienced hand.

For example, the loan agreement might require the borrower to designate an experienced business consultant, acceptable to the Bank, to advise the borrower on an on-going basis, and temporarily turn over management of the business to that consultant (or some other independent business expert chosen by the Bank), if (i) the borrower falls behind in its loan payments or gives the Bank other reasonable grounds for insecurity and (ii) the Bank elects to require the management change. These arrangements would of course require the agreement of the specified consultant and experts, but that agreement could be obtained in advance. The loan agreement could also provide mechanisms for choosing replacements in case the designated individuals become unable or unwilling to serve.

In all events, it would be essential for the consultant and the expert to remain independent of the Bank. If the Bank controls them, they could be deemed the Bank's agents and *Cargill* could apply by attribution. The loan agreement should therefore provide that the consultant and the expert will each (i) work for and be paid by the borrower, not the Bank and (ii) have a duty to serve the best interests of the borrower, not the Bank. It should also

22. The tactical objective is intended to make possible the pursuit of another objective — increasing the bank's lending to minority- and female-owned businesses.

23. It might be possible to propose additional options for the Bank by challenging the rationale. That approach is not pursued here, however, because that kind of analysis presupposes considerable familiarity with the way businesses function.

provide that the Bank will have no right to control the advice given or the decisions made by either the consultant or the expert. The rationale and importance of these provisions should be explained to those Bank employees who deal with the borrower, so that the Bank's conduct (through those employees) conforms to these restrictions.

This structure is admittedly more cumbersome than Hornet's proposal and certainly provides less direct control for the Bank. The structure's virtue is that it significantly reduces the Bank's legal exposure while still serving the basic tactical objective of Hornet's plan.[24]

24. This approach will not work, however, if the Bank's objectives include causing the borrower to prefer the Bank's claims over the claims of other creditors. If that is an objective, *Cargill* exposure is probably inevitable and appropriate.

PART TWO

Partnerships

7

Introductory Concepts in the Law of General Partnerships

§7.1 The Role and Structure of the Uniform Partnership[1] Act

§7.1.1 History and Prevalence of the UPA

The Uniform Partnership Act ("UPA") is the backbone of partnership law. Promulgated in 1914 by the National Conference of Commissioners on Uniform State Laws, the Uniform Partnership Act has been adopted in 49 states.[2] Through more than 40 sections the UPA provides rules for:

- determining whether a partnership exists,
- governing the relationship between the partnership and its partners with outsiders (and making all partners personally liable for the debts of the partnership),

1. U.S. law encompasses two forms of partnership: general partnerships and limited partnerships. Whenever this book uses the term "partnership" by itself, the term refers to general partnerships. For a discussion of limited partnerships, see Chapter Twelve.

2. Louisiana is the lone hold out. The District of Columbia, Guam, and the Virgin Islands have also adopted the UPA. Some states have adopted nonuniform provisions, and a few states have adopted the recently-promulgated Revised Uniform Partnership Act. The Revised Act is discussed in section 7.1.3.

- governing the relationship among the partners and between the partners and the partnership, and
- determining when a partnership ceases to exist and what happens then to the partners' interests, the partnership's assets and the partnership's liabilities.

Although this book describes many UPA provisions in detail and analyzes several in depth, *no secondary source can ever replace your own careful reading of the statute*. Each time you consider a section of this book which deals with a section of the UPA, you should compare this book's analysis with the statute's actual language.

Case law is also extremely important in the law of partnerships, perhaps more than one might expect in a field covered by an apparently comprehensive statute. This phenomenon has at least three causes. First, the UPA incorporates certain areas of judge-made law. The statute provides generally that "In any case not provided for in this act the rules of law and equity, including the law merchant, shall govern"[3] and specifically that the law of estoppel and of agency "shall apply under this act."[4] In particular, "the rights and liabilities of partners with respect to each other and to third persons are largely determined by agency principles"[5] or by UPA provisions consistent with those principles.

Second, flaws in the UPA's language have invited and even necessitated judicial clarification. A few UPA provisions are so vague or recondite as to be virtually unintelligible. Third, many of the UPA rules are "default" rules that can be displaced by agreement.[6] Numerous cases consider the existence and effect of such agreements.

§7.1.2 UPA Flexibility: Default Rules and Agreements Among Partners

The rules of the UPA can be divided into two categories:

- those that govern the relationship among the partners (inter se rules), and
- those that govern the relationship between the partnership (and its partners) with outsiders (third party rules).

These categories carry an important practical distinction. Inter se rules are "default" rules, applicable only in the absence of a contrary agreement

3. UPA §4.
4. UPA §5.
5. Restatement §14A, comment *a*.
6. For a more detailed discussion of this point, see section 7.1.2.

Table 7-1. Default and Mandatory Rules

Rules Governing Inter Se Relationships	Rules Governing Relationships with Third Parties
"default rules"	"mandatory rules"
can be changed by agreements among partners	cannot be changed by agreements among partners
<u>Examples:</u> UPA §18(a) (partners share profits equally) UPA §18(e) (all partners have equal right to manage partnership and its business)	<u>Examples:</u> UPA §13 (partner's wrongful act binds the partnership) UPA §15 (all partners personally liable for debts of the partnership)

among the partners. Such an agreement may be express or implied, written or oral.[7]

To the extent the default rules are changed by the initial partnership agreement, unanimous consent is required. As a matter both of partnership and contract law, *adopting* a partnership agreement always requires unanimity. However, a partnership agreement can provide for its own amendment on a less-than-unanimous basis (e.g., majority vote of the partners). With such a provision in place, subsequent changes to the default rules can be accomplished with less-than-unanimous consent.

In contrast, third party rules are mandatory rules. An agreement among the partners cannot change them.[8] See Table 7-1.

The UPA's default structure provides a basic set of operating rules for partners who do not want to spend the time and money to develop their own "rules of the game." At the same time, the default approach provides great flexibility. To the extent partners wish to accept the default rules, they may do so.[9] But partners who wish to deviate from the default structure may tailor their relationship virtually as they see fit.

The special tailoring does have some limits. Deviating too far from the default rules may negate the existence of a partnership. For example, if an

---

7. According to the weight of authority, the statute of frauds does not apply to most inter se agreements. It may apply to agreements to enter into a partnership, or to admit someone into a partnership, if (1) the partnership is alleged to have a term of more than one year, or (2) the admission is allegedly conditioned on some performance by the would-be partner and that performance cannot be accomplished within a year.

8. As a matter of contract law, a third party may agree with a partnership or a partner to waive rights created under one of UPA's mandatory, third party rules.

9. Indeed, those who become partners by inadvertence are stuck with those rules wholesale, at least initially. (Formation of a partnership requires no special formalities and may occur even though the participants in a business relationship are unaware that the law labels their arrangement a partnership. See section 7.2.2.)

agreement labels a person a partner but denies that person any share in the profits, that person would not be a partner.[10] In addition, rules dealing with partner-to-partner fiduciary duty can be shaped by agreement but not abrogated.[11]

These limitations are rarely problematic, however. Flexibility in structuring inter se relationships is a prime attraction of the partnership form.

§7.1.3 *The Revised Uniform Partnership Act*

In 1992 the National Conference of Commissioners on Uniform State Laws adopted a Revised Uniform Partnership Act ("RUPA"). It made changes to the new Act in 1993 and approved a final version in 1994.[12] RUPA contains some improvements over UPA. RUPA §203, for example, contains useful rules for determining whether particular property belongs to the partnership or the individual partners. Section 201(a) seeks to provide a straightforward answer to the question of whether a partnership is merely an aggregate of individuals or an entity unto itself. While the UPA has taken a schizoid approach, RUPA declares, "A partnership is an entity."[13]

In other respects, RUPA's provisions are more difficult to evaluate. For example, RUPA contains elaborate, new procedures for handling the dissociation of a partner from the partnership[14] and a significant reformulation of a partner's fiduciary duty to fellow partners.[15] In still other respects, RUPA carries forward some of UPA's major drafting disasters. For example, RUPA §301, dealing with the power of a partner to bind the partnership, repeats almost verbatim the confusing wording of UPA §9(1).[16]

It is unclear how RUPA will fare in state legislatures. To date only three states have adopted RUPA, while 46 states and the District of Columbia have enacted statutes authorizing a new form of business entity — the *limited liability company*. This new entity threatens to make general partnerships obso-

---

10. See section 7.2.3. However, if a third party knew of the label, the person might be liable to that third party *as if* a partner. See section 7.5 (partnership by estoppel).

11. See section 9.9.1.

12. The National Conference refers to RUPA as "UPA (1994)," but most commentators style the new Act as the "Revised Uniform Partnership Act" or "RUPA." For clarity's sake, this book uses "UPA" to refer to the original Act, promulgated in 1914, and "RUPA" to refer to the new Act, finalized in 1994.

13. RUPA §201. See section 7.2.7.

14. For a detailed discussion of this topic under the UPA and highlights of RUPA's new approach, see Chapter Eleven.

15. For a detailed discussion of this topic under the UPA and highlights of RUPA's new approach, see Chapter Nine.

16. See section 10.2.

lete, because a limited liability company (i) is taxed like a partnership,[17] (ii) can be structured much like a partnership, and yet (iii) has all the liability protections of a corporation.[18] As limited liability companies gain widespread acceptance, general partnerships may cease to be an entity of choice and come into existence only through inadvertence or poor legal advice. With this possibility in view, some legislatures may be unwilling to invest the time to seriously consider a new partnership act.

That future, however, is neither here nor certain. Moreover, another, even newer statutory development points in the opposite direction. Within the past few years nearly 15 states have authorized *limited liability partnerships*, which are essentially ordinary general partnerships with a corporate-like liability shield.[19] The limited liability partnership may suit many businesses as well or better than a limited liability company. If so, state legislatures may indeed have good reason to consider RUPA.

In any event, RUPA is a major development in partnership law, even though the full impact of that development is as yet unclear. Accordingly, this book concentrates on the current state of the law — UPA — and provides highlights of what RUPA may augur for the future.

§7.2 Partnership Described

§7.2.1 Key Characteristics

Partnership is the label that the law applies to a particular kind of business relationship. In the words of the UPA, "A partnership is an association of two or more persons to carry on as co-owners a business for profit."[20] The paradigmatic partnership is:

- an unincorporated[21] business, intended to make a profit,
- which has two or more participants, who may be either individuals or entities,
- each of whom "brings something to the party," such as efforts, ideas, money, property, or some combination,

17. As discussed in section 7.3.2, favorable tax status is one of the prime reasons for doing business as a general partnership.

18. For a more detailed discussion of limited liability companies, see section 12.2.

19. For a more detailed discussion of limited liability partnerships, see section 12.3.

20. UPA §6(1).

21. A business that complies with the formalities necessary to become a corporation cannot be a partnership, even if in every other respect the business matches the key characteristics of a partnership.

- each of whom co-owns the business,
- each of whom has a right to comanage the business, and
- each of whom shares in the profits of the business.

Partnerships appear in a wide variety of forms and engage in a wide variety of businesses. Some partnerships have only two partners; others have hundreds.[22] Some partnerships are based on complicated partnership agreements. Others arise from a handshake or a course of conduct. Many small retail establishments are partnerships, as are many businesses that own real estate. At one time, lawyers wishing to combine their efforts and share profits had no choice but to form partnerships, and even today most law firms, as well as other professional practices, are organized as partnerships.[23]

Creating a partnership involves no special formalities. There are no magic words that must be said or documents that need be signed or filed. If a business structure has the essential characteristics of a partnership, then the business *is* a partnership.

§7.2.2 *The Consent Characteristic*

The UPA refers to a partnership as "an association."[24] That term connotes voluntariness, and the law has always considered a partnership to be a consensual relationship. For a partnership to exist, there must be a business relationship whose participants intend the kind of arrangement that the law calls a partnership. The participants must agree to that arrangement, either expressly or by their conduct.

It is not necessary, however, that the participants intend or agree to the *legal label* of partnership. A partnership can exist even though the participants have no idea that the legal label applies to them. Indeed, a partnership can exist among participants who have expressly disclaimed the partnership label.

Example: Sid has fallen on hard times. He receives the following letter from his brother, Jules:

---

22. Partnerships with large numbers of partners are uncommon. Partners are personally liable for the debts of the partnership, and the partnership is liable for the misconduct of its partners. See section 7.3 and Chapter Ten. The larger the number of partners, the greater is this risk of vicarious liability. Also, partnerships are susceptible to dissolution, and increasing the number of partners increases the problems inherent in that susceptibility. See Chapter Eleven.

23. See section 7.3.2 (restrictions on business forms available to professionals).

24. UPA §6(1).

Dear Sid,

I am sorry to hear that you've lost your job. Things are very tight here, otherwise I'd be happy to send you some money to tide you over.

I do have another idea, though. You know that land I own up by the lake? I think it would make a good resort, if I could just get some cabins built on it. If you'd be willing to move up there with your family and build the cabins, I would pay for all the materials, and for food and necessities for you and your family. I couldn't afford to pay you any wages, but once we got the resort up and running I'd give you half of the profits for the first 5 years.

Let me know how you feel about this.

/s/ Jules

Sid's letter may be the blueprint of a partnership.

Example: Caesar lends money to Julio, who personally owns a company that produces and markets cheese. The loan agreement provides that, until the money is repaid Caesar (i) will receive a share of the company's profits in lieu of interest, (ii) may have the marketing rights for 50 percent of the company's output, and (iii) may have his own accountant check the company's finances weekly and approve any payments to be made by the company in excess of $100. The loan agreement also expressly states that Caesar and Julio are not partners in the cheese company but rather are creditor and debtor. Nonetheless, a court may find that a partnership exists.[25]

Partnerships that arise inadvertently are likely to be problematic. The parties will have created a legal relationship without having thought about, much less worked through, key business issues. At least initially, UPA default rules will govern their relationship,[26] but those rules may fail to match the deal the parties would have made for themselves. In any event the applicability of those rules will come as quite a surprise.

When a partnership arises despite an express disclaimer, there is another unpleasant consequence. Disputing the disclaimer is worthwhile only when money is at stake, so in these situations the label "partner" is invariably costly. In the cheese company Example above, for instance, if Caesar is deemed a partner of Julio, then Caesar will be personally liable for the cheese company's debts.[27]

25. The parties' self-description is not necessarily useless. The parties' label can be influential in "close call" situations. See section 7.4.3.

26. As explained in section 7.1.2, the partners can displace the default rules, but they can do so only by agreement.

27. See section 7.4.2 (contesting and establishing the existence of partnerships).

§7.2.3 *The Profit Sharing Prerequisite*

For participants in a business to be partners they must have the right to share in the business's profits. It is not necessary that the business actually have profits, and profit sharing is not irrefutable evidence of partner status,[28] but the right to share whatever profits exist is a necessary precondition to being a partner.

> ***Example:*** Carolyn opens an art supply store in a building she rents from Sylvia. As part of her rent, Carolyn pays Sylvia 30 percent of Carolyn's monthly revenues. Carolyn and Sylvia are not partners because they do not share profits.

Since sharing in revenues does not satisfy the profit-sharing prerequisite, it is important to understand the difference between profit sharing and revenue sharing. A business's revenue (or proceeds, or receipts, or gross income) consists of all the money the business takes in. A business's profit equals the amount of its revenue, less the amount of expenses the business has incurred in generating that revenue.

> ***Example:*** The Acme Widget Company manufactures and sells widgets. In 1994 it sold 50,000 widgets, for which it received $500,000. In order to make and sell the widgets, in 1994 the Company spent $100,000 on materials, $150,000 on salaries, wages and sales commissions, $20,000 in energy costs and $30,000 in legal fees for total expenses of $300,000. In 1994, the Company had $500,000 of revenue (or gross receipts), but only $200,000 of profits ($500,000 minus $300,000 of expenses equals $200,000).[29]

Having a share of profits tends to produce a different attitude than having a share of revenues. Someone with a share merely of revenues tends to focus on making sales, worrying little about the rest of the enterprise. For someone who shares profit, in contrast, sales (and revenues) are only part of the equation; a profit will exist only if the whole business is functioning well.

> ***Example:*** Sylvia is a partner in the Acme Widget Company with a right to ten percent of the profits. Phil is a salesperson for the Company, with a five percent commission on all revenue collected from the sales

---

28. See sections 7.4.3 and 7.4.4, which discuss other business relationships that may involve profit sharing.

29. For simplicity's sake, the example lists only a few of the costs an actual company would incur. The concepts being illustrated would apply as well in a realistically complicated situation.

he makes. Phil has a customer who is willing to buy 5,000 widgets if Acme can ship within two weeks. Acme can make that deadline only by paying its workers substantial amounts of overtime pay. For Phil the main concern is booking the order and seeing that Acme meets the shipping deadline. Sylvia, in contrast, wants to know how much the extra overtime costs will add to the cost of manufacturing.

The profit-share prerequisite thus fits well with two other key partnership characteristics: comanagement and co-ownership. Those who share profits tend to view their economic fate as linked with the fate of the enterprise as a whole. As a consequence, they will wish to involve themselves in controlling the enterprise and will tend to see the enterprise as belonging in part to them.

§7.2.4 *The Role of Loss Sharing*

Express agreements to share losses certainly intensify the comanagement and co-ownership inclinations just discussed,[30] and in all jurisdictions such agreements are very strong evidence of a partnership. In some jurisdictions, an express agreement to share losses is actually a prerequisite to a finding of partnership.

The majority rule, however, is to the contrary. The UPA's definition of partnership does not mention loss sharing. Instead, the UPA implies an agreement to share losses as a consequence of partnership status.[31]

Example: Carolyn opens an art supply store in a building she rents from Sylvia. As part of her rent, Carolyn agrees to pay Sylvia 20 percent of Carolyn's yearly profits. The agreement says nothing about Sylvia's obligation to pay Carolyn if Carolyn loses money. Under the UPA, the absence of an express agreement to share losses does not preclude a finding that Carolyn and Sylvia are partners.

Example: Julie and Evelyn operate a dance school as partners. They specifically agree to share profits 50/50, but do not consider what will happen if they lose money. The UPA implies an agreement to share losses 50/50.[32]

---

30. Section 7.2.3.

31. UPA §18(a) (losses to be shared in the same proportion as profits are shared). See section 8.3.1.

32. UPA §18(a).

§7.2.5 A Meaning for "Co-Ownership"

Co-ownership is a key characteristic of a partnership, but the concept can be quite confusing. The confusion results because the UPA does not define the term and because the concept has a different meaning depending on whether it is used (i) to help determine whether a partnership exists or (ii) to describe certain legal rights that follow from partner status. In the former sense, the concept of co-ownership is an entrance criterion to the legal box[33] labeled "partnership." In the latter sense, the concept is a consequence of being in that box.

To understand co-ownership as an entrance criterion to partnership status,[34] consider two entrepreneurs who go into business together. They agree (as partners do) that they will jointly control whatever property the business uses ("the assets") and will decide together what property to select, what use to make of those assets, and whether, when, and for what price to dispose of the use and control of that property. They also agree that they will share the economic benefit (or detriment) that eventuates from their control, use, and disposition of those assets (i.e. they will share profits).

Without regard to formal questions of title, in a functional sense the two entrepreneurs co-own the assets of the business. By their agreement they have arranged to share the two predominant characteristics of property ownership: the right to control use and disposition, and the right to benefit (or suffer) economically from the exercise of that right of control. Such functional co-ownership is characteristic of a partnership.

§7.2.6 Partnership Types and Joint Ventures

Partnership types. There are three basic types of partnership, categorized according to when the partnership rightfully comes to an end.[35]

- *Partnership at will* — each partner has the right to cause the partnership to come to an end, at any time and without having to state or have "cause."[36]

---

33. See Introduction, supra, Figure 1. In the other nomenclature provided in the Introduction, co-ownership is sometimes part of an "If" statement and sometimes part of a "Then" statement. Id. For example:

If the following characteristics exist (. . . *co-ownership* . . .), *then* a partnership exists.

If a partnership exists, *then* the individual partners have the following rights (. . . *co-ownership* . . .).

34. For a discussion of the co-ownership "consequences" of partnership, see Chapter Eight.

35. Recall from sections 4.1.3 and 4.1.6 the difference between *power* and *right*. Each partner always has the *power* to call an end to the partnership. See section 11.1.1.

36. A partner's fiduciary duty may limit this right. See section 11.6.1.

- *Partnership for a term* — the partnership comes to an end at the end of the time period specified in the partners' agreement.
- *Partnership for a particular undertaking* — the partnership comes to an end when the particular task or goal specified in the partners' agreement has been accomplished.

Example: Paul, Suzanne, and Sarah form a partnership to practice law. They make no agreement about the duration of the partnership. Each partner has the right to leave the partnership at any time, causing the partnership to come to an end. The partnership is at will.

Example: Paul, Suzanne, and Sarah form a partnership to invest in a strategically located parcel of real estate. They agree that the partnership will hold the property for five years, after which the partnership will sell the property and come to an end. The partnership is for a term.

Example: Paul, Suzanne, and Sarah form a partnership to develop a subdivision of single-family houses. They agree to remain partners until all construction is complete and all the houses have been sold. The partnership is for a particular undertaking.

Joint ventures. The term *joint venture* provides more confusion than enlightenment. Under the law of most states, a joint venture is distinguished from a partnership by having a more narrow scope than a partnership formed to conduct an on-going business. But that distinction makes little sense, since the UPA recognizes limited-scope partnerships as partnerships for a particular undertaking. Moreover, under the law of most states, joint ventures are analogized to partnerships and therefore governed by partnership law.

§7.2.7 *Entity or Aggregate? (And Why Care?)*

The question of "entity vs. aggregate" has long vexed the law of partnerships. Is a partnership a separate legal person, with a legal identity distinct from its individual partners? Or is a partnership merely an aggregation of its individual partners, with no separate legal identity of its own?

The problem inheres in the UPA. When the Act was being drafted reasonable minds differed on the issue. As the drafting project began, the principal drafter favored the entity approach. He died, however, in the middle of the project, and his replacement favored the aggregate view.

The UPA as promulgated includes both approaches. Some provisions reflect an entity concept. UPA §9(1), for example, begins: "Every partner is an agent of the partnership. . . ." Other provisions reflect the aggregate notion. For instance, UPA §29 characterizes partnership dissolution as "the change in the relation of the partners caused by any partner ceasing to be associated in the carrying on . . . of the business." Still other provisions combine the two approaches.[37]

Understanding that the UPA embodies two discordant themes helps make sense of some of the Act's provisions. The themes can also have an impact in determining how nonpartnership law treats partners and partnerships.

> ***Example:*** A state statute prohibited banks from making loans to their own directors. A bank made a loan to a partnership in which one of the bank's directors was a partner. A court held that the bank had not violated the statute, since the partnership was an entity separate from its partners. A court in another state reached the opposite conclusion in an essentially identical situation. The state had a similar statute, but this court considered the partnership to be a mere aggregation of individuals. As a result, the court saw the bank's loan to the partnership as a loan to each individual partner, of whom one was a director of the lending bank.

§7.3 The Hallmark Consequence of Partnership: Partners' Personal Liability for the Partnership's Debts

The most important consequence of partner status is simply this: *All partners are personally liable for debts and other obligations of the partnership.* It does not matter whether a particular partner participated or approved the conduct that creates the obligation. The liability results merely from the status of "partner" and is automatic, strict, and vicarious.

In the modern commercial world, this situation is remarkable and — for partners and potential partners — harrowing. Being a partner is tantamount to giving a personal guarantee to everyone with a claim or potential claim against the business.

§7.3.1 Exhaustion, Joint and Several Liability, Inter Se Loss Sharing

The rule of personal liability has three separate areas of complexity: an exhaustion rule, a set of rules relating to joint and several liability, and the issue of how partners' liability to third parties relates to partners' obligations to share losses among themselves.

---

37. E.g., UPA §25 (partners have no individual rights in property owned by the partnership but do have collective rights to use and possess the partnership's property for partnership purposes).

Exhaustion rule. In some jurisdictions, a creditor of the partnership may not pursue individual partners without first exhausting the assets of the partnership.

Joint liability and joint and several liability. In most jurisdictions, partners are jointly and severally liable for certain kinds of debts and jointly liable for others. Under UPA §15, partners are jointly and severally liable for partnership debts arising from partner misconduct and merely jointly liable for all other partnership debts.[38]

The distinctions between the two types of liability relate not to the extent of each partner's personal responsibility but rather to the steps a creditor must take to pursue the partners. Under both forms of liability, each partner may be held individually responsible for the full amount of the partnership's debt.[39] When the liability is joint *and* several, the creditor may pursue any one of the partners individually. That is, the creditor does not need to include all the partners as defendants in the same lawsuit. Moreover, the creditor may release its claim against one of the partners without undermining its claim against the others. In contrast, when the liability is joint *but not* several, the creditor must sue all of the partners in order to sue any of them. Likewise, if the liability is merely joint, the creditor's release of any partner releases all of them.

> ***Example:*** Burt and Aretha form a partnership to practice law. As a result of Burt's negligence, the firm is liable for malpractice. As to this obligation, Burt and Aretha are jointly and severally liable. The injured client may sue one of them without the other and may release one of them without releasing the other.

> ***Example:*** Burt and Aretha form a partnership to practice law. The partnership buys a photocopier through an installment sales agreement. The firm's obligations on the agreement do not arise from partner misconduct, so Burt and Aretha are jointly liable. To sue either, the vendor must sue both. Releasing either will release both.

> ***Example:*** Burt and Aretha form a partnership to practice law. As a result of an associate's negligence, the firm is liable for malpractice. The firm's obligations result from respondeat superior, not partner miscon-

---

38. For a discussion of how a partner's misconduct could give rise to a partnership debt, see sections 10.5 and 10.6. For a discussion of other ways in which partners can bind their partnership to third parties, see section 10.2.

39. Of course the creditor cannot collect more than the amount owed. That amount will be reduced to judgment. Once the creditor has collected the full judgment amount, the judgment is satisfied.

duct, so Burt and Aretha are jointly liable. To sue either, the injured client must sue both. Releasing either will release both.

Relationship of partners' liability to third parties and partners' inter se loss sharing. As discussed in Chapter Eight, partners typically share losses among themselves. Their inter se loss sharing has, however, absolutely no effect on a third party's claim against any particular partner.

> ***Example:*** Under their partnership agreement, Larry, Moe, and Curley agree to share losses 60/20/20. Shemp has a $100,000 claim against the partnership on which each partner is jointly and severally liable. Shemp sues only Larry, seeking to recover the entire amount. Larry cannot defend by saying, "At most, my liability is $60,000 [i.e., 60 percent]."[40]

§7.3.2 Why Risk It?

Why would anyone form a general partnership instead of a corporation? Forming a corporation is a simple matter, and the corporate entity shields its owners from the debts of the business. Of course even with the corporate form, owners of start-up businesses often have to give personal guarantees to particular, important creditors (e.g., banks, major suppliers). However, such particularized guarantees cause far less exposure than does the simple fact of partner status. Why would anyone take the risk of partnership?

That question has a five-part answer: (i) tax advantages; (ii) greater flexibility in structuring the "deal" among the participants; (iii) legal restrictions on the business forms available to professionals; (iv) inadvertence; (v) poor or no legal advice. The first answer is of great, although now waning importance. The second and third are for the most part mere vestiges of past practices. The fourth and fifth have perhaps the greatest lasting significance.

Tax advantages. For decades, tax advantages have been a substantial reason for organizing a business as a partnership rather than a corporation. Most corporations are taxable entities and therefore face double taxation when distributing profits. The standard corporation can pay dividends to its shareholders (i.e., distribute profits to its owners) only in after-tax dollars. In essence, the corporation must first pay corporate income tax on its corporate

---

40. Larry will, however, be entitled to indemnity from the partnership and, if the partnership lacks the necessary funds, will have a claim against Moe and Curley for their respective shares of the loss. See sections 8.4 (partner's right to indemnity) and 8.3.1 (loss sharing applied when third party has collected from one partner and the partnership has failed to indemnify).

profits before distributing any of those profits as dividends. The shareholders must in turn pay income tax on the dividends.

A partnership, in contrast, is a "pass through" entity. Tax law treats the partnership's profits as allocated among (i.e., passed through to) the partners. The partnership pays no tax; only the partners do. Partners thus face only a single level of taxation.

> ***Example:*** Sachs Paper Bag Partnership ("the Partnership") is a partnership with two partners who divide the profits 50/50. In 1992 the Partnership made \$100 of profits, distributing \$50 to Partner Irv and \$50 to Partner Selma. Each partner is in the 30 percent tax bracket,[41] so each pays \$15 of tax. The partnership pays no tax, so all told taxes have taken \$30 of the original \$100 (\$50 × 30 percent = \$15; \$15 × 2 partners = \$30).
>
> In contrast, a competitor bag company, Ziegler Corporation ("the Corporation"), is organized as a corporation. The Corporation has two shareholders, Todd and Jeff. Todd and Jeff each own half the stock in the Corporation and have a right to half of whatever profits the Corporation distributes. In 1992, the Corporation, like the Partnership, made \$100 in profit. However, unlike the Partnership, the Corporation had to pay a corporate income tax of 40 percent (\$40). The Corporation then distributed the remaining \$60 to its two shareholders. Todd and Jeff each received \$30. Like Irv and Selma, both Todd and Jeff are in the 30 percent tax bracket. Each therefore paid \$9 in taxes (\$30 × 30 percent = \$9). All told taxes have taken \$58 of the original \$100 (corporate tax of \$40, plus Todd's individual tax of \$9, plus Jeff's individual tax of \$9). Thus the tax bite on Ziegler Corporation and its shareholders has been nearly twice as large as the tax bite on the Sachs Bag Partnership and its partners.

Pass-through status brings partnerships other tax advantages as well. For example, losses also pass through. When a partnership loses money, the partners obtain tax deductions for use on their own income taxes.

Corporations whose shareholders all work in the business can eliminate most or all double taxation by arranging to "zero out," that is, to pay out all of the "might have been" profits to their shareholders in the form of salaries. The shareholder/employees must of course pay tax on the salary, but the corporation does not pay corporate income tax on the salary amount.[42]

---

41. For simplicity's sake this Example does not use actual tax rates.

42. Tax law does limit this approach. Salaries must be reasonable; otherwise they are taxable to the corporation as a disguised distribution of profits. In any event, the corporation must pay various payroll taxes on salaries.

Corporations that can elect to be taxed under Subchapter S of the Internal Revenue Code can do even better. Profits and losses of a Subchapter S corporation pass through to the shareholders, eliminating double taxation and allocating loss deductions to the shareholders. A Subchapter S corporation is not a complete pass-through entity, however. In a number of esoteric ways, partnership tax status is superior to Subchapter S. In addition, not all corporations can qualify for Subchapter S status. Eligibility requirements are quite restrictive, limiting inter alia the number of shareholders (35 or fewer), the characteristics of the shareholders (e.g., no nonresident aliens, no corporations), and the way the shareholders structure their relationship with each other (e.g., only one class of stock).

For some businesses, the tax advantages of a partnership have been substantial enough to warrant the risks of personal liability. This has been especially so when the risks are either small or insurable.

However, tax advantages have recently begun to wane in importance. This is not because partnership tax status is less attractive but rather because that status is now available to some businesses with a corporate-like liability shield. The advent of limited liability companies, mentioned previously,[43] has undercut and may eventually eliminate the tax rationale for doing business as a general partnership.[44]

Greater flexibility in structuring the deal. As discussed previously,[45] partners have almost unlimited flexibility in structuring their relationship with each other. With this flexibility, they may predetermine the various aspects of their deal. For example, they may agree in advance which partners will work in the business and how much, if any, extra remuneration those partners will receive for doing so. They may, in contrast, establish a flexible mechanism for allocating profits. They may subject particular business decisions to the veto of each partner, or they may give complete management authority to one or more managing partners.

At one time, the corporate form did not allow comparable flexibility. Some courts invalidated predetermined deals as attempts to "sterilize" the corporation's directors, who under traditional corporate norms are supposed to exercise independent judgment in managing corporate affairs. Modern court decisions and modern corporate statutes have changed matters, however. In most jurisdictions, shareholders in a closely-held corporation (i.e., a corporation with few owners) can do just as much predetermination as the partners in a partnership. In these jurisdictions, business people who want

43. Section 7.1.3. For a more detailed discussion, see section 12.2.1.

44. Something of the same approach has been available for decades through the limited partnership, in which only one partner need be personally liable for the debts of the business. See section 12.1.4.

45. Section 7.1.2.

to set their deal in advance no longer have to expose themselves to the personal liability that comes automatically with partner status.

Restrictions on business forms available to professionals. At one time, states prohibited professionals from practicing in corporate form. Professional status was seen as carrying a special responsibility, so the corporate liability shield was inappropriate for a professional practice. According to this view, professionals were properly saddled with the all-encompassing, vicarious liability of a partner. Professionals who wished to practice together and co-own their practice had only one organizational choice — a partnership.

Today, in contrast, states allow professionals to practice in a special form of corporation known as a "professional association" or "professional corporation."[46] Within the past few years, a number of states have also authorized professionals to practice as professional limited liability companies. A limited liability company combines the liability shield of a corporation with the tax status of a partnership. Even more recently, a few states have authorized professionals to practice as limited liability partnerships. A limited liability partnership is a general partnership with the liability shield of a corporation.[47] Consequently, professionals who today choose the partnership form do so for reasons other than necessity.

Inadvertence. Since creating a partnership requires no special formalities, partnerships can arise inadvertently.[48] Thus many partners assume the harrowing risk of personal liability without understanding that they are doing so.

Poor or no legal advice. Some persons knowingly become partners without appreciating the liability risk that accompanies partner status. These persons have either not sought legal advice or have received bad advice.

§7.4 Contesting and Establishing the Existence of a Partnership

§7.4.1 *Why a Contest?*

Some of the most important partnership cases involve disputes over whether a particular business relationship constitutes a partnership. These disputes

46. A few state supreme courts have held the corporate liability shield inapplicable to attorneys practicing in a professional corporation.

47. For a discussion of these new business entities, see section 7.1.3 and also Chapter Twelve.

48. See sections 7.2.2 and 7.4, and also Chapter Eight.

usually relate to one of two major attributes of partnership status: the fact that partners are personally liable for the debts of the partnership and the fact that partners share profits with each other.

The liability attribute interests creditors seeking a "deep pocket." If the party who owes a debt cannot pay, the creditor may seek a more solvent business associate of the debtor and try to characterize that business association as a partnership.

> ***Example:*** A manufacturing plant defaults on its obligation to buy power from a power company. Another creditor of the plant has exerted some control over the plant's business and has received a share of the plant's profits. The power company claims that the other creditor is in fact a partner in the plant's operations and as such personally liable for the plant's debt.

The profit-sharing attribute interests those seeking a bigger piece of a business's pie. If a person who participates in a business can establish partner status, that person stakes a potentially valuable claim. As a partner, the person is entitled to a share not only of profits made in the future but also of any profits distributed in the past (i.e., while the individual was in fact a partner although not recognized as such).

> ***Example:*** Bob owns and operates a tree farm. He induces Ted to work on the farm as manager, and Ted holds that position for six years. Ted then claims that Bob had promised him a 50/50 partnership after three years. During years 4 through 6 Bob took $200,000 in profit out of the business. A court sides with Ted and orders Bob to pay Ted $100,000 in back profits. (After that payment, Bob's profit from years 4 through 6 will be reduced to $100,000, so the two partners will have profited equally.)

§7.4.2 *The Pivotal Question: The Character of the Profit Sharing*

The right to share profits is a prerequisite to partner status, and the UPA gives profit sharing a pivotal role in most disputes concerning the existence *vel non* of a partnership:

> The receipt by a person of a share of the profits of a business is prima facie evidence that he is a partner in the business, but no such inference shall be drawn if such profits were received in payment:
>
> (a) As a debt by installments or otherwise,
> (b) As wages of an employee or rent to a landlord,

(c) As an annuity to a widow or representative of a deceased partner,
(d) As interest on a loan, though the amount of payment vary with the profits of the business,
(e) As the consideration for the sale of the good-will of a business or other property by installments or otherwise.[49]

Under this provision disputes about the existence of a partnership have a typical structure:

1. The party asserting the existence of a partnership has the burden of proof (because under U.S. law the party asserting a claim ordinarily has the burden of establishing the elements of the claim).
2. Evidence of a right to share in profits will ordinarily be enough to get the case to the finder of fact.[50]
3. Assuming that profit sharing exists, attention will shift to characterizing it. Does the profit share reflect the remuneration of a co-owner (a partner) or does it fit within one of the business relationships described in clauses (a) through (e) of UPA §7(4)?

Since no one can be a partner without a right to share in profits, disputes about the existence of partnership inevitably focus on the characterization issue.

§7.4.3 *Factors in the Contest of Characterization*

There is, unfortunately, no bright line test for resolving disputes over the characterization of profit sharing. It is, however, possible to identify the following five factors which tend to influence courts.

Control. Comanagement is a key characteristic of a partnership. The more an alleged partner participates in management decisions or exercises control over the business, the more likely is a finding of partnership. The control factor can be especially problematic for creditors who receive profits "[a]s

49. UPA §7(4).

50. Prima facie evidence means that the party with the burden of proof has submitted enough evidence to satisfy that burden, if the evidence happens to persuade the finder of fact. Prima facie evidence does not shift the burden of proof; only a presumption does that. In unusual circumstances, evidence of profit sharing might not be enough to avoid summary judgment. If the evidence supporting one of the exceptions was so strong as to compel any reasonable fact finder to find an exception, then — as a matter of law — no partnership would exist.

interest on a loan."[51] Many loan agreements permit the creditor a voice in or even control over management decisions if the debtor has trouble making payments. A creditor who takes a profit share and then exercises such rights faces substantial risks if the debtor's business fails. *Other* creditors will use that exercise of control to characterize the profit sharing as a partner's remuneration. Since all partners are liable for the partnership's debts, this characterization will make the profit-sharing creditor liable *on the other creditor's claims* against the debtor.

Control is a less useful factor when the alleged partner provides the business full-time services, rather than money or credit. Many key employees exercise substantial discretion in the conduct of their employer's business. Some key employees even have contract rights which oblige the employer to respect that discretion. Control can therefore be equivocal when trying to distinguish between profits received as a partner and profits received "[a]s wages of an employee."[52]

Agreements to share losses. As previously explained,[53] an express agreement to share losses is strong evidence of a partnership. Such agreements rarely, if ever, exist in the arrangements between creditor and debtor, employer and employee, or in any of the other relationships that, according to UPA §7(4), involve profit sharing but not partnership.

Business participants can and sometimes do share losses without having an express agreement to do so. That course of conduct probably implies a loss-sharing agreement and in any event is itself strong evidence of a partnership.

Contributions of property to the business. If a party has contributed property to the business, that contribution favors the partnership characterization. As discussed more fully in Chapter Eight, partners often "buy into" a partnership by transferring ownership of something such as land, patents, or money to the business.[54] They give up ownership rights in the property in return for a share of the profits and a right to receive back the value of the property (but not the property itself) if and when the partnership comes to an end.

A contribution of property is not a prerequisite to a finding of partnership, and many partners bring only their talents, skills, and labor.[55] However, a property contribution does tend to rule out any of the UPA §7(4)

51. UPA §7(4)(d).

52. UPA §7(4)(b).

53. Section 7.2.4.

54. See sections 8.1 and 8.6.

55. See section 8.7.

relationships. Property transfers do occur in some of those relationships, but the transfers are of a different nature. For example, a landlord transfers to a tenant the property right to occupy and use the leased premises, but: (i) the transfer is only temporary, (ii) the landlord has a right to regain the same property and not just its value, and (iii) the return of the property ordinarily occurs at a time certain or upon specified notice, not merely when the partnership happens to come to an end. Similarly, a lender transfers to a borrower the right to use and dispose of the loaned funds, but the timing of the repayment ordinarily does not depend on the ending of the partnership.

The extent to which the profit share constitutes the recipient's only remuneration from the business. If a profit recipient receives no other remuneration from the business, that fact favors the partnership characterization. If, in contrast, the profit share is just a bit of "icing" on top of some other payments, courts are more inclined toward one of the relationships listed in UPA §7(4).

> ***Example:*** Sylvia manages the widget factory of the Acme Widget Company. She receives no salary. Her only compensation is a 20-percent share of profits. (She can "draw" a certain amount each month against her profit share, but if at the end of the year her draws have exceeded her share she must repay the excess.) Phil, the national sales manager of the company, receives a salary of $50,000 per year, plus one percent of the Company's profit as an incentive. A court is far more likely to find Sylvia to be a partner than Phil. All of her remuneration comes in the form of profits. For Phil, the profit share is small and is a mere add-on to his salary.

> ***Example:*** The First National Bank lends Acme $500,000. The Bank thinks that the loan is a bit risky. As compensation for that risk, it insists on a high interest rate *plus* a three percent profit share while the loan is outstanding. The bank's loan officer explains, "Since we're going to take this risk on you, we want a little bit of the 'up side' if things go well." Even if Acme does do well, the interest payment will be roughly three times as large as the profit share. Unless other factors point strongly to the contrary, a court is likely to characterize the profit sharing as "interest on a loan."[56] The existence of interest payments suggests that the bank is a creditor, not a partner. The relative sizes of the interest payments and the profit share also support that characterization.

The parties' own characterization of their relationship. Although the parties' own labels are never dispositive, in close situations some courts look

56. UPA §7(4)(d).

to how the participants in a business relationship have characterized that relationship. This factor is probably more influential when the characterization dispute involves only the participants. When someone outside the relationship (e.g., a creditor seeking to find a deep pocket) challenges the participants' self-labelling, courts are more likely to see the label as self-serving.

§7.4.4 *Handling the Factors (A Mode of Analysis)*

Legal analysis involving factors is always difficult. Which factor is the most important? What if one factor points strongly in one direction, while two other factors point weakly in the other? Unfortunately, no simple, mechanical paradigm exists for ordering the characterization factors. However, you may find the following perspective helpful.

All disputes about the character of profit sharing are either/or disputes. The parties do not contest generally the paradigm of a partnership but instead struggle over whether a particular person is a partner or merely a participant in one of the nonpartnership relationships listed in UPA §7(4). In one case, for example, the alleged partner will be either a partner or a wage earner receiving profits as wages. In another case, the alleged partner will be either a partner or a lender receiving profits as interest.

To decide these either/or questions, courts can look to the factors discussed in section 7.4.3. If all the factors point in the same direction, the analysis is simple and the answer is clear. The analysis gets complicated only when the factors point in opposite directions.

You can handle that complexity by thinking of each type of either/or choice as a multi-layered continuum. Each layer reflects one of the five char-

Table 7-2. Partner Versus Wage Earner

"Partner" ←		→ *"Wage Earner"*
participates in all important decisions	*Control*	obeys instructions; has no important discretion
has expressly agreed to share losses	*Express Loss Sharing Agreement*	has never agreed to share losses; when losses occur, payout does not change
contributed property to the business	*Contribution*	merely works in the business
all payout via profit share	*Importance of Profit Share*	profit share is only icing on the cake
called a partner	*Self-Labelling*	called an employee

acterization factors. At one end of the continuum sits the "ideal type"[57] of a partner. At that end, at each layer of the continuum, the facts indicate "partner." At the other end of the continuum sits the "ideal type" of the arguably applicable exception from UPA §7(4). At that end, at each layer of the continuum, the facts indicate "wage earner," or "lender," or whatever the exception may be. For example, when the characterization choice is either "partner" or "wage earner," the continuum might look like Table 7-2.

Although in any particular case one factor (or layer) or another may predominate, courts rarely decide on the basis of one factor alone. Instead, they look at the overall picture: The more each layer of the disputed situation leans toward one end of the applicable continuum, the more likely the court is to come down on that side of the either/or fence.

The analysis is inevitably imprecise. Since the law declines to make one factor (or combination of factors) dispositive, courts are left essentially to decide whether the disputed situation "looks" more like one end of the continuum or the other.

§7.5 Partnership by Estoppel

§7.5.1 *The Basic Approach*

It is possible for a person to have partner-like liability for an enterprise's obligations without truly being a partner. The applicable rule is *partnership by estoppel*. Unfortunately, the UPA's rule on partnership by estoppel is exceedingly intricate and requires painstaking reading. The basic concept, however, is fairly simple and is consistent with ordinary estoppel principles:

If
- a person represents itself as being a partner in an enterprise (or allows others to make the representation)

and
- a third party reasonably relies on the representation and does business with the enterprise,

---

Then
- the person who was represented as a partner is personally liable on the transaction, even though that person is not in fact a partner, and
- others who have either made or consented to the representation are bound by the person's acts as if they were partners with that person.

The rule rests on common beliefs about a partner's responsibilities and powers. It is well known that all partners are personally liable for the part-

57. An "ideal type" possesses all the key attributes described by a concept; it epitomizes the concept.

nership's debts. To represent oneself as a partner (or to allow someone else to make the representation) is therefore to impliedly promise to be "good for" any debts of the enterprise. When a false representation induces a third party to deal with the enterprise, the third party cannot invoke genuine partner liability against the person whose status was misrepresented. (That person is not, in fact, a partner.) The third party can, however, invoke partnership by estoppel, which will function to make good that person's implied promise of responsibility.

The "power to bind" aspect of the rule rests on a similar rationale. It is well known that partners have certain powers to bind the partnership.[58] When a person is represented to be a partner with others, third parties will naturally believe that the person can bind the partnership and, on account of each partner's personal liability, can bind those others as well. To the extent that those others consent to the representation, a partner-like power to bind should apply.

§7.5.2 *The Details*

Liability of person whose status is misrepresented (UPA §16(1)). This part of the rule is straightforward in concept:

If:
- a person represents itself, or consents to others representing it, as a partner in an enterprise, and
- a third party relies on that representation and enters into a transaction with the supposed partnership,[59]

Then:
- the person is liable to the third party on the transaction.

The reliance element has two components. The third party must believe the misrepresentation, and the misrepresentation must cause the third party to act.

> ***Example:*** Rachael and Samuel are partners in The Egg Company, a chicken farming operation. Together with Carolyn, the partnership's farm manager, Samuel goes to the local feedstore to buy chicken feed. At the store Samuel explains that he is a partner in the Egg Company and that the Egg Company wishes to buy chicken feed on credit. The store owner is initially reluctant to make a credit sale but then sees Carolyn and says, "Oh, is she one of you?" Samuel nods his head, and Carolyn says nothing. The store owner then agrees to sell on credit. Carolyn is personally liable on the sale. By her inaction she consented

58. For a discussion of the rules that underlie this perception, see Chapter Ten.

59. UPA §16(1) refers specifically to liability to a third party "who has, on the faith of such representation, given credit." Case law has expanded the liability to favor those who have detrimentally relied in other ways.

to being misrepresented as a partner; in reliance on that representation a third party entered into a transaction.

If a person's status as partner has been misrepresented publicly, either by the person or with the person's consent, then a third party may rely on the reverberations of that public misrepresentation. That is, a third party may invoke UPA §16(1) without having relied on a misrepresentation *directly* made or *directly* consented to by the person whose status is being misrepresented.

> ***Example:*** Rachael and Samuel send Carolyn to a chicken auction to buy baby chickens for The Egg Company. So that Carolyn will have no trouble getting her bids accepted, Rachael and Samuel indicate on the bidder's registration form that Carolyn is a partner. Carolyn acquiesces in this tactic. The chicken auction provides all auctioneers and registered sellers a list of registered bidders and their status. Although Carolyn may be unaware of this list, the listing of her as a partner will satisfy the misrepresentation element of UPA §16(1).

UPA §16(1) attaches liability only to the person whose status was misrepresented. If others have made or consented to the misrepresentation, then UPA §16(2) will impose liability on them.

Liability of others who make or consent to the misrepresentation (UPA §16(2)). UPA §16(2) imposes liability on those who misrepresent another person's status as partner or who consent to that misrepresentation. The nature of the liability depends on whether a genuine partnership exists and, if so, whether all the genuine partners have made or consented to the misrepresentation. The following three-part rule restates the recondite formulation found in UPA §16(2).

1. *If*:
   - a partnership exists, and
   - all the partners make or consent to the misrepresentation of a person's status as partner,

   Then:
   - the partnership is liable on the transaction, and
   - the partners are each liable under the ordinary rules of partner liability — i.e., UPA §15.
2. *If*:
   - a partnership exists, but
   - not all the partners make or consent to the misrepresentation,

   Then:
   - the partnership is not liable, and
   - those partners who made or consented to the misrepresentation are jointly liable on the transaction.

3. *If*: no partnership exists,
Then: those who made or consented to the misrepresentation are jointly liable on the transaction.

> ***Example:*** Recall the chicken feed Example above. Samuel is jointly liable with Carolyn under UPA §16(2), since he made the misrepresentation. UPA §16(2) does not apply to Rachael, since she neither made nor consented to the misrepresentation.[60]

> ***Example:*** Recall the chicken auction Example above. UPA §16(2) will apply to make all of Carolyn's bids binding on the partnership. A genuine partnership does exist, and all the partners have consented to the misrepresentation.

Relationship between §16(1) liability and §16(2) liability. It is possible for a person to be liable under UPA §16(1) without anyone being liable under UPA §16(2).[61] It is likewise possible for someone to be liable under UPA §16(2) for misrepresenting some other person's status as partner without that other person being liable under UPA §16(1).

> ***Example:*** Rachael and Samuel send Carolyn, their chicken farm manager, to the hardware emporium to buy chicken wire. The Egg Company has a charge account at the emporium, but the cashier seems reluctant to allow Carolyn to use the account. Carolyn says, "It's okay. They made me a partner." The cashier then approves the charge. UPA §16(1) imposes liability on Carolyn, but UPA §16(2) does not affect either Rachael or Samuel. Carolyn made the misrepresentation, but neither Rachael nor Samuel consented to it.[62]

> ***Example:*** Recall the first chicken feed example, in which Samuel misrepresents Carolyn as a partner and Carolyn consents by inaction. Assume, instead, that Carolyn is out of the room when Samuel makes the

---

60. However, if Samuel's act in buying the feed bound the partnership, then Rachael will be liable on this transaction as for any other partnership obligation. UPA §15(b). For the power of partners to bind the partnership, see Chapter Ten.

61. Doctrines of ratification and unjust enrichment may create liability, however, if an actual partnership accepts the benefits of the transaction. See section 2.6.

62. If Carolyn had power as an agent to bind the partnership, then both Rachael and Samuel will be liable on this transaction as for any other partnership obligation. UPA §15(b). For an agent's power to bind, see Chapter Two.

misrepresentation. Samuel would then be liable under UPA §16(2), but Carolyn would not be liable under UPA §16(1).

PROBLEM 63

Ralph wants to open a riding stable but does not have enough money. He approaches Sally, who has both experience managing start-up businesses and some money to invest. They agree that: each will own a half-interest in the business; Ralph will run the day-to-day operations while Sally will "handle the books"; all major decisions will be made jointly; Sally will invest $50,000; Ralph will get 40 percent of the profits and Sally 60 percent. Sally is concerned with the liability that comes with being a partner, so the agreement between Ralph and Sally states clearly: "This relationship shall not be deemed to be a partnership." What legal effect will that disclaimer have on claims by creditors?

EXPLANATION

The disclaimer will be useless. Sally and Ralph have created precisely the type of business relationship that the law considers to be a partnership. They co-own, they comanage, and they share profits. In the face of a claim by a creditor, the disclaimer will be disregarded as inaccurate and self-serving.

PROBLEM 64

Mark is the treasurer of the Zenith Vending Machine Company. In that capacity he prepares all the Company's tax returns. The Company is a partnership, and each year its partnership tax returns list the partners as Allen, Betty, Charlotte, and Ralph.[63] As part of his remuneration, Mark receives a share of Zenith's profits. If he later claims that he is a partner in the company, what role will the partnership tax returns play in the dispute?

EXPLANATION

The returns will argue strongly against him, because they list the partners and do not include Mark. As the preparer of the returns, Mark evidently assented to the exclusion. This situation therefore differs from efforts to use disclaimers against third parties.

PROBLEM 65

For ten years Paul has operated "Paul's," an automobile salvage business. The business buys wrecked automobiles from insurance companies or at auction

63. Even though partnerships do not pay taxes, see section 7.3.2, they must nonetheless file tax returns.

and then either rebuilds them or cannibalizes them for parts. Paul's sells rebuilt and used parts to car dealers, service stations, and the public.

For the past three years Eli has been working in the business with Paul. Eli has only a third grade education but is an excellent, street smart auto mechanic. He is active in almost all aspects of the business: bidding at auctions, buying cars from insurance companies, and fixing cars and parts. Only Paul, however, sets the prices on cars and parts that the business sells. Paul also maintains all the business's records and takes care of the business's various tax returns.

Paul first approached Eli to come to work with him when Paul learned that Eli had won $9,000 at the racetrack. Eli gave the money to Paul, who used it to buy cars at an auction. Those cars were then used in the salvage business. Paul promised Eli 50 percent of the business's profit for as long as Eli would "work as hard, sweat as much, and do as much as I do."

Ever since Eli began work at Paul's, the company's records have shown him as an employee. His salary has been calculated based on 50 percent of the profits, and social security has been withheld from his checks. The company has paid social security and unemployment compensation taxes on account of Eli and has maintained worker's compensation coverage for him. Both the company's various tax returns and its insurance policies list Eli as an employee.

Is Eli an employee of or a partner in Paul's?[64]

Explanation

Eli is a partner. He shares in the profits and has made a capital contribution. Although Paul has exclusive responsibility in two areas, Eli shares management authority over other areas that are crucial to the business.

The company's books and tax returns do describe Eli as an employee, but that fact does not undermine Eli's partner status. Parties' self-descriptions can give insight into their intents, but only when the parties genuinely assent to the description. There is no evidence that Eli was aware of the way he was described in the company's records, other than the withholding of social security from his checks. With his lack of formal education, Eli was probably unaware of what that withholding implied about his status at Paul's.

PROBLEM 66

Mousetrap, Inc. ("Mousetrap"), a small start-up company, has developed the proverbial better mousetrap, but is having great difficulties breaking through

---

64. This question will have great practical importance if, for example, Paul attempts to "fire" Eli. See sections 11.3.2 (partner's right to compel liquidation of partnership business), 11.6.1 (partner's right to damages for dissolution done in bad faith), and 11.4.3-11.4.4 (partner's right to distribution upon dissolution).

in the marketplace. Convinced that it needs vibrant and cogent marketing leadership, Mousetrap persuades Dorothy to leave her position as national marketing manager for a large corporation and become Executive Vice President of Marketing at Mousetrap. Dorothy is widely considered to have great talent, and she is leaving a prestigious job and a large salary. Mousetrap cannot match Dorothy's current salary, but does promise her: (i) a 300 percent increase in Mousetrap's current budget for sales and marketing efforts, (ii) complete discretion over that budget, (iii) a salary of $100,000, and (iv) as an incentive, an annual bonus equal to five percent of the increase in Mousetrap's gross sales revenues over the preceding year.

Dorothy's first year on the job is tough. Mousetrap has difficulty raising the money necessary to increase the sales and marketing budget, and Dorothy actually loans Mousetrap $50,000. The next year things get much better. Annual sales jump, and Dorothy receives a bonus that almost equals the net profit made by Mousetrap. The next year Mousetrap again makes progress, and Dorothy's bonus actually exceeds Mousetrap's profit. The following year is not so successful, as Dorothy increasingly indulges in grandiose marketing schemes. By the end of the fifth year, the bubble has burst, Mousetrap is insolvent, and Mousetrap's creditors are looking for someone else to sue. Might Dorothy be liable to Mousetrap's creditors on a partnership theory?

Explanation

The creditors might try to allege a partnership between Mousetrap and Dorothy, but they would fail. Although many of the paradigmatic characteristics are present (e.g., sharing control via discretion over the budget, "bringing something to the party" via essential services and working capital), the most important characteristic is missing: Dorothy has a right to share in gross returns, not profits. As a result, Dorothy cannot be a partner.

PROBLEM 67

As a sole proprietor, Dave runs a dry-cleaning store called "Dave's Drycleaning." He is in deep financial trouble. His bank will no longer give him any credit and is threatening to call his loans (i.e., demand immediate payment of all money owed). Dave also owes money to various trade creditors (i.e., businesses which have supplied him goods and services). Dave approaches Susan, a well-known venture capitalist, and asks her to refinance his business. Susan reviews his books and his operations and says, "Listen, you're a great dry cleaner but a lousy businessman. I'll bail you out, but we have to divide up the responsibilities a bit. If we're going to make this business work, we have to be more hardnosed about it. First, no more credit to law professors. They're lousy risks. Second, I want to determine who gets paid when. One of the arts of staying in business is stretching out your accounts payable. So, before you pay anyone, you check with me. Also, I want some upside potential. So long as you owe me money, I want 12 percent interest on what you owe or 10 percent of the profits, whichever is higher. You pay me the 12 percent monthly, and quarterly I'll decide whether to keep the past three months' interest or take my share of the past three months' profits."

Dave accepts Susan's terms, with one condition: "We have to pay our people [i.e. the employees] on time. If we have the money, we pay them." Susan accepts Dave's condition, pays off the bank, and provides additional working capital to the business.

The business continues to operate under the same name, and no one except Dave knows of Susan's role in the business. Dave stops extending credit to law professors. Each month Susan reviews Dave's accounts payable and sets the priorities for payment as follows: (i) pay Susan the interest owed her, (2) pay overdue bills from people Dave intends to buy from again, (3) pay overdue bills from other people who are threatening suit, (4) pay others. Susan never does take a percentage of the profit, because the 12 percent interest figure is always higher.

Dave makes all decisions about which tradespeople to buy from. He also makes all personnel decisions (e.g., hiring, firing, salaries). After a year the business fails. Dave owes Susan $350,000; he owes creditors a total of $175,000 (trade creditors — $150,000; three employees — $25,000 in back wages). Dave has no money.

Can these other creditors collect from Susan? Consider Chapter Six as well as Chapter Seven in analyzing this Problem.

Explanation

Two different theories hold promise for the creditors — partnership law and constructive agency under Restatement §14O. If the creditors can establish that Susan is Dave's partner, UPA §15(b) will make Susan jointly liable with Dave for the partnership's debts. If the creditors successfully invoke §14O, Susan will be liable to the creditors as Dave's principal.

Although it is unlikely that Dave and Susan thought of their relationship as a partnership, they may nonetheless have formed one. Their thoughts on the subject are largely immaterial. What matters is the nature of the business relationship they have intentionally created.

The other creditors will contend that the business relationship fits most of the paradigmatic characteristics of a partnership. Most importantly, Susan has a right to share profits. That right — rather than the actual receipt of profits — is the fundamental prerequisite to partner status. Susan has also "brought something to the party" — not only essential working capital, but also key management services. Moreover, like a paradigmatic partner, Susan has helped run the business, exercising management control over key financial issues. She has not contributed any property, because she has a contractual right to be repaid her loan. But not all partners contribute property. There is no express agreement to share losses, but most jurisdictions do not require one. Dave and Susan have shared control over the business and its assets and have linked their economic fate to each other and to the business by agreeing to share profits. In doing so, they have arranged to "carry on as co-owners a business for profit."[65].

Susan's response will be to characterize her right to share profits as mere "interest on a loan" and therefore not probative of partner status.[66] Both the profit-sharing agreement and the circumstances leading up to that agreement support this characterization. Susan's agreement with Dave gave her the right to take either interest at a fixed rate or a profit share. This arrangement demonstrates that profits, if chosen, were to take the place of conventional interest. The origins of the profit right indicate likewise. Susan did not seek an interest in Dave's business, but rather demanded an option on profits as a condition to making a loan.

The biggest problem with Susan's argument is the type of control she exercised. While many loan agreements give the lender extraordinary power over the debtor's affairs in the event of a default, Susan asked for, obtained, and began exercising *mundane* control *as a condition of granting the loan*. This deviation from standard lending practice may well tip the balance against Susan.

In any event, Susan has troubles under agency law. If a creditor asserts enough control over a debtor to take over the management of the debtor's business, Restatement §140 makes the creditor liable for the debts of the business. Mere veto power is not enough; extensive involvement is necessary.

Susan may well have asserted the necessary control and undertaken the necessary involvement. She was certainly involved in the business; she spoke specifically of "divid[ing] up the responsibilities." Moreover, she controlled some very important aspects of the business — namely, when and what accounts would be paid and what customers would be allowed to buy services on credit. Susan can, however, point to large areas of the business that she did not control, namely, all personnel matters and the selection of vendors.

With the fact question of control a close one, a court may be influenced by the striking similarity between Susan's situation and the situation in *Cargill*. The creditor in *Cargill* kept the Warren grain elevator in business, obtaining grain while the elevator's debts to farmers mounted. Susan kept the dry cleaning enterprise in business and then used her control to make sure that she was paid before all creditors other than employees. In both situations, the creditor

---

65. UPA §6(1) (definition of partnership).

66. UPA §7(4)(d).

used its control to obtain a benefit at the expense of other creditors. Such an abuse of power simultaneously (a) demonstrates that the creditor did substantially interfere with the management of the debtor's business and (b) provides a policy reason for making the controlling creditor liable to the other creditors.

If Susan is liable under Restatement §140, the extent of that liability depends on whether the court follows *Cargill* or *Nash-Finch*.[67] *Cargill* follows §140 faithfully and makes the creditor-principal liable for all debts incurred in the business after the creditor took control. Under *Cargill*, therefore, Susan would be liable to all creditors for all amounts arising after she refinanced and took control of the business.

Under *Nash-Finch*, in contrast, the principal's liability extends only to debts arising within areas of the business controlled by the creditor. Under that approach, Susan would not be liable to the three employees. She did not control their selection, training, supervision, or payment. She did control payment to trade creditors and would be liable to them.

PROBLEM 68

From 1979 to 1993 attorneys Smith and Jones practiced law as a partnership. They had their offices on the tenth floor of a downtown office building. Outside their office they hung a beautiful mahogany sign that read:

SMITH & JONES
Attorneys at Law

In 1993 Smith and Jones terminated their partnership. They continued to share offices and office staffs, however. They also left in place their mahogany sign. They considered taking the sign down but decided "it was too beautiful to remove."

In 1994 a bookseller, J. A. Proofrock, came to Smith's office and sold her a new, expensive treatise on limited liability companies. Smith failed to pay and later became insolvent. Can Proofrock hold Jones liable for the debt? What additional facts would Proofrock have to prove?

EXPLANATION

Proofrock may be able to hold Jones liable on a theory of partnership by estoppel. By allowing the sign to remain up, Jones represented that he and Smith were partners. Proofrock would also have to prove that "on the faith

67. See section 6.3.3 n.16.

of such representation" she extended credit to Smith.[68] That showing has two components: (i) that Proofrock believed Smith and Jones to be partners, and (ii) that the belief caused Proofrock to enter into the transaction. Both components concern Proofrock's state of mind. The facts provide a little outward evidence on the first component. The shared office space and staff show that Proofrock had no reason to disbelieve the sign. The facts provide no outward evidence on the causation issue.

PROBLEM 69

Burt and Heathcliffe are brothers who own adjacent farms. They farm as sole proprietors and have never held themselves out as partners. Burt contacts Nelson's Cropdusting Service to arrange for aerial pesticide spraying during the next growing season. Nelson's fee schedule provides a large discount for large farms, but Burt's farm alone does not qualify. The following conversation ensues between Burt and Nelson.

Nelson: Too bad you and your brother don't come in on this together. Then I could give you a real good discount.

Burt: Well, why don't you do both the farms and give us the discount?

Nelson: I can only do that if Heathcliffe comes in and gives his okay. That's his farm and his business.

Burt: Well wait a minute. Over this past winter Heathcliffe and I decided to go into business together. We're partners in the farming operations.

Nelson: Well, in that case, okay. You get the best rate.

Burt later tells Heathcliffe of the deal and the circumstances. Heathcliffe is outraged; in fact, no partnership exists. Heathcliffe angrily tells his brother to "never do such a thing again." Heathcliffe does not, however, contact Nelson.

During the following growing season, Nelson provides aerial spraying for both farms per his agreement with Burt. Heathcliffe never objects to the spraying but refuses to pay any of the bill. Can Nelson nonetheless collect from Heathcliffe? If so, how much?

EXPLANATION

A claim of unjust enrichment should allow Nelson to recover from Heathcliffe the fair value of the spraying over Heathcliffe's land. A claim of ratification may make Heathcliffe liable for the entire contract price. A purported principal

68. UPA §16(1).

who knows of an unauthorized act can affirm through inaction, that is, by failing to repudiate the act "under such circumstances that, according to the ordinary experience and habits of men, one would naturally be expected to speak if he did not consent."[69] Partnership by estoppel probably does apply, because Heathcliffe neither made nor consented to Burt's misrepresentation prior to the third party's reliance on that misrepresentation.[70] It could be argued to the contrary that the third party's reliance continued up to the moment of spraying and that Heathcliffe consented by inaction. That argument fits better into the ratification analysis, however.

69. Restatement, §94, comment *a*. See section 2.6.2.

70. UPA §16(2). In contrast, UPA §16(1) will apply to Burt and make him accountable for the full contract price. Burt will also be liable for breach of the warranty of authority. He represented himself as having the authority to bind a partnership that did not exist. See section 4.2.2.

RUPA HIGHLIGHTS

RUPA:

- introduces some permissive formalities, allowing public filings of a Statement of Authority (delimiting authority of partners), a Statement of Dissociation (indicating that a partner has dissociated from the partnership), and a Statement of Dissolution (indicating that the partnership has dissolved); the filings serve as constructive notice with regard to partnership transactions in real property, certain on-going liabilities of dissociated partners, the fact of partnership dissolution and certain limitations on partner authority that follow from dissolution; for all other purposes the filings are merely a possible source of actual notice, RUPA §§303, 704 and 805
- unequivocally labels a partnership an entity, RUPA §201
- changes the nature of partners' personal liability, making all liability joint and several and requiring creditors of the partnership to first exhaust the partnership assets, RUPA §§306 and 307
- modifies slightly the rules for determining whether a partnership exists, by
  - — stating that profit sharing creates a rebuttable presumption of partnership rather than mere prima facie evidence, and
  - — adding new categories of protected relationships, where profit sharing does not indicate partnership status (e.g., services provided by an independent contractor, mortgage arrangements in which the mortgagee has an equity participation). RUPA §202(c)(3)
- makes clear that partnership by estoppel (renamed "Liability of Purported Partner") benefits not only those who "extend credit" but rather all who enter into transactions, RUPA §308

8

Financial Aspects of a Partnership (Creation and Operation)

§8.1 The Practical Background

Like any other business, a partnership needs two types of inputs in order to function: the working efforts of human beings ("labor") and the use of at least some property, be it as elaborate as a $30 million factory or as simple as paper on which to write out bills ("capital"). Partnerships can and often do obtain inputs from outsiders (i.e., from nonpartners). A partnership can, for example, rent office space from a landlord, borrow money from a bank, and engage servant agents (colloquially called *employees*), nonservant agents, and even nonagent independent contractors.

Partnerships also depend on inputs from the partners. A partnership typically obtains both labor and capital from its partners, although not every partner necessarily provides both.[1] Of course, a partner who provides something of value to the partnership will want something in return. The UPA includes a comprehensive set of default rules that determine how and when

1. In some partnerships, for example, one partner provides all the capital, while the other partner provides only labor. See section 8.7.

partners receive a return,[2] and this chapter discusses how those rules apply to the creation and operation of a partnership.[3]

§8.2 The Partner's Basic Return

Absent a contrary agreement, a partner's financial return has two components: (1) a right to share in the profits of the partnership, if any, and (2) a right, when the partnership ends, to receive the value of any property that the partner *contributed* to the partnership.[4] A partner also has the right to be indemnified against expenses and liabilities incurred in the service of the partnership.[5]

A partner may also have other financial arrangements with the partnership. For example, a partner may rent property to the partnership or loan it money. But such arrangements result from particular agreements between the partner and the partnership. They do not inhere in partner status.

§8.3 Rules for Sharing Profits and Losses

§8.3.1 The Size of the Share (Percentages)

Profits. The UPA has a simple default rule on the size of each partner's profit share. Absent a contrary agreement, each partner receives an equal share.[6] The rule applies regardless of how much individual partners have contributed to the partnership and regardless of how much individual partners work for the partnership.

> ***Example:*** Larry, Moe, and Curley form a partnership to manufacture and sell whoopee cushions. To get the business started, Larry and Curley each contribute $10,000. They each work in the factory 60 hours per week. Moe, in contrast, contributes $0 and works 20 hours per week "closing big deals." Despite these differing contributions and efforts, the partners share profits equally (i.e., a third each). Absent a contrary agreement the default rule applies.

---

2. As explained in section 7.1.2, default rules apply except to the extent the partners have agreed otherwise.

3. UPA §18 contains most of the default rules relevant to this chapter. When a partnership comes to an end, other financial aspects surface and other UPA provisions become relevant. Chapter Eleven discusses those aspects and provisions in detail.

4. As discussed in detail in section 8.6, a partner contributes property to the partnership by transferring ownership of the property to the partnership.

5. See section 8.4.

6. UPA §18(a).

Losses. Absent a contrary agreement, partners share losses in the same percentage as they share profits. UPA §18(a) states: "Each partner . . . must contribute towards the losses . . . sustained by the partnership according to his share in the profits." If there is no inter se agreement addressing profits or losses, then — because the default rule on profits provides for equal profit sharing — the partners will share losses equally. If a partnership agreement establishes profit-sharing percentages but neglects to address loss sharing, the loss sharing percentages will mirror the profit-sharing percentages.

> ***Example:*** Larry, Moe, and Curley form a whoopee cushion partnership. The partnership agreement gives Moe a 60 percent share of profits and Larry and Curley each a 20 percent share. The agreement does not mention losses. If the partnership suffers losses, the partners will share the losses 60/20/20. Because the default rule applies, the loss shares match the profit shares.

No impact on third party claims. Loss sharing arrangements *among* partners do not affect the personal liability of each partner to creditors. Regardless of the inter se situation, each partner is either jointly liable or jointly and severally liable for each partnership debt.[7]

Inter se arrangements can, however, affect what happens if a creditor does succeed in collecting a partnership debt from an individual partner. If the partnership lacks the funds to indemnify that partner,[8] then the inter se arrangements will determine how much each of the other partners must compensate the partner who took the hit.

> ***Example:*** The Larry-Moe-Curley partnership goes out of business. A creditor of the partnership subsequently collects from Curley a $21,000 debt owed to the creditor by the partnership. The partnership has no funds to reimburse Curley. The partners had agreed to share losses equally. Curley has a right to collect $7,000 each from Larry and Moe.

§8.3.2 Timing

Determining when profits are paid. The UPA's default provision on profit sharing does not specify how often profits are to be calculated and distributed. The provision can be read to suggest that a partnership must repay the value of all contributions and discharge all liabilities before it pays out any profit:

---

7. UPA rules governing relationships with outsiders cannot be changed by agreements among partners. See section 7.3.1 (relationship between partners' liability to third parties and partners' inter se loss sharing).

8. See section 8.4.

"Each partner shall be repaid his contributions . . . and share equally in the profits and surplus remaining *after* all liabilities . . . are satisfied. . . ."[9]

In practice, however, such an approach would be extremely unusual. Partnerships typically repay contributions only when a partner withdraws from the partnership or when the partnership business comes to an end.[10] Profits, in contrast, are typically recognized and distributed on an annual basis.[11]

This annual approach is sometimes by express agreement and sometimes by custom. Likewise by agreement or by custom, partners in many partnerships make "draws" throughout the year against their anticipated annual profit share. Under most such arrangements, matters are evened up at year's end. If a partner has overdrawn, the partner must repay the excess. If a partner has drawn too little, the partner may then withdraw the remainder.

Annual reconciliation is not mandatory. For example, a partnership agreement can appoint a later time for the "evening up" process or provide that overdraws simply be subtracted from the value of any contributions the partner has made to the partnership.[12] Likewise, a partnership agreement could allow partners to leave in some or all of their profit share and have that amount treated as if the partners had contributed it back to the partnership.[13]

Determining when losses are "shared." The UPA does not specify the timing of loss sharing. Typically the partnership's books keep track of loss allocations, and the recorded losses affect what each partner receives when the partnership comes to an end.[14]

§8.4 A Partner's Right to Indemnity

UPA §18(b) states, as a default rule, that:

> The partnership must indemnify every partner in respect of payments made and personal liabilities reasonably incurred by him in the ordi-

9. UPA §18(a) (emphasis added).

10. See Chapter Eleven.

11. The typical approach is consonant with tax law requirements. Although a partnership pays no tax, it must annually provide each partner a "K-1" form. This form indicates each partner's share of profits or losses from the past tax year.

12. See section 8.6.3 (contributions) and section 11.4.3 (capital accounts).

13. Profit draws are thus quite different than salary and wages. Salary and wages reflect a definite commitment by the partnership to pay a fixed amount, regardless of how much profit (if any) the partnership makes. Absent a contrary agreement, no partner has a right to wages or salary for work done for the partnership. See section 8.5.

14. Section 11.4.3 explains both the recordkeeping process and the eventual effect of the allocated losses.

> nary and proper conduct of its business, or for the preservation of its business or property.

This rule closely resembles an agent's right of indemnity from its principal.[15]

> ***Example:*** In the Larry, Moe, and Curley whoopee cushion partnership, all partners share in the marketing work. A potential customer comes to town to discuss the possibility of placing a large order. Moe spends $300 wining and dining the customer, but the customer decides against placing the order. The partnership must reimburse Moe. His efforts were reasonable in light of the shared marketing responsibilities, and the amount of expense was reasonable in light of the potentially large order.

> ***Example:*** Same situation, except the partners have agreed that Larry alone will handle marketing efforts and sales promotion.[16] That agreement means that Moe's wining and dining expenses have not been "reasonably incurred." He is therefore not entitled to reimbursement.

§8.5 Remuneration for Labor Provided by Partners to the Partnership

If partners spend time and effort furthering the partnership's business, what compensation do they receive? Under UPA §18(f), the default rule is simple. Absent a contrary agreement — be it express or implied — they receive nothing beyond their share in the profits: no wages, no salary, no extra compensation of any kind.[17]

> ***Example:*** Larry, Moe, and Curley form a partnership to manufacture and sell whoopee cushions. They agree to share profits equally. To get the business started they each contribute $5,000 to the partnership. Larry and Curley each work in the factory 60 hours per week. Moe works 20 hours per week "closing big deals." Larry and Curley contend that they should get "something extra" for working more. They are incorrect, unless they can show either an express or implied agreement.

15. See section 4.3.1.

16. For the enforceability of such agreements inter se the partners, see Chapter Nine. For the effect of such agreements on the *power* of partners to bind the partnership to third parties, see Chapter Ten.

17. This rule has one exception. If the partnership comes to an end and a sole surviving partner winds up the partnership's affairs, that partner is entitled to reasonable compensation for the winding up efforts. UPA §18(f).

Although in concept the mechanism for determining whether a partner has a right to additional compensation is clear-cut, in practice fact disputes about alleged implied or oral agreements can be quite intense.

§8.6 Remuneration for Capital Provided by Partners to the Partnership

§8.6.1 Overview

Providing capital may be some or all of what a partner brings to the table when forming or entering a partnership.[18] The UPA default rules on remunerating partners for capital are far more complicated than the rules for remunerating partners for labor because partners can provide capital to the partnership in three different ways:

- They may *contribute* property, transferring their ownership interest in the property to the partnership.
- They may *furnish* property, providing the partnership only the use of the property for either the duration of the partnership or some other period of time, retaining title to the property and receiving no remuneration beyond a share in the profits.
- They may *lease* or *loan* the property, providing the partnership the use of the property for either the duration of the partnership or some other period of time, retaining title to the property and receiving rent, interest, or royalties as compensation.

The property involved can be any property — real or personal, tangible or intangible — in which the partner holds an interest.

> ***Example:*** Larry, Moe, and Curley form a partnership. Larry *contributes* \$10,000 in cash. Moe has a right under a lease to occupy certain business premises, and he *furnishes* those premises to the partnership. Curley *leases* his truck to the partnership.

The remuneration rules vary depending on the mode a partner has used to provide capital.

18. Absent a contrary agreement, a partnership cannot compel those already partners to provide *additional* capital.

§8.6.2 Distinguishing the Modes of Providing Capital

In general.[19] The UPA contains no rules for distinguishing the modes of providing capital.[20] The rules come from the case law, which is plentiful. Whether a partner has leased, loaned, furnished, or contributed property to a partnership depends on the intent of the parties, that is, of the partner providing the property and the partnership. Intent is a question of fact, to be determined objectively from the parties' manifestations. Express agreements provide the clearest manifestation.

In the absence of an express agreement, a court is unlikely to find a lease or a loan unless the partnership has in fact made payments that can be fairly construed as rent, interest, or royalties. As for distinguishing *contributed* property (ownership transfers to the partnership) from merely *furnished* property (partner retains ownership), the following factors indicate *contribution*:

- the use of the property in the partnership business, especially if the property is crucial or central to that business;
- the use of partnership funds in improving, maintaining, insuring, or paying taxes on the property;
- indications in the partnership's books that the property belongs to the partnership; and
- nonreceipt of rent or other compensation by the partner who provided the property.

Why title is not dispositive. The factors just listed do not include the partnership holding formal legal title to the property. There are at least two reasons. First, only real property and a few forms of personal property (e.g., motor vehicles, stocks) even *have* record title. Second, in many states, prior to the enactment of the UPA a partnership could not hold title to real property in the partnership's name.[21] It was therefore common for individual partners, or for partners jointly, to hold title to real estate that in a functional and equitable sense belonged to the partnership. As a result of custom and inertia, such arrangements continue even under the UPA.

---

19. This section is drawn from Kleinberger & Wrigley, Who Owns the Christmas Trees? The Disposition of Property Used by a Partnership, 39 Kansas L. Rev. 245, 256-57 (1991).

20. UPA §8(2) does provide a rule for characterizing property purchased with partnership funds. "Unless the contrary intention appears, property acquired with partnership funds is partnership property."

21. This disability reflected the aggregate approach to partnerships. See section 7.2.7.

§8.6.3 Remuneration Rules for Property Provided to the Partnership

Each remuneration rule has two aspects: (i) what compensation, if any, the partner receives for providing property to the partnership, and (ii) whether the partner ever receives back the property provided. Inherent in the second question are two more questions: (i) if the property depreciates while being used by the partnership, who bears the loss? (ii) if the property appreciates, who takes the gain?

For property leased or loaned. A partner who leases or loans property to the partnership receives compensation according to the terms of whatever agreement establishes the lease or loan. When the lease or loan period ends, the property returns to the partner. Absent a contrary agreement, if the value of the property has decreased (for reasons other than abuse) or increased during the loan/lease period, that detriment or benefit belongs to the partner who owns the property.

> ***Example:*** A partner leases to the partnership several new pieces of construction equipment, and the partnership agrees to pay rent of $5,000 per month. After five years, the partnership comes to an end and the lease terminates. The partner regains the right to possess, use, and dispose of the equipment. Although the equipment is now far less valuable than it was originally, the partnership is not obliged to compensate the lessor/partner for the decrease.[22] Absent a contrary agreement, the risk of diminishing value stays on the party who owns the leased property.

For property merely furnished. A partner who merely furnishes property to the partnership receives no compensation beyond a share in the profits; allowing the partnership to use the property is part of what the partner brings to the party in return for that profit share. When the partnership ends, the property returns to the partner who furnished it. Absent a contrary agreement, if the value of the property has decreased (for reasons other than abuse) or increased, that detriment or benefit belongs to the partner who owns the property.

> ***Example:*** A partner furnishes to the partnership the royalty-free use of a patent. After five years the partnership dissolves, and the partner regains full rights in the patent. In that five years, the patent has become more valuable because a major competitive product has been discon-

22. Of course, if the lessor/partner has figured the lease payments rationally, those payments will have taken the depreciation into account. Nonetheless, as a formal matter the risk of depreciation stays with the owner.

tinued as unsafe. The partnership has no right to share in that increased value. Absent a contrary agreement, the benefits of increasing value stay with the party who owns the property.

For property contributed. A partner who contributes property to the partnership receives no on-going compensation beyond a share in the profits — no lease payments, no royalties, no interest.[23] However, when the partnership comes to an end, the partnership owes the contributor the ***value*** of the contribution, measured as of the time contribution occurred.[24] In a well-run partnership the partners specify that value by agreement. Otherwise, if a dispute occurs, valuation becomes a question of fact.

Absent a contrary agreement, the contributor has no right to the return of the property itself. If after contribution the property has decreased or increased in value, that detriment or benefit belongs to the partnership.[25]

> ***Example:*** To help the Larry-Moe-Curley partnership get started making whoopee cushions, Moe contributes equipment worth at the time $500,000. A year later the equipment breaks down and becomes worthless. When the partnership later comes to an end, the partnership owes Moe $500,000.

> ***Example:*** Larry contributes to the partnership land worth $400,000. The land appreciates during the partnership's existence and is worth $1,000,000 when the partnership comes to an end. Larry has no right to the return of the land; it belongs to the partnership. Larry does have a right to the return of the original value of his contribution, that is, $400,000. The $600,000 in appreciation belongs to the partnership.[26]

§8.7 Special Problems with K-and-L Partnerships

§8.7.1 *K-and-L Partnerships Described*

A partner may "buy into" a partnership by providing or promising to provide capital, labor, or both. There is no requirement, however, that each partner

---

23. UPA §18(d).

24. There may be other facts which create debits or offsets against this amount. See section 11.4.3.

25. To keep track of their financial rights and obligations, partners use a device called "capital accounts." Although the term may seem frightening to those unfamiliar (or phobic about) accounting, it merely labels a set of conventional rules for tracking what is due each partner from the partnership and vice versa. Section 11.4.3 explains capital accounts in more details and illustrates their function.

26. Larry may receive some of the $600,000 as shared profits. See section 11.4.3.

provide both capital and labor. In some partnerships one partner provides all the capital (the *K* partner) and another partner provides all the labor (the *L* partner).[27] In the context of such K-and-L partnerships, courts occasionally have difficulties applying the UPA's default rules on remuneration and loss sharing.

§8.7.2 Problems with Loss Sharing

The UPA's default provisions apply regardless of the inputs the partners provide to "buy into" the partnership. Therefore, if a K-and-L partnership loses money, the *L* partner (i.e., the one who provided only labor) will receive nothing from the partnership (since there will be no profits to share and since UPA §18(f) precludes any other compensation for *L*'s labor). In addition, the *L* partner will have to pay the *K* partner so as to share losses with that partner (since UPA §18(a) provides for loss sharing).[28]

> ***Example:*** Cliff and Lilith form a partnership to run a dating service. They do not make any agreements displacing the remuneration and loss default rules. Lilith provides $250,000 in start-up money and does not work in the business. Cliff works full-time in the business, but contributes no capital. The partnership comes to an end after a year, having lost $250,000. (That is, the partnership manages to pay off all creditors, but then has nothing left over. Since the partnership began with $250,000, the partnership has suffered a $250,000 loss.) For his year of work, Cliff has received nothing. There are no profits, and UPA §18(f) bars any other form of compensation. Lilith appears to have lost $250,000, but the UPA's default rule on loss sharing is in effect. That rule provides that Cliff and Lilith share losses as they would have shared profits; that is, equally. For Cliff's *out-of-pocket* losses to equal Lilith's, $125,000 must make its way from Cliff to Lilith. Cliff will pay $125,000 to the partnership, which will then distribute that amount to Lilith. Both Cliff and Lilith will then have lost $125,000.

This result may appear harsh. After all, without loss sharing Cliff and Lilith appear each to have lost roughly comparable value. They have lost, that is, the value they provided the partnership in return for becoming partners. (The UPA default rules seem to assume that those values are roughly comparable, because under those rules Cliff and Lilith qualified for equal shares

27. In the shorthand used by economists, *K* represents capital and *L* represents labor.

28. Technically, the *L* partner would pay the partnership, which would then distribute the money to the *K* partner. See section 11.4.3.

of the profits.) Accordingly, if Cliff has to transfer $125,000 to Lilith, his loss of value will exceed hers.

Seeking to avoid such apparently harsh results, some courts have held that the *L* partner shares losses only if he or she has expressly agreed to do so. Appearances can mislead, however, and those courts have misunderstood the balance of losses between K-and-L partners. In the example above, Cliff lost whatever value he could have derived from using his labor elsewhere during the partnership's year of operation. Lilith had a parallel loss — whatever income she could have derived from investing the $250,000 elsewhere for a year. In addition, without loss sharing, Lilith also lost the $250,000 itself.

Whether the UPA default rule is unfair to Cliff (or perhaps unfair to Lilith) will depend on how the value of Cliff's forgone labor opportunity compares with the value of Lilith's forgone capital opportunity. If Lilith could have earned 10 percent interest by investing her money elsewhere for a year, and if Cliff's lack of skills and odd personality mean that he could have earned no more than $20,000 in salary in some other position, then even after Cliff pays Lilith $125,000 Lilith will have suffered greater detriment than Cliff. Cliff will have lost $125,000 out-of-pocket, plus the forgone opportunity to earn $20,000 by working elsewhere for the year. Total detriment: $145,000. Lilith will have lost $125,000 out-of-pocket ($250,000 contributed, offset partially by Cliff's $125,000), plus the forgone opportunity to earn $25,000 interest on her capital. Total detriment: $150,000.

In any event, at least in jurisdictions that have adopted the UPA, the express language of UPA §18(a) mandates loss sharing.

§8.7.3 *Problems with Appreciation*

Under the UPA's default remuneration rules, when a partner contributes property to the partnership and that property subsequently increases in value, the partnership — not the partner — benefits.[29] Eventually, when the partnership realizes the appreciation, that value either offsets business losses or adds to profits. To the extent the appreciation adds to profits, all partners share in the benefit according to their respective profit shares. The partner who originally contributed the property has no special claim on the appreciation.

Occasionally, courts dealing with K-and-L partnerships ignore or misunderstand the default rules and allocate all the appreciation to the *K* partner (i.e., the partner who contributed the property). They do so either by miscalculating the amount they award each partner or by returning the appreciated asset itself to the *K* partner.

29. See section 8.6.3.

Example: Cliff and Lilith form a partnership to raise chickens, agreeing to share profits equally. Cliff contributes a small farm worth $50,000. Four years later the partnership comes to an end. By selling all of its assets other than the farm the partnership has enough cash to exactly pay off its debts. During the life of the partnership land values have increased sharply, so the partnership manages to sell the farm for $200,000. How the proceeds are divided will depend on whether the court follows the UPA:

- *Applying the UPA's Default Rules* — The partnership pays $50,000 to Cliff, returning to him the value of his contribution.[30] The remaining $150,000 represents postcontribution appreciation and is therefore profits. Cliff and Lilith each receive half.
- *Overcompensating the* K *Partner* — The partnership either allocates all $200,000 to Cliff or simply transfers ownership of the farm back to him. In either event, Cliff gets the benefit of all the appreciation.

§8.8 Property Interests in Partnership Law

§8.8.1 A Hybrid Set of Concepts

So far this chapter has discussed UPA rules that deal with partners, partnerships, and property in an economic and financial sense. UPA also approaches the matter using formal concepts of property. A partnership can own property of its own, and its partners have specified property interests in the partnership.

§8.8.2 Partnership Property

Reflecting the entity approach,[31] the UPA allows partnerships to own property, and partnerships typically do so. Partnerships acquire ownership of property either by accepting contributions or by purchase. Funds for purchase can come from contributions, from business operations (including the sale of other partnership property), or from loans.

§8.8.3 Partner's Property Rights in the Partnership

According to UPA §24, each partner has three property rights in the partnership: "(1) his rights in specific partnership property, (2) his interest in the

30. Id.

31. See section 7.2.7.

partnership, and (3) his right to participate in the management." This approach borders on the bizarre. As to the first and third rights, the "property" label is quite misleading; the rights relate to management prerogatives, not property interests. Only the second right, the so-called partner's interest, has the direct economic value normally associated with property. However, labelling that interest a property right does nothing to clarify the interest or augment the value.

The partner's interest — the partner's economic rights. A partner's interest consists of a right to share in the profits of the partnership and the right to receive, when the partnership ends, the value of any property contributed to the partnership.[32] Although labelling these rights "property" is not misleading, it is redundant. UPA §18(a) independently establishes that being a partner involves having a right to share in the profits of the business. Likewise, UPA §18(a) provides that "[e]ach partner shall be repaid his contributions."[33]

Management prerogatives disguised as property rights. A partner's property rights include two management prerogatives: (i) the right to use the assets of the partnership in furtherance of the partnership's business (UPA §25); and (ii) the right to participate in the management of the partnership (UPA §24). The "property" label is ill-suited to describe these rights. The key to understanding the UPA approach is therefore to disregard the label and attend instead to the specific content of the rights being described.

The essence of UPA §25 is a fairly straightforward and common sense notion. Absent a contrary agreement each partner has the right to possess and use partnership property for the purposes of the business, but no partner has the right to use partnership property for other purposes. Unfortunately, UPA §25 states this notion in an unnecessarily intricate way. Taking an aggregate approach, the provision describes the right to use business assets for business purposes as "co-tenancy in partnership."

As for a partner's property right in a management role, UPA §24(3) merely superimposes a property label on what UPA §18(e) establishes directly — a partner's "equal rights in the management and conduct of the partnership business."[34]

---

32. UPA §26 (share of profits and surplus).

33. As for a partner's right to receive back the value of its contribution, see section 8.6.3 and section 11.4.3 (describing how UPA §40 implements UPA §18).

34. Sections 9.2, 9.3, 9.4.2, and 9.5.1 discuss UPA §18(e) in detail.

§8.8.4 *Assignability and Creditors Rights*

Assignability. Of all the so-called property rights of a partner, under the UPA's default rules only a partner's economic rights are freely assignable. A partner may not assign to someone else the right to participate in management or the right to use partnership property for partnership purposes, unless an agreement among the partners allows the assignment. Such an agreement may be made in advance and apply generally or may consist merely of consent to a particular assignment.

> ***Example:*** Larry wants to assign his right to receive profits in the Larry-Moe-Curley partnership to the First National Bank. The Bank wants the assignment as security for a loan it is about to make to Larry. The Bank also wants the right to exercise Larry's management rights. The partnership agreement is silent on the subject. To assign the management rights to the Bank, Larry needs the consent of Moe and Curley.

> ***Example:*** The partnership agreement of the Larry-Moe-Curley partnership states that all partners must agree on any purchase whose price exceeds \$10,000. The agreement also provides: "If a partner assigns all of his interest in profits, the partner may also assign to that same assignee the right to vote on proposed purchases whose price exceeds \$10,000." Under that provision, when Larry assigns his profit interest to the First Bank, he may — without further consent from Moe and Curley — also assign the right to vote on purchases in excess of \$10,000.

The UPA's default approach to assignment is consistent with the statute's default approach to adding new partners. To assign management and asset-use rights is tantamount to bringing the assignee into the partnership. Under UPA §27(1) a partner cannot assign a complete partnership interest (and thereby make the assignee effectively a member of the partnership) "in the absence of agreement" with the copartners. Likewise, under UPA §18(g), absent a contrary agreement: "No person can become a member of a partnership without the consent of all the partners."[35]

Agreements among partners can also work to restrict transferability, limiting or eliminating partners' rights to assign their economic interests.

Creditors' rights — the charging order. Creditors seeking to collect on a claim against an individual partner may reach only the partner's economic

35. An assignment of a complete partnership interest would not effectively admit a new partner if the assignee were already a partner. However, UPA §27(1) applies regardless of whether the assignee is already a partner.

rights.[36] The creditors may not attach or levy on the partnership's property, for an individual partner's rights to that property are inalienable without the agreement of the other partners.[37]

To reach a partner's economic rights, the creditor must use a *charging order*, a special device created by UPA §28. The charging order first functions as a type of garnishment. The creditor applies to a court for an order that, if granted, obligates the partnership to pay to the creditor any amounts that would otherwise be paid to the debtor partner.

A charging order also functions as a judgment lien. The other partners can use their own, separate funds to redeem the charged rights, and partnership funds may be used with "the consent of all the partners whose interests are not so charged or sold."[38] If "the circumstances of the case . . . require,"[39] the court may order the charged interest foreclosed and sold. In that event, the economic rights of the debtor partner are sold just like any other property subject to a judgment lien. Any third party has a right to buy the interests, as do the partners individually. The partnership may buy only with the unanimous consent of the partners whose interests have neither been charged nor sold.

> ***Example:*** The Larry-Moe-Curley partnership owns considerable property, including a modern factory and a large inventory of whoopee cushions. Moe personally owes Shemp $500,000, and that amount has been reduced to judgment. Shemp cannot levy against the factory or the inventory, since that property belongs to the partnership. Shemp can, however, obtain a charging order against Moe's economic rights in the partnership. With that order in place, Shemp will receive any distributions the partnership would otherwise make to Moe.

A charging order and any foreclosure and sales relate only to the debtor partner's economic rights. Neither the creditor nor any foreclosure purchaser obtains any rights to participate in the management of the partnership or to possess or use partnership property.

> ***Example:*** Although the Larry-Moe-Curley partnership enjoys good long-term prospects, the business is not currently making any profits. Shep wishes to collect on his judgment now and persuades a court to foreclose the charging order. The charged interest is sold at auction to

---

36. UPA §§28(1), 26.

37. UPA §25(2)(c). Creditors seeking to collect a debt of the partnership can, in contrast, levy on the partnership's property. Id.

38. UPA §28(2)(b).

39. UPA §28(1).

Lucille, who in essence now owns whatever economic interests Moe had as a partner. However, neither the foreclosure nor the sale make Lucille a partner or entitle her to participate in the operation and management of the business.

PROBLEM 70

The partnership agreement of a law firm provides a complicated formula for determining each partner's annual profit share. The formula takes into account billable hours, payments actually received on account of work billed, and work brought into the firm ("rainmaking"). At the end of one year, one partner seeks "a more egalitarian approach" and contends that the UPA requires partners to share profits equally. Is that partner correct?

EXPLANATION

No. UPA §18(a) provides for equal profit shares but only as a default rule. When partners displace the default rule by agreement, the agreement governs.

PROBLEM 71

Paul and Dennis operate a basketball camp as a general partnership. Theirs is a handshake deal, they have no written agreement.

A camper who is hurt at the camp successfully sues the partnership for negligence and recovers a judgment of $250,000. The partnership has no money, and the camper collects the entire amount from Paul. Assuming that the partnership has sustained no other losses but has no money with which to reimburse Paul, how much, if anything, can Paul collect from Dennis? Can Dennis successfully argue that "the losses should lay where they fall"?

EXPLANATION

Dennis owes Paul $125,000. Absent a contrary agreement, partners share losses as they do profits — equally. Collection by a third party does not change how losses are allocated.

PROBLEM 72

In 1983, Larry, Moe, and Curley became partners in an entertainment business. Their partnership agreement set a term of ten years and stated:

> Profits shall be calculated and paid on an annual basis, with the fiscal year being the calendar year. For any profit made in any fiscal year,

> Larry will receive 60%, Moe 25%, and Curley 15%. Losses will be shared as provided in the Uniform Partnership Act.

Each year in the period 1983 through 1987, the partnership broke even. In 1988, the partnership lost $100,000. How should that loss be apportioned?

EXPLANATION

The loss should be apportioned 60/25/15. Under UPA §18(a), absent a contrary agreement losses are apportioned the same way as profits.

PROBLEM 73

Suzanne and Bernard run a dance school as a partnership. The school serves children between the ages of 4 and 14. The highlight of each year is a splendiferous dance recital held at a public auditorium rented by the partnership. Suzanne takes care of the business side of operations, and Bernard has agreed that Suzanne alone has the right to sign checks and make payments for the partnership. Bernard handles the artistic side of the business.

This year disaster threatened the school. On the night of the big recital Bernard arrived at the auditorium and found it locked. After some frantic telephoning he located the auditorium manager who said that she had never received the dance school's rental check. (It had apparently been lost in the mail.) The manager refused to open the auditorium without a check in hand. Suzanne was out of town, so Bernard wrote a personal check for the rental fee. Is Bernard entitled to reimbursement from the partnership, or does his foray into the business side of the partnership disqualify the expense?

EXPLANATION

UPA §18(b) provides for reimbursement for "payments made . . . for the preservation of [the partnership's] business or property." Cancelling or rescheduling the recital at the last minute could have been disastrous for the dance school's business. Therefore, Bernard is entitled to reimbursement.

PROBLEM 74

Rachael and Rebecca go into partnership together to own a natural foods store. They each put up $5,000 and jointly select a store front to rent. During the first year Rebecca is the "silent" partner. She does no work for the business. Rachael, in contrast, works about 50 hours per week in the store, with no vacation. At the end of the year, the partnership has made a profit of $30,000. Rachael proposes a profit split of $20,000 for herself and $10,000 for Rebecca. She explains, "I put in at least 2,500 hours this year, and our lowest paid clerk got $4 per hour. I figure I'm worth at least that. Four times 2,500 is $10,000, leaving another $20,000 which we split equally." Is Rebecca obliged to agree to Rachael's proposal?

Explanation

No. Absent a contrary agreement, Rachael's work in the partnership business brings her no right to extra remuneration.[40] Absent a contrary agreement, the partners split profits equally.[41]

PROBLEM 75

Joseph owns 500 acres of land on which he grows pine trees for harvest and for sale each year at Christmas time. The land is worth $500,000, and land values in the region are increasing steadily. Joseph asks Charles to operate the Christmas tree business for him. In return for Charles' promise to stay for five years, Joseph promises Charles an annual salary of $10,000 plus half the profits.

Assume that (i) Charles makes a number of changes to the land, including harvesting some trees, planting others, and building a few dirt roads; (ii) at all times relevant title to the land is in Joseph's name; and (iii) a court finds that the arrangement between Joseph and Charles constitutes a partnership with a five-year term. At the end of the five years, will Joseph still own the land?

Explanation

The answer depends on whether Joseph has contributed the land to the partnership or merely furnished its use. The land was of central importance to the partnership, and the partnership did (through Charles) make some improvements to the property.

However, it seems unlikely that Joseph intended to give up ownership of the land. In most states, a partnership can own land in its own name, and Joseph never transferred title to the partnership. More importantly, to view the land as contributed is to construe into existence an extraordinary sweetheart deal for Charles. Charles brought to the partnership only his labor, for which he received not only a salary but also a share of profits. At minimum, Joseph furnished the use of land worth $500,000 and contributed any trees that Charles harvested from the land. For that, Joseph received in return less than Charles — merely a profit share.

---

40. UPA §18(f).

41. UPA §18(a).

If Joseph *contributed* the land, then the deal is even sweeter for Charles. The land itself belongs to the partnership; any appreciation will belong to the partnership; and Charles will have a right to half of that appreciation. That deal seems too good to be either true or intended.

PROBLEM 76

This Problem is based on a children's poem by Eugene Field:

> Wynken, Blynken, and Nod one night
>   Sailed off in a wooden shoe —
> Sailed on a river of crystal light,
>   Into a sea of dew.
> "Where are you going, and what do you wish?"
>   The old moon asked the three.
> "We've come to fish for the herring fish
>   That live in this beautiful sea;
>   Nets of silver and gold have we!"
>   Said Wynken,
>   Blynken,
>   And Nod.

Assume that Wynken, Blynken, and Nod are partners. Last year, before the partners divided profits, the "nets of silver and gold" were purchased using some of the revenues generated by the sale of herring fish. Wynken is taking her family fishing and wants to take one third of the nets with her on the outing. Does she have the legal right to do so?

EXPLANATION

No — not without the consent of her fellow partners. The nets belong to the partnership, not to the partners. "Unless the contrary intention appears, property acquired with partnership funds is partnership property."[42] Under UPA §25(2)(a), Wynken has an equal right to possess partnership property but only for partnership purposes. To use partnership property for personal purposes requires the consent of the other partners.

PROBLEM 77

Although the Rachael/Rebecca health food store partnership is doing well enough, Rebecca has fallen on hard times. One of her personal creditors is about to sue her. To avoid that embarrassment, Rebecca persuades the creditor to release the claim in return for "an assignment of all of my rights in the

---

42. UPA §8(2).

partnership I co-own with Rachael." The creditor then approaches Rachael and insists upon a voice in running the health food store. Is Rachael obliged to accede?

Explanation

No. Absent a contrary agreement, Rebecca may assign her economic rights in the partnership but cannot assign her rights to participate in management.[43]

PROBLEM 78

Samuel, Philip, and Sylvia operate a dental supply business as partners. Samuel and Philip are the "outside salesmen," and Sylvia runs the office. Samuel and Philip both do a lot of driving, and every two years, partnership money is used to buy them each a new car. Title to the cars is in the partnership's name, and the partnership pays for the car insurance. However, the price of the each car is reported as profit on Samuel's and Phil's respective K-1 forms. A judgment creditor of Samuel's tries to levy on the car he currently drives. What result?

Explanation

The levy will be successful only if the car is not partnership property. A personal creditor of a partner cannot levy on partnership property.[44]

Several factors suggest that Samuel's car is partnership property. Partnership funds were used to purchase and to insure it. Title is in the partnership's name. Moreover, the car is of central use in the partnership's business.

The question is, however, ultimately one of the partners' intent, and the K-1 forms argue strongly that the car is Samuel's personal property. By treating the price of the car as profit allocated to Samuel, the K-1 form effectively characterized the car as his personal property. It is hard to dismiss that characterization as self-serving or artificial, because (i) it was integrally connected with the way the partners structured their relationship and (ii) it created tax liability for Samuel.[45]

---

43. UPA §27(1).

44. UPA §25(2)(c).

45. See section 7.3.2 (profits allocated to a partner are taxable income for that partner).

RUPA HIGHLIGHTS

RUPA:

- writes into the statute a system of capital accounts, RUPA §401(a)[46]
- suggests even more strongly than the UPA that, in the default mode, profits are not distributed prior to dissolution, RUPA §401(a)(1)
- allows all partners (not just the sole surviving partner) reasonable compensation for winding up the affairs of the partnership, RUPA §401(h)
- provides somewhat more detailed rules for determining whether property used by the partnership or held in the partnership name is in fact partnership property, RUPA §204
- eliminates the "tenancy in partnership" concept, producing the same rules directly through a description of partner management rights, RUPA §401(g), and partner ownership interests, RUPA §§501 and 502
- applies the label "partner's transferable interest" to the assignable, economic aspects of a partner's interest (i.e., the right to share profits and losses, the right to receive distributions), RUPA §502
- makes the charging order available not only to creditors of a partner but also to creditors of the partner's assignee (renamed "transferee"), RUPA §504
- makes clear that the charging order is the exclusive remedy by which the creditor of a partner or a partner's transferee may proceed against the partner's interest in the partnership, RUPA §504(e)[47]

46. The statutory formulation reflects current practices under UPA. See section 11.4.3 for an explanation of capital accounts.

47. Some states have special statutory mechanisms for enforcing family support orders, and Comment 5 to §504 notes that those mechanisms may apply to partnerships.

9

Management Issues and Fiduciary Duties

§9.1 The Panoply of Management Rights

Comanagement is a key attribute of a partnership, and — under the UPA's default rules — each partner has a full panoply of management rights:

- the right to know what is going on in the partnership,
- the right to be involved in conducting the business,
- the right to commit the partnership to third parties,[1]
- the right to participate in decision making, and
- the right to veto certain decisions.

§9.2 The Right to Know

Each partner has a right to obtain from the partnership and from fellow partners full and complete information concerning the partnership and its business. This right rests on four sources. UPA §§19 and 20 provide the most direct authority. UPA §19 states that "every partner shall at all times have access to and may inspect and copy any of [the partnership books]." UPA

1. Just as an agent can have the *power* to bind its principal without having the right to do so, see section 2.1.3, a partner can have the *power* to bind its partnership without having the *authority* to do so. Section 9.4 considers a partner's authority to bind. Chapter Ten considers the power.

§20 states: "Partners shall render on demand true and full information of all things affecting the partnership to any partner. . . ."[2]

UPA §18(e) provides authority by implication. That provision gives each partner an equal right "in the management and conduct of the partnership business," and a partner who lacks information cannot meaningfully manage or conduct business. For the UPA §18(e) right to be meaningful, therefore, it must by implication encompass access to all relevant business information.

The concept of fiduciary duty also provides authority by implication. As discussed below,[3] partners are mutual fiduciaries. Each partner owes fellow partners a duty of loyalty, which includes a duty of candor. If Partner *A* owes Partner *B* a duty of candor, by implication Partner *B* has a right to whatever information Partner *A* is duty bound to provide.

§9.3 The Right to be Involved in the Business

Each partner has the right to be involved in the business: to get his, her, or its[4] hands dirty, to actually take part in the work of the partnership. This right brings no extra compensation, because under the default rule of UPA §18(f) working in the business does not increase a partner's remuneration. The right to participate can, however, be psychologically important. Moreover, working in the business can be a very effective way to keep "in the know."

The right to be involved rests on two provisions of the UPA. UPA §18(e) states the right expressly: "All partners have equal rights in the management and *conduct* of the business."[5] UPA §25(2)(a) buttresses the point with its concept of cotenancy in partnership: Each partner has, as a property right, "an equal right with his partners to possess specific property for partnership purposes."

§9.4 The Right to Bind the Partnership

§9.4.1 The Issue's Significance

A partner's right to bind the partnership is significant in two contexts. First, the right affects the power to bind. When a partner acts with authority (i.e.,

2. In some situations, a partner has an affirmative duty to disclose information to a fellow partner, even without a demand. Section 9.8 discusses those situations.

3. Section 9.8.

4. A partner that is an organization (e.g., a corporation) would take part through its agents.

5. Emphasis added.

with the right to act), the partner's act binds the partnership. However, unauthorized acts may bind the partnership as well. In logical terms, authority is sufficient but not necessary to bind the partnership. See Figure 9-1.

Second, the question of authority is significant inter se the partners. A partner who enters into a transaction without authority risks several negative consequences. If the unauthorized act binds the partnership to the partnership's detriment, the partner will be liable to the partnership for damages. If, to the contrary, the unauthorized act does not bind the partnership, the partner will be liable to the third party for damages.[6]

In addition, a partner who acts without authority ordinarily acts without a right to indemnity. UPA §18(b) provides for indemnification "in respect of payments made and personal liabilities *reasonably* incurred by [a partner] in the ordinary and *proper* conduct of [the partnership's] business."[7] It will rarely be reasonable or proper for a partner to act without authority.[8]

Figure 9-1. Authority to Bind the Partnership Is Sufficient But Not Necessary for the Power to Bind the Partnership

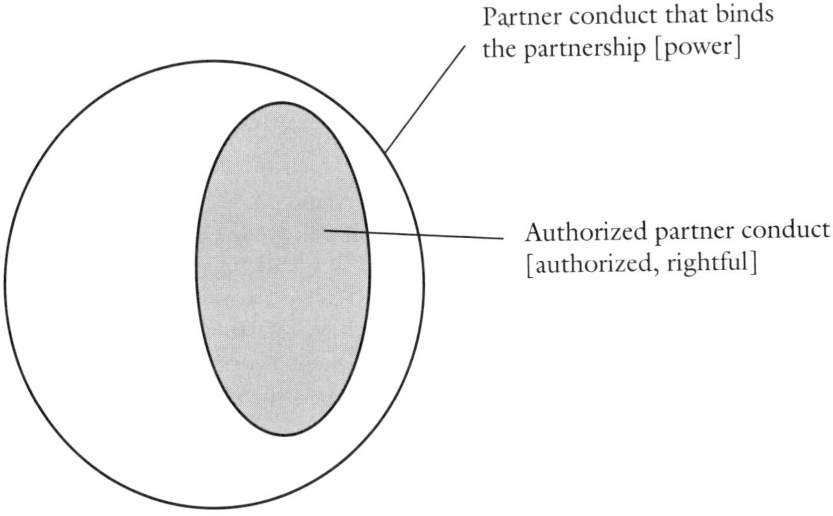

6. If the partner made the commitment while purporting to bind the partnership, the partner would be liable for a breach of the warranty of authority. See 4.2.2. If the partner made the commitment in its own name, without reference to the partnership, the partner would be liable directly on the contract. See section 4.2.1 (agent liable on the contract when principal is undisclosed).

7. Emphasis added. Section 8.4 discusses a partner's right to indemnity.

8. If a partner acts without authority but "reasonably . . . for the preservation of [the partnership's] business or property," indemnification should be available. UPA §18(b).

§9.4.2 Deducing the Extent of Actual Authority

The basic scope. Partners may by agreement define the authority of each partner to bind the partnership, and partnership agreements often do so. Such definition is wise, for the UPA default rules are deficient in this area; they do not directly address the subject. Fortunately, UPA §§9(1), 18(e), 18(b), and 18(h) combine to imply the default scope of each partner's authority.

Although §9(1) deals primarily with a partner's power to bind a partnership, it does contain a clause relating to authority: "Every partner is an agent of the partnership for the purpose of its business. . . ."[9] An agent has implied actual authority to commit its principal to third parties as the agent reasonably believes necessary to achieve the objectives of the agency. In the default mode, therefore, a partner has the authority to make commitments the partner reasonably believes necessary to further the partnership's business.

UPA §§18(e) and 18(b) support this position from a different angle. As a practical matter, at least one partner must have *some* authority to bind the partnership. As a legal matter, UPA §18(e) provides that *all* partners have "equal rights in the management and conduct of the partnership business." Therefore, absent a contrary agreement, *all* partners have *some* authority to bind the partnership.

The extent of that authority is suggested by §18(b). That provision delimits the acts that qualify for indemnification. Presumably the acts that qualify for indemnification are the acts that are authorized, and vice versa. If so, absent a contrary agreement, a partner is authorized to make those commitments "reasonably [made] in the ordinary and proper conduct of [the] partnership's business."

An implied but important limit. A partner's authority to bind the partnership has an important limit. Absent a contrary agreement, no partner has the authority to commit the partnership *when* aware that another partner does or would disagree with the proposed commitment, *until* or *unless* the partnership has voted on the proposed commitment.

This limitation follows from UPA §18(h) and the law of agency. Under UPA §18(h), disputes among partners are to be settled by a vote of the partners.[10] Under agency law, an agent's authority ceases when the agent no longer has reason to believe that the authority exists. Since partnership law mandates a vote on disputed matters, a partner's awareness of a disagreement means that the partner can no longer reasonably believe the authority exists.

9. Under both pre- and post-UPA case law, a partner's agent status is that of a general agent. Restatement §14A, comment *a*. See section 2.5.2 for a definition of a general agent.

10. See section 9.5 for a detailed discussion of UPA §18(h).

Example: Rachael, Sam, and Carolyn form a chicken farming partnership, but the partnership agreement does not specify who may commit the partnership to sell chickens. One day Carolyn overhears Sam discussing a sale of 500 chickens to an established customer. Before Sam can close the deal, Carolyn says, "I don't think we should sell to that customer. They're on the verge of bankruptcy." Sam has no authority to make the deal. He must refer the matter to a vote of the partners.

Example: Sam does have the partners' vote, and he and Rachael vote in favor of continuing to sell to that customer on a "C.O.D." basis. Sam closes the deal with the customer. The next week Carolyn learns that Sam proposes to sell another 1,000 chickens to the customer. She again objects. Since a partner vote has already settled the matter, Sam's awareness of Carolyn's objection does not remove Sam's authority.[11]

§9.5 The Right to Participate in Decision Making and to Veto Some Decisions

§9.5.1 *The Basic Default Structure*

The basic approach. When partners disagree, under the UPA's default rules:

- the partners resolve the disagreement by a vote,[12]
- each partner has one vote, regardless of how much each partner has contributed to the partnership and regardless of how much each partner works in the partnership's business,[13] and
- some disputes are resolved by majority vote, while other actions require unanimity.[14]

Determining what vote is required. Three UPA provisions comprise the default rules for determining the vote required for resolving disagreements among the partners. UPA §§9(3) and 18(g) list particular matters requiring unanimous consent. UPA §18(h) provides a general rule for disagreements not covered by UPA §§9(3) or 18(g).

---

11. These Examples address Sam's *authority* to commit the partnership. For a discussion of a partner's *power* to bind the partnership, see Chapter Ten.

12. UPA §18(e).

13. UPA §18(e).

14. UPA §§18(h) and 9(3).

Particular matters requiring unanimous approval. Under UPA §9(3), unless a partnership agreement provides otherwise, the following actions require unanimous approval:

- assigning the partnership's property in trust to creditors or in return for the assignee's promise to pay the partnership's debts;
- disposing of the good will of the business;
- doing any other act which would make it impossible to carry on the partnership's ordinary business;
- confessing a judgment against the partnership;
- submitting a claim by or against the partnership to arbitration.

UPA §18(g) adds another management decision that requires unanimous consent: "No person can become a member of a partnership without the consent of all the partners."

The general rule of UPA §18(h). For matters not covered by UPA §§9(3) or 18(g), the general rule of §18(h) appears simple enough:

> Any difference arising as to ordinary matters connected with the partnership business may be decided by a majority of the partners; but no act in contravention of any agreement between the partners may be done rightfully without the consent of all the partners.

Example: Rachael, Sam, and Carolyn form a partnership to raise chickens. Each works full-time in the business. Rachael contributes $60,000 in start-up money. Sam contributes $10,000 worth of chickens. Carolyn contributes the use of a small farm, which the partners agree to value at $30,000. Some time later, the partners disagree about where to buy their chicken feed. Rachael wants to buy from Eli's Feed and Stock. Both Sam and Carolyn prefer Rebecca's Ranching Necessities. On this ordinary matter, covered by neither UPA §9(3) nor §18(g), Sam and Carolyn will prevail. Each partner has one vote, UPA §18(e), and a majority vote controls, UPA §18(h).

Example: The Rachael-Sam-Carolyn partnership buys chicken feed from Rebecca's Ranching Necessities. Later a dispute develops over the quality of the feed. Rebecca proposes submitting the dispute to binding arbitration. Sam and Carolyn think arbitration is a good idea, but Rachael objects. Rachael's objection means that none of the partners has the right to agree to the arbitration. Under UPA §9(3) unanimity is necessary.[15]

---

15. As for the power to commit the partnership to binding arbitration, see section 10.2.6.

§9.5.2 *Issues under UPA §18(h)*

The problem of the omitted category. The rule of UPA §18(h) is problematic, because its language omits a category of conduct: matters that are not "ordinary" (i.e., that are highly unusual or significant) but that do not involve "an act in contravention" of a partnership agreement. See Figure 9-2.

> ***Example:*** For five years the Rachael-Sam-Carolyn partnership profitably raises and sells chickens. Then Rachael and Sam decide the partnership should "branch out" into raising cattle. Cattle raising involves significantly different equipment, feed, skills, and contacts than chicken farming and would require the partnership to invest a substantial amount of money in purchasing equipment and stock. Carolyn objects to the change, but nothing in the partnership agreement limits the scope of the partnership's business. The decision on expansion is not "ordinary," but neither would expansion contravene an express provision of the partners' agreement.

The case law has resolved this conundrum by generally holding that extraordinary changes require unanimous consent. Some cases hold that a decision to depart substantially from past practices actually does contravene an agreement, because the past practices imply an agreement among the partners. Other cases pay less homage to the language of §18(h), recognize the omitted category, and establish a rule for it. Noting that a partnership is a

Figure 9-2. How the Set of "Extraordinary" Matters Overlaps Only Partially the Set of "Acts in Contravention"

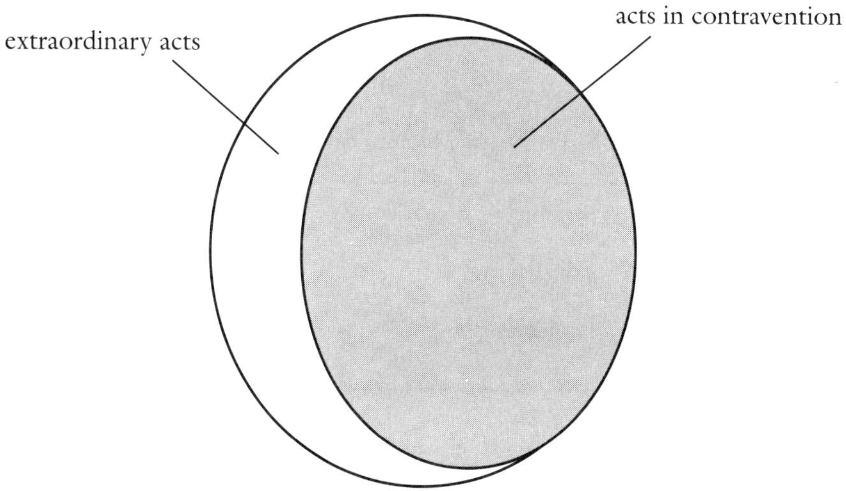

voluntary association and that each partner is *personally* liable for debts arising from the partnership's operations, these cases hold as a matter of policy that each partner must consent to any fundamental change in a partnership or its operations. Figures 9-3 and 9-4 illustrate how the cases resolve the problem of UPA §18(h)'s omitted category.

The boundary between "ordinary" and "extraordinary." The precise boundary between "ordinary" and "extraordinary" is easier to find in a diagram than in actual cases or other real-life situations. A few generalizations are possible, however. Substantial changes to the nature of the partnership's business are likely to require unanimous consent. So too are decisions to increase substantially the size of the business, where that increase requires a significant increase in the liability exposure of each partner. Changes in the standards for admitting new partners or expelling old ones probably also require unanimity.[16]

Figure 9-3. Resolving the Conundrum by Equating Extraordinary Acts with Acts in Contravention

The Universe of Matters on Which Partners Might Disagree

<table>
<tr><td>ordinary

{majority vote}</td><td>acts in contravention [including extraordinary acts, which are deemed to contravene an agreement implied by the ordinary course of events]

{unanimous consent}</td></tr>
</table>

Figure 9-4. Resolving the Conundrum by Stating a Separate Rule for Extraordinary Acts

The Universe of Matters on Which Partners Might Disagree

<table>
<tr><td rowspan="2">ordinary matters

{majority vote}</td><td>acts in contravention

{unanimous consent}</td></tr>
<tr><td>extraordinary acts
{unanimous consent}</td></tr>
</table>

16. For a discussion of partner expulsion, see section 11.6.2.

Example: Robert, Martin, and John have a partnership that invests in real estate. Each partner contributed $50,000 to get the business going, and for the five years of its existence the partnership has invested in properties averaging approximately $100,000 each in value. The partnership agreement does not mention any limit on the size of any single investment. Robert and Martin wish to have the partnership buy a large apartment building that has just come on the market. To buy the building, the partnership will have to assume a $1.2 million mortgage. Although the purchase would not contravene any express provision of the partnership agreement, it would fundamentally change the nature of the partnership business and significantly increase each partner's exposure to personal liability. Most likely, Robert and Martin need John's consent to rightfully make this extraordinary decision.

§9.5.3 *The Special Problem of Defrocking a Partner*

As explained previously,[17] absent a contrary agreement each partner has the authority (i.e., the right vis-à-vis fellow partners) to commit the partnership to third parties. Suppose that the other partners wish to take away that right, that is, they wish to defrock the partner. As between the partners,[18] may they do so by majority vote? Or is unanimous consent necessary?

Defrocking most likely requires unanimous consent. Recall that, absent a contrary agreement, each partner has an equal right to "conduct" the partnership business. Conducting business typically involves making binding commitments to third parties. Therefore, taking away a partner's right to bind the partnership would seem to constitute an extraordinary act. Moreover, if the particular partner has for some time exercised the right to bind, that pattern of conduct may imply an authority-granting agreement. In that event, defrocking would constitute "an act in contravention." Under either view, unanimity is required.

The would-be defrockers are not totally without recourse. If a partner's irresponsible actions are getting the partnership in trouble, the fellow partners may bring the partnership to an end.[19] If the irresponsible actions focus on one particular area of the business or one particular third party, a less drastic

17. Section 9.4.

18. As to whether taking away the right will affect the defrocked partner's power to bind the partnership, see section 10.2.7.

19. In an at-will partnership, any partner may bring on the partnership's end at any time. In a partnership for a term or undertaking, the would-be defrockers could ask a court to end the partnership under UPA §32(1)(c) or (d) (partner conduct that prejudices the partnership; partner conduct that makes it unreasonable to carry on the business with that partner). Bringing the partnership to an end does have disadvantages, however. See Chapter Eleven.

alternative may be available. As a matter of ordinary business operations, the fellow partners may by majority vote deprive all partners of the authority to do business with that particular third party or may oblige all partners to seek approval before committing the partnership in that particular area.

Example: In the Rachael-Sam-Carolyn chicken raising partnership, Rachael and Sam decide that Carolyn is "too soft" when buying chicken feed from Rebecca's Ranching Necessities. By a majority vote, Rachael and Sam can have the partnership decide to stop buying from Rebecca's Ranching Necessities. Carolyn would thereafter lack authority to make further purchases from that vendor.

Example: Carolyn's buying problems arise whenever she makes a major purchase. By a majority vote, Rachael and Sam adopt a rule requiring a vote of all partners before making a purchase for more than $500. Carolyn would thereafter lack authority to make such purchases without prior approval.[20]

§9.5.4 The Special Problem of Management Deadlock

What happens when the partners are in disagreement, a majority vote is necessary to resolve the disagreement, and no majority is possible? This problem arises most often in two person partnerships.

Example: Alice and Ariel have a partnership that operates a grocery store. They have for several years purchased bread from National Bakery. Alice decides that the bread is inferior and the price too high. She wants to find a new supplier. Ariel thinks that both the bread and the price are fine. This is certainly an "ordinary" matter, but neither partner can muster a majority vote.

The cases hold that the partner proposing the change loses. As one authority put it, "[I]f the partners are equally divided, those who forbid a change must have their way."[21] This rule is consistent with the statute, which requires at least a majority to take action in the event of a dispute. How the rule works in practice, however, can depend on how the partners conceptualize the matter in dispute.

---

20. These Examples address Carolyn's *authority* to commit the partnership. For a discussion of a partner's *power* to bind the partnership, see section 10.2.7.

21. Lindley, A Treatise on the Law of Partnership, ch. II, §24-8 at 403 (1924), quoted in Summers v. Dooley, 481 P.2d 318, 321 (Idaho 1971).

Example: Alice and Ariel are meeting to discuss Alice's opposition to buying bread from National Bakery. Ariel says, "What's at issue is your idea that we discontinue using National. I vote no. There's no majority, so you lose." Alice says, "Oh no. You don't understand. What's at issue is where we buy bread this week. You're proposing National. I vote no. There's no majority, so you lose. And there will be no majority until you agree on another supplier."

If the deadlock concerns a substantial matter, the partners can resolve the problem by dissolving the partnership.[22]

§9.6 Agreements That Change Management Rights

§9.6.1 Importance and Ubiquity

The UPA's default management rules are not for everyone. One of the great advantages of the partnership form is its flexibility, and almost every partnership with a formal partnership agreement varies the management rules in some way. Moreover, the course of conduct among partners can imply agreements about management rights.

The following is a nonexclusive list of important areas in which partners often vary the UPA default management rules:[23]

- delegating to one partner or a committee of partners some or all decisions on the conduct of the business
- changing the "one partner/one vote" rule (e.g., weighting each partner's vote proportionally to capital contributed to the partnership, or allocating more votes to partners who work full time in the business)
- changing the unanimous consent requirements (e.g., allowing the admission of new partners on a two-thirds vote of the current partners, or by approval of a management committee)
- requiring super-majority votes for important decisions (e.g., major financial commitments)
- creating a right to expel partners
- requiring partners to seek approval before making certain kinds of commitments on behalf of the partnership
- delegating to a management or executive committee the right to bind the partnership to any significant obligations

---

22. See the discussion supra note 19, and in Chapter Eleven.

23. Partners may also by agreement alter the other default rules, such as the rules on profit sharing, no remuneration for labor. See generally Chapter Eight.

Example: The partnership agreement of Sachs & Harris, a 100-partner law firm, provides for the annual election of a five-partner "Management Committee" and includes the following two provisions:

> *Admission of New Partners:* The Management Committee shall in its sole discretion determine whether to admit any new member to the partnership. A vote of four of the five members of that Committee is necessary to admit a new partner. . . .
>
> *Authority to Advance Costs:* Whenever a partner begins representation on a new matter, that partner will report in writing to the Management Committee whether in that partner's judgment it will be necessary for the firm to advance costs in the matter.[24] If the partner wishes to have authority to advance costs, the report must identify the types of costs to be incurred and state an estimate of the total costs to be advanced prior to final disposition of the matter. The Management Committee will promptly set a maximum amount of costs which may be advanced on the matter and will inform the partner of that authority. No partner has authority to advance any costs except as authorized consistent with this procedure.

Agreements among partners can go very far to change the management structure of a partnership. Beyond even delegating management authority, inter se agreements can even delegate the right to amend the partnership agreement itself.

Example: The partnership agreement of Sachs & Harris contains the following provision:

> *Amendments:* This Partnership Agreement may be amended only upon a majority vote of the members of the Management Committee followed by a 2/3 majority vote of all Partners.

§9.6.2 Limits on Inter Se Agreements

Agreements that restructure management face three constraints. First, although agreements can waive certain fiduciary duties and define others, no agreement among partners can remove totally the fiduciary obligation that partners owe each other.[25] Second, the more fundamental the obligation involved, the more likely is judicial scrutiny. For example, a court will examine

24. Law firms often pay third parties for costs such as court filing fees and transcripts of depositions, and then re-bill the clients for those costs. This practice is known as *advancing costs*.

25. Section 9.8 discusses partners' fiduciary duty, and section 9.9 focuses on agreements which waive, limit, or define fiduciary duty.

carefully any agreed-upon restrictions on a partner's right to information.[26] A restriction is most likely to be upheld if it (i) has some important justification, (ii) is not overbroad, and (iii) does not leave the partners who lack access vulnerable to oppression.

Third, dicta in at least one noted case suggests that partners may have the ***nondelegable*** right to consent to fundamental changes in the partnership agreement.[27] That is, if a proposed amendment will fundamentally alter either the nature of the partnership or the partner's stake in the venture, then:

- even though the partnership agreement purports to allow amendment with less than unanimous consent,
- nonetheless each partner may have to consent to the amendment.[28]

> ***Example:*** The Sachs & Harris Partnership Agreement provides for amendment upon a majority vote of the Executive Committee, coupled with a 2/3 vote of all partners. The Agreement initially provided that any partner could be expelled without cause upon a 4/5 majority vote of the Executive Committee, confirmed by a 2/3 majority vote of all partners. The expelled partner had a right to be "cashed out" of the partnership within 30 days of the expulsion date. An amendment to the Partnership Agreement, adopted by a majority vote of the Executive Committee and a 2/3 vote of the partners, changed the expulsion provision in three important ways: (i) the votes required were reduced to a simple majority of the Executive Committee and the partners, (ii) the partnership was given the right to cash out the expelled partner through installment payments over a two-year period, and (iii) the cash out amount was reduced. If a partner who voted against the change challenged the amendment, a court might hold the amendment invalid. Because the amendment so significantly increased the risks of expulsion for individual partners, perhaps — despite the amendment procedure stated in the Partnership Agreement — each partner had a right to veto the change.

§9.6.3 *Effect of Inter Se Agreements on Third Parties*

In some circumstances partners' inter se management agreements can increase a third party's ability to hold the partnership liable. In other, more restricted circumstances, an inter se agreement can undercut a third-party claim.

---

26. See section 9.2 (partner's right of access to information) and section 9.8.3 (full disclosure).

27. McCallum v. Asbury, 393 P.2d 774 (Or. 1964).

28. Id. *McCallum* has been noted by commentators but not followed by courts. Indeed, a few cases flatly contradict it.

Increasing the third party's ability to hold the partnership liable. If a partnership agreement gives a partner the right to act for the partnership on particular matters, then within that specified scope the partner has actual authority. A partner who acts within actual authority binds the partnership as a matter of agency law. There is no need to rely on any of the special and intricate rules that partnership law contains for binding the partnership to third parties.[29]

Undercutting a third party's claim. Just as a partnership agreement can convey actual authority, so too an agreement can negate authority. If a partner who lacks actual authority purports to bind the partnership to a third party, and that third party knows of the lack of authority, then the partnership is not bound.[30]

§9.7 Management Duties

§9.7.1 Duty to Furnish Services

Does and should a duty exist? As previously discussed,[31] absent a contrary agreement each partner has a right to participate in partnership affairs. Is there also a duty to participate? Is each partner obligated to furnish labor, services, or some other form of effort to the partnership business?

Some, mostly older cases suggest that such a duty exists. The UPA, however, contains no support for the notion, and the case law authority may reflect an antiquated notion of the typical partnership. Perhaps at one time it made sense to imply a duty to provide services, because with only rare exceptions partnerships consisted exclusively of active partners. For a partner to decline to serve, therefore, defeated the reasonable expectations of the copartners.

Today, however, it makes far less sense to imply a duty to serve merely from partner status. While partnerships with exclusively active partners still predominate, passive partners are by no means rare. Of course, partners may by express agreement create a duty to be active, and their behavior in the formation or conduct of the partnership may imply a duty as well.[32] But no duty should be presumed on account of partnership status alone.

Remedies for breach of the duty. A partner who breaches a duty to provide services may be held liable for the cost of hiring someone else to perform

29. Chapter Ten discusses those rules. Of course, if actual authority is not conceded, the cautious lawyer (and law student) will also consider the partnership law rules.

30. UPA §9(4).

31. See section 9.3.

32. For example, it seems reasonable to expect services from a partner who has contributed neither money nor other property to the partnership.

the services or for the reasonable value of the services withheld. If the withheld services are crucial to the business, the copartners may obtain a court order bringing the partnership to an end.[33] In that case, the breaching partner would probably be liable for damages caused by the partnership's premature demise.

§9.7.2 *Duty of Care*

When a partner does work in the partnership business, does the partner have a duty to the partnership to do so carefully? If a partner's mistake damages the partnership, is the partner liable to the partnership for the resulting harm?

Some commentators argue that the answer to these questions should be "no." They assert that partners can adequately protect themselves by carefully choosing and then carefully monitoring their copartners. The weight of authority, however, is to the contrary. Partners have a duty of care, although the duty is less than that of a paid agent.[34] Partners have a duty to avoid gross negligence and wilful misconduct. They are not, however, liable for ordinary mistakes in judgment.

> ***Example:*** Alvin, a partner in a partnership of surgeons, makes a mistake during an operation and is later found to have committed malpractice (i.e., ordinary negligence). Under UPA §13 the partnership is liable to the patient,[35] and the plaintiff chooses to collect from the partnership rather than Alvin personally. The partnership cannot recover from Alvin. Alvin would be liable to the partnership only if the partnership could show that he had been grossly negligent or had engaged in wilful misconduct.

§9.8 Partner's Fiduciary Duty of Loyalty

§9.8.1 *The Beauty, Ubiquity, Influence, and Vagueness of Cardozo's Language*

Partners owe each other a fiduciary duty of loyalty, and the touchstone of analysis in this area is a beautiful passage in Justice Cardozo's opinion in *Meinhard v. Salmon:*[36]

---

33. UPA §32(1)(d) requires a court to dissolve a partnership if "[a] partner wilfully or persistently commits a breach of the partnership agreement, or otherwise so conducts himself in matters relating to the partnership business that it is not reasonably practicable to carry on the business in partnership with him."

34. Paid agents have a duty to exercise ordinary care. See section 4.1.4.

35. See section 10.5.

36. 164 N.E. 545 (N.Y. 1928).

> Joint adventurers, like copartners, owe to one another, while the enterprise continues, the duty of the finest loyalty. Many forms of conduct permissible in a workaday world for those acting at arm's length, are forbidden to those bound by fiduciary ties. A trustee is held to something stricter than the morals of the market place. Not honesty alone, but the punctilio of an honor the most sensitive, is then the standard of behavior.

Although *Meinhard v. Salmon* actually involved a joint venture rather than a partnership, the principle articulated by Cardozo is equally applicable to partnerships.[37] Indeed, Cardozo's beautiful words are probably the most often quoted passage in all of partnership law. They instruct courts to approach partner selfishness with a critical eye.

Beyond that general instruction, however, Cardozo's words are quite vague. It is one thing to say in general, "be your brother's keeper," but how does the principle apply when, for instance, your brother wants to watch the opera, you want to watch the football game, and your house has only one TV and no VCR? What does "the punctilio of an honor the most sensitive" mean when the two partners in an at-will partnership are discussing a change in profit shares because one partner believes she is bringing in most of the business?[38]

The law of partner loyalty can be divided into two categories, and in one of those categories some pretty specific rules augment and define Cardozo's "punctilio." The first category consists of issues relating to the conduct or interests of the partnership's business. In that category partner selfishness is not allowed. The second category consists of issues relating to differences of interests between or among partners. In that category the rules are less stringent and less clear. Section 9.8.2 discusses "partner versus partnership" issues, and section 9.8.3 discusses "partner versus partner" issues. Section 9.9 examines the extent to which partner agreements can change, waive, or eliminate partner fiduciary duties.

§9.8.2 Partner Versus Partnership Fiduciary Duties

In matters relating to partnership affairs, a partner may not profit at the expense — either direct or indirect — of the partnership. In particular, a partner may not:

---

37. As explained in section 7.2.6, in most jurisdictions the law of joint ventures is essentially identical to the law of partnerships.

38. Recall from section 7.2.6 that in an at-will partnership any partner has the right to call an end to the partnership at any time. That right will have an inevitable impact on negotiations between partners.

- compete with the partnership
- take business opportunities from which the partnership might have benefitted or which the partnership might have needed
- use partnership property for personal gain
- engage in conflict-of-interest transactions

Noncompetition. UPA §21(1) contains a very broad noncompete provision:

> Every partner must account to the partnership for any benefit, and hold as trustee for it any profits derived by him without the consent of the other partners from any transaction connected with the formation, conduct, or liquidation of the partnership. . . .

To engage in a competing business is to engage in "transaction[s] connected with the . . . conduct . . . of the partnership."[39] The "account/trustee" language in §21 means that a partner who violates the noncompete rule must disgorge to the partnership any profits made through the violation.

> ***Example:*** Michael is a partner in a company that provides business consulting services throughout the United States. While on a skiing vacation in Colorado, Michael meets Dorothy, who seeks some business advice. Michael at first declines, explaining, "I'm on vacation." He suggests that Dorothy use the services of another partner and offers to call his office and arrange matters. Dorothy, however, insists on Michael's services and offers to pay double his usual charges. Michael finally agrees. He takes a day out of his vacation, provides Dorothy the advice she needs, and pockets a large fee. The fee belongs to the partnership, even though (i) Michael did the work "on his own time," (ii) Michael tried to steer Dorothy to another partner, and (iii) Dorothy insisted on Michael performing the services and rejected Michael's suggestion that she consult with another partner. None of those facts are relevant under UPA §21. The work Michael did was precisely the type of work the partnership does, and Michael's dealings with Dorothy therefore constituted a "transaction connected with the . . . conduct . . . of the partnership." UPA §21. For Michael to retain the fee would be to set himself as a competitor to the partnership.

A partner may escape the noncompete strictures by having the copartners consent. In the default mode, the consent must be unanimous. The law does not require the consent to be in writing, although prudence militates for

---

39. In some circumstances, the competition might relate to formation or liquidation of the partnership.

written evidence. The consent may relate specifically to a particular transaction or may be given in advance with regard to broad categories of transactions. Often, for instance, partnership agreements will authorize partners to engage in competing activities. In any event, the consent is effective only if the partner obtaining the consent has fully disclosed all material information to the copartners. That is, the consent must be informed.

Taking business opportunities. A partner's duty of loyalty also prevents a partner from taking business opportunities from the partnership, unless the copartners consent. Protected opportunities include not only those from which the partnership might have profited but also those which the partnership might have needed. The business opportunity duty somewhat overlaps the noncompetition duty: to compete with the partnership is to seek and take opportunities (i.e., customers) from which the partnership might have benefitted. But the opportunity rule also has independent scope.

> ***Example:*** Alice, a partner in a biotechnology partnership, knows that the partnership is looking to rent new office and laboratory space. She happens to know of a building, in the ideal location, suitable to house the firm's special equipment. She learns that the owner is willing either to lease or to sell. Alice decides that the building would make a fine personal investment, so she buys it for herself. She leases the building to a company that does not compete with the partnership, and later she resells the building at a profit. She must account to the biotechnology partnership for whatever profit she made on the building. Although Alice did not engage in directly competitive activity, the building could have been a fruitful opportunity for the partnership. Under UPA §21, Alice must therefore "hold as trustee . . . any profits derived . . . from [this] transaction connected with the . . . conduct . . . of the partnership."

Like the noncompete duty, the opportunity rule can be waived by copartners' informed consent. In addition, a partner may be able to avoid the default requirement of unanimous consent by presenting the opportunity to the partnership and having the partnership vote on taking the opportunity for itself. Arguably such a decision is an ordinary matter, and a majority vote will control.[40] If the majority rejects the opportunity and a partner then proceeds individually, the partnership will have a difficult time persuading a court to order disgorgement.

Using partnership property for personal gain. UPA §25(2)(a) prohibits a partner from using partnership property for personal purposes without

40. UPA §18(h). See section 9.5.2.

copartner consent, and UPA §21 requires a partner to disgorge any personal gain obtained "without the consent of the other partners . . . from any use by him of [the partnership's] property."

> ***Example:*** Alex is a partner in a landscaping company that works exclusively on commercial projects. On weekends, without the permission of his copartners, Alex uses company equipment to do landscaping at private homes. He must disgorge his profits to the partnership. They result from his use of partnership property.

This rule is subject to a *de minimis* requirement. For example, a partner in an accounting firm who occasionally uses the firm's telephones to talk with a stockbroker will not have to disgorge profits made from stock trading.

Conflict of interest. A partner has a conflict of interest when the partner causes or allows the partnership to do business with:

- the partner itself,
- a closely-related member of the partner's family, or
- an entity in which the partner has a material financial interest.

> ***Example:*** Alice is a partner in a biotechnology partnership that is looking to rent new laboratory space. Alice happens to own a building, in the ideal location, suitable to house the firm's special equipment. If Alice leases or sells the building to the partnership, she will be "on both sides of the deal." She has a conflict of interest.

Transactions like the one just described are often called *self-dealing*. Under §21, self-dealing breaches a partner's duty of loyalty unless the other partners give informed consent.

Remedies. A partner who breaches the fiduciary duty of loyalty must disgorge all profits gained through the disloyal act. It is not necessary for the partnership to prove damages in order to obtain disgorgement. However, if the partnership can prove damages, the partnership may also bring a damage action. In a self-dealing situation, the partnership may rescind any executory portion of a contract tainted with partner conflict-of-interest.[41]

§9.8.3 Differences of Interest Between and Among Partners

According to Cardozo, partners may not use tactics appropriate to "arm's length" transactions in their inter se dealings. But even if partners are never

---

41. For the procedures to be followed in bringing both damage actions and claims for equitable relief, see section 9.10 (action for accounting).

at arm's length, they are nonetheless occasionally on opposite sides of the negotiating table. These occasions come in two categories

- partner-to-partner transactions (when partners engage each other in partnership-related financial transactions), including:
  - — formation of the partnership
  - — renegotiation of profit shares, particularly in an at-will partnership
  - — sale or purchase of a current partner's interest in the partnership
- partners' exercise of discretion vis-à-vis copartners, including:
  - — exercise of a right created by the partnership agreement to expel a partner "without cause"[42]
  - — calling an end to an at-will partnership, when the end disadvantages one partner and advantages another

On any such occasion, one partner's interests will inevitably be adverse to another's. For example, if several partners seek to buy out one of their copartners, that copartner will want as high a buy-out price as possible. The would-be buyers, naturally enough, will want a low price. Similarly, when one partner wishes a higher profit share, any gain must come at the expense of some other partner or partners.

The issues raised by no-cause expulsion and ending an at-will partnership are more complicated. In each situation, the acting partner or partners apparently have absolute discretion. The law appears to entitle them to act for any reason they choose — even if their actions benefit them to the prejudice of copartners.

When partners' interests are potentially or actually adverse, a partner's duty of loyalty requires: (i) full disclosure (which is a well-defined concept) and (ii) "fair dealing" (which is not).

Full disclosure. As explained previously,[43] each partner has a right to information concerning partnership affairs. UPA §19 gives each partner a right of access to the partnership books, and UPA §20 obligates each partner to "render on demand true and full information of all things affecting the partnership to any partner. . . ." A partner who blocks that access or fails to respond "on demand" has breached the duty of loyalty.

---

42. Partnership agreements often authorize a specified majority of partners (or in some agreements a specified majority of a management committee) to expel a partner without having to state or possess "cause." Under such agreements, if the required majority decides that a partner should be out, the partner is out. There is no obligation to prove that the partner did anything wrong. See the more detailed discussion in this section and in section 11.6.2.

43. See section 9.2.

In partner-to-partner transactions. Additional disclosure obligations arise when partners have adverse interests, particularly when partners are buying from or selling to each other interests in the partnership. A partner involved in such a transaction has an affirmative duty to disclose any material information that:

- relates to the value of the partnership interest or the partnership itself, and
- could not be learned by examining the partnership books.

The partner who possesses the information must volunteer it. "You didn't ask" is no excuse.[44]

> ***Example:*** Samantha and Todd are partners in a real estate investment partnership. The partnership has a term of ten years, but after five years Samantha wants to get her money out. Todd offers to buy her out and names what appears to be a reasonable price. Samantha does not know, however, that Todd has received a very good offer on one of the partnership's parcels. Todd does not volunteer the information, and Samantha accepts Todd's offer. Samantha has a claim against Todd. He breached his fiduciary duty by failing to disclose information relating to the value of the partnership which could not be learned by reviewing the partnership's books.

When partners exercise discretion vis-à-vis copartners. When a partner calls an end to an at-will partnership, the general disclosure requirements continue as the partnership comes to an end.[45] When partners expel a copartner, the expelled copartner's right to information may, in contrast, be quite restricted. The same provision of the partnership agreement that authorizes the expulsion may expressly or implicitly deny the expelled partner any right to an explanation for the expulsion.[46]

Fair dealing. "Fair dealing," a far vaguer concept than full disclosure, has two aspects: process and substance. The process aspect concerns the manner in which partners deal with each other. The substance aspect concerns the fairness of the outcome of partner-to-partner dealings.

---

44. The partner's obligation differs substantially from the situation of a party to an arm's length transaction. In an arm's length transaction, a party may not misrepresent information, but — absent some special relationship — the party has no duty to volunteer. Partnership is a special (i.e., fiduciary) relationship.

45. Chapter Eleven discusses in detail the process by which a partnership comes to an end.

46. For a detailed discussion of expulsion, see section 11.6.2.

In partner-to-partner transactions. As a matter of *process*, partners are obliged to deal with each other in a candid, noncoercive manner. They have, as just discussed, a duty of full disclosure. They must also avoid exacting agreements through threats or other forms of intimidation. Conduct which in an arm's-length relationship would *not* amount to actionable duress or procedural unconscionability may suffice to invalidate a transaction between partners.

As a matter of *substance,* the cases speak of a partner's obligation to provide a "fair price" in partner-to-partner transactions. However, almost without exception "unfair price" cases are also "nondisclosure" cases. That is, the partner who agreed to the bad deal did so in the absence of material information that the other partner possessed and failed to disclose. It seems unlikely that a court would use "unfair price" to overturn a partner-to-partner deal if the partner who benefitted from the deal made full disclosure and avoided any abusive negotiating tactics.

In deference to freedom of contract, a partner who complies with the process aspect of "fair dealing" in a partner-to-partner transaction should not have to worry about the substantive aspect. Any *post hoc* attack on the fairness of the outcome should be rejected as "buyer's (or seller's) remorse" or "20/20 hindsight."

When partners exercise discretion vis-à-vis copartners. The process aspect of "fair dealing" has little relevance to a partner's right to end an at-will partnership. To cause the end of the partnership, a partner must manifest *express will.*[47] This manifestation typically involves giving notice to fellow partners, but there is no fiduciary duty to consult with them before making the decision or to hear them out if they object to ending the partnership. Process-fair dealing likewise has little relevance when a partner is expelled under a partnership agreement. Those doing the expelling must comply with any process requirements stated in the agreement, but fiduciary duty does not impose additional requirements. Unless the partnership agreement so provides, fair dealing does not mean "due process," a warning, an opportunity to be heard, or even a statement of reasons. Substance-fair dealing has slightly greater impact in controlling partners' exercise of discretion. Partners may not end an at-will partnership or effect an expulsion for the malicious purpose of depriving a fellow partner of benefits, if:

- the fellow partner had a right to expect the benefits,
- the benefits would have naturally accrued to the fellow partner absent the exercise of discretion, and
- the exercise of discretion transfers the benefits to the partner or partners exercising the discretion.

47. UPA §31(1)(b).

Succeeding with a claim based on this substantive aspect of fair dealing is not easy. The claimant partner must show conduct amounting to expropriation or unjust enrichment.[48]

§9.9 The Impact of Agreements on Partner Fiduciary Duty

§9.9.1 Limits on Agreements

Like other facets of partners' inter se relationships, partner fiduciary duties are subject to contrary agreement. Unlike other inter se facets, however, these duties are not completely default rules. There is a limit to the changes agreements can make.

Unfortunately, the extent of those limits is unclear. Some duties can be completely waived and therefore may also be changed or limited. For example, the duties under UPA §21(1) (prohibiting competition, usurpation of business opportunities, self-dealing, and personal use of partnership property) all give way with "the consent of the other partners." In contrast, attempts to waive process fair dealing in partner-to-partner transactions will likely be ineffective, as will attempts to authorize the expropriating use of discretion. Where the UPA does not expressly authorize a complete waiver, an agreement can at least define if not eliminate the duty at issue.

§9.9.2 Oral and Implied Agreements

There is no legal requirement that waivers of fiduciary duty be in writing, but alleged oral agreements can produce wasteful and expensive "swearing contests." Courts tend to construe oral waivers strictly, because the interests protected by fiduciary duties are so important and partners' fiduciary relations are so fundamental to a partnership.

Courts can infer waivers from the conduct of the partners, but such inferences do not come easily. Courts usually insist on clear and definitive evidence and in particular are reluctant to make too much out of tacit acquiescence to past conduct.

> ***Example:*** Alice, a partner in a biotechnology partnership, knows that the partnership is looking to rent new office and laboratory space. She happens to know of a building, in the ideal location, suitable to house the firm's special equipment. She learns that the owner is willing either

48. For further discussion of this vague and rarely-satisfied standard, see section 11.6.1.

to lease or to sell. Alice decides that the building would make a fine personal investment, so she buys it for herself. Her partners later discover the transaction but make no objection. Two years later, when the partnership is looking for additional laboratory space Alice again buys an opportune location for herself. This time her partners object, and under UPA §21 their objection is valid. Their acquiescence to the first transaction did not waive Alice's duties as to the second transaction.

§9.10 Enforcing Inter Se Obligations: Action for an Accounting

When one partner raises a breach of duty claim against another, the resulting dispute can be exceedingly complicated. Any situation nasty enough to produce litigation is likely to signal the end of the partnership. If so, it may be impossible (or at least extremely difficult) to determine the breach of duty of claim without also settling accounts generally among all the partners.[49]

To keep this complexity within bounds, partnership law provides an equitable action for an accounting. The accounting sorts out the partners' various claims and rights and avoids piecemeal adjudication. An accounting is generally a condition precedent to bringing a claim for damages arising out of the partnership's affairs or business.

Example: The whoopee cushion partnership of Larry, Moe, and Curley has fallen on hard times. Larry accuses Moe of failing to use his best efforts, as promised in the partnership agreement, to secure new clients. Curley claims Larry has taken excessive draws against profits and owes money to the partnership. Moe believes that the partnership owes him $5,000 in reimbursement for customer entertainment expenses. None of the partners can pursue their claims unless their prayer for relief includes an accounting.

Some exceptions do exist to the condition precedent rule, including claims between the partners that do not relate to the partnership business and claims that are so simple that no accounting is necessary.

PROBLEM 79

A 30-partner law firm has a partnership agreement that delegates most management decisions to a five-partner Executive Committee elected annually by

49. Sections 11.4.3-11.4.5 discuss the rules that apply to settle partner accounts when the partnership comes to an end.

all the partners. The partnership agreement states a formula for determining each partner's profit share and allocates to the Executive Committee the exclusive authority to apply the formula and determine the profit shares. The formula allows the Executive Committee some discretion but depends very heavily on objective factors such as billable hours, payments received from clients, and clients brought to the firm.

A partner is dissatisfied with the profit share he received this year and wishes to see the partnership records the Executive Committee used in determining shares for all the partners. The Committee claims that this information "relates to the individual performance of the several partners and is therefore confidential." The Committee offers to show the partner only the records directly relevant to him. The partner accurately points out that the formula requires the Committee to compare the performance of all the partners. He insists on seeing all the relevant records. Who is right?

EXPLANATION

The partner. Under UPA §20, "[p]artners shall render on demand true and full information of all things affecting the partnership to any partner." The partner has made demand, and the records are connected to the fundamental partnership question of profit shares. Given that connection, they certainly contain "information of . . . things affecting the partnership."

The delegation of management authority to the Executive Committee makes no difference to this issue. A partner's right to information can perhaps be waived by agreement, but the agreement must be specific to be effective.[50]

PROBLEM 80

Rachael and Rebecca have a partnership that owns and operates a health food store. For the first three years of the partnership (and the health food) store, Rachael did all the hands-on work — managing both the store and the partnership's books. For the past several weeks Rebecca has been coming into the store and "rolling up my sleeves and getting my hands dirty — really taking part in what we do."

Rachael sees Rebecca's efforts as incompetent and interfering. She wants to return to the good old days, when Rebecca was the silent partner. What are Rachael's options?

---

50. There is a counterargument, based on the delegation of management authority to the Executive Committee. That delegation establishes a system of profit allocation that, arguably at least, requires confidentiality in order to work. When the partners agreed to the delegation of authority, they implicitly agreed to the necessary confidentiality.

Explanation

The law will not allow Rachael to force a return to the status quo ante. Her best option is to approach Rebecca openly, to voice her concerns, and to try to reach a mutually agreeable solution.[51]

Absent a contrary agreement, Rebecca has a right to hands-on involvement. UPA §18(e) gives her "equal rights in the management and conduct of the business," and a court is unlikely to see her past acquiescence to Rachael's management control as a permanent waiver of those equal rights. Moreover, since the facts state no particular term or undertaking for this partnership, the partnership is probably at will. If Rachael pushes Rebecca too hard, Rebecca may simply exercise her right to end the partnership.[52]

Rachael does have some legal arguments, if Rebecca is indeed incompetent. To injure the partnership through gross incompetence is to breach the duty of care. To insist on performing work for which one is incompetent is to place one's own selfish desires above the partnership's welfare. Such selfishness arguably breaches the duty of loyalty.

Rachael's remedies, however, are unattractive. If the partnership is at will, she can call an end to the relationship and seek an accounting for any damages caused by Rebecca. If the partnership is not at will, she can invoke UPA §32(1)(d) and ask a court to end the partnership because Rebecca has "so conduct[ed] [her]self in matters relating to the partnership business that it is not reasonably practicable to carry on the business in partnership with [her.]" Either approach is draconian. Rachael would be better off first trying to talk.

PROBLEM 81

Bernard and Suzanne form a partnership to run a dance school for children ages 4 to 14. Their partnership agreement delegates all artistic control to Bernard, and states that "all business decisions shall be decided by Suzanne in her sole discretion." The school sells ballet and tap shoes to its students, at a very healthy mark-up. Bernard thinks the shoes should be sold at cost. "We make our money from our teaching," he says. "We are not shopkeepers." Does Suzanne have a right to continue to sell at a mark-up, despite Bernard's objections?

Explanation

Yes. Although under UPA §18(h) partners decide "ordinary matters" by majority vote, that provision is a default rule. These partners have agreed to

51. See also UPA §25(2)(a) (each partner has the right to possess partnership property for partnership purposes).

52. Absent a contrary agreement, Rebecca would then be able to force liquidation of the partnership business. See section 11.3.2.

allocate all business decisions to Suzanne. Therefore, on matters such as the price of shoes Bernard no longer has "equal rights in the management and conduct of the partnership business."[53]

PROBLEM 82

Larry, Moe, and Curley form a partnership to operate a whoopee cushion factory. Larry invests $100,000, Moe, $80,000, Curley, $20,000. They agree that (i) each will work full time in the business, (ii) each will receive a salary of $20,000 (separate from whatever profits they may receive), and (iii) none will withdraw their capital for at least three years. They make no other specific agreements.

At the end of the first year of operation, the partnership has a profit (after salaries) of $100,000. Larry and Moe want to distribute profits in proportion to the partners' respective contributions — 50 percent to Larry, 40 percent to Moe, and 10 percent to Curley. They assert that profits are an ordinary part of partnership business and that therefore a majority vote controls. Are they correct?

EXPLANATION

No. UPA §18(a) provides for partners to share profits equally, "subject to any agreement between them." To change the default rule requires unanimous consent, not a mere majority vote.

PROBLEM 83

This Problem is based on a children's poem by Eugene Field:

Wynken, Blynken, and Nod one night
Sailed off in a wooden shoe —
Sailed on a river of crystal light,
Into a sea of dew.
"Where are you going, and what do you wish?"
The old moon asked the three.
"We've come to fish for the herring fish
That live in this beautiful sea;
Nets of silver and gold have we!"
Said Wynken,
Blynken,
And Nod.

53. UPA §18(e). Without the partnership agreement, the partners would be deadlocked. See section 9.5.4.

Assume that Wynken, Blynken, and Nod are partners. Since the inception of the partnership, Wynken, Blynken, and Nod have always given the same answer to the old moon's question. If Wynken and Blynken want to have the partnership take up vegetable farming, and Nod opposes the idea, what result?

Explanation

Absent a contrary agreement, UPA §18(h) governs this type of situation. If the dispute over vegetable farming is an "ordinary matter," then the majority rules and Wynken and Blynken will prevail. If the dispute is in contravention of the partnership agreement (or, arguably, a "nonordinary" matter), taking up vegetable farming will require unanimous consent and Nod will prevail.

The facts suggest that Nod will prevail. The partners' repeated answers to the old moon would support a finding that the ordinary business of the partnership is fishing. Moreover, the same facts could be evidence of an implied-in-fact agreement among the partners that the partnership will confine itself to fishing. In either case, UPA §18(h) would require unanimous agreement to take up vegetable farming.

PROBLEM 84

Oscar is a partner in a partnership formed, in the words of the partnership agreement, "for the purpose of investing in real estate." The agreement contains no other limitation on the scope of the partnership's business. In the five years since its formation, the partnership has invested exclusively in residential real estate located in either Minnesota or Iowa. While on vacation in Hawaii, Oscar comes across an attractive investment opportunity in an office building located there. Without informing his partners or obtaining their consent, Oscar uses his own money and buys the building. Two years later, while the partnership is still in existence, Oscar sells the building and makes a profit of $300,000. When the other partners learn of the transaction they insist that Oscar share the profits with the partnership. Must he?

Explanation

Probably. The profits certainly come from "investing in real estate," and so appear "connected with the . . . conduct of the partnership." Oscar's partners will therefore prevail under UPA §21, unless Oscar can show that the partnership's practice of investing solely in residential real estate impliedly limited the scope of the partnership business.

PROBLEM 85

Same facts as Problem 84, except that:

(1) Two weeks before his trip to Hawaii, Oscar attended a partnership meeting at which the partners reviewed the partnership's then-current finances.
(2) During that review, it was apparent that the partnership had on hand only sufficient funds to meet operating expenses and did not have any cash available to make any further investments.
(3) Before purchasing the Hawaii building, Oscar telephones you, his attorney, and asks "Am I going to be in trouble with that partnership if I buy this building?"

What advice should you give Oscar?

EXPLANATION

Despite the partnership's current "cash poor" situation, the Hawaii building may still be a partnership opportunity. If made aware of the opportunity, the partners may choose to raise the necessary cash by, for example, selling some of the partnership's current holdings or borrowing against those holdings. Oscar's safest course therefore is to disclose the situation to his copartners and either (i) obtain their unanimous consent for him to take the opportunity personally or (ii) obtain a vote of the partners rejecting the opportunity.

If Oscar can obtain unanimous consent, the first approach is better. It has the virtue of certainty. The second approach rests on the argument that (i) a decision to take or reject a business opportunity is an ordinary matter and is therefore subject to a majority vote under UPA §18(h), and (ii) the fact that a partner wishes to take the opportunity individually does not transform the decision into an extraordinary matter requiring unanimous consent.

PROBLEM 86

Same facts as Problem 84, except that:

(1) At a partnership meeting that took place three weeks before the Hawaii trip, the partners rejected by a vote of 3-2 a proposal to invest in an office building in Minneapolis.
(2) One of the partners who voted against the proposal expressed the opinion that the partnership should "stick with residential real estate."

Will these new facts change the outcome of the partnership's disgorgement claim?

Explanation

No. Neither the partnership's decision to reject an opportunity nor one partner's opinion on the subject generally will change the scope of matters "connected with the . . . conduct of the partnership."[54] If that scope does in fact include commercial real estate, then only an amendment to the partnership agreement can put such investments beyond the partnership's reach.

PROBLEM 87

Same facts as Problem 84 except that:

(1) The office building is located in Minneapolis.
(2) Oscar first discovers the building while inspecting several apartment complexes owned by the partnership and while driving in a car owned by the partnership.
(3) The partnership agreement limits investments to residential real estate.

Will these new facts change the outcome of the partners' disgorgement claim?

Explanation

Yes. Oscar will not have to disgorge, even though his investment is tangentially "connected with the . . . conduct . . . of the partnership [and ensues] from . . . use by [Oscar] of its property." UPA §21. Oscar discovered the opportunity while engaged in the partnership's business and while driving the partnership's car. However, a de minimis rule applies to UPA §21. Because the connection is so insubstantial, and because the opportunity is so clearly beyond the partnership's scope, the partnership has no claim.

PROBLEM 88

Same facts as Problem 84, except that:

(1) Instead of making a profit of $300,000, Oscar loses $100,000.
(2) The partnership agreement provides that all investment decisions will be made by majority vote.
(3) The partnership agreement requires all partners to share partnership losses equally.

Can Oscar get any reimbursement from his copartners?

---

54. UPA §21.

EXPLANATION

No. The reach of UPA §18(b), the UPA's indemnification provision, is different than the reach of UPA §21. UPA §18(b) obligates the partnership to "indemnify every partner in respect of payments made and personal liabilities reasonably incurred by him in the ordinary and proper conduct of its business, or for the preservation of its business or property." Oscar's investment satisfies neither condition. He acted outside the "ordinary and proper conduct" of the partnership business (i.e., without the authority of a partner vote) and did not act to preserve partnership "business or property." Oscar therefore must bear his losses alone, even though he might have been obliged to share his profits.

PROBLEM 89

Sweeney & Todd, a large metropolitan law firm, has been growing steadily and now has 50 partners. Plans call for adding another 40 partners over the next five years. Under the current partnership agreement all partners have one vote on all matters, including the annual election of the firm's management committee. Some of the more senior partners wish to give greater control to partners who have been with the firm at least ten years. Is such an arrangement lawful? If so, how might it be accomplished?

EXPLANATION

Such an arrangement is certainly lawful. UPA §18 is a default rule and allows partners to shape their management structure virtually as they see fit. The partnership agreement could, for example, give extra votes to partners who have been with the firm at least ten years. Or, the agreement could create two separate classes of partnership interests, allocate the "senior" interests to partners who have been with the firm at least ten years, and reserve specified management matters to partners holding senior interests.

To establish either structure, the partners would have to amend the partnership agreement. Unless the agreement provides for amendment on a less-than-unanimous basis, all the current partners will have to agree to any change.

PROBLEM 90

In addition to its 50 partners, Sweeney & Todd has 50 associates and 125 other employees. The partnership agreement dates from when the firm had only ten partners and requires unanimous consent for any amendment.

The firm's elected Management Committee wishes to implement a firm sexual harassment policy for dealing with complaints from firm employees.[55] Upon the advice of counsel experienced in employment law, the Committee wishes to implement a policy that provides for confidential investigations of employee complaints and allows the Committee to impose discipline, either confidential or public, on any employee found to have engaged in harassing conduct. (This particular policy will not apply to partners. The Committee hopes soon to propose a policy on that subject.)

The Committee is quite concerned about confidentiality. "Leaks" can discourage employees from making complaints, ruin on-going investigations, and subject the firm to damages for defamation. The Committee wants to make sure that only partners on the Management Committee will have access to information relating to complaints made, determinations reached, and sanctions imposed under the policy.

Are there any partnership law "wrinkles" to the Committee's concern?

EXPLANATION

Yes. UPA §20 may give each partner a right to the information the Committee seeks to protect. Claims of sexual harassment are exceedingly serious, and their proper handling is essential to the welfare of the partnership. Obversely, poor handling of a complaint could imperil both the partnership and the partners.[56] The complaint information is therefore "information of . . . things affecting the partnership" and subject to disclosure to any partner on demand.

Since the partnership agreement can only be amended through unanimous consent, the only solution to this problem is to have each partner waive his or her right to the problematic information.

PROBLEM 91

Same facts as in Problem 90, except that the partnership agreement provides: "This Agreement may be amended at any time upon the vote of 3/5 of the

---

55. Title VII prohibits various types of discrimination in employment, including sex discrimination, which in turn includes sexual harassment. An employer, such as the firm in this Problem, can be liable in damages to an employee if one of the employer's supervisors engages in *quid pro quo harassment* or if the employer allows a *hostile environment* to exist. Quid pro quo harassment occurs when a supervisor seeks to force a subordinate to engage in sexual activities either by offering job-related inducements or threatening job-related penalties. A hostile environment exists when an employer knows or should know that harassment is occurring and fails to take appropriate remedial measures. Whether Title VII applies to protect the firm's *partners* is a complicated question. Individuals who possess the paradigmatic attributes of partner status are not covered by Title VII or by any other statute that seeks to protect "employees." See section 11.6.2.

56. Recall that partners are personally liable for the debts of the partnership. UPA §15. See section 7.3.

members of the Management Committee and the vote or written consent of a majority of all partners." Can Sweeney & Todd protect the complaint information through a nonunanimous amendment of the partnership agreement?

Explanation

Probably. There is some dicta to the effect that, despite agreements to the contrary, all partners must consent to changes that affect their fundamental rights. That dicta should not be problematic here. Although the duty to render information is a core fiduciary duty, the contemplated waiver is limited in scope, is well defined, and will clearly serve the partners' overall interests.

RUPA HIGHLIGHTS

RUPA:

- affirmatively requires the partnership and partners to render to each partner "without demand, any information concerning the partnership's business and affairs reasonably required for the proper exercise of the partner's rights and duties," RUPA §403(c)(1)[57]
- omits UPA §9(3), which contains a list of transactions requiring unanimous consent or actual authority
- fixes the problem of the "omitted category" under UPA §18(h); "An act outside the ordinary course of business" requires unanimous consent, RUPA §401(j)
- explicitly recognizes a duty of care for partners, but that duty "is limited to refraining from engaging in grossly negligent or reckless conduct, intentional misconduct, or a knowing violation of law," RUPA §404(c)
- creates an intricate and complex set of rules on partners' duty of loyalty, including:
  - the duties stated in the statute purport to be exhaustive, RUPA §404(a)
  - a partner's duty to "account for" profits, etc. [UPA §21] no longer includes profits and benefits related to the formation of the partnership, RUPA §404(b)(1)
  - a partner's obligation not to compete ends at dissolution, not termination, RUPA §404(b)(3)
  - a partner must discharge duties and exercise rights in accordance with "the obligation of good faith and fair dealing," RUPA §404(d)[58]
  - a partner does not breach any duty "merely because the partner's conduct furthers the partner's own interest," RUPA §404(e)
- sets certain nonwaivable limits on the power of partners to change their inter se relationship by agreement, including:
  - prohibiting any unreasonable reduction in the duty of care, the elimination of the duty of loyalty, and the elimination of the obligation of good faith and fair dealing, RUPA §103(b)(3)(4) and (5), but

57. Essentially the same duty exists under the UPA as a matter of case law.

58. This obligation is borrowed from Uniform Commercial Code §1-203 ("Every contract or duty within this Act imposes an obligation of good faith in its performance and enforcement.")

- — allowing partners to "authorize or ratify, after full disclosure of all material facts, a specific act or transaction that otherwise would violate the duty of loyalty," RUPA §103(b)(3)(ii),[59] and to "identify [by agreement] specific types or categories of activities that do not violate the duty of loyalty, if not manifestly unreasonable," RUPA §103(b)(3)(i)[60]
- allows partners to bring suit without having to seek an accounting, RUPA §405(b)

59. UPA §21 and its case law provide essentially the same rule.

60. In the scholarly debate over RUPA, considerable controversy has centered around RUPA's provisions on the duty of loyalty and on the relationship between that duty and the partnership agreement.

10

The Power to Bind the Partnership

§10.1 Overview

The UPA uses five major sections[1] to explain how the acts of an individual partner may bind the partnership:

- §9 (Partner Agent of Partnership as to Partnership Business)
- §11 (Partnership Bound by Admission of Partner)
- §12 (Partnership Charged with Knowledge of or Notice to Partner)
- §13 (Partnership Bound by Partner's Wrongful Act)
- §14 (Partnership Bound by Partner's Breach of Trust)

Of these five attribution rules, UPA §9 requires the most attention. It is by far the most difficult to follow because it is intricate and very poorly drafted.[2] It is also the most fundamental. It provides rules for binding the partnership in contract and is therefore the key provision for analyzing most business transactions. Moreover, it provides the conceptual basis for some of

1. UPA §10 (Conveyance of Real Property of the Partnership) contains special rules for transferring real property owned by a partnership. Those rules rest on the more general provisions of UPA §9(1) and relate mostly to the formalities of title transfer.

2. However, once you have mastered UPA §9 you will find the other provisions discussed in this chapter comparatively straightforward.

the other attribution rules. The reach of UPA §11, for instance, depends on how that provision interacts with §9.[3]

§10.2 Binding the Partnership Through a Partner's Consensual Acts (UPA §9)

§10.2.1 *The Paragon of Complexity*

UPA §9 provides:

§9. Partner Agent of Partnership as to Partnership Business

(1) Every partner is an agent of the partnership for the purpose of its business, and the act of every partner, including the execution in the partnership name of any instrument, for apparently carrying on in the usual way the business of the partnership of which he is a member binds the partnership, unless the partner so acting has in fact no authority to act for the partnership in the particular matter, and the person with whom he is dealing has knowledge of the fact that he has no such authority.

(2) An act of a partner which is not apparently for the carrying on of the business of the partnership in the usual way does not bind the partnership unless authorized by the other partners.

(3) Unless authorized by the other partners or unless they have abandoned the business, one or more but less than all the partners have no authority to:

(a) assign the partnership property in trust for creditors or on the assignee's promise to pay the debts of the partnership,

(b) dispose of the good-will of the business,

(c) do any other act which would make it impossible to carry on the ordinary business of a partnership,

(d) confess a judgment,

(e) submit a partnership claim or liability to arbitration or reference.

(4) No act of any partner in contravention of a restriction on authority shall bind the partnership to persons having knowledge of the restriction.

The difficulty in mastering UPA §9 comes from three sources: (1) the section states an extremely intricate set of rules, (2) the section compounds

3. See section 10.3. See also UPA §10 (providing rules for the conveyance of a partnership's real property and repeatedly referring to "the provisions of paragraph (1) of section 9").

the complexity by using language carelessly, and (3) the case law is for the most part superficial and unenlightening.

The intricacy exists because UPA §9 contains multiple rules and those rules run in opposite directions. UPA §9's basic structure reflects an execrable but common tendency of lawyers to write rules in the mode of "two steps forward, but one step back." Asked to define a bagel, for example, a lawyer might say, "A bagel is a disc of baked dough, provided however that, notwithstanding the foregoing, the center of the disc does not contain dough."[4] UPA §9 follows this "cha-cha" approach by providing two rules that establish a partner's power to bind and three rules that confine that power:

- *the "agency law" empowering rule (§9(1), first clause),* which invokes the law of agency, although ultimately to very little effect
- *the "apparently/usual" empowering rule (§9(1), second clause),* which constitutes partnership law's novel contribution to the "power to bind" rubric
- *the "not apparently/usual" constraining rule (§9(2)),* which looks like the "flip side" of the "apparently/usual" empowering rule but which serves to substantially undercut the "agency law" empowering rule
- *the "no authority" constraining rule (§9(1), third and fourth clauses, §9(4)),* which is apparently so important that the UPA states it twice
- *the "unanimous consent" constraining rule (§9(3)),* which is the clearest of all five rules

As for careless use of language, UPA §9 deals sometimes with the power to bind, sometimes with the right to bind, and sometimes with both at once. Worse, the section does not always make clear when it is doing which. As for unenlightening case law, many of the cases apply UPA §9 without much analysis, neglecting important nuances and focusing on individual parts of the rules out of context. It is impossible to construe UPA §9 in a way that reconciles all or even most of the cases.

Some of the case law confusion relates to the role of agency law under UPA §9. The provision's first clause seems to incorporate all of agency law's attribution rules,[5] and many courts invoke those rules uncritically. As a result, many cases fail to consider how, if at all, the rest of UPA §9 constrains the application of agency law rules.

To avoid the same failing, the following analysis begins with the components of UPA §9 that belong exclusively to partnership law.

---

4. A less intricate definition might be "a ring of baked dough."

5. That clause reads: " Every partner is an agent of the partnership for the purpose of its business. . . ." See also UPA §4(3) ("The law of agency shall apply under this act.")

§10.2.2 The "Apparently/Usual" Empowering Rule

The basic rule. The second clause of §9(1) reads in pertinent part: "the act of every partner . . . for apparently carrying on in the usual way the business of the partnership of which he is a member binds the partnership. . . ." A third party claimant who seeks to use this language must that show that:

- at the time of the transaction
- it reasonably[6] appeared to the claimant that the partner's act was:
  — for carrying on the business of the partnership and
  — for doing so "in the usual way."

The apparently/usual rule is generally seen as partnership law's counterpart to apparent authority and, like apparent authority, concerns itself with appearances, reasonably interpreted, rather than reality as it actually exists.[7]

> ***Example:*** Ventura Company is a partnership that trades agricultural commodities, and for many years the Company has traded in tobacco. This year, on personal moral grounds, the partners unanimously decided to stop. Subsequently, however, one of the partners backslides and makes a contract for the partnership to buy 50,000 pounds of tobacco. The apparently/usual power of UPA §9(1) probably binds the partnership to the contract. Although a tobacco contract is no longer "the usual way" for Ventura to do business, the contract likely appeared "usual" to the third party. If so, the partnership is bound.[8]

The apparently/usual rule's focus on appearances gives rise to four questions: (1) Must the partner's act appear "usual" for that particular partnership, or merely for partnerships of the same type? (2) Does the rule apply when the partnership does not appear at all, that is, when the partnership's involvement is undisclosed? (3) Does the rule apply even though both the appearances

6. Although the statute does not mention reasonableness, the case law does.

7. Some cases treat the apparently/usual power as reflecting inherent agency power, but these cases have difficulty making sense of the word "apparently."

8. A company that "trades" commodities buys and sells the right to take delivery of the commodities. Occasionally the company may itself take delivery of an order, but usually the company tries to match each "take delivery" contract with a "make delivery" contract. If the company correctly predicts how prices will move, it matches well and profits. For example, on Monday the company buys from a farmer the right to receive 5,000 bushels of sunflower seeds for $5.79 per bushel. On Wednesday, after a big storm damages crops in sunflower country, the company is able to sell its right to receive those 5,000 bushels for $6.00 per bushel. The company has made a profit of $1,050 (less commissions charged for the buying and selling). If the company predicts poorly, it will lose money.

and the acting partner are deceiving, that is, when the partner purports to act for the partnership but instead takes personally the benefits of the transaction? (4) Are some actions so extraordinary that they can never be apparently/usual? These questions highlight separate sub-issues that may arise when a third party seeks to invoke the "apparently/usual" power of UPA §9(1).

Subissue #1: Whose usual way? The phrase "the usual way" is ambiguous. Possible interpretations vary both as to the proper referent (i.e., the particular partnership or partnerships engaged in similar activities) and as to whether usualness with regard to one referent can be established with evidence relating to the other.

Three plausible intepretations hold that the third party must establish that the partner's act appeared usual *for the particular partnership:*

1. The third party must show that the act appeared usual for the particular partnership, and evidence concerning similar partnerships is irrelevant.
2. The third party must show that the act appeared usual for the particular partnership. Evidence concerning similar partnerships is relevant if that evidence tends to show either what the third party believed about the particular partnership or that the third party's belief about the particular partnership was reasonable.[9] However, the third party cannot rely exclusively on "similar partnership" evidence.
3. The third party must show that the act appeared usual for the particular partnership. However, "similar partnership" evidence is sufficient to create an appearance as to the particular partnership, unless the third party was aware of contrary evidence about the particular partnership.

Two other plausible intepretations hold that the third party must or may establish that the partner's act appeared usual *for similar partnerships:*

4. The third party must show that the act appeared usual for similar partnerships. Evidence concerning the particular partnership is relevant nonetheless, because the particular partnership is an example of a partnership engaged in similar activities.
5. The third party must show that the act appeared usual either for the particular partnership or for similar partnerships. Evidence concerning either is relevant.

---

9. A third party might, for example, testify: "I did not know anything in particular about Ventura Company's trading practices, other than it was a commodities trading firm. I know what customary trading practices are for most such firms, and I assumed that Ventura followed customary practices."

The following Example shows the tension between two of these five possible interpretations.

> ***Example:*** Al, a partner in the Ventura Company, purports to purchase on Ventura's behalf 50,000 bushels of sunflowers from Acme Agriculture. Ventura Company later repudiates the transaction, asserting that Al had no right to commit Ventura to such a large purchase. Acme invokes the apparently/usual power of §9(1) and offers to prove that: partners in commodities trading partnerships often make 50,000 bushel commitments, so therefore at the time of the transaction it appeared to Acme that Al was acting "in the usual way" for partnerships engaged in similar activities. [Interpretation #4.] In contrast, according to Ventura, Acme should instead prove that at the time of the transaction it appeared to Acme that Al was acting "in the usual way" *for the Ventura Company*, and, in proving that appearance Acme should not be able to rely solely on the custom of similar partnerships. [Interpretation #2.]

The case law is divided. Most courts will consider evidence relating to similar partnerships, and some courts will allow third parties to rely exclusively on "similar partnership" evidence.

Subissue #2: The partnership must be apparent. A partner may transact business on behalf of a partnership without disclosing the partnership's existence to the third party. In those circumstances, other attribution rules may bind the partnership to the third party,[10] but the "apparently/usual" power will not. Whatever "the usual way" means, the statute certainly requires that the partner's act appear to be "for . . . carrying on . . . the business of the partnership of which he is a member."

> ***Example:*** Al, a partner in the Ventura Company, buys a computer for the partnership to use in its offices. It is quite usual for Ventura partners to make such purchases, and indeed Ventura partners have previously made such purchases from this seller. However, the seller does not know that Al is a partner in Ventura, and Al does not mention the partnership. Instead, Al signs an installment contract in his own name. The apparently/usual power will not bind the partnership,[11] because the seller cannot satisfy the "appearance" element. The partnership was undisclosed, and the seller could not reasonably have believed that the purchase was connected in some way with the business of a partnership.

---

10. For example, a partner with actual authority may bind the partnership even though the partnership is undisclosed. See section 10.2.4.

11. Other doctrines probably will. See sections 10.2.4 and 10.2.8.

Subissue #3: The partnership need not benefit.[12] Since appearance is what matters, the apparently/usual rule may apply even though the partner's act actually benefits the partner rather than the partnership.[13]

> ***Example:*** Al is a partner in the Ventura Company. Purporting to act for the Company, Al buys a computer on credit from a computer store. Ventura partners have made such purchases from the computer store in the past. This time, however, Al does not deliver the computer to the partnership. Instead, he resells the computer to a friend and pockets the cash. The computer store may nonetheless collect from the Ventura Company. From the perspective of the computer store Al's act in buying the computer was "for apparently carrying on in the usual way the business of the partnership." The partnership is therefore bound.

This interpretation is not universally accepted, but it (i) seems compelled by the language of the statute, (ii) finds support in the case law, and (iii) comports with analogous tenets of apparent authority.[14] Moreover, the interpretation serves basic notions of efficiency and fairness. It is generally easier for members of a partnership to monitor each other than for third parties to inquire deeply into the bona fides of every partner who reasonably appears to be acting for the partnership. If a partner's dishonesty causes loss, that loss should fall on those better positioned to avoid it.

Subissue #4: Acts considered not "apparently/usual." Through the early twentieth century, partnership law used an overarching concept to address the apparently/usual issue — namely, the concept of a "trading" partnership. Trading partnerships were involved in trade; their businesses consisted of buying and selling goods. In contrast, nontrading partnerships sought profits through means then considered less mercantile, such as the provision of services. In the view of many courts, certain commercial acts, such as borrowing money, could be "apparently/usual" for a trading partnership but were quite out of character for a nontrading partnership.

Today, even partnerships of professionals are intensely commercial in their outlook, and the trading/nontrading distinction is obsolete. Lawyers do marketing studies, physicians face a "health care financing system," and architects think about their bottom line. Services providers of all types worry

---

12. The cases and the commentators do not all agree on this point.

13. While the *first* clause of UPA §9(1) empowers a partner to act only "for the purpose of [the partnership's] business," the "apparently/usual" rule contains no such restriction. The first clause of §9(1) is discussed at section 10.2.4.

14. See section 2.3.4 and Problem 7 (apparent authority can bind apparent principal even though apparent agent takes all benefits personally).

about "cash flow," and borrowing money under a line of credit is hardly extraordinary.[15]

The demise of the trading/nontrading distinction leaves the apparently/usual rule without any overarching tool of analysis. The case law does, however, suggest that the following categories of acts are not "apparently/usual" regardless of the type of partnership involved:

- having the partnership guaranty the debts of some other person or entity
- paying or assuming the debt of a partner
- giving away significant partnership property

This list is not exhaustive, nor is each category a per se rule. Ultimately, the apparently/usual issue is always a question of fact.

§10.2.3 The "Flip Side" Constraining Rule: Not "Apparently/Usual" and No Actual Authority

Under UPA §9(2) a partner lacks the power to bind the partnership if:

- the partner is not "authorized by the other partners" (i.e., if the partner lacks actual authority), and
- the partner's act "is not apparently for the carrying on of the business of the partnership in the usual way."

Example: Sara is a partner in Ventura Company. Under the partnership agreement, Sara has no authority to commit Ventura to any trades. Sara makes a purchase of soybeans in her own name from a farmer who is unaware of the partnership's existence. Under UPA §9(2), Sara's act cannot bind Ventura, because (i) the act was not "apparently/usual" and (ii) Sara lacked actual authority.[16]

Although both the "apparently/usual" empowering rule of UPA §9(1) and the "not apparently/usual" constraining rule of UPA §9(2) have a com-

---

15. Under a line of credit, a borrower may borrow as it sees fit (typically from a bank) for the purposes specified in the line of credit agreement, so long as the amount borrowed does not exceed the credit limit stated in the agreement and the customer makes timely payments of the interest required by the agreement.

16. If, however, the partnership later accepts the benefits of the deal, the partnership will be bound to some extent. Acceptance may indicate ratification, which would bind the partnership to the deal itself. Short of ratification, acceptance may oblige the partnership to respond in quantum meruit for the reasonable value of benefits accepted. See section 10.2.8.

mon component, the constraining rule does not follow automatically from the empowering rule. The empowering rule states conditions under which a partner's act binds the partnership, but that rule does not itself foreclose other empowering conditions — UPA §9(2) performs that function. Taken together the two "apparently/usual" rules mean that:

- a partner who has actual authority binds the partnership within the scope of that authority, regardless of what appears to the third party, and
- a partner who lacks actual authority can bind the partnership only by satisfying the "apparently/usual" empowering rule.

§10.2.4 *The Agency Law Empowering Rule*

The first clause of UPA §9(1) states: "Every partner is an agent of the partnership for the purpose of its business. . . ." This clause invokes agency law principles as a separate basis for holding a partnership responsible for the acts of a partner. When a partner acts "for the purpose of [the partnership's] business," the partner *qua* agent may bind the partnership.[17] Thus, even when the "apparently/usual" power does not work, a partnership may still be bound under agency rules unless a UPA §9 constraining rule provides to the contrary.

This section analyzes a partner's *agency* power to bind the partnership, considering in turn a partner's actual authority, apparent authority, and inherent power.

Actual authority. Although in many instances a partner who triggers the "apparently/usual" rule also acts with actual authority, sometimes a partner's authorized act is not "for apparently carrying on in the usual way the business of the partnership." However, the "not apparently/usual" constraining rule specifically excepts authorized acts. A partner who acts with actual authority[18] binds the partnership regardless of appearances.

> ***Example:*** Al is a partner in the Ventura Company and has the actual authority to make equipment purchases for the partnership. Without mentioning the Company, he buys a computer for the Company to use in its offices. He even signs an installment contract in his own name. The partnership is obligated on the contract, even though the "appar-

17. The entity/aggregate debate, see section 7.2.7, sometimes surfaces in this context, with some authorities contending that each partner is an agent for all the other partners. UPA §9(1) takes an express entity approach, referring to the partner's act as binding "the partnership."

18. Section 9.4 discusses the actual authority of a partner.

ently/usual" power does not apply. Agency law attributes Al's act to the partnership, and Al's actual authority defeats the "not apparently/usual" constraining rule of UPA §9(2).

Apparent authority. For apparent authority to exist, a manifestation of the apparent principal must cause a third party to reasonably believe that the apparent agent is authorized to act for the apparent principal. In the partnership context:

- a partner would be the apparent agent,
- the partnership would be the apparent principal, and
- the manifestation would have to be the act of some other partner (or nonpartner agent) attributable to the partnership.[19]

At first glance, apparent authority seems a likely source of a partner's power to bind the partnership. Although in most circumstances a partner's "apparently/usual" power will overlap the partner's apparent authority, in some circumstances apparent authority could extend further.

Example: Al, a partner in the Ventura Company, approaches Acme Agricultural and offers to buy 100,000 bushels of birdseed for the partnership. Acme's Vice President of sales knows from experience that Ventura deals only in commodities suitable for human consumption. The Vice President telephones Beatrice, Ventura's Managing Partner, who says, "It's okay. We've authorized Al to try a few experiments in birdseed. It's not our usual practice, but this trade is okay." Satisfied, the Vice President agrees to Al's offer. Ventura Company later repudiates the deal, and Acme learns that, contrary to Beatrice's assertion, Al had no actual authority. The partnership agreement expressly limits the partnership to trading commodities suitable for human consumption.

Is Ventura Company bound? Al had no actual authority. The Ventura Partnership Agreement expressly limits the company's business to trading in human consumables and prohibits the Managing Partner from authorizing other kinds of trading. Acme cannot invoke Al's "ap-

19. With one limited exception, the partner who is the apparent agent could not provide the manifestation attributable to the partnership. The manifestation must come from the apparent principal, not the apparent agent. See section 2.3.3. For the limited exception, see section 2.3.3 (a genuine agent has the actual authority to accurately describe the scope of its authority; that description is attributable to the principal and can form the basis of apparent authority). Perhaps the mere fact that a partner is a partner constitutes a manifestation from the partnership. By admitting the partner into the partnership, the partnership gives the partner apparent authority by position. See section 2.3.4. If such apparent authority exists, however, it is probably coterminous with the "apparently/usual" power.

parently/usual" power, because it did *not* appear to the Vice President that Al's act was "for apparently carrying on in the usual way the business of the partnership."

A claim of apparent authority seems more promising. By placing Beatrice in the position of Managing Partner, the partnership gave her the apparent authority to describe to third parties the authority of her fellow partners, including Al.[20] Her statement to the Vice President concerning Al's authority was therefore a manifestation attributable to the partnership. From that manifestation Acme (through its agent, the Vice President) reasonably believed that Al was authorized to bind the partnership. Al seems therefore to have had apparent authority, and the partnership should therefore be bound.

Things are, however, not always as they seem, and the analysis cannot end without considering UPA §9(2). That constraining rule states: "An act of a partner which is not apparently for the carrying on of the business of the partnership in the usual way does not bind the partnership unless authorized by the other partners." Since Al's act was *not* "apparently/usual," and since Al had only *apparent* authority, under UPA §9(2) Al's act "does not bind the partnership."

The same analysis will apply in any situation comparable to the Example.[21] Indeed, due to UPA §9(2), an apparently authorized act of a partner which is "not apparently usual" can bind the partnership only if the act is actually authorized as well. Thus, despite its initial promise apparent authority adds nothing substantively to the power of a partner to bind the partnership.[22]

Inherent agency power. Like the concept of apparent authority, at first glance the doctrines of inherent agency power seem a likely source of a partner's power to bind the partnership. Those doctrines include several that

---

20. For a discussion of apparent authority by position, see supra note 19 and section 2.3.4. Beatrice certainly lacked actual authority to give the description she gave, since she could not reasonably have believed that the partnership wished her to incorrectly describe Al's authority.

21. This analysis applies only to the apparent authority of partners. Apparent authority could enable a nonpartner agent (or even a nonpartner who was merely an apparent agent) to bind the partnership.

22. Apparent authority can, however, provide a procedural benefit to a third party claimant, because the UPA §9(2) "constraining rule" appears to state a defense. The partnership therefore has the burden of proof. Assume that (i) a claimant can carry its burden of proof to establish apparent authority but not to establish apparently/usual power, and (ii) the partnership cannot carry its burden of proving "not apparently/usual," that is, the facts on apparently/usual are too close to call. The claimant will not be able to show apparently/usual power but will establish apparent authority. The partnership will be unable to prove its defense (i.e., the "not apparently/usual" constraint). The claimant will therefore prevail on a claim of apparent authority.

extend a general agent's power to bind the principal beyond the scope of the agent's actual authority, and most partners are general agents.[23]

A partner's inherent agency power would be most significant when the partnership is undisclosed. Actual authority may of course exist, but what if the partner acts beyond that authority? Neither apparently/usual power nor apparent authority can exist, because both presuppose that the third party knows of the partnership. Inherent power, in contrast, might apply. According to the Restatement:

> A general agent for an undisclosed principal authorized to conduct transactions subjects his principal to liability for acts done on his account, if usual or necessary in such transactions, although forbidden by the principal to do them.[24]

The impediment here, however, is the same as with apparent authority — namely, UPA §9(2).

Example: In the Rachael-Sam-Carolyn chicken-breeding partnership, each partner has the authority to purchase chickens for the partnership. During a cash flow crunch, however, the partners by a 2-1 vote decide not to buy any chickens for the next 30 days. Two days later, however, Carolyn finds what she considers a "golden opportunity" to purchase 500 chicks, cheap. Without disclosing to the seller that she is a partner, she agrees to buy the chicks.

Is the partnership bound? Actual authority did not exist, because the 2-1 vote on an ordinary matter deprived Carolyn of actual authority to make the purchase. There was no apparently/usual power, because the partnership was undisclosed and therefore Carolyn's act could not have appeared to be "in the usual way" of a partnership. There was no apparent authority, because no partnership manifestation reached the third party.

---

23. According to the Restatement:

> A general agent is an agent authorized to conduct a series of transactions involving a continuity of service. Restatement §3(1). . . .
>
> One who is an integral part of a business organization and does not require fresh authorization for each transaction is a general agent. Comment a to Restatement §3.

As section 9.4 explained, absent a contrary agreement among the partners, each partner has the ongoing authority to enter into transactions on the partnership's behalf. Therefore, absent a contrary agreement, each partner is a general agent of the partnership. See Restatement §14A, comment *a*.

24. Restatement §194. Similar inherent power exists when the principal of the general agent is disclosed. Restatement §161. However, in the partnership context that power probably does not reach any situations other than those already covered by the apparently/usual power.

Inherent agency power seems the seller's only hope for recovering against the partnership. "Although forbidden by the principal [i.e., the partnership]," Carolyn's act was "usual" for the type of transactions she was authorized to conduct as the partnership's general agent.

Unfortunately for the seller (and for all similarly situated claimants), the same constraints that apply to apparent authority claims likewise vitiate claims of inherent agency power. When the partnership's involvement is not disclosed, a partner's act cannot be apparently/usual. According to UPA §9(2), when a partner's act is neither authorized nor apparently/usual, not even inherent agency power can bind the partnership.

In sum, inherent agency power adds nothing to a partner's power to bind the partnership.[25]

§10.2.5 *The "No Authority" Constraining Rule*

UPA §9(4) and the last lines of §9(1) state the same rule. Regardless of the "apparently/usual" empowering rule, the partnership is not bound if (i) the partner acts without actual authority, and (ii) at the time of the act the third party knows of the lack of authority.

Example: To finance its commodities purchases the Ventura Company establishes a $4 million line of credit with the First National Bank. When Ventura applies for the line of credit the Bank asks for and receives a copy of the Partnership Agreement. The Agreement specifies that the signatures of two partners are necessary to commit the partnership to borrow money. Four months later, Al approaches the Bank to arrange a loan outside the line of credit to finance the partnership's purchase of a $10,000 mini-computer. A loan officer approves the loan, and Al signs the loan agreement on behalf of the partnership. The partnership is not bound. Although Al's act may appear "apparently/usual," according to the Ventura Partnership Agreement he lacks the actual authority to borrow the money. Having received a copy of the Partnership Agreement, the bank knows of that lack.[26] According to both §§9(1) and 9(4), therefore, the partnership is not bound.

---

25. Inherent authority does not even provide the "burden of proof" advantage explained supra note 22. If the partnership is undisclosed, the partnership automatically meets its UPA §9(2) burden of showing "not apparently/usual." See section 10.2.7.

26. As for how a bank could "know" something, see sections 2.2.4 and 2.2.8.

§10.2.6 *The "Unanimous Consent" Constraining Rule*

Under UPA §9(3), unless the other partners have abandoned the business, a partner needs either *actual* authority or unanimous consent from copartners to:

(a) assign the partnership property in trust for creditors or on the assignee's promise to pay the debts of the partnership
(b) dispose of the good will of the business
(c) do any other act which would make it impossible to carry on the ordinary business of a partnership
(d) confess a judgment
(e) submit a partnership claim or liability to arbitration or reference

In these specified areas, a partner who lacks the authority to bind the partnership also lacks the power to bind.

If a partner lacks actual authority, the copartners' unanimous consent can remedy the situation. If the consent precedes the partner's act, the consent creates actual authority. If the consent follows the act, the consent amounts to ratification. In either event, the partner's act becomes rightful and can therefore bind the partnership.

> ***Example:*** The Ventura Company, a commodities trading partnership, has a dispute with one of its customers. The customer suggests to Sara, one of Ventura's partners, that the parties settle the dispute through binding arbitration. The Ventura Partnership Agreement makes no mention of arbitration, and the other partners have not authorized Sara to agree to arbitration. Nonetheless, Sara agrees. At this point, regardless of what might appear apparently/usual to the customer, Ventura is not bound. UPA §9(3)(e).
>
> Sara later discusses the matter with her fellow partners and, at her insistence, they all agree to the arbitration. Now the Ventura Company is bound to arbitrate. The partners' unanimous consent ratified Sara's initially unauthorized act.

§10.2.7 *The Problem of "Defrocking" a Partner*

Suppose a partner begins to run amok, committing the partnership in inappropriate transactions. Can the partnership eliminate that partner's *power* to bind the partnership?

The only sure method is to trigger the no-authority constraining rule of UPA §9(4). To securely "defrock" a partner, the partnership must (i) eliminate the partner's *authority* to bind the partnership, and (ii) make sure that potential third parties know of the lack of authority.

Eliminating a partner's authority to bind the partnership is certainly problematic and arguably impossible, unless the partnership agreement provides for such action.[27] Even if the partnership manages to end the authority, disseminating that information can be a daunting task. If the partnership has kept good records, it can notify current and past customers and vendors.[28] But what about the world at large? Unlike other provisions of UPA, §9(4) does not provide for public notice as a substitute for knowledge.[29]

In sum, defrocking a fellow partner of authority is fully effective only against third parties who get the message. Actual authority claims will be cut off regardless, but the apparently/usual power will be unimpaired wherever the message fails to reach. In an extreme situation, the only practical recourse may to be bring the partnership to an end.[30]

§10.2.8 *The Import of the Partnership's Receipt of Benefits*

Under ordinary contract and agency law principles, a partnership's acceptance of benefits from a transaction can bind the partnership to that transaction under theories of ratification,[31] quantum meruit, or unjust enrichment.

§10.3 Binding the Partnership Through Partner Admissions (UPA §11)

§10.3.1 *The Rule*

An admission is (i) a statement by a party to a lawsuit, (ii) made outside of court (and typically before the trial), (iii) which is subsequently recounted in court (by someone who heard the statement),[32] (iv) to be used as evidence against the person who originally made the statement. UPA §11 attributes to the partnership any "admission or representation made by any partner concerning partnership affairs within the scope of his authority as conferred

27. See section 9.5.3.

28. Under UPA §3 notice is not equivalent to knowledge, but a properly sent communication should raise a strong inference that the recipient has actual knowledge.

29. See, e.g., UPA §35(1)(b)(II) providing for advertising the fact of dissolution "in a newspaper of general circulation."

30. See section 9.5.3.

31. See section 2.6.

32. Or, in the case of a written admission, by someone who has read the admission.

by this act" and makes the attributed information admissible in court as "evidence against the partnership."[33]

§10.3.2 *The Reach of the Rule*

The reach of UPA §11 depends on two questions of interpretation, both related to the phrase "within the scope of his authority as conferred by this act." The first question concerns the meaning of the word *authority*. In other UPA contexts, *authority* signifies *actual authority*. Here, the cases and commentaries make clear, the word means *power,* particularly a partner's power to bind the partnership as reflected in UPA §9.[34]

The second question is more difficult and concerns the referent for the problematic phrase as a whole. Does the phrase "within his authority as conferred by this act" refer to "an admission or representation" or to "partnership affairs"?

If the former, then UPA §11:

- is to be interpreted as if it began: "An admission or representation *made* by a partner within the scope of his authority as conferred by this act. . . ."
- applies only if "this act" (i.e., UPA §9) separately recognizes the partner's power to bind the partnership *by making the statement.*
- does *not* apply if the partner lacks the power under UPA §9 to make a binding statement, even if the partner has power to act for the partnership in matters of the type being described in the partner's statement.
- is therefore totally redundant to UPA §9.

Example: Al, a partner in the Ventura Company trades in soybeans and has actual authority to do so. He has, however, no authority to discuss any disputes that may arise from his trades. Under the Company's Partnership Agreement, he must refer any disputes to the Managing Partner. Acme Agricultural is aware of this aspect of Ventura's practices. However, when a dispute arises between Acme and Ventura over one of Al's trades, Acme's Vice President telephones Al and says, "You know that you promised delivery by June 1, not September 1." Al responds, "Yes, I did." Under the construction of UPA §11 just discussed, Acme may not use Al's statement against the Ventura Com-

33. This rule is significant, because it allows litigants to enter out-of-court statements into evidence without having to satisfy the exceedingly complex rule on "hearsay."

34. A partner's *power* to bind the partnership includes both the partner's actual authority, section 10.2.4, and the partner's "apparently/usual" power, section 10.2.2.

pany. The statement was not "within the scope of his authority as conferred by this act." Al lacked actual authority to comment on a disputed trade, and Acme knew of that lack. UPA §9(4). The fact that Al had actual authority to make trades is irrelevant.

UPA §11 has a broader reach if the phrase "within the scope of his authority as conferred by this act" modifies the phrase "partnership affairs." In that case, UPA §11:

- is to be interpreted as if it began: "An admission or representation made by a partner concerning partnership affairs *which are* within the scope of his authority as conferred by this act. . . ."
- applies if under UPA §9 the partner has power to act for the partnership in matters of the type being described in the partner's statement, even if UPA §9 does not empower the partner to make a binding statement concerning that subject matter.[35]
- is not redundant to UPA §9.

Example: In the Example just above, Al's statement ("Yes, I did.") is "within the scope of his authority as conferred by this act." Although Al had neither actual authority nor apparently/usual power to make a binding statement concerning a disputed trade, he had both actual authority and apparently/usual power to make trades. His statement referred to a matter within his power under UPA §9 and is therefore admissible against the partnership under UPA §11.

The cases favor the latter, broader interpretation, as does the Official Comment to §11.[36] As a result, comments made by a partner incidental to any "empowered" transaction bind the partnership. So do comments made after a transaction by a partner with the power to engage in that type of transaction.

Example: The Rachael-Sam-Carolyn chicken-breeding partnership is disputing with Eli's Feed and Stock the amount still outstanding on a chickenfeed bill. Each partner has the power to enter into such transactions, although Carolyn actually placed the order in question. In a discussion with the partnership's bookkeeper, Sam says, "And, oh yes, we still owe $500 to Eli's." UPA §11 applies to Sam's statement.

---

35. If the partner lacks power to act in the matters referred to but somehow has power under §9 to make binding statements, then UPA §9 will likely bind the partnership to the statement.

36. The Comment states: "Admissions . . . concerning a particular matter should bind the partnership only where the partner has authority to act in the particular matter."

§10.3.3 Two Places Where UPA §11 Will Not Reach

Admissions that a partnership exists. An alleged partner's admission that a partnership exists is not admissible against the other alleged partners to prove that the partnership does in fact exist. This rule follows from the language of UPA §11, which refers to statements "made by any partner." To successfully invoke UPA §11, therefore, the third party must first show — at least prima facie[37] and through independent evidence — that a partnership did exist and that the maker of the admission was in fact a partner in that partnership.

Admissions that conduct is ordinary partnership business. As discussed below,[38] determining whether a partner's tortious act was "in the ordinary course of business" can be crucial to determining whether the partnership is vicariously liable for the partner's tort. According to the case law under UPA §11, a third party cannot use a partner's admission to establish "ordinary course."

> *Example:* Carolyn decides that the Rachael-Sam-Carolyn chicken-breeding partnership should consider expanding to raise turkeys. She drives over to a local turkey farm to make some inquiries. On the way back she carelessly runs off the road and injures Farmer Brown's cow. During discovery in Farmer Brown's lawsuit against the partnership, Carolyn says in her deposition, "My trip to the turkey farm was part of the partnership's ordinary business. We're always considering new possibilities." Under UPA §11, Carolyn's statement is not admissible against the partnership to prove "ordinary course." Farmer Brown will have to find some other way to satisfy UPA §13.

§10.4 Binding the Partnership Through Information Possessed by a Partner (UPA §12)

§10.4.1 The Attribution Rules

UPA §12 attributes to the partnership "notice" made to a partner and "knowledge" possessed by a partner. The relevant substantive law determines the significance of any attributed information.

---

37. For an explanation of prima facie, see section 7.4.2, n. 50.
38. See section 10.5.1.

Example: Dorothy buys 500 chickens from the Rachael-Sam-Carolyn chicken-breeding partnership. She later claims damages, asserting that she had a particular purpose in mind, that the partnership knew of that purpose, and that the chickens were not suitable to that purpose. Carolyn did, in fact, know of that purpose. UPA §12 will determine whether Carolyn's knowledge binds the partnership. The law of sales will determine what significance, if any, that attributed knowledge has for Dorothy's claim.

Rule for attributing notice. UPA §12 attributes to the partnership almost any notice properly made to a partner:

> Notice to any partner of any matter relating to partnership affairs . . . operate[s] as notice to . . . the partnership, except in the case of a fraud on the partnership committed by or with the consent of that partner.

UPA §3(2) provides that a party gives "notice" of a fact to a partner (and to any other person) by either:

> (a) stat[ing] the fact to such person, or
> (b) deliver[ing] through the mail, or by other means of communication, a written statement of such fact to such person or to a proper person at his place of business or residence.

For the purposes of UPA §3(2),

- When a party gives notice by delivering a written statement to the intended recipient, it is irrelevant whether the intended recipient actually reads the notice.
- When a party gives notice by making delivery through "a proper person at [the intended recipient's] place of business or residence," it is irrelevant whether that "proper person" actually conveys the written statement to the intended recipient.[39]

For the purposes of UPA §12, subject only to the fraud exception (discussed below),[40] it is irrelevant whether the partner who receives a notice conveys the information to the partnership or to fellow partners.

---

39. An intended recipient who does not receive the statement will likely dispute whether delivery actually occurred and, if so, whether delivery was made to a "proper person."

40. See section 10.4.2.

> ***Example:*** The First Regional Bank has extended a line of credit to the Ventura Company but now wishes to deny the Company any additional borrowing against the credit. The line of credit agreement requires the Bank to give the partnership written notice. When Al, a Ventura partner, comes to the Bank to make a deposit, the Bank manager gives him a written statement about "no further borrowing." Al neglects to read the statement and neglects to inform his fellow partners. The Bank has nonetheless given notice to the partnership. Under UPA §3(2)(b) the bank gave notice to Al by delivering the written statement to him. Under UPA §12 notice to Al is notice to the partnership, regardless of whether Al actually passes the notice on.

Rule for attributing knowledge. The attribution analysis for partner knowledge is more complicated than for notice. The UPA's definition of *knowledge* is clear enough; it is the attribution rule that is complex.

According to UPA §3(1):

> A person has "knowledge" of a fact . . . not only when he has actual knowledge thereof, but also when he has knowledge of such other facts as in the circumstances shows bad faith.

According to UPA §12, the attribution rule varies depending on whether the partner with knowledge is "acting in the particular matter":

> . . . the knowledge of the partner acting in the particular matter, acquired while a partner or then present to his mind, and the knowledge of any other partner who reasonably could and should have communicated it to the acting partner, operate as . . . knowledge of the partnership, except in the case of a fraud on the partnership committed by or with the consent of that partner.

If the partner *is* acting in the matter, the partner's knowledge inescapably binds the partnership. UPA §12 attributes both (i) knowledge "acquired while a partner" and (ii) knowledge acquired earlier if at the time of the action the acting partner still retains the knowledge.[41]

The knowledge of a partner *not* acting in a particular matter binds the partnership only if the partner "reasonably could and should have communicated it to the acting partner." The Official Comment to §12 explains the rationale:

> It seems clear that . . . the partnership should be charged [with the nonacting partner's knowledge] only when the partner having

41. Id. The precise language is: "acquired while a partner or then present to his mind."

> "knowledge" had reason to believe that the fact related to a matter which had some possibility of being the subject of partnership business and then only if he was so situated that he could communicate it to the partner acting in the particular matter before such partner give[s] binding effect to his act.[42]

Example: At a trade show Rebecca happens to meet Sam of the Rachael-Sam-Carolyn chicken-breeding partnership and mentions to him that she "buys supplies for a new regional restaurant chain, Fast Food, Inc." Rebecca is only one of dozens of people Sam meets at the trade show. Moreover, Fast Food's restaurants are far away from the partnership's breeding farm. Sam therefore does not mention Rebecca to his fellow partners.

A month later Rebecca contacts Rachael and commits to buy 5,000 chickens. Although Rebecca is in fact acting as agent for Fast Food, Inc., she does not disclose that fact to Rachael. When Rachael commits the partnership to sell the chickens, Rachael believes that the contract is with Rebecca.

Fast Food later repudiates the contract, and Rebecca so informs Rachael. Acting for the partnership, Rachael insists that Rebecca personally honor the contract. (Rachael correctly asserts that an agent who executes a contract on behalf of an undisclosed principal is personally liable on the contract.[43]) Rebecca responds that the principal was not undisclosed, that Sam knew of her relationship with Fast Food, and that Sam's knowledge binds the partnership.

Rebecca's argument will most likely fail. Sam was not "acting in the particular matter" of the contract, UPA §12, and at the time of contract formation Sam did not have "reason to believe that the fact [of Rebecca's agent status] related to a matter which had some possibility of being the subject of partnership business." UPA §12, Official Comment. Sam's knowledge, therefore, is not attributable to the partnership.

---

42. The rationale here parallels the rationale for attributing to a principal an agent's knowledge concerning a matter within the agent's actual authority while not attributing an apparent agent's knowledge concerning a matter within the apparent agent's apparent authority. In the former situation, the agent has a duty to communicate the information to the principal. In the latter, the apparent agent has no such duty. See sections 2.2.4 (attribution rule for knowledge and actual authority), 2.3.8 (nonattribution rule for knowledge and apparent authority), and 4.1.5 (duty of agent to provide information to its principal).

43. See section 4.2.1 (liability of agent who enters into a contract on behalf of an undisclosed principal).

§10.4.2 *The "Partner Fraud on the Partnership" Exception*

The attribution rules of UPA §12 do not apply "in the case of a fraud on the partnership committed by or with the consent of [the] partner" whose knowledge or receipt of notice is to be attributed. In this context the concept of "fraud" probably includes a breach of the partner's duty of loyalty (sometimes called "equitable fraud"). Fraud blocks the attribution even if the third party was ignorant of the fraud and has no reason to know of it.

> ***Example:*** Seeking to preclude the Ventura Company from additional borrowing against its line of credit, the First Regional Bank delivers a written "no more borrowing" notice to Al, a partner. For some time Al has been borrowing from the line of credit in the partnership's name but for his own personal benefit. Neither the Bank nor the partnership are aware of Al's misconduct. Because Al is committing "a fraud on the partnership," notice to him is not notice to the partnership.

§10.5 Binding the Partnership Through a Partner's Tortious Acts (UPA §13)

§10.5.1 *The Attribution Rule*

UPA §13 states a rule for attributing certain "wrongful" acts or omissions of a partner to the partnership. The provision is often invoked to sue a partnership of professionals for the malpractice of one the partners, or to sue a partnership for damages caused by an auto accident involving a partner. If UPA §13 attributes a partner's act to the partnership, "the partnership is liable therefor to the same extent as the partner so acting or omitting to act." The partnership's liability includes "any penalty . . . incurred." The attribution rule applies both to torts of negligence and intentional torts but does not apply to wrongs by one partner to another.

To be attributable under UPA §13, that is, to bind the partnership, the partner's act or omission must be "wrongful" and must be done or omitted either: (i) "in the ordinary course of the business of the partnership," or (ii) "with the [actual] authority of [the] co-partners."

Wrongful but ordinary? How can an act or omission be wrongful and still be "in the ordinary course" or actually authorized? Whenever a claimant invokes §13, won't the partnership argue that, while the "rightful" version of the partner's conduct may be "ordinary course" or authorized, the wrongful conduct is not? Won't the partnership say, for example, "Yes, it's normal and proper for our partners to describe our products, but it is both extraordinary and unauthorized for them to make misrepresentations when doing so"?

Although superficially attractive, such arguments should fail. The proper question under UPA §13 is not whether the specific *wrongful* act *is* "ordinary course" or authorized, but rather whether that *type* of act, *if done rightfully, would be*. For example, the question is not whether attending a Chamber of Commerce luncheon and then driving negligently back to the office meets the scope requirement, but rather whether attendance and nonnegligent driving would do so. Similarly, the question is not whether a partner's inaccurate disparagement of a competitor's product meets the scope requirement, but rather whether an accurate criticism of the product would be "ordinary course" or authorized.[44]

> ***Example:*** Al, a partner in the Ventura Company, believes that the partnership should branch out and begin importing *paté de fois gras*. The other Ventura partners are not so sure, but they do agree that Al should journey to Paris to investigate possible vendors. While driving to the airport, Al negligently hits another car, causing $10,000 in damages. The partnership is liable under UPA §13. Although Al's trip was not "in the ordinary course of the business of the partnership," he was making the trip "with the authority of his copartners."

> ***Example:*** In the course of discussing a soybean trade with a customer, Al offers to sell (for the partnership) 20,000 bushels "99% free of vermin infestation." Al knows that the soybeans in question actually have a troublesome eight-percent infestation rate. The partnership is legally responsible for Al's misstatement. Since Al's intentional misrepresentation (a wrongful act) occurred "in the ordinary course of the business of the partnership," UPA §13 attributes the misrepresentation and any resulting liability to the Ventura Company partnership.

> ***Example:*** At a cocktail party, a purely social event unrelated to his work, Al is asked, "Are people honest in your business?" He responds, "Some are. Some aren't. For instance, Honest Abe Traders lie every chance they get." Although Al may be personally liable for defamation, that defamation is probably not attributable to the partnership. There is no indication that Al's copartners had authorized him to comment on Honest Abe[45] and no indication that such comments are within the

44. This distinction parallels rules of agency law. See section 2.5.3 (agent has inherent power to bind principal with inaccurate statement if agent has actual authority to make accurate statement on the same subject).

45. There is no indication that Al had express authority, and no suggestion that Al reasonably believed the comment appropriate for furthering the partnership's interests. See section 9.4.

partnership's ordinary course. Al's statement was not connected with any partnership dealings and was neither intended nor likely to further the partnership's interests. Al's allegedly wrongful act occurred, therefore, outside the scope of UPA §13.

§10.5.2 UPA §13 Compared with "Apparently/Usual" Power

The attribution rule of UPA §13 differs from the "apparently/usual" empowering rule of §9(1) in two important respects. First, appearances are irrelevant to UPA §13. What matters are the actual ordinary practices of the partnership business, not what the tort victim believed about those practices. Likewise, copartner authorization under §13 must be actual; apparent authority does not suffice.

This distinction makes sense. The "apparently/usual" rule protects third parties who enter into transactions based on certain appearances. Appearances rarely induce tort victims to subject themselves to harm.[46]

The second distinction concerns wrongfulness. Wrongfulness is irrelevant to the "apparently/usual" rule of UPA §9(1) but is a precondition to liability under UPA §13. That precondition suggests, for instance, that UPA §13 will not attribute strict liability to the partnership.[47]

§10.5.3 UPA §13 Compared to Respondeat Superior

UPA §13 states a rule of vicarious liability, and in that general respect resembles the agency doctrine of respondeat superior:[48] One legal person (the partnership or the master, as the case may be) becomes liable on account of the tortious acts or omissions of another person (the partner or the servant agent), without the claimant needing to establish that the first person is at fault or directly responsible for the claimed harm. All that a claimant need show is:

- that the second person (the partner or the servant agent) incurred tort liability, and
- that the first and second person stand in a particular relationship to each other (partner and a partnership or servant agent and master).

The two rules do, however, differ in one major respect. Under respondeat superior the claimant must show that the master had the right to control the

---

46. But see section 3.3.4 (negligence of apparent servants).

47. In RUPA §305 the phrase "or other actionable conduct" supplements the word "wrongful," so that the attribution rule will apply to "no-fault torts." Official Comment to RUPA §305.

48. For a discussion of respondeat superior, see section 3.2.

means by which the tortfeasor performed his, her, or its functions. Such a showing is crucial to establishing servant status.[49] The partnership rule has no parallel requirement. UPA §13 applies regardless of whether the tortfeasor is the lowliest and most subservient junior partner or the most senior, powerful, and dictatorial managing partner.

§10.6 Binding the Partnership Through a Partner's Breach of Trust (UPA §14)

§10.6.1 *The Attribution Rule*

If a partner misapplies (e.g., steals, converts, loses) a third party's money or other property, UPA §14 attributes the loss to the partnership if either:

- the *partner* received the money or other property while "acting within the scope of his apparent authority," §14(a), or
- the *partnership* received the money or other property "in the course of its business" and the partner misapplies the property "while it is in the custody of the partnership," §14(b).

The second prong of UPA §14's either/or criterion applies to situations in which the partnership and its business are truly connected to the third party's property. The first prong applies to situations in which the partnership and its business merely appear to be involved.

> ***Example:*** Beatrice, the Managing Partner of Ventura Company, tells Ben, "We'll be happy to set up an account for you and execute trades on your behalf. Any one of our trading partners can help you." Later Al, a partner in Ventura Company, contacts Ben and persuades him to set up an account and deposit $10,000 with the firm to be used in trades that Al will have the discretion to make. Al then takes the money for his personal use. Ben later learns of Al's misapplication. Ben also learns that Al had no authority to set up such a "discretionary" account, that the Ventura Company never opens discretionary accounts for its customers, and that it is highly unusual for commodities trading partnerships to use discretionary accounts.
>
> Ben may nonetheless have a valid claim against the Ventura Company. Because Al had neither actual authority nor "apparently/usual" power to receive the $10,000, the partnership never received nor had custody of the money. UPA §14(b) is therefore inapplicable. However,

49. For a discussion of the criteria for establishing servant status, see section 3.2.4.

Beatrice's statements to Ben constituted a manifestation attributable to the partnership, and that manifestation probably clothed Al in apparent authority to receive Ben's money. Therefore, Ben may be able to recover from the partnership under UPA §14(a).

Example: Chris, an attorney in a law partnership, represents a hospital in a malpractice case. Chris arranges a settlement, and the hospital sends a check, made out to the partnership, to cover the settlement amount and Chris's fees. Chris takes the entire amount for himself.

The law partnership is liable to the hospital. The position of partner in a law firm probably creates by itself the apparent authority to receive settlement checks. If so, UPA §14(a) applies. In any event, UPA §14(b) applies because (i) receiving settlement checks is undoubtably within "the course of [a law partnership's] business," (ii) Chris probably had actual authority and undoubtedly had "apparently/usual" power to receive the check for the partnership, so under UPA §9(1) the partnership received and had custody of the check, and (iii) Chris misapplied the check while it was "in the custody of the partnership."

Many, perhaps most, of the cases brought under UPA §14 concern misapplications by partners in professional partnerships.

§10.6.2 *Why Is UPA §14 Necessary? (Won't UPA §13 Suffice?)*

A partner's misapplication of funds or other property is certainly a "wrongful act." Why doesn't UPA §13 cover such defalcations?

Indeed, it covers many. If handling third-party property meets the scope requirement of UPA §13,[50] the partner's breach of trust will trigger §13. The partnership will doubtlessly argue that, while handling property may be "ordinary course" or authorized, misappropriating property is not. As explained previously,[51] however, that argument should fail. If so, any situation actionable under UPA §14(b) (property received by "partnership in the course of its business") is also actionable under §13.

What UPA §13 does not cover, however, are some of the situations that UPA §14(a) was designed to reach. If a partner defalcates after receiving funds:

---

50. The scope requirement will be satisfied if handling third-party property is part of "the ordinary course of the business of the partnership," or if a partner handles a third party's property "with the authority of his copartners." See section 10.5.1.

51. See section 10.5.1.

- not "in the ordinary course of the business of the partnership," UPA §13, and
- not "with the authority of his copartners," §13, but
- *with* apparent authority,

then only UPA §14(a) can provide a remedy.

§10.6.3 *Closing Potential Loopholes (Property Received Under Actual Authority or "Apparently/Usual" Power)*

The language of §UPA 14 provides arguable loopholes when a partner receives property (i) with actual but not apparent authority, or (ii) with apparently/usual power but outside the course of the partnership's business.[52] Consider first a partner who:

- receives property from a third party with actual but not apparent authority,
- never turns over possession of the property to anyone else connected with the partnership, and then
- takes the property for personal use.

In the third party's suit against the partnership, UPA §14(a) will be to no avail. That provision specifically requires "apparent authority," and the doctrine of *inclusio unius est exclusio alterius* suggests that actual authority will not suffice.[53]

UPA §14(b), however, should work for the third party. If the partner acts with actual authority, the partnership has probably received the property "in the course of its business" and the partner's authorized possession of the

---

52. Where the "equities" favor an innocent claimant, most courts will stretch the statutory language as necessary to catch the miscreant. On occasion, such results-oriented interpretation distorts the statute, producing a ripple effect of unintended and unforeseen consequences for parties and transactions outside the case at hand and beyond the court's contemplation. The analysis that follows in the text seeks to show that no such stretching is necessary here.

53. The doctrine is one of statutory interpretation, meaning "The inclusion of one is the exclusion of another." According to Black's Law Dictionary (6th ed.) at 763:

> This doctrine decrees that where law expressly describes particular situation [sic] to which it shall apply, an irrefutable inference must be drawn that what is omitted or excluded was intended to be omitted or excluded.

Compare the scope requirement of §11, which is satisfied by "*any* authority as conferred by this act" (emphasis added).

property constitutes "custody of the partnership." The partner's misapplication therefore renders the partnership liable.[54]

Consider now a partner who:

- receives property from a third party with apparently/usual power but without actual or apparent authority,
- never turns over possession of the property to anyone else connected with the partnership, and then
- takes the property for personal use.

With UPA §14(a) unavailing,[55] the third-party claimant would turn to §14(b) and seek to show that the partnership received the property "in the course of its business" and that the partner misapplied the property "while it [was] in the custody of the partnership." Under UPA §9(1) the partner's apparently/usual receipt of the property "binds the partnership," which means that the partnership (through the partner) has "custody." The same analysis will not work, however, for the "course of its business" requirement. That requirement relates to actual, not apparent reality. Unless independent evidence shows that the partner's receipt of the property was not only "apparently/usual" but also "in the course," UPA §14(b) will not help the third party.[56]

All is not necessarily lost, however. The third party can perhaps recover against the partnership by combining UPA §9(1) and the law of bailments. When under UPA §9(1) the partner's "apparently/usual" receipt of the property "binds the partnership," the partnership (through the partner) becomes a bailee of the property. From that moment the partnership itself owes the third party a contract-like duty to safeguard the property. If, due to the

---

54. It can be argued, with reference to agency law, that the moment the partner contemplates misapplication, the partner's possession of the property no longer constitutes "custody" of the partnership. (When an agent acts contrary to the principal's interest, the agent acts without actual authority.) If so, it might be argued that the partner's eventual misapplication will not occur "while [the property] is in the custody of the partnership." UPA §14(b). The argument would be ingenious, but specious. If the partner's "cheating heart" means that possession of the property has shifted from the partnership (through the partner's authorized possession) to the partner, that switch itself is an actionable misapplication that occurs "while [the property] is in the custody of the partnership."

55. UPA §14(a) would be unavailing because by hypothesis the partner did not receive the property with apparent authority.

56. UPA §13 will not help, because the partner's handling of the property is neither (i) "with the authority of his copartners" [according to the initial hypothesis, the partner received the property without actual authority] nor (ii) "in the ordinary course of the business of the partnership" [by hypothesis, the third party claimaint cannot establish "course of its business" for UPA §14(b) purposes and so cannot establish "ordinary course" under UPA §13].

partner's defalcations, the partnership cannot return the property to the third party or use it as the third party intended, the partnership has breached its contract-like duty and is liable to the third party for damages.[57]

§10.6.4 *A Core Concern of UPA §14 — Defalcations by Professionals*

Many of the most interesting cases under UPA §14 involve defalcations by partners in professional partnerships. A partner in a law firm induces a grieving widow to entrust him with the investment of her late husband's estate and then steals the funds. A partner in an accounting firm supervises a client's accounts receivable and then embezzles funds collected from the client's customers. In each case the partnership, while perhaps sympathizing with the victim, asserts that the fund handling involved is foreign to the normal business of the partnership.

The older leading cases deny recovery against the partnership. Rationales include:

- The mere fact of partner status does not constitute a "holding out" that a partner is authorized to handle the funds on behalf of the partnership. Therefore, without some other manifestation of authority attributable to the partnership, no apparent authority exists. Therefore no §14(a) liability.
- The fund handling is not within "the course of [the partnership's] business." Therefore no §14(b) liability.
- The fund handling is not "within the ordinary course of the business of the partnership" and is not "authorized by [the] copartners." Therefore no UPA §13 liability.

Some of the newer cases allow recovery, or at least reverse summary judgments that had favored the defendant partnership. Rationales include:

- Apparent authority should be determined from the perspective of the client, not the profession. It may, for instance, be unreasonable for a fellow lawyer to believe that a partner in a law firm has authority to act as an investment advisor. But the proper question is whether a *client* might reasonably have that belief.

---

57. R. Brown, The Law of Personal Property §11.2 at 260 (3d ed. 1975) ("A growing number of courts . . . take the position that since the bailee, by virtue of his relationship to the bailor, owes the latter the specific duty of caring for his goods, the bailee cannot escape from this obligation by entrusting its performance to servants. The liability of the bailee is really contractual and his freedom from negligence is therefore immaterial.")

- In modern professional practices, handling funds may indeed occur "in the course of [the partnership's] business," especially when the client entrusts the funds to a partner in connection with advice or services that themselves clearly constitute traditional "course of business" matters.
- When professionals are involved, the need to protect the public and to hold professionals to high standards of responsibility argue for an expansive interpretation of vicarious liability provisions.

Example: Brad is a partner in a law firm partnership. Shirley retains Brad to help her business "work out" from some serious financial difficulties. She entrusts Brad with $100,000, to be used for legal fees and for paying Shirley's creditors. Brad suggests to Shirley that, rather than letting the money "sit around," she should allow him to invest it for her. "We do it all the time," he says, "especially when a client has a lot of money just waiting." Shirley agrees. Brad then uses the money for his own purposes. When Shirley discovers the loss, she learns that the firm never invests funds for clients and that Brad had no authority from the firm to accept the money for investment purposes.

The partnership is probably liable to Shirley. From her perspective, Brad may have had apparent authority to receive the funds on the partnership's behalf. If so, UPA §14(a) applies. UPA §14(b) may also apply. Shirley proffered the money in connection with traditional legal work to be done by Brad, so arguably at least the partnership received the money "in the course of its business." UPA §14(b). If Brad's acceptance of the money was "apparently for carrying on the business of the partnership . . . in the usual way," UPA §9(1), his possession of the money gave the partnership "custody." If so, under UPA §14(b) "[t]he partnership is bound to make good the loss."

PROBLEM 92

In the aftermath of a bitter divorce, Ronald goes into partnership with Robert in a donut shop. Ronald wishes to hide his income from his ex-wife, so he and Robert agree that Ronald will be a very "silent" partner. Ronald will provide 60 percent of the capital and will share in all major decisions. Robert will handle all transactions with third parties. He will appear to third parties as the sole owner of the business. Accordingly, after consultation with Ronald, Robert signs a long-term lease for a building in which the donut shop will operate.

The business eventually fails, and only afterwards does the lessor discover the relationship between Robert and Ronald. Can the lessor hold the partnership liable on the lease?

Explanation

Yes. The arrangement between the partners gave Robert actual authority to sign the lease on behalf of the partnership. The fact that the partnership was undisclosed is therefore immaterial.

PROBLEM 93

The Ventura Company partnership agreement gives wide-ranging authority to Beatrice, the partnership's managing partner. However, all decisions to initiate or settle litigation must be approved by a majority vote of the partners. On two occasions during the past five years, Beatrice has recommended to the partners that the partnership arbitrate a dispute, and on each occasion the partners approved.

Ventura has a dispute with Central California Soybean ("CCS") concerning a particular trade. No suit has been filed, but litigation seems inevitable. Aware that Ventura has arbitrated disputes in the past, CCS proposes arbitration. Beatrice agrees, this time without consulting the other partners. Is Ventura bound to arbitrate the dispute?

Explanation

No. Under UPA §9(3)(e), no partner has the power to "[s]ubmit a partnership claim or liability to arbitration" unless either all the partners consent or the partner agreeing to arbitration has actual authority to do so. In this instance, the other partners have not consented, and under the partnership agreement Beatrice lacks actual authority to agree to arbitration on her own. The partnership's past practices conform with and confirm this interpretation of the partnership agreement. To obtain actual authority, Beatrice needs the consent of a majority of her partners.

CCS may well have believed that Beatrice's agreement to arbitrate was apparently/usual. However, since UPA §9(3) applies, the apparently/usual question is immaterial.

PROBLEM 94

Two brothers, Caleb and Adam, operate a farm as a general partnership, known as AdCal Farming Company. The two brothers are well respected. Their partnership is well known in the community, as is the fact that each partner regularly makes equipment purchases for the partnership business.

One day, Caleb goes to the local Ford dealer and buys a $25,000 Ford pick-up truck on credit, signing the purchase agreement "AdCal Farming Company, by Caleb, general partner." In fact, the truck has nothing to do with the partnership business. Caleb has decided to give up farming and go "on the road." The truck is for his personal use. May the Ford dealer hold *Adam* liable on the purchase agreement?

EXPLANATION

Yes — assuming that in the relevant jurisdiction, courts allow the apparently/usual analysis to consider evidence relating to the particular partnership. If so, Adam is liable under UPA §15(b) because the partnership is liable under UPA §9(1). Caleb's truck purchase was "for *apparently* carrying on in the usual way the business of the partnership."[58] The dealer knew Caleb to be a partner and saw nothing unusual in an individual AdCal partner committing the partnership to an equipment purchase. To the contrary, the partnership had a reputation for doing business this way. Moreover, Caleb asserted that he was acting for the partnership, and nothing in Caleb's reputation gave the dealer any reason to doubt that assertion.

PROBLEM 95

Hiview Company is a partnership that operates a drive-in movie theater. Rachael, its managing partner, purports to sell the land where the theater is located to a development company. The partnership agreement authorizes the managing partner to "make all management decisions in the ordinary course of the business." Has Rachael's action bound the partnership?

EXPLANATION

No, for three reasons: (1) Her "ordinary course" actual authority does not extend to the extraordinary decision to sell the crucial assets of the business. (2) Her doing so could not have appeared "apparently/usual" to the buyer. (3) Her doing so runs afoul of UPA §9(3)(c) (partner lacks power to do "any . . . act which would make it impossible to carry on the ordinary business of a partnership," unless partner has actual authority or all partners agree).

PROBLEM 96

Illegitimus, Non, and Carborundum have formed a partnership as a "handshake deal" and gave explicit thought to only two issues. First, they agreed that the sole purpose of the partnership would be to function as a locator of "spot" grapes for the makers of wine. Second, they agreed that they would share equally all profits from the partnership.

Locators of spot grapes play an important part in the production of

58. UPA §9(1) (second clause, emphasis added).

nonvintage wines.[59] From time to time vineyards producing nonvintage wine find themselves short of a particular type of grape that they want to add to a mixture of other grapes. Locators of spot grapes are in the business of knowing which vineyards have a need for which types of grapes and which vineyards have a surplus of that type of grape. Based on this knowledge they act to get surplus grapes to the vineyards that need them.

The overwhelming majority of locators act only as agents, never taking a position in grapes. This means that when they have a customer who needs a particular type of grape, they locate a supply of those grapes in another vineyard. Then, acting merely as the agent of the customer who needs the grapes, they arrange for the sale of grapes from the vineyard with the surplus to the vineyard with the need. In this conventional approach, the locator never takes title to the grapes and never commits itself to pay for the grapes.

The partnership carries on its business at variance with this typical pattern. On occasion, it will buy and take title to surplus grapes held by a vineyard, speculating that it (i.e., the partnership) can find another vineyard to which it can resell the grapes. Although with this approach the partnership faces greater risk than it would if it followed the conventional pattern, the potential rewards are greater. Where it takes a position and then resells the grapes, the partnership charges a mark-up that exceeds the amount of commission the partnership would have received for simply acting as a locator agent.

When Illegitimus, Non, and Carborundum began the partnership they needed start-up capital. Illegitimus contributed $30,000. Non and Carborundum each contributed $10,000. Each year the partners have fully drawn out all profits. They have never withdrawn any capital.

Last spring Non and Carborundum became concerned about some of the deals that Illegitimus had made. At a regularly scheduled partnership meeting, they voted to prohibit Illegitimus from making any further purchases of grapes on behalf of the partnership. They expressly allowed him to continue arranging deals of the more conventional sort, that is, where the partnership would act only as an agent. Illegitimus objected to and voted against the limitation.

Soon after the meeting, Illegitimus took a buying tour out into the countryside and visited Schekainery Vineyard. The owner of the vineyard, Sally Schekainery, knew generally of the partnership and of Illegitimus's status as a partner. She had no particular knowledge about the partnership or about its business practices, and had never done business with the partnership before. During the visit Illegitimus learned that the Schekainery Vineyard had several tons of surplus of a particular variety of red grape. Illegitimus believed, and reasonably so at the time, that several regular clients of the partnership would soon need this grape. Over dinner he began to negotiate with Sally for a price,

59. The practices described in this Problem do not necessarily correspond to actual commercial practices.

and eventually Illegitimus and Sally agreed to a price of $5,000 per ton for 8 tons, to be delivered within the next 30 days. The next morning Sally wrote a memorandum expressing the deal, and Illegitimus signed on behalf of the partnership.

As it turned out, several of the clients whom Illegitimus had in mind did not need that particular variety of grape. Moreover, throughout the entire valley, vineyards that needed to purchase the grapes were able to purchase easily at a price significantly below the price Illegitimus had committed to pay. When Non and Carborundum learned what Illegitimus had done, they wrote to Sally (1) explaining that Illegitimus had no authority to act for the partnership in this matter and (2) stating that the partnership had no interest in purchasing the grapes. As evidence of Illegitimus's lack of authority, they enclosed a certified copy of the minutes of the meeting at which Non and Carborundum voted to "defrock" Illegitimus of his authority to enter into this particular type of transaction.

Sally consulted an attorney, who advised her to warn the partnership (1) that she intended to hold them to the contract and (2) that if they did not take delivery as agreed, she would mitigate her damages by selling the grapes elsewhere and would then file suit against the partnership for any difference between the mitigation price and the contract price. Hearing no response from the partnership, she proceeded as she had indicated. The difference amounted to $20,000. Sally sued the partnership. What result?

Explanation

The partnership will be liable if either (i) Illegitimus's act was "apparently/usual," or (ii) Illegitimus had actual authority to make the deal.

Sally's apparently/usual claim will fail. She cannot show that Illegitimus's act appeared "in the usual way," UPA §9(1), regardless of how the relevant jurisdiction interprets that phrase. If the jurisdiction requires evidence as to the appearance of similar partnerships, industry practices suggest that Illegitimus's act should have appeared quite unusual. If the jurisdiction requires or allows evidence as to the appearance of the particular partnership, Sally has none to offer. She knew nothing in particular about this partnership. She could only suppose that its commercial practices resembled those of similar partnerships.

Sally will probably fare better with her actual authority claim. Illegitimus certainly had authority to make comparable deals when the partnership began, and it is unlikely that a mere majority vote of the partners could have ended that authority. Defrocking a partner seems an extraordinary act, requiring unanimous consent. The partners' 2–1 vote did not suffice.[60]

---

60. The facts about capital contributions are red herrings. In the default mode, capital contributions have no impact on partner voting power. Absent a contrary agreement, each partner has a single vote. UPA §18(e). See section 9.5.1.

The partnership could, however, advance a less aggressive interpretation of the 2–1 vote that, ironically, could give Sally difficulty. The partnership could argue that (i) the vote and the discussion that preceded it informed Illegitimus that his partners would differ with him anytime he contemplated making a purchase of spot grapes; (ii) Illegitimus therefore knew that any grape purchase he might contemplate would involve a "difference arising as to ordinary matters," to be decided in each particular instance by majority vote, UPA §18(h); and (iii) as with any such difference, knowledge of the difference eliminated the acting partner's authority pending resolution "by a majority of the partners." Id.

If this latter interpretation prevails, the partnership will not be liable.

PROBLEM 97

For many years Harry has owned and operated a delivery service. When Harry's son, Joe, turns 21, Harry takes him into the business as a partner. Father and son agree to split profits 70/30. They have a clear understanding that, for at least the next five years Harry is in charge of all dealings with customers, and that Joe's role is to make deliveries and pick-ups and to maintain the partnership's books.

One day Joe delivers a truckload of sensitive environmental testing equipment to an environmental clean-up company. The next day the company's manager calls Joe to complain that the equipment is damaged, apparently from having been bounced around in transit. Joe says, "Ah . . . that must have happened when I hit that giant pothole on Route 66." If the clean-up company sues the partnership for damage to the equipment, will Joe's statement be admissible as a partnership admission?

Explanation

Yes. Joe had authority to make deliveries, so his statement was "[a]n admission made by [a] partner concerning partnership affairs within the scope of his authority as conferred by this act." UPA §11. His admission is therefore "evidence against the partnership." Id.

The partnership might argue that (i) the phrase "within the scope of his authority as conferred by this act" refers not to the subject matter of the partner's comment but rather to comment-making itself; (ii) the agreement between Joe and Harry deprived Joe of actual authority to comment to customers, and therefore (iii) if the clean-up company wants to use Joe's comment against the partnership, the clean-up company has to show that Joe had other "authority as conferred by this act," that is, "apparently/usual" power to make comments.

That argument should fail. It rests on an interpretation of UPA §11 that ignores the provision's Official Comment and, moreover, would make the provision redundant of UPA §9(1).

PROBLEM 98

For the past 15 years Lucille, Phyllis, and William have operated a fishing guide business from a piece of lakefront property near the Canadian border. They operate the business as a general partnership, share in all the work, make business decisions by consensus, and share profits equally.

The partnership rents rather than owns its lakefront location. The lease has a two-year term and renews automatically unless either party gives written notice of nonrenewal "at least 90 days but no more than 120 days in advance of the renewal date."

The lease was up for renewal last January 1. On the preceding September 15th the lessor handed a written notice of nonrenewal to William. The notice was in an envelope and the lessor did not say specifically what the envelope contained. The lessor did say, "William, this is important. Don't put it aside."

Unfortunately, William did just that. Unbeknownst to the lessor or William's partners, William was suffering a relapse into alcoholism. He lost the envelope, forgot its existence, and never mentioned it to Lucille or Phyllis. The first they learned of the lessor's intention was on November 15th, when the lessor telephoned to discuss "transition issues." The November 15 conversation occurred too late to constitute valid notice of nonrenewal. Did the lost letter constitute valid notice to the partnership?

EXPLANATION

Yes. Under UPA §3(2)(b), the lessor gave notice to William by "deliver[ing] a written statement" to William. It is irrelevant that William never read the statement. Under UPA §12, "[n]otice to any partner of any matter relating to partnership affairs . . . operate[s] as notice to . . . the partnership." It is also irrelevant that the partner never mentioned the notice to any other partner. UPA §12 contains an exception applicable "in the case of a fraud on the partnership committed by or with the consent of [the] partner" receiving notice. However, William's dereliction of duty does not constitute fraud.

PROBLEM 99

Same facts as Problem 98, except that when the lessor handed William the notice (i) the lessor was aware of William's history of alcoholism, and (ii) William was visibly intoxicated.

EXPLANATION

As to UPA §12 alone, the change in facts should not change the outcome. UPA §12 appears to take a per se approach to attributing notice.

UPA §12 should not, however, apply alone. UPA §4(2) incorporates the law of estoppel, and UPA §5 states: "In any case not provided for in this act the rules of law and equity . . . shall govern." The partnership can argue that the lessor is equitably estopped from asserting a notice that the lessor knew would never reach any partner capable of taking note of it. See UPA §3(1) ("A person has knowledge of a fact . . . when he has knowledge of such other facts as in the circumstances shows bad faith.")

PROBLEM 100

Their dispute over the nonrenewal notice convinces Lucille, Phyllis, and William to buy a piece of lakefront property. After William regains sobriety, the three partners locate an apparently suitable parcel on another lake. They negotiate with the parcel's owner ("the seller") and eventually sign a contract on behalf of the partnership. During the negotiations, the seller assures all three partners that "this lake is real quiet. There's no rule against motorboats, but almost no one ever uses them here." That representation is central to the partners' decision to have the partnership buy the land.

After the contract is signed, Phyllis learns that motorboats are quite common on the lake and that during the summer months waterskiing is the dominant lake activity. The partnership seeks to rescind the contract, asserting fraud in the inducement.

In the jurisdiction, a party asserting fraud in the inducement must show not only a material misstatement and reliance, but also that the reliance was reasonable. The seller contends that the partnership could not have reasonably relied on his assertions because "Two years ago William was over here all the time, and he saw all the motorboats and the water skiing all over the lake."

His memory prompted by that claim, William acknowledges it as true. Just as truthfully he states that (i) he visited the lake on vacation and not on partnership business, and (ii) his recent bout with alcohol had suppressed all memory of that vacation.

Assuming that the seller's representations about the quiet and the lack of significant motorboat activity were false and material, what result on partnership's fraud in the inducement theory?

EXPLANATION

The partnership will lose.

The outcome turns on UPA §12 and its rule for attributing a partner's knowledge to the partnership. William was "acting in the particular matter," so the rule will attribute to the partnership any "knowledge acquired while a partner or then present to his mind." UPA §12. Although at the time of the negotiations and contract formation, William's knowledge about the motor boats was not "present to his mind," that phrase is in the disjunctive with the phrase "acquired while a partner." That is, any knowledge the acting partner acquires while a partner is attributed to the partnership, regardless of whether the acting partner happens to remember the information at the critical moment. The phrase "then present to his mind" serves only to limit attribution of information acquired before the partner became a partner. Therefore, William's dormant knowledge of the motor boat traffic is attributed to the partnership and defeats the partnership's claim of reasonable reliance.

PROBLEM 101

Since graduating from law school five years ago, Able, Baker, and Charlene have practiced law in a partnership. The partners "cover" for each other during vacations, and the partnership has in place a system for avoiding conflicts of interests. Otherwise, however, each partner is responsible for his or her own files. Three years ago, Attorney Able filed a consumer fraud lawsuit in state district court against Defendant, Inc. Consumer fraud was one of Able's principal areas of practice, but in this instance the claims were frivolous. Able had signed the complaint without having made any investigation into the facts.

Neither Baker nor Charlene had any involvement in the case. Indeed, Baker was not even aware that the case had been filed. The court eventually dismissed the lawsuit and, citing and quoting Rule 11 of the state Rules of Civil Procedure, ordered Able to pay Defendant, Inc. the $7,000 in attorney's fees which Defendant, Inc. had incurred in defending the lawsuit. The court specifically found that Able had violated Rule 11 by "failing to make a 'reasonable inquiry' into the facts before filing a complaint that was neither 'well grounded in fact' nor 'warranted by existing law or a good faith argument for the extension, modification, or reversal of existing law.' " The court of appeals affirmed the award against Able. Can Defendant, Inc. hold Baker and Charlene personally liable for the Rule 11 award?

EXPLANATION

Baker and Charlene are liable jointly and severally under UPA §15(a), because the partnership is liable for the award under UPA §13.[61]

To establish the partnership's liability under UPA §13, Defendant, Inc. must show that (i) it suffered harm from a partner's wrongful act or omission, and (ii) the conduct occurred either (a) in the ordinary course of the partnership's business or (b) with the authority of the other partners. Able was a partner, and filing a frivolous lawsuit is clearly a wrongful act. Defendant will therefore have no trouble on the first element of UPA §13. As to the second element, Defendant can actually meet both requirements of the either/or test.

61. This liability may be subject to an exhaustion requirement. See section 7.3.1 (some jurisdictions require third parties to exhaust partnership assets before asserting UPA §15 claims against individual partners).

The business of the partnership ordinarly included the filing of lawsuits. Therefore, when Able filed the frivolous claim, he was "acting in the ordinary course of business of the partnership." Able was also acting with actual authority. UPA §18(e) gives all partners "equal rights in the . . . conduct of the partnership business." The partners augmented this statutory authority by granting each partner autonomous authority over his or her own files. It is not clear from the facts whether the partners agreed to this grant expressly, but the way they conducted their business certainly implied an agreement.

The fact that Baker and Charlene had no part in this misconduct is irrelevant to Defendant, Inc.'s claim. UPA §13 states a rule of vicarious liability, and UPA §15 states a rule of liability by status.

PROBLEM 102

Mrs. Rouse recently lost her husband. He left a small estate, mostly in cash. The widow is an elderly lady who throughout her life had left business affairs to her husband. She confides to her lawyer, Mr. Pollard, that she does not know how best to invest the funds.

Mr. Pollard has been a lawyer for 20 years, and for the past 15 years has served as the Rouse family lawyer. For the past 16 years he has been a partner in the law firm of What, Me and Worry. The firm is organized as a general partnership. Mr. Pollard tells Mrs. Rouse, "My dear lady, I would be delighted to handle your investment decisions for you. Place yourself in my hands. Entrust your funds to our firm. We have quite a bit of experience in such matters."

Mrs. Rouse agrees to "put the money with the firm." She writes a check for almost the entirety of her assets. At Mr. Pollard's direction, she makes the check payable to him.

Unfortunately, Mr. Pollard is a crook. The law firm of What, Me and Worry does not handle investments for clients. Indeed, law firms in general do not ordinarily serve as investment advisors. Mr. Pollard deposits Mrs. Rouse's check in his personal checking account and appropriates her money to his own use. For a few months he sends her checks drawn on his personal account purporting to represent a return on her investments. Then his financial house of cards topples, and his fraud is exposed.

Mr. Pollard goes into bankruptcy and thence into jail. Mrs. Rouse sues the law firm partnership for return of the money she entrusted to Mr. Pollard. What result?

EXPLANATION

Whether Mrs. Rouse will prevail depends on how modern a view the court takes of UPA §14.

UPA §13 cannot help Mrs. Rouse. To successfully invoke that provision she must show either that Mr. Pollard handled her funds "in the ordinary course of the business of the partnership," or that he did so "with the authority of his copartners." As to the latter requirement, the authority must be actual authority. Mrs. Rouse can make neither showing. The law firm never acted as an investment advisor and never authorized Mr. Pollard to do so.

For similar reasons Mrs. Rouse will be unsuccessful invoking UPA §14(b). For that provision to apply, the partnership must have received the money "in the course of its business." Arguably at least, the *partnership* never received the money at all. Moreover, "the course of its business" did not include investing clients' funds.

Mrs. Rouse may fare better under UPA §14(a). She can certainly show that Mr. Pollard, a partner, misapplied her money. It is only doubtful whether she can show that Mr. Pollard received the money "within the scope of his apparent authority." UPA §14(a).

Under the older case law, Mrs. Rouse would likely lose on this point. The older cases suggest, almost as a matter of law, that no reasonable client can believe that a lawyer has the authority to handle client funds for investment purposes. More modern cases, however, treat the question as one of fact. They do not simply assume that every reasonably prudent client understands the limitations on a law firm's business.

Mrs. Rouse may therefore be able to prevail by proving that (i) Mr. Pollard had apparent authority by position, and (ii) despite Mr. Pollard's direction that the check be made out to him personally, Mrs. Rouse was reasonable in believing that Mr. Pollard's authority extended to handling client funds for investment. Mr. Pollard's assertions about the firm's business and his own authority would not suffice as manifestations of the firm, but they could help show the reasonableness of Mrs. Rouse's belief. The long relationship of trust and confidence between Mr. Pollard, as a partner of the firm, and the Rouse family would also support Mrs. Rouse's reasonableness argument.

If Mrs. Rouse prevails on the apparent authority issue, under UPA §14(a) "[t]he partnership is bound to make good the loss."

RUPA HIGHLIGHTS

RUPA:

- changes UPA §9 by:
  - rephrasing the apparently/usual power to refer to acts of a partner "for apparently carrying on in the *ordinary course the partnership business or business of the kind carried on by the partnership,*" RUPA §301(1) (emphasis added)
  - deleting UPA §9(3)'s list of transactions requiring unanimous consent or actual authority
- provides for the filing of a Statement of Partnership Authority, which may contain statements of partner authority and limitations on that authority, unless cancelled or limited by a subsequent filing or cancelled by operation of law: (i) statements of authority are binding on the partnership to the benefit of any third party who has given value, unless the third party knew the statement to be incorrect; (ii) statements limiting authority provide constructive knowledge to third parties only as to transactions in real property, RUPA §303
- omits any specific provision on partner admissions
- limits "knowledge" to actual knowledge, RUPA §102(a), but expands the concept of "notice" to situations in which a person "has reason to know [a fact] exists from all of the facts known to the person at the time in question," RUPA §102(b)(3)
- attributes to the partnership "[a] partner's knowledge, notice, or receipt of a notification of a fact relating to the partnership," without distinction between a partner who is acting in the relevant matter and one who is not and subject only to the fraud on the partnership exception, RUPA §102(f)
- combines and modifies UPA §§13 and 14, so that:
  - a partner's "actionable" conduct is attributable even if not wrong-

ful, thereby encompassing, for example, strict liability claims, RUPA §305(a)

— a partner's actionable conduct is attributable if apparently authorized, even if the partner lacks actual authority and is not acting "in the ordinary course of business of the partnership," RUPA §305[62]

62. The language of RUPA does not expressly make this point, but the official Comment does: "The partnership is liable for the actionable conduct or omission of a partner acting in the ordinary course of its business or 'with the authority of the partnership.' This is intended to include a partner's apparent, as well as actual, authority, thereby bringing within [RUPA] Section 305(a) the situation covered in UPA Section 14(a)." UPA §14(a) covers misappropriation of funds received by a partner with apparent authority. However, the Comment to RUPA §305 will do far more than replicate UPA §14(a) within RUPA §305. If "authority" in RUPA §305 includes "apparent authority," then, for instance, the partnership will be liable for the defamatory statements of a partner who acted with apparent authority — even if the partner lacked actual authority and made the statements outside the ordinary course of the partnership's business.

11

Ending the Partnership — Dissolution and Winding Up

§11.1 Foundational Notions

§11.1.1 Four Fundamental Concepts

Partnership dissolution raises complex and interrelated issues. To keep those issues straight, you must keep in mind four fundamental concepts: (i) the dissociation of any partner causes dissolution of the partnership; (ii) dissolution does not end the partnership but instead puts the partnership into a period of winding up; (iii) the eventual end of a partnership is not necessarily the end of the partnership's business; (iv) a partner always has the power (but not necessarily the right) to dissolve the partnership.

Dissociation causes dissolution. The UPA has a long list of "Causes of Dissolution,"[1] but the core concept is that the dissociation of any partner

1. UPA §31, titled "Causes of Dissolution," lists in its six paragraphs nine different events or actions that cause dissolution. The list is actually longer, however, because UPA §31(6) incorporates another list of causes from UPA §32. The eight different

from the partnership triggers dissolution. Dissolution "is the change in the relation of the partners caused by any partner ceasing to be associated in the carrying on . . . of the business."[2]

Although you should familiarize yourself with all the listed causes of dissolution, you may want to note particularly the following situations:

- *Express Will Dissolution of an At-Will Partnership* — If the partners have not agreed to continue the partnership until the end of some particular term or undertaking, then each partner has the power and the right to cause dissolution at any time simply by withdrawing, resigning, retiring, or otherwise making known his, her, or its *express will*.[3]
- *Express Will Dissolution of a Partnership for a Term or Undertaking* — Even if the partners have agreed to a partnership for a "definite term or particular undertaking,"[4] each partner retains the *power* to cause dissolution merely by making known his, her, or its express will.[5] The partner will have caused dissolution prematurely and wrongfully, that is, "in contravention of the agreement between the partners,"[6] but dissolution will occur nonetheless.[7]
- *Dissolution by Expelling a Partner* — An expelled partner has been dissociated, so expulsion causes dissolution. A partnership agreement can authorize expulsion, but it cannot prevent expulsion from causing dissolution.[8]
- *Dissolution by the Death or Bankruptcy of a Partner* — Death obviously changes the deceased's relationship to fellow partners. The changes caused by bankruptcy are less permanent but sometimes are just as

---

causes listed in UPA §§31(1)-31(5) are all automatic and "self-actuating." If a listed event or action occurs, the partnership is dissolved. In contrast, UPA §32 lists grounds upon which "the court shall decree dissolution." A claim of dissolution under UPA §31 can nonetheless result in judicial intervention. Partners sometimes litigate over whether a dissolving event did in fact occur. See sections 11.3.2, 11.4.4, and 11.4.5 (significance of the distinction between wrongful and rightful dissolution). They also litigate in an effort to sort out the consequences of dissolution. See section 9.10 (action for accounting).

2. UPA §29. Although UPA does not itself mention *dissociation*, the term is probably the best shorthand for "any partner ceasing to be associated." In RUPA *dissociation* is a fundamentally important term. See infra RUPA Highlights.

3. UPA §31(1)(b).

4. UPA §31(1)(a).

5. UPA §31(2).

6. Id.

7. For the distinction between wrongful and rightful dissolution see infra this section. For the consequences of the distinction, see sections 11.3.2, 11.4.4, and 11.4.5.

8. UPA §31(1)(d) (dissolution is caused "[b]y the expulsion of any partner from the business bona fide in accordance with such a power conferred by the agreement between the partners"). For a discussion of expulsion issues, see section 11.6.2.

fundamental. Either event causes dissolution. In neither event is the dissolution wrongful.[9]

- *Expiration of a Term or Undertaking* — If the partnership agreement includes a specific term or a particular undertaking, the expiration of the term or the accomplishment of the undertaking automatically causes dissolution.[10]

Dissolution does not end the partnership. Dissolution is not itself the end of the partnership; it is merely the beginning of the end. Dissolution means that the partnership as a legal entity has no future, other than to finish in one way or another the work it has already begun and to settle accounts among the partners.

The finishing of business and the settling of accounts is called "the *winding up* of partnership affairs,"[11] and dissolution automatically puts the partnership into the winding up phase. To wind up its business with outside *obligees,* the partnership must perform or otherwise satisfy the obligations. If, for example, dissolution occurs with a project underway for a customer, during winding up the partnership will complete the project, arrange to have someone else (including one of the partners or a successor partnership) complete the project, or obtain the customer's permission to abandon the project.

For outside *obligors,* during winding up the partnership will receive performance, assign the right to receive performance or release performance of the obligation. For example, during winding up a partnership will try to collect all of its accounts receivable (i.e., money which customers owe the partnership for products sold or services rendered). For amounts owed but not yet due, the partnership may try to collect early, offering to accept a reduced amount in return for early payment. Or, the partnership may sell to someone else (including one of the partners or a successor partnership) the right to collect the debt when it comes due.

Winding up also involves settling accounts among the partners. If the partners have an agreement on the subject, that agreement will govern. Otherwise, UPA default rules will control this final reckoning.

When winding up has finished, the partnership is actually and legally at an end. There are no papers to be filed or magic words to be said.[12] The end of function marks the end of existence.

---

9. UPA §§31(4) (death) and 31(5) (bankruptcy).

10. UPA §31(1)(a).

11. UPA §30.

12. In this respect the death of a partnership resembles its creation. See section 7.2 (no special formalities needed to create a partnership). There may, however, be some paperwork following dissolution. To protect themselves against future liabilities, partners of a dissolved partnership may wish to give notice of the dissolution to third parties who have done business with the partnership. See section 11.2.3.

The end of the partnership is not necessarily the end of the partnership business. There is a difference between the legal construct the law calls a partnership and the business that can be carried on under the partnership form. As both a theoretical and a practical matter, the "partnership business" is distinct from the legal form. It is therefore possible for a particular partnership to dissolve, wind up, and terminate while the partnership business continues.

Whether the business continues depends on whether the partners have so agreed. In the default mode, the UPA gives every partner the right to require liquidation,[13] but partners often relinquish this right by agreement. Such agreements can be made either before or after the dissolution. Often the same agreement that forms the partnership also dictates what will happen after dissolution.

Whenever made, business continuation agreements typically provide for a successor partnership to take over from the dissolved partnership. The successor partnership may consist of some or all of the members remaining from the dissolved partnership and may also include some "new blood."

A partner always has the power (but not necessarily the right) to dissolve a partnership. Among the inevitable causes of dissolution is the "express will" of a partner. Under UPA §§31(1)(b) and 31(2), any partner can dissolve the partnership at any time simply by manifesting a desire to do so. For centuries the law has characterized partnership as a voluntary arrangement, and a partner's power to dissolve reflects and preserves that character.

The power cannot be eliminated by agreement. Indeed, the power exists even when its exercise will breach an agreement. "[T]he express will of any partner at any time" dissolves a partnership, even though the dissolving partner is acting "in contravention of the agreement between the partners."[14]

Having the power to dissolve is not, however, the same as having the right to dissolve. Dissolutions that contravene a partnership agreement are "wrongful" rather than "rightful."[15] Moreover, in some jurisdictions an opportunistic dissolution can be wrongful even though the dissolving partner has not breached any specific provision of the partnership agreement. As will be discussed in detail below,[16] the wrongful/rightful distinction can significantly influence the nature of the winding up process.

---

13. In liquidation, the partnership sells off all its assets (e.g., its buildings, equipment, accounts receivable, good will) either as a whole or piecemeal. See section 11.3.1. If a partner *wrongfully* dissolves the partnership, that partner may lose the right to compel liquidation. See section 11.3.2.

14. UPA §31(2).

15. A comparable distinction exists between wrongful and rightful terminations of agency relationships. See section 5.2.

16. See sections 11.3.2, 11.4.4, and 11.4.5.

§11.1.2 *Following the Three-Ring Circus: Three Pathways of Postdissolution Concerns*

Understanding what happens when a partnership dissolves is a lot like watching a three-ring circus. Three different things are happening at once, and it is almost impossible to have them all in view simultaneously. It is nonetheless useful to understand that they are all occurring. In partnership law, the three postdissolution rings (or pathways) concern: (i) how the partnership is managed during winding up, (ii) what happens to the partnership business, and (iii) what happens to the partners. The following sections deal with each pathway in turn.

§11.2 Management Issues During Winding Up

When a partnership dissolves, it does not immediately disappear. It lingers to wind up its affairs. Winding up can occur quickly, as when a successor partnership takes over, or may be quite lengthy, as when an extensive and complicated business is sold off in pieces. In any event, the same two basic categories of management issues exist both during winding up and before dissolution: (i) inter se the partners, who has the right to manage the business and make commitments on its behalf; (ii) as between the partnership and third parties, what acts of individual partners suffice to bind the partnership.

§11.2.1 *Inter Se Issues*

Authority to manage the partnership during winding up. UPA §37 states the default rule: "the partners who have not wrongfully dissolved the partnership [have] the right to wind up the partnership affairs."[17] The partners may by agreement change this rule, either to conform postdissolution authority to predissolution authority, or to change the allocation of authority upon dissolution.

> ***Example:*** A partnership agreement states: "The business and affairs of this partnership, including winding up upon dissolution, are to be managed by the Managing Partner. . . ."
>
> ***Example:*** The Larry-Moe-Curley racehorse partnership has a partnership agreement that states in part: "During winding up, Moe will have

17. When no partners survive into the winding up period, "the legal representative of the last surviving partner, not bankrupt" may wind up. UPA §37.

the sole authority to dispose of partnership assets." Under the agreement, when dissolution occurs, Moe's authority expands and Larry's and Curley's constricts.

UPA §37 does not say what happens if those partners disagree, but presumably UPA §18(h) applies. Under UPA §18(h) differences over "ordinary matters" are settled by majority vote, while acts "in contravention of any agreement between the partners" require unanimous consent.[18]

As explained previously,[19] UPA §18(h) fails to provide a rule for matters not "in contravention" but nonetheless extraordinary. During winding up, this omitted category may cause serious problems. Some winding up matters will be clearly ordinary — for example, deciding where to buy supplies. Others, such as deciding whether to compromise a claim or sell an important partnership asset, may be unprecedented.

Some courts have solved the problem by holding that extraordinary matters can become ordinary during the winding up process.

Example: Larry, Moe, and Curley have an at-will partnership that owns and races a single racehorse. Fed up with Moe's abuse, Curley quits. The partnership accordingly dissolves, and Moe insists on liquidation. A third party offers $100,000 for the race horse. Larry and Curley vote yes. Moe votes no. Predissolution, selling the partnership's key asset would have required unanimity. But in winding up, selling off assets is probably "an ordinary matter." If so, Larry and Curley's majority vote prevails.

UPA §37 also provides that "any partner, his legal representative or his assignee, upon cause shown, may obtain winding up by the court." The provision does not specify what constitutes cause, but courts have held that waste, fraud, and gross mismanagement justify the appointment of a receiver to wind up the partnership. Whether mere dissension among the partners justifies appointing a receiver is an open question. Even a partner who wrongfully dissolved the partnership can seek court intervention under UPA §37.

Authority to commit the partnership to new business. Dissolution deprives all partners of actual authority to transact new business. "Except so far as may be necessary to wind up partnership affairs to complete transactions begun but not then finished, dissolution terminates all [actual] authority of any partner to act for the partnership."[20]

---

18. See section 9.5.1.
19. See section 9.5.2.
20. UPA §33.

The precise timing of the deprivation depends on the cause of dissolution. If the act of some partner is responsible, then each partner's "new business" authority terminates upon knowledge of the dissolution.[21] When a partner's death or bankruptcy causes dissolution, each partner's "new business" authority ends upon knowledge or notice of the death or bankruptcy.[22] With all other causes, "new business" authority ends at the moment of dissolution.[23] The end of "new business" actual authority does not necessarily end the partners' power to bind the partnership on new business.[24]

§11.2.2 *The Power to Bind the Partnership After Dissolution*

UPA §35 describes the postdissolution power of a partner to bind the partnership. UPA §35(1) states empowering rules, and UPA §35(3) states constraining rules.[25] For a partner's postdissolution act to bind the dissolved partnership, the act must (i) qualify under one of the rules of UPA §35(1) and (ii) not be disqualified under any of the rules of UPA §35(3).

The empowering rules of UPA §35(1). The empowering rules of UPA §35(1) establish two categories of postdissolution partner acts: (i) acts "appropriate for winding up partnership affairs or completing transactions unfinished at dissolution,"[26] and (ii) acts that would bind the partnership if dissolution had not occurred.[27]

Under UPA §35(1)(a), acts in the former category bind the partnership, subject to the constraining rules of UPA §35(3).

> ***Example:*** A partner in a dissolved autobody partnership orders paint so the partnership can finish work on cars already in the shop. This is an "act appropriate for . . . completing transactions unfinished at dissolution," and UPA §35(1)(a) applies.

> ***Example:*** The same partner, with a view toward settling the partners' accounts with each other, hires an accountant to put a value on part-

21. UPA §§33(1)(b) and 34(a).
22. UPA §§33(1)(a) and 34(b).
23. UPA §33(1)(a).
24. UPA §§33(2) and 35(1)(b). See section 11.2.2.
25. UPA §35(2) limits the personal liability of individual partners for certain postdissolution obligations of the partnership, and UPA §35(4) makes clear that UPA §35 does not affect liability created under UPA §16 (partnership by estoppel). For an explanation of partnership by estoppel, see section 7.5.
26. UPA §35(1)(a).
27. UPA §35(1)(b).

nership assets. This is an "act appropriate for winding up partnership affairs," and UPA §35(1)(a) applies.

Example: The same partner accepts a new, "rush" order on a '67 Corvette and hires a "detailing" expert to do the fancy paintwork. Neither the rush order nor the new hire qualifies under UPA §35(1)(a).

The rule for the second category — "transactions which would bind the partnership if dissolution had not taken place" — is considerably more complicated. The rule has two branches, depending on whether the third party extended credit to the partnership before dissolution. If so, under UPA §35(1)(b)(I), the third party must show that (i) absent dissolution the partner's act would have bound the partnership, and (ii) at the time of the partner's act the third party had "no knowledge or notice of the dissolution."[28]

Example: A partner in a dissolved bodyshop partnership accepts a new, "rush" order on a '67 Corvette and hires a detailing expert to do the fancy paintwork. The expert has worked for the partnership before, always billing the partnership after completing the work. No one has notified the expert that the partnership is dissolved, and she is unaware of that fact. Assuming that the partner's act of hiring the expert would have bound the partnership before dissolution, UPA §35(1)(b)(I) applies.

If the third party did not extend credit to the partnership before dissolution, under UPA §35(1)(b)(II) the third party must show that (i) it knew of the partnership prior to dissolution, (ii) at the time of the partner's act it had no knowledge or notice of the dissolution, (iii) at the time of the partner's act there had been no public notice of the dissolution (through advertisement in a newspaper of general circulation in the partnership's place(s) of business), and (iv) absent dissolution the partner's act would have bound the partnership.[29]

Example: A partner in a dissolved bodyshop partnership accepts a new, "rush" order on a '67 Corvette, and the owner of the Corvette seeks to hold the partnership to the deal. Another partner has sent letters announcing the partnership's dissolution to all the bodyshop's suppliers and customers and has published the announcement in the city's main newspaper. The Corvette's owner has never been a customer before, never received a copy of the letter, never read the newspaper announce-

28. UPA §35(1)(b)(I).
29. UPA §35(1)(b)(II).

ment, and was unaware of the dissolution when the first partner accepted the rush order. However, even assuming the first partner's act of accepting the order would have bound the partnership before dissolution, UPA §35(1)(b)(II) does not apply. The owner had not extended credit to the partnership before dissolution, and "the fact of dissolution had . . . been advertised in a newspaper of general circulation in the place . . . at which the partnership business was regularly carried on."[30]

Under both branches of UPA §35(1)(b), the third party must show that the partner's act would have bound the partnership absent dissolution. To make that showing, the third party invokes the same rules that apply predissolution — namely, UPA §9.

The constraining rules of UPA §35(3). UPA §35(3) contains three constraining rules. The first two are straightforward. A partner's postdissolution act cannot bind the partnership if (i) dissolution occurred because it was unlawful to carry on the partnership business and the partner's act is not appropriate for winding up (UPA §35(3)(a)), or the partner doing the act is bankrupt (UPA §35(3)(b)).

Example: A partner in an autobody partnership files for personal bankruptcy, causing the partnership to dissolve. The same partner then orders paint so the partnership can finish work on cars already in the shop. Although this is an "act appropriate for . . . completing transactions unfinished at dissolution," UPA §35(1)(a) does not bind the partnership. Because the acting partner is bankrupt, the partnership can invoke UPA §35(3)(b) to override UPA §35(1)(a).

Example: One of the partners in a five-partner law firm is disbarred for misconduct. State law prohibits lawyers from practicing law in a partnership that includes nonlawyer partners. The disbarment is therefore an "event which makes it unlawful . . . for the members to carry [the business of the partnership] on in partnership"[31] and therefore dissolves the partnership. The firm's managing partner, figuring that the remaining four partners will have to increase their efficiency, orders a new computer network for the office. The act would have bound the partnership before dissolution but cannot do so now. Even assuming the seller can satisfy UPA §35(1)(b), the partnership can invoke UPA §35(3)(a) to defeat liability. Dissolution occurred because it was unlawful to carry on the partnership business, and the network purchase is not appropriate for winding up.

---

30. UPA §35(1)(b)(II).

31. UPA §31(3).

The third constraining rule is more important as a practical matter and decidedly more complex. The third rule determines whether a partner's ***unauthorized*** postdissolution act binds the partnership. Like the empowering rule of UPA §35(1)(b), this constraining rule of UPA §35(3)(c) has two branches, depending on whether the third party extended credit to the partnership before dissolution. If so, UPA §35(3)(c)(I) bars a third party from recovering only if the third party had "knowledge or notice of [the partner's] want of authority." If the third party had not extended credit to the partnership before dissolution, UPA §35(3)(c)(II) bars a third party from recovering if either the third party had "knowledge or notice of [the partner's] want of authority" or there has been public notice of the partner's lack of authority (through advertisement in a newspaper of general circulation in the partnership's place(s) of business).

> ***Example:*** Larry, Moe, and Curley have a partnership that owns and races a single racehorse. The partnership agreement provides that (i) the partnership has a term of five years, (ii) after dissolution Moe will handle all discussions with third parties interested in buying the horse, and (iii) any decision to sell the horse following dissolution will be made by a majority vote of the partners. When the partnership dissolves, it places an announcement in all the major racing publications. The announcement states in part: "We are dissolving our partnership and looking for buyers for our horse. All interested parties should contact Moe."
>
> Despite the partnership agreement, Curley starts looking for potential buyers on his own. He finds a hot prospect who has never previously done business with the partnership, has not seen the announcement in the trade papers, and is unaware that Curley is acting for a dissolved partnership. After a half-hour of hard bargaining, Curley and the prospect agree that the prospect will buy the horse for $75,000.
>
> Despite the partnership agreement and the public announcement, the partnership is bound. Curley's act is "appropriate for winding up partnership affairs,"[32] and so qualifies under the empowering rule of UPA §35(1)(a). Curley's lack of authority does not negate this power, because under UPA §35(3)(c)(II) the prospect had "no knowledge or notice of [Curley's] want of authority" and the public notice about Moe was not in a newspaper of general circulation. (Since the third party had not extended credit to the partnership before dissolution, UPA §35(3)(c)(II) is the relevant constraining rule.)

32. UPA §35(1)(a).

§11.2.3 *Partner Self-Protection: The Importance of Notice*

What a third party knows or has notice of often determines whether a partner's postdissolution act binds the partnership to the third party. Therefore, following dissolution a partnership can limit its liability for unauthorized acts by promptly "spreading the word" both about the dissolution and about any limitations on the winding up authority of particular partners.[33]

To spread the word effectively, the partnership should (i) run an advertisement, stating the fact of dissolution and detailing any limitations of partner authority, in "a newspaper of general circulation" published in the partnership's regular place(s) of business, and (ii) send a letter, containing the same information as the advertisement, to all third parties that have provided goods or services to the partnership. The advertisement will limit claims by those who have not previously extended credit to the partnership.[34] Technically, the letter need only go to those who have previously "extended credit to the partnership,"[35] but it may be difficult to determine from the partnership records which businesses have extended credit and which have acted solely on a cash basis. It is better to be overinclusive and safe than underinclusive and sorry.

§11.3 The Fate of the Partnership Business

§11.3.1 *The Fundamental Decision: Whether to Liquidate*

The most fundamental decision after any dissolution is whether the partnership business will be liquidated or continued.[36] From a business standpoint, liquidation usually produces inferior results. Unless a buyer can be found for the business as a whole, the partnership will have to sell off its assets piecemeal. Usually, a business is much more valuable as a going concern, so a piecemeal sale will produce an inferior payout. Moreover, liquidation sales are often in the nature of fire sales — everything must go within a relatively short period of time, and potential buyers know it. As a result, the seller rarely gets top dollar.

---

33. A partner can also spread the word and would be well advised to do so if the partnership fails to act promptly.

34. UPA §§35(1)(b)(II) and 35(3)(c)(II).

35. UPA §§35(1)(b)(I) and 35(3)(c)(I).

36. A decision to continue the business does not relieve the dissolved partnership of its obligations to its creditors or release the partners of the dissolved partnership from their personal liability on those obligations. See section 11.4.2. The decision does, however, affect the way in which the partners settle accounts with the outside world and with each other. See sections 11.4.3-11.4.5.

Despite the practical problems with liquidation, the UPA default rules conduce toward that result. Following a rightful dissolution, absent a contrary agreement UPA §38(1) gives every partner the right to have the assets of the partnership liquidated and the partners paid in cash.[37] In the default mode the right to compel liquidation also exists following a wrongful dissolution, unless all of the partners who did not wrongfully dissolve agree to carry on the business of the partnership and meet certain other statutory requirements.[38]

§11.3.2 Who Decides

Although the decision whether to liquidate or continue affects third parties, the decision itself is an inter se matter. Like all inter se matters, it is subject to the agreement of the partners. Agreement may precede or follow the dissolution.

> ***Example:*** A 50-partner law firm has a written partnership agreement that states in part:
>
> **Article IX — Continuation of the Firm After Withdrawal of a Partner**
>
> If any Partner withdraws or is expelled from the partnership for any reason, the business of the partnership will not be liquidated but instead will be continued in a successor partnership, consisting of all of the members who have not withdrawn from the prior partnership. The successor partnership will be governed by the terms of this agreement, except that the withdrawing partner will be entitled to receive, as full settlement of his or her rights, the amount specified in Article XV. . . .

> ***Example:*** The Cheyenne Investment Company is a general partnership formed for the purposes of investing in the stock market. The partnership agreement provides in part:
>
> **Article Five: Partnership Term; No Liquidation Upon Premature Dissolution**
>
> This partnership has a term of ten years ("the Commitment Period"). If the partnership dissolves for any reason before the end of the Commitment Period:

37. In extraordinary circumstances, courts may divide the partnership's assets in kind. In general, however, valuation problems cause the law to disfavor in-kind division of assets. See section 11.4.3.

38. UPA §§38(2)(b), 38(2)(c)(II). A wrongful dissolution occurs when a partner dissolves in violation of the partnership agreement. See section 11.1.1. In some jurisdictions a breach of fiduciary duty can also cause a wrongful dissolution. See section 11.6.

a. Unless a majority of the partners vote to liquidate the partnership business, the partnership business will not be liquidated but instead will be carried on by a successor partnership which will have a term equal to the remainder of the Commitment Period. The successor partnership will consist of all partners of the dissolved partnership except any partner whose dissociation from the dissolved partnership caused the former partnership to dissolve. The successor partnership will be governed by the same terms as stated in this document.
b. As to any partner whose dissociation causes dissolution before the end of the Commitment Period, that partner will receive as full payment of its interest in the dissolved partnership an amount calculated according to Article Seven of this agreement. . . .

Example: Rachael, Sam, and Carolyn have a partnership that operates a chicken-breeding farm. There is no written partnership agreement and no commitment to continue the partnership for any particular time or undertaking. One day Carolyn decides that she is getting out of chicken farming and going to attend art school. Carolyn's friend, Suzanne, expresses an interest in joining the business. After discussing the matter, Rachael, Sam, Carolyn, and Suzanne agree that Suzanne will buy "Carolyn's share." Suzanne joins the business, Carolyn leaves for art school, and chicken breeding continues through the successor partnership of Rachael, Sam, and Suzanne. Carolyn's withdrawal has dissolved the old partnership, but Rachael, Sam, and Carolyn have each agreed not to compel liquidation.

In the absence of any agreement, the UPA provides default rules, which differ depending on whether the dissolution was rightful or wrongful.

Following a *rightful* dissolution, liquidation is the typical default result. Under UPA §38(1), "each partner . . . , unless otherwise agreed, may have the partnership property applied to discharge its liabilities, and the surplus applied to pay *in cash* the amount owing to the respective partners."[39] An exception exists when "dissolution is caused by expulsion of a partner, bona fide under the partnership agreement." In that event, the expelled partner has no right to force liquidation if the continuing partners (i) "cash out" the expelled partner without liquidating the business[40] and (ii) cause the expelled partner to be released from (not merely indemnified for) personal liability for the debts of the dissolved partnership.[41] Authority is divided as to whether

39. Emphasis added.

40. For how the cash-out amount is calculated, see section 11.4.3.

41. For the difficulties involved in obtaining a release, see section 11.4.2 (effect of dissolution on the liabilities of partners). Absent a contrary agreement, each of the nonexpelled partners retains the right to compel liquidation. Ordinarily, however, the same agreement that provides for expulsion overrides UPA §38(1) generally. As a result, the nonexpelled partners lose their right to compel liquidation, and the expelled partner may lose the right to be released from partnership liabilities.

the estate of a deceased partner can force liquidation. The language of UPA §38(1) implies that the estate has no such right, but language in UPA §41(3) points the other way.[42] The cases are also divided.

Following a *wrongful* dissolution, the analysis is a bit more complicated. Under UPA §38(2), the first choice belongs to the partners who did not wrongfully dissolve:

> The partners who have not caused the dissolution wrongfully, if they all desire to continue the business in the same name, either by themselves or jointly with others, may do so, during the agreed term for the partnership. . . .[43]

The remaining partners must agree unanimously and in addition must "indemnify [the wrongful dissolver] against all present or future partnership liabilities" (with the indemnity backed by a bond approved by a court) ***and either*** cash out the wrongful dissolver immediately[44] ***or*** promise to pay the cash-out amount at some later date and obtain a court-approved bond to secure the payment. If these criteria are met, the continuing partners "may possess the partnership property" and use it for the rest of the dissolved partnership's original term.[45]

If the criteria are not met, each partner — including the wrongful dissolver — has the right to demand liquidation just as if the dissolution had been rightful.[46]

42. UPA §38(1) states only that "each *partner*" has a right to compel liquidation. The right does not extend to "persons claiming through [partners] in respect of their interests in the partnership." That latter category (persons claiming through partners) includes the estate of a deceased partner. In contrast, UPA §41(3) refers to "the business of the dissolved partnership [being] continued . . . *with the consent of* the retired partners or *the representative of the deceased partner*." (Emphasis added.)

43. UPA §38(2)(b).

44. For how the cash-out amount is calculated, see section 11.4.3 (settling accounts among partners following wrongful dissolution).

45. UPA §38(2)(b).

46. UPA §38(2)(a)(I) (following wrongful dissolution, "Each partner who has not caused dissolution wrongfully shall have (I) All the rights specified in paragraph (1) of this section . . .) and §38(2)(c)(I) (following wrongful dissolution, if the partnership business is not continued under §38(2)(b), wrongful dissolver has "all the rights of a partner under paragraph (1)," subject to any claims for damage on account of wrongful dissolution).

§11.3.3 *Continuing the Business Through a Successor Partnership (An Example)*

The following Example may help you follow the various issues inherent in a decision to continue the business of a dissolved partnership through a successor partnership.

> ***Example:*** Three law students, Charlotte, Paul, and Sophie, form a partnership to sell used law textbooks. They place no term on the partnership, agreeing instead to continue "just as long as we all want to." The three partners rent a room in their law school, take books from fellow students on consignment, open a partnership checking account, and do a profitable business. After a year, Sophie is nearing graduation and wants to "get her money out." She dissolves the partnership.
>
> Charlotte and Paul want to continue the bookstore business and decide to bring in Jacob to take Sophie's place. To carry on the bookstore business, Charlotte, Paul, and Jacob form a successor partnership. Although Sophie has the legal right to force liquidation of the dissolved partnership's business, Charlotte and Paul convince her to take a cash settlement instead. As part of the winding up process of the dissolved partnership:
>
> 1) the dissolved partnership settles Sophie's accounts by cashing her out (that is, by paying her the settlement amount);
> 2) Charlotte and Paul take rights in the successor partnership as settlement of their respective accounts in the dissolved partnership;[47]
> 3) the dissolved partnership arranges to transfer its rights and obligations (including, e.g., its lease with the law school) to the successor partnership; and
> 4) the successor partnership agrees to hold Sophie harmless from any liabilities arising from either the dissolved or successor partnership.[48]
>
> When winding up ends, the Charlotte-Paul-Sophie partnership terminates; it no longer exists. Its business, however, continues on. With the same suppliers, the same customers and two of the same partners, Charlotte, Paul, and Jacob operate that business "at the same old stand."

The following terms will be useful in keeping straight the legal issues raised when the partnership business continues despite dissolution:

---

47. For a detailed discussion of settling accounts among partners, see section 11.4.3-11.4.5.

48. This undertaking is part of the settling of accounts among the partners. See section 11.4.4.

- *Dissociated Partners* — Partners of the dissolved partnership, who are not continuing in the business as members of the successor partnership. In the Example above, Sophie is a dissociated partner. (The UPA calls such withdrawal "retirement," a term which is confusing because of its lay association with senior citizen status and warm climates.)
- *Continuing Partners* — Partners of the dissolved partnership, who are continuing in the business as members of the successor partnership. In the Example above, Charlotte and Paul are continuing partners.
- *New Partners* — Partners of the successor partnership, who were not members of the dissolved partnership. In the Example above, Jacob is a new partner.

§11.3.4 Settling Accounts with Third Parties

The dissolution of a partnership does not abrogate obligations between the dissolved partnership and third parties. Indeed, half of the winding up process consists of resolving those obligations.[49]

When the partnership business is being liquidated. If the partnership business is being liquidated, resolving relations with third parties is theoretically quite simple. Winding up continues until the partnership has completed all performance as an obligor and received all performance as an obligee.

As a practical matter, however, such completion may be difficult and time consuming. For example, not all amounts owed the partnership can be collected immediately. Some obligations may not be due yet, and some obligors may be "slow pays." To the extent prompt collection is impractical, the partnership may either sell the right to collect to a third party, assign the collection right to one of the partners,[50] or simply abandon the obligation.

For obligations the dissolved partnership owes to third parties, two pathways exist. The partnership can either pay off or otherwise perform its obligations, or it can delegate the responsibility to someone else. Delegation may be especially attractive for long-term obligations, such as constructing a building. For a dissolved partnership that has long-term obligations, delegation is the only alternative to a very extended period of winding up.[51]

---

49. The other half consists of settling accounts among the partners. See sections 11.4.2-11.4.5.

50. Typically as part of an agreed-upon settling of accounts among the partners.

51. Delegating an obligation does not by itself release the dissolved partnership or its partners. If the delegatee fails to perform, the obligor may proceed against those partners — even if the dissolved partnership has long since ceased to exist. Moreover, if the obligation arises from a contract, the contract may purport to prohibit or restrict delegation. See section 4.4.3 for a discussion of these issues in the agency context.

When the partnership business is being continued. When the partnership business is being continued by a successor partnership, the theoretical structure is far more complex, although from a practical perspective the transition from the dissolved partnership to the successor partnership can be seamless.

Resolving obligations owed to the dissolved partnership is simple enough: The dissolved partnership assigns its rights to the successor partnership. Resolving obligations owed to third parties is more complicated. The dissolved partnership could in theory perform all these obligations. However, if the obligations are large relative to the assets of the business, that approach would require at least partial liquidation, which in turn would cripple the successor partnership's ability to function. Moreover, as discussed above, some obligations require drawn out performance. Typically, therefore, the dissolved partnership resolves its obligations to third parties by delegating them to the successor partnership.

Contract law applies to these delegations. In some instances the transfer of responsibility may require the obligee's consent.[52] In all instances, the mere transfer of responsibility does not discharge the dissolved partnership from its obligations. As a matter of contract law, discharge occurs only if the obligee consents to a novation with the successor partnership.[53] An economically rational obligee will not agree to a novation without receiving something in return.

> ***Example:*** Alex, Bernice, Carl, and Donald form a partnership to do carpentry work. To equip themselves they borrow $10,000 from First State Bank at the then current rate of 15 percent. Two years later Alex dissolves the partnership. He is willing to let the others continue the business, so long as he is released from any personal liability to the bank. Over the past two years interest rates have risen, so the going rate is now 18 percent. If Bernice, Carl, and Donald are creditworthy without Alex, then the bank may well release Alex, provided the interest rate on the loan is reset nearer to or at 18 percent.

§11.3.5 *Successor Liability When a Successor Partnership Continues the Business of a Dissolved Partnership*

If a successor partnership continues the business of a dissolved partnership, then both contract law and partnership law make the successor partnership

52. Some contracts expressly prohibit delegation without the obligee's consent, and contract law sometimes validates such provisions. See section 4.4.3 (delegation of performance to an agent).

53. See section 2.6.5. As a matter of partnership law, delegation to the successor partnership may lead to release of dissociated partners, i.e. those partners of the dissolved partnership who are not members of the successor partnership. See section 11.4.2.

liable for the obligations of the dissolved partnership. The agreement transferring the business typically calls for the successor partnership to assume the obligations of the dissolved partnership, and, as a matter of contract law, creditors of the dissolved partnership can enforce the assumption agreement as third party beneficiaries. Even without an assumption agreement, if the successor partnership includes any continuing partners (i.e., any members from the dissolved partnership), UPA §41 makes the successor partnership liable for the debts of the dissolved partnership as a matter of partnership law.[54]

This successor liability extends to the partners in the successor partnership,[55] with one exception. The liability created by ***partnership law*** for ***new partners*** is limited. Under UPA §41(7), "The liability of a third person becoming a partner in the partnership continuing the business, under this section, to the creditors of the dissolved partnership shall be satisfied out of partnership property only." Although the language of the statute is confusing, the phrase "a third person" refers to persons who are members of the successor partnership but were not members of the dissolved partnership. In other words, newcomers have no personal liability for the debts of the dissolved partnership. The entire value of their interest in the successor partnership may be consumed in paying those old debts, but those debts do not put a newcomer's personal assets at risk.[56]

UPA §41(7) expressly limits its reach to "liability . . . under this section," so a newcomer's protection relates only to liability arising from UPA §41. Since successor partnerships typically agree to assume the obligations of the dissolved partnership, liability typically arises not only from UPA §41 but also from contract law. The protections of UPA §41(7) do not extend to liability arising from contract law.

> ***Example:*** Charlotte, Paul, and Sophie form a partnership to operate a used bookstore in the law school. When Sophie nears graduation, she dissolves the partnership. Jacob joins Charlotte and Paul, and they form a successor partnership to carry on the business of the dissolved partnership. En masse the professors assign new editions, the market for used books plummets, and the bookstore goes under. The business can no longer make its lease payments to the law school.
>
> Under UPA §41(1), "the creditors of the . . . dissolved partnership are also creditors of the partnership . . . continuing the business."

---

54. UPA §§41(1), (2), (3), (5), and (6). If the entity continuing the business includes no continuing partners, then the successor entity is liable for the debts of the dissolved partnership only if it has promised to assume those debts. UPA §41(4).

55. This personal liability follows from UPA §15.

56. Those assets are at risk, of course, for all other debts of the successor partnership. UPA §15.

Therefore, the law school can pursue the successor partnership for the lease payments. Under UPA §15, the law school can also pursue the successor partnership's partners.[57] If the law school bases its claims solely on UPA §41, the personal assets of Jacob (the newcomer) are not at risk, due to UPA §41(7). Jacob's protection under UPA §41(7) will be of no use, however, if the successor partnership contractually assumed the lease obligation of the dissolved partnership. (In any event, Charlotte, Paul, and Sophie are liable as partners of the dissolved partnership.)[58]

§11.4 The Impact of Dissolution on the Partners

§11.4.1 Impact on Partners' Fiduciary Duties

Since dissolution does not end the partnership, dissolution does not end the partners' reciprocal fiduciary duties.[59] Indeed, these duties can take on a special importance if the partners seek to negotiate an agreement to continue the business or to buy each other out.[60]

§11.4.2 Impact on Partners' Personal Liability

Dissolution by itself does nothing to change the partners' personal liability for the debts of the dissolved partnership. In the words of UPA §36(1), "The dissolution of the partnership does not of itself discharge the existing liability of any partner." Discharge *will* occur, however, under two circumstances that may follow from dissolution.

Postdissolution discharge by agreement with the creditor. UPA §36(2) states "A partner is discharged from any existing liability upon dissolution of the partnership by an agreement to that effect between himself, the partnership creditor, and the person or partnership continuing the business. . . ." Presumably under such an agreement "the person or partnership continuing the business" will assume responsibility for the discharged partner's obligations.

At first glance, UPA §36(2) may seem unnecessary. If the creditor agrees to release the partner, and the person or partnership continuing the business

57. In some jurisdictions, the law school will first have to exhaust partnership assets. See section 7.3.1.

58. See section 11.4.2.

59. For a discussion of these duties, see section 9.8.

60. For a more detailed discussion of this point, see section 9.8.3.

provides consideration for that release by agreeing to assume the obligation, then the release should be enforceable as a matter of contract law. But contract law may not suffice to validate the release, unless all the partners of the dissolved partnership agree to the release. If the liability being released is joint and several,[61] then the release of one partner may increase the burden facing the partners who remain liable. Arguably at least, therefore, without the statute all the partners would have to agree to the release of any.

UPA §36(2) also provides that an agreement to discharge a member of the dissolved partnership "may be inferred from the course of dealing between the creditor having knowledge of the dissolution and the person or partnership continuing the business." The statute provides no guidance on what factors support an implied agreement. At least one case suggests, however, that a creditor risks implied discharge by acting as if the dissociated partner is no longer liable.

> ***Example:*** A farmer borrowed money from a finance company and secured the debt by giving the finance company a mortgage on some farmland and a security interest in some farm equipment. The farmer subsequently sold the land and equipment (subject to the financing company's interests) to a partnership on credit. One of the partners then withdrew from the partnership, and the other continued the business. The dissociated partner assigned all his interests in the partnership to the continuing partner. From this the court implied an agreement by the continuing partner to assume the obligations of the dissociated partner. The court found an implied agreement by the farmer to release the dissociated partner based on the following facts: (i) the farmer learned that the dissociated partner had withdrawn from the partnership business; (ii) the continuing partner signed an agreement to assume the farmer's obligations to the finance company, but the dissociated partner did not and apparently the farmer did not insist on the dissociated partner's signature; (iii) when the continuing partner was unable to make a payment on the debt to the finance company, the continuing partner and the farmer agreed to sell off some farm equipment to reduce that debt. The dissociated partner was not consulted.[62]

Discharge by material alteration in the obligation. Under UPA §36(3) a creditor may inadvertently discharge partners from their predissolution liabilities. Discharge occurs if (i) an individual or an entity has agreed to assume the obligations of the dissolved partnership, (ii) the creditor knows of the agreement, and (iii) the creditor consents to a material change in the obligation.

---

61. See section 7.3.1.

62. *Gjovik v. Strope*, 401 N.W.2d 664 (Minn. 1987).

Most of the cases under UPA §36(3) concern the meaning of "material alteration." Many of those cases use analogies from surety law.[63] Changes found to be material under UPA §36(3) include: extension of time to pay a debt; renewal of a promissory note, agreement to surrender leased premises in advance of the surrender date stated in the original lease. Changes found not to be material include: assignment to creditor of accounts receivable as additional security for the debt (no change in the nature of the obligation, no possible prejudice to dissociated partner); failure of creditor to immediately sue business to collect on overdue account (no consented-to change in the obligation).

§11.4.3 *Settling Accounts Among Partners When the Business Is Liquidated*

When the business is being liquidated, settling accounts among the partners is a crucial part of winding up. An agreement among the partners can govern this inter se matter.

> ***Example:*** Burt and Dorothy form a partnership to raise and race thoroughbred horses. The partnership has a term of five years. Burt provides all the money to buy the horses, and Dorothy contributes her considerable expertise as a trainer. Profits are split 60 percent to Dorothy, 40 percent to Burt. The partnership agreement states in part:
>
> > *Distribution of assets following dissolution:* Upon dissolution the partnership shall pay or secure the discharge of all liabilities which it owes. Any remaining partnership property — other than horses — shall be sold and the net proceeds divided according to the partners' respective profit shares. All horses shall become the property of Burt.

In the absence of an agreement UPA §§38, 40, and 42 supply the default rules. Which particular rules apply vary depending on whether the business is being continued or liquidated and on whether the dissolution was wrongful or rightful.

When the partnership business is to be liquidated following a rightful dissolution, UPA default rules provide a theoretically simple approach for distributing the assets of the partnership and settling accounts among the partners. Property that a partner has merely loaned or rented to the partnership

63. Absent a contrary agreement, a creditor releases a surety if the creditor and principal agree to a material change in the underlying obligation.

returns to the partner as the partnership business comes to an end.[64] The assets that belong to the partnership are marshalled and liquidated.[65] From those assets:

- outside creditors are paid off;
- inside creditors (i.e., partners who have made loans or leased property) are paid off;
- partners are repaid their invested capital (i.e., the value of any property they have contributed to the partnership, plus any profits previously allocated to the partners and left in the business, less any returns of capital previously made); and
- any remaining funds are divided, as profit, according to each partner's ordinary profit percentages.[66]

If the partnership has insufficient funds to pay its creditors and repay capital contributions, then the partners must pay into the partnership according to their respective obligations to share losses.[67]

The UPA expressly provides for the settling of accounts among partners in cash.[68] Division of assets in kind raises significant problems of valuation and so is disfavored. Partners may of course agree to settle accounts with each other through an in-kind asset distribution, but absent such an agreement in-kind distribution is permissible only to avoid great unfairness or extraordinary waste.

> ***Example:*** A partnership grew Christmas trees on land rented from one of the partners. When the partnership dissolved, growing trees, not ready for harvest, were a substantial partnership asset. Liquidation was impractical; to order the trees harvested and sold would have wasted the asset. Instead the court divided the growing trees between the partners.

The function of partners' capital accounts in dissolution. As part of the settling up process, partners are paid the amounts owed "in respect of capital."[69] "Capital accounts" are the bookkeeping devices which track the

---

64. See sections 8.6.2-8.6.3 (distinguishing property contributed to the partnership from property merely loaned, leased or furnished).

65. UPA §38(1).

66. UPA §40(b). The UPA rule that sets priorities among creditors has little practical significance. For the UPA rule to be significant, the partnership must lack sufficient funds to pay all its creditors. In that event, however, the partnership would be bankrupt and federal bankruptcy law would preempt the UPA's rule on creditor priority.

67. UPA §§40(a)(II) and 40(d).

68. UPA §38(1).

69. UPA §40(b)(III).

amount the partnership owes each partner "in respect of capital. . . ." Property contributed to the partnership increases the contributing partner's capital account by an amount equal to the fair market value of the asset as of the time of contribution. Payments made to partners as return of capital decrease their respective capital accounts. Postcontribution depreciation or appreciation of a contributed asset does not affect the contributing partner's capital account. The contribution severs the contributor's direct connection to the asset; subsequent vicissitudes in the asset's value are for the partnership's account.[70]

When the partnership dissolves and the partners settle accounts, each partner receives as a return of capital the amount in his, her, or its capital account. If the partnership has neither made nor lost money, has experienced neither depreciation nor appreciation in its assets, and has generated no saleable good will, then the sum of the capital accounts at dissolution will equal the net worth of the firm.

Such equality is by no means the norm, however. If, for example, the firm's assets have appreciated in value, then the net worth of the firm will exceed the sum of the partners' capital accounts. Any surplus remaining after paying creditors and discharging the capital accounts is profit — to be distributed according to the partners' respective profit shares.

In contrast, if the firm has lost money or its assets have depreciated, then at dissolution the sum of the capital accounts will exceed the firm's net worth. The loss or depreciation will have affected the firm's assets, but not the separate claims of the partners to be repaid the value of their respective contributions. The partners will have to contribute additional funds to the partnership, either to permit a full return of capital or at least to adjust the capital accounts so that losses are shared appropriately.[71]

The following Example, modeled in simplified form on *Langness v. "O" Street Carpet Shop, Inc.*,[72] illustrates how capital accounts and UPA §§38(1) and 40 determine each partner's return when the partnership business is liquidated following rightful dissolution.

> ***Example:*** Three individuals, *A, B,* and *C,* form a partnership. They agree to share profits equally. *A* contributes $14,000. *B* contributes the vendee's interest in a real estate purchase agreement. At the time, the fair market value of the real estate is $65,000. The purchase agreement sets a price of $56,000, so the value of the contribution is $9,000. *C* makes no capital contribution, providing instead legal services in the

70. See section 8.6.3.

71. UPA §40(d). Absent a contrary agreement, partners share losses equally. UPA §18(a). See section 8.3.1.

72. 353 N.W.2d 709 (Neb. 1984).

drafting of the partnership agreement. At that point the capital accounts would stand as follows:

A	$14,000
B	9,000
C	0

(*C*'s providing of legal services qualifies *C* for a share of the profits, but not for any credit in *C*'s capital account.)[73]

An Interim Return of Capital: Soon after, by agreement, *B* receives $8,000 as a return of capital. The capital accounts would then stand at:

A	$14,000
B	1,000
C	0

Interim Capital Contributions: The partnership later purchases the property subject to the purchase agreement, and *B* and *C* each contribute $2,000 in cash to be used toward the down payment. The capital accounts would then stand at:

A	$14,000
B	3,000
C	2,000

Interim Losses: The next year the partnership suffers a $6,000 operating loss. The partners have no explicit agreement on loss sharing, so under UPA §18(a) they share losses "according to [their respective] share in the profits." The capital accounts would then stand at:

A	$12,000
B	1,000
C	0

Dissolution and Settling up Among the Partners: Later the partnership sells the real estate, making a profit of $46,000 on the sale. The partnership then dissolves, owing $3,000 to outside creditors. The sale profits are the partnership's only asset. Under UPA §40(b)(I), the "first" $3,000 of the $46,000 goes to pay the creditors. Then, under UPA §40(b)(III), *A* and *B* receive the value of their respective capital accounts. The three partners then divide the remaining $30,000 equally, according to their original agreement on sharing profits.

73. UPA §18(f). See section 8.5.

Assets of the partnership	\$46,000
Less payment to creditors; per §40(b)(I)	(3,000)
Available prior to return of capital	43,000
Less discharge of *A*'s capital account; per §40(b)(III)	(12,000)
Less discharge of *B*'s capital account; per §40(b)(III)[74]	(1,000)
Remaining for distribution as profits; per §40(b)(IV)	30,000

Per agreement, each partner receives one third (\$10,000) of the profits. Total payout per partner:

A	\$22,000	(capital account of \$12,000, plus profits of \$10,000)
B	11,000	(capital account of \$1,000, plus profits of \$10,000)
C	10,000	(no capital to return; profits of \$10,000)

Settling accounts following wrongful dissolution. If the business is being liquidated following a wrongful dissolution, the settling of accounts among the partners is the same as if the dissolution were rightful — except that the wrongfully dissolving partner's share may be decreased by the amount of damages due the other partners "for breach of the [partnership] agreement."[75]

§11.4.4 Settling Accounts Among Partners When the Business Is Continued: Rightful Dissolution

Settling accounts by express agreement. For the partnership business to continue after dissolution, there must be some agreement among the partners. The agreement can be made before or after dissolution, and, if the dissolution is wrongful, need not include the wrongful dissolver. But some agreement there must be; the default mode is liquidation.[76]

The agreement that provides for the continuation of the business will normally govern how the partners will settle their accounts. Indeed, any business continuation agreement should at minimum address the following five topics:

i. the transfer of the rights and obligations of the dissolved partnership to the successor partnership;
ii. the conversion of the continuing partners' rights in the dissolved partnership to rights in the successor partnership;
iii. the compensation of the dissociated partner for that partner's rights in the dissolved partnership;

---

74. The capital claims of *A* and *B* have equal priority.

75. UPA §38(2)(c)(I) and (2)(a)(II). In addition, the wrongful dissolver has no right to wind up the partnership. UPA §37. See section 11.2.1.

76. See section 11.3.2 (partners' rights to compel liquidation).

iv. the indemnification or (if possible) the release of the dissociated partner for debts of the dissolved partnership; and
v. the indemnification of the dissociated partner for debts of the successor partnership.

The possibility of a tacit agreement to continue the business. If a partner rightfully dissociates from a partnership and fails to seek liquidation of the partnership business, a court may decide that the partner tacitly consented to a continuation of the business. One case found implied consent even though, throughout the period of supposed acquiescence, the dissociated partner sought to have the continuing partners buy out his interest. Such a result is not preordained, however. For example, in another case another court rejected the tacit consent argument even though liquidation was delayed for years following dissolution. During the delay a lawsuit was pending, challenging the partnership's ownership of important assets. The court treated the delay as a long, drawn-out wind up.

Compensating the dissociated partner. A finding of tacit agreement does stave off liquidation but leaves open, among other issues, the question of how to compensate the dissociated partner.[77] The same issue exists when all the partners expressly agree to continue the business but neglect the compensation issue.[78]

For these situations, UPA §42 provides a default rule, essentially treating the value of the dissociated partner's interest in the dissolved partnership as a loan to the successor partnership. Under UPA §42:

a. the value of the dissociated partner's interest in the dissolved partnership is calculated as of the date of dissolution;
b. as compensation for the business's use of that value from the date of dissolution to the date the successor partnership cashes out the dissociated partner, the dissociated partner receives (at the dissociated partner's election) either:
    i. interest on that value, or
    ii. a share of the profits attributable to the successor partnership's "use of [the dissociated partner's] right in the property of the dissolved partnership."

77. In theory, a finding of tacit agreement also leaves open the question of what interests the continuing partners will have in the successor partnership. In practice, however, the conduct of the continuing partners often reflects an understanding on that point. If not, it seems reasonable to assume that the continuing partners intend their respective interests to be the same in the successor partnership as they were in the old.

78. The same issue also exists when the business of a wrongfully dissolved partnership is continued without the agreement of the wrongful dissolver. See section 11.4.5.

The language of UPA §42 leaves open at least seven important questions. The relevant case law is scarce, and much of the reasoning is muddy. Following are the seven troubling questions and the author's view of the answers.

1. *How long may the successor partnership wait to cash out the dissociated partner?* In some circumstances, the dissociated and continuing partners may expressly or impliedly agree on a pay-out deadline. If not, the law must give the successor partnership some breathing room. An obligation to immediately cash out the dissociated partner could force the continuing partners to liquidate the business in order to come up with the necessary cash.[79]

2. *Must the successor partnership make interim payments to the dissociated partner pending the cash out?* The cases do not contemplate interim payments, because they all involve actions for an accounting.[80] In each of these actions, the continuing partners had disputed the cash out amount and had made no interim payments. Nothing in the cases penalizes the continuing partners for failing to make interim payments. Nor does anything in the law prevent the partners from agreeing on interim payments.

3. *When does the dissociated partner elect between the interest option and the profit sharing option?* The dissociated partner may wait until an accounting reveals both the value of the partnership at dissolution and the value of the dissociated partner's interest. If the dissociated partner has to bring an accounting action to obtain the cash out, then the dissociated partner can delay the election until the partner can determine which option will be the more lucrative. The dissociated partner's right to delay election creates an incentive for the continuing partners to cash out the dissociated partner as soon as possible.

4. *May the dissociated partner change the election?* A representative of a deceased partner's estate may lack the authority to make a binding election before an accounting has revealed the value of the partnership and the value of the deceased partner's interest. Otherwise, it appears that a dissociated partner is stuck with the election once made. It does not make sense for a dissociated partner to make an election prior to cash out unless the continuing business is making interim payments.

5. *How is the interest rate determined?* There is very little authority on this point. Among the arguable positions: the legal rate for interest on judgments, the legal rate for prejudgment interest, and the amount the successor partnership would have to pay to borrow funds in an arm's length transaction.

6. *How is the profit share calculated?* The case law and commentaries indicate that the profit share equals the ratio of the value of the dissociated partner's interest in the partnership at dissolution to the value of the entire

---

79. The cases do not directly address this question, because they do not concern disputes about the timing of the cash out. Instead, they involve disputes relating to the amount of the payment due or whether any payment was due at all.

80. For an explanation of the action for an accounting, see section 9.10.

partnership at dissolution, regardless of the profit share enjoyed by the dissociated partner prior to dissolution.

> ***Example:*** When Sophie dissolves her used bookstore partnership with Charlotte and Paul, the partnership's net worth is $10,000 and Sophie's capital account is at $5,000. Sophie agrees that the business will be continued without liquidation but no agreement is made on compensating Sophie for her interest. If Sophie chooses the profit sharing option, her share of the successor partnership's profits will be 50% ($5000/$10,000), even though in the dissolved partnership the partners shared profits equally.

7. *How long may the business continue before fully cashing out the dissociated partner?* Under the aegis of UPA §42 the successor partnership may continue the business indefinitely, subject of course to the power of the members of the successor partnership to dissolve that partnership. If the continuing partners do not pay the dissociated partner the cash out amount (plus interest or profit), then the dissociated partner can sue to collect the amount due. The dissociated partner can proceed against both the partners of the dissolved partnership and against the successor partnership and its members.[81] But the dissociated partner will proceed "as an ordinary creditor"[82] and will therefore have no special rights to compel liquidation of the business of the successor partnership.

§11.4.5 *Settling Accounts Among Partners When the Business Is Continued: Wrongful Dissolution*

The default "package" for the wrongful dissolver. Following a wrongful dissolution, the partnership business may be continued either (i) by agreement of all of the partners or (ii) under UPA §38(2)(b), by the unanimous consent of the partners who did not wrongfully dissolve. In the former instance, the partners' agreement will likely set the pay-out rights of the wrongful dissolver. In the latter instance, UPA §38(2) provides the wrongful dissolver a compensation package consisting of three elements:

- the right (at the option of the continuing partners) either to be cashed out immediately or to be cashed out later (with the delayed payment guaranteed),
- the right to be protected against personal liability for partnership debts,
- if the cash-out payment is not immediate, the right to compensation on account of the delay.

81. See section 11.3.5.

82. UPA §42.

Calculating the cash-out amount. When the default package applies, UPA §38(2)(c)(II) requires that "the value of [the wrongful dissolver's] interest in the partnership" be ascertained. The calculation proceeds as if the dissolution were rightful,[83] with two important exceptions:

- "in ascertaining the value of the [wrongfully dissolving] partner's interest the value of the good-will of the business shall not be considered,"[84] and
- the value of the wrongful dissolver's interest is to be decreased by "any damages caused to his co-partners by the [wrongful] dissolution."[85]

Timing and securing the payment. If the wrongful dissolver has a large stake in the partnership, requiring immediate payment of the cash-out amount might interfere with or even preclude the continuation of the business. The UPA therefore allows the continuing partners an option: They can either pay the wrongful dissolver immediately, or they can delay payment until the end of the original term of the dissolved partnership.

If the continuing partners delay payment, they must "secure the payment by bond approved by the court."[86] That is, they must obtain a guarantee from a bonding company stating that, if the successor partnership fails to pay the cash out amount when due, the bonding company will make payment to the wrongful dissolver. The statute does not specify whether the bond must be for the full amount of the obligation and does not indicate whether the bond can require the wrongful dissolver to first try to collect from the members of the successor partnership. Presumably the court granting approval to a proposed bond would consider such matters.

Except for the bond, a wrongful dissolver awaiting payment has the status of "an ordinary creditor."[87] UPA §42 applies, and the wrongful dissolver appears to have no greater rights to interim payments than does any rightfully dissociated partner who becomes subject to that provision.[88]

Protecting the wrongful dissolver from partnership debts. UPA §38(2)(b) plainly requires that the continuing partners "indemnify [the wrongful dissolver] against all . . . future partnership liabilities." The statute's approach to current liabilities is less clear. UPA §38(2)(b) requires indemnification "against

83. See section 11.4.4.

84. UPA §38(2)(c)(II).

85. Id.

86. UPA §38(2)(b).

87. UPA §42.

88. See section 11.4.4 (UPA §42 governs when rightfully dissociated partner agrees to have the partnership business continue without liquidation but overlooks the compensation issue).

all present . . . partnership liabilities," but UPA §38(2)(c) entitles the wrongful dissolver "to be released from all existing liabilities of the partnership." Neither the statute nor its official comments explain the inconsistent language. The major commentators note but do not resolve the problem.

From the perspective of the wrongful dissolver, the release approach is certainly superior. The indemnity does nothing to the underlying obligation; the obligee is still entitled to pursue the wrongful dissolver. The indemnity is therefore only as good as the solvency of the indemnitor.

From the perspective of the continuing partners, the release approach may be impractical. Generally, obligees are unwilling to release partners without receiving full payment or perhaps an increase in interest rates. After all, why should the obligee give up something — the right to pursue the wrongful dissolver — without getting something in return?

Rationale for protecting the wrongful dissolver from liability. It makes sense for the continuing partners to protect the wrongful dissolver against future partnership liabilities, because the wrongful dissolver will have no part in the creation of those liabilities. At most, if the cash-out payment is delayed, the wrongful dissolver will relate to the continuing business as an ordinary creditor.

The rationale for protecting the wrongful dissolver against existing liabilities is more complex and is best explained with an Example.

Example: George, Bernard, and Shaw form a partnership with a term of five years to sell widgets. They agree to share profits equally. After three years George wrongfully dissolves the partnership. Bernard and Shaw decide to continue the business under UPA §38(2).

The value of George's interest (the cash-out amount) must therefore be ascertained. The partnership's assets, other than good will,[89] are as follows:

Assets	
Cash	$50,000
Accounts Receivable	35,000
Orders in, but not yet billed	5,000
TOTAL	$90,000
Liabilities	
Loan due to the bank	$25,000
Accounts payable	5,000
TOTAL	$30,000
VALUE OF PARTNERSHIP: $90,000 – $30,000 =	$60,000

89. Good will is excluded from the calculation. UPA §38(2)(c)(II). See supra.

To keep the analysis as simple as possible, assume that none of the partners has anything in his capital account.[90] The $60,000 value is therefore all surplus (i.e., as yet undistributed profit) to be divided equally per the original partnership agreement. George's share is $20,000. This figure is reached by *subtracting liabilities from assets* and then dividing by 3. In effect, the $20,000 figure assumes that the partnership will pay its $30,000 in liabilities, and George's cash-out amount has been decreased by his share of those liabilities. In essence, therefore, George has already "paid" his share. He should be protected against having to pay again.

§11.5 Avoiding Dissolution by Agreement (A Specious Idea)

According to the language of the UPA, certain events automatically and inevitably cause dissolution. Under UPA §31(4), for example, "Dissolution is caused . . . by the death of any partner." Under UPA §31(1)(d) the expulsion of a partner under a power conferred by the partnership agreement likewise causes dissolution. Unlike many other provisions of the UPA, these provisions are not by their terms subject to contrary agreement by the partners. Despite any partnership agreement to the contrary, the occurrence of the specified event triggers dissolution.

Nonetheless, some partnership agreements seek to avoid disruption to the partnership business by ignoring the statutory language. These agreements provide that the dissociation of a partner does not cause dissolution.

> ***Example:*** The law firm of Tinkers, Evers, and Chance has a partnership agreement which provides, in part:
>
> > Neither the death, retirement, resignation, or withdrawal of any partner shall dissolve this partnership but the partnership will buy out the dissociated partner's interest in the partnership as provided in paragraph *Z* of this agreement.

Although there are cases upholding these agreements in disputes among the partners, such agreements are dangerous. The conflict between the language of the agreement and the language of the statute invites litigation.

Moreover, ignoring the UPA's approach to dissolution subjects the dissociated partner to an added risk of personal liability if the partnership business continues. The UPA provides a panoply of protections for the dissociated partner, but all those protections revolve around the concept of dissolution:

90. For an explanation of capital accounts, see section 11.4.3.

i. UPA §§33 and 34 end the authority (though not the power) of the continuing partners to bind the dissolved partnership (and thereby the dissociated partner) on obligations related to new business.[91]
ii. UPA §35 limits the power of the continuing partners to bind the dissolved partnership (and thereby the dissociated partner).[92]
iii. UPA §36 provides, under certain circumstances, for the dissociated partner to be discharged from personal liability for debts of the dissolved partnership.[93]
iv. UPA §15 imposes personal liability on the dissociated partner only for the debts of the dissolved partnership and not for the debts of the successor partnership which dissolution causes the continuing partners to create.[94]

If dissolution does not occur, these protections do not arise.

The answer for partners trying to avoid business disruption is to provide for rather than preclude dissolution. A well-drafted partnership agreement ensures continuity by providing for the partnership business to be continued even as the partnership itself is wound up and terminated.[95]

§11.6 Wrongful Dissolution Without Breach of Agreement

§11.6.1 Wrongful Dissolution of a Partnership at Will

As indicated throughout this chapter, the distinction between rightful and wrongful dissolution has great significance. The simplest and clearest example of a wrongful dissolution is dissolution "[i]n contravention of the agreement between the partners . . . by the express will of any partner."[96] For instance, a partner who purposely withdraws from a term partnership before the end of the term is a wrongful dissolver.[97]

It might seem impossible to have a wrongful dissolution of a partnership at will. After all, the essence of an at-will partnership is that every partner has

91. See section 11.2.1.

92. See section 11.2.2.

93. See section 11.4.2.

94. See section 7.3 (partner's personal liability results from status as a partner in the partnership).

95. See section 11.3.2.

96. UPA §31(2).

97. The dissolution is not wrongful, however, if the partner dissociates through death or bankruptcy. UPA §§31(4) and 31(5).

the right as well as the power to dissolve the partnership at any time. Yet a few cases have held to the contrary. These cases all involved egregious situations, in which the dissolution either promised a substantial and unfair economic advantage for the dissolving partner or threatened significant and unfair economic disadvantage to the other partners.

The cases that have granted relief have dealt with the at-will issue in one of two ways: (i) by finding an implied agreement for a particular term or undertaking, or (ii) by holding that partners have an implied agreement not to injure each other through breach of fiduciary duty. *Vangel v. Vangel*,[98] for example, considered a partnership formed by three brothers to purchase and operate a citrus ranch. One brother was unable to furnish his share of the down payment for the ranch, so the other two brothers advanced his share. The borrower was to repay his brothers "only out of funds accumulated from the operation of the ranch or realized from its sale."[99] The court acknowledged that the partnership agreement "does not mention the term of the partnership."[100] It held, however, that the borrowing arrangement "seems to negate any idea of a partnership at will for it cannot be assumed that it was the intention of the parties that the borrower was at liberty to walk out of the partnership until the loan had been repaid from either the operation or the sale of the ranch."[101] This holding meant that the partnership was for a particular undertaking[102] and made the dissolution premature and wrongful.

Other decisions have gone further, implying a fiduciary duty limit on dissolution even in partnerships that are genuinely at will. *Page v. Page*[103] is perhaps the leading case. It involved a linen supply partnership, which after eight unprofitable years seemed about to turn the corner; the air force had established a base in the vicinity. Just then, one of the partners dissolved the partnership. The other partner feared that his own weak financial position and lack of management experience in the business would enable the dissolving partner to pick up the business of the dissolved partnership without providing fair compensation.

The California Supreme Court rejected the claim that the partnership had an implied term to continue until the losses of previous years had been recouped. It held instead that:

> If . . . it is proved that [the dissolving partner] acted in bad faith and violated his fiduciary duties by attempting to appropriate to his own

98. 254 P.2d 919, 925 (Cal. App. 1953), *appeal (on other grounds) after remand,* 282 P.2d 907 (Cal. App.), *rev'd in part and aff'd in part,* 291 P.2d 25 (Cal. App. 1955).

99. 254 P.2d at 921.

100. Id. at 925.

101. Id.

102. UPA §31(1)(a). The undertaking was the paying off of the loan.

103. 359 P.2d 41 (Ca. 1961)(en banc).

> use the new prosperity of the partnership without adequate compensation to his co-partner, the dissolution would be wrongful and the [dissolving partner] would be liable under [the California equivalent of UPA §38(2)(a)] (rights of partners upon wrongful dissolution) for violation of the implied agreement not to exclude defendant wrongfully from the partnership business opportunity.[104]

§11.6.2 *Wrongful versus Rightful Dissolution in the Context of Expulsion*

Under UPA §31(1)(d), "the expulsion of any partner from the business bona fide in accordance with such a power conferred by the agreement between the partners" automatically dissolves the partnership. Such dissolution is ordinarily rightful, even if the agreement allows "no cause" expulsion.[105]

Example: The partnership agreement among nine physicians who practice medicine together states in part:

> *Expulsion*: A partner will be expelled from the partnership if six of the partners vote to expel that partner. There is no requirement that the partners voting for expulsion state a reason or give the expelled partner an opportunity to be heard. The expulsion will take effect when notice of the vote is given the expelled partner. As full compensation for his or her interest in the partnership, the expelled partner will receive an amount determined under Paragraph *X* of this Agreement.

Although such "guillotine" provisions may at first glance seem harsh, they rest on a solid rationale. The success of a partnership often depends on the ability of the partners to work together. If, as sometimes happens, one of the partners becomes troublesome or is otherwise undermining the business, an expulsion provision allows the partnership to save the business without destroying it.[106]

The "no cause" aspect of an expulsion provision can be very important, because otherwise the partnership may have to go through the time-consuming, costly, and bitter process of proving partner misconduct. No-

---

104. Id. at 45.

105. Under most no-cause provisions, the expelling partners need not even state a reason, or give the expelled partner an opportunity to be heard. They just have to prove that the agreed upon number of partners voted for expulsion.

106. To be useful, the provision must be accompanied by an agreement allowing the remaining partners to continue the business of the old partnership. Otherwise, unless the continuing partners can get the expelled partner released from personal liability on the debts of the dissolved partnership, the expelled partner will have the right to force liquidation of the business. UPA §38(1). See note 41. Getting the expelled partner released from liability may be very difficult. See section 11.4.2.

cause provisions help avoid litigation (what is there to litigate about?) and allow for the immediate, surgical removal of a problem partner. No-cause provisions also reflect the idea that if — for whatever reason — most of the partners decide they no longer want to work with one of their colleagues, then that decision by itself is adequate reason to separate the unwanted partner from the business.

The notion of wrongful "no-cause" expulsion. In a few reported cases, expelled partners have challenged their expulsion as wrongful, asserting that the expelling partners have breached fiduciary duty by acting either in bad faith or without "due process." These challenges have generally failed, with the courts holding either that the plain language of the partnership agreement allows no-cause expulsion or that the expelled partner has failed to prove bad faith.

A claim for wrongful dissolution might exist if an expelled partner could prove the type of expropriating bad faith contemplated in *Page,* supra. *Page* involved dissolution of an at-will partnership rather than no-cause expulsion, but the situations seem analogous. The rationale that led the *Page* court to constrain a partner's seemingly absolute discretion to dissolve an at-will partnership might apply to constrain partners' seemingly absolute discretion to vote expulsion.

For very large partnerships and those with very "junior" (i.e., powerless) partners, there may be another constraint as well. If the expelled partner is a member of a protected class, he or she may be able to contest the expulsion under federal and state anti-discrimination laws. These statutes generally protect "employees," and, formally at least, partners are not employees. However, the larger the partnership and the more junior the partner, the more the situation resembles employment. Most of cases raising this issue have involved large law firms and large brokerage houses, and the courts have focussed primarily on the amount of management authority and responsibility enjoyed by the partner claiming employee status. So far most decisions have gone against the plaintiff, but the courts' analysis has left the door open.

PROBLEM 103

John, Jacob, and Susan form an investment partnership with a term of five years. For the first two years everything goes fine. Then Jacob says to his partners, "I want out. I want my money out — now." Is the partnership dissolved? If so, was the dissolution wrongful or rightful?

EXPLANATION

Even though the partners (Jacob included) promised each other to maintain the partnership for five years, Jacob's "express will" causes a dissolution. Because that dissolution breaches Jacob's promise — that is, because the dissolution is in contravention of the partnership agreement — the dissolution is wrongful. UPA §31(2).

PROBLEM 104

John, Jacob, and Susan form a five-year investment partnership. Two years later John dies. Is the partnership dissolved? If so, was the dissolution wrongful or rightful?

EXPLANATION

The death of a partner automatically dissolves the partnership. UPA §31(4). John's death and the resulting dissolution disappoints the expectations of Jacob and Susan but does not breach the partnership agreement or violate some other legally enforceable duty owed by John to his partners. Therefore, the dissolution is rightful.

PROBLEM 105

John, Jacob, and Susan form an investment partnership with a five-year term. One of the partnership's assets is a classic car, which is in basically good shape but will require considerable mechanical work if it is to be profitably sold. Two years into the partnership John causes a wrongful dissolution. He then hires a mechanic to prepare the classic car for sale. The mechanic is unaware of the dissolution and was not previously aware of the partnership. Is the partnership bound by John's act?

EXPLANATION

Most likely yes. If the partnership is to be wound up through liquidation, John's act is probably "an act appropriate for winding up partnership affairs." Under UPA §35(1)(a) such acts bind the dissolved partnership. Because the mechanic is unaware of the dissolution, the constraining rules of UPA §35(3)(c) cannot apply.

The answer under UPA §35(1)(a) might be different if Jacob and Susan plan to continue the partnership business under UPA §38(2)(b) and intend to wind up the affairs of the dissolved partnership by transferring them (and the dissolved partnership's assets) to a successor partnership. In that case, John's act would not be appropriate for winding up purposes.

PROBLEM 106

Assume that Jacob and Susan do plan to liquidate the partnership business and that John's act does bind the partnership. The mechanic John hires charges the partnership $2,000 more than it would have been charged by any other mechanic of comparable skill and experience. Do Jacob and Susan have any recourse?

Explanation

Yes. Under UPA §37 John, as a wrongful dissolver, lacked authority to act for the partnership in the winding up phase. He is therefore liable to the partnership for any damages resulting from his unauthorized actions.[107]

PROBLEM 107

Able and Baker have a partnership at will which buys finished cloth from mills and resells it to garment manufacturers. For the past two years the partnership has regularly bought cloth from Inventive Design Outlet, Inc. ("IDO"), using purchase orders signed by either partner. The terms of the sale have been "net 30 date of shipment," that is, payment is due 30 days after the goods are shipped.

On January 15, Baker says to Able, "This partnership is over." On that day the partnership has a few outstanding obligations to provide cloth to various manufacturers, and the partnership has sufficient cloth in stock to cover those obligations.

On January 17 Able signs and sends a purchase order to IDO for $50,000 worth of wool cloth. IDO promptly wires back its acceptance. Two days later the president of IDO telephones the partnership's offices to express appreciation for the order. Able is not in, so the president speaks to Baker. Upon hearing of the order Baker exclaims, "That order is no good. Able had no right to issue it. We dissolved this partnership two days before." The president of IDO quite accurately explains that IDO "knew nothing of any dissolution" and asserts, "That order is good. You're stuck with it."

Did Able's purchase order bind the partnership?

Explanation

The partnership is bound. While under UPA §33 Able lacked authority to bind the partnership in matters of new business, under UPA §35(1)(b) she had the power to do so. Her actions in sending the purchase order bound the partnership under UPA §35(1)(b)(I).

Since the partnership was at will, Baker's January 15 statement caused a dissolution. Dissolution being caused by an act of the partner, Able lost her authority to bind the partnership for new business as soon as she knew of the

---

107. John's liability is analogous to the liability of an agent who exceeds its authority. See section 4.1.2. The result might be different if Jacob and Susan had known about the mechanic being hired and failed to object. See section 2.2.2 (actual authority by acquiescence).

dissolution — immediately. UPA §§33(1)(b) and 34(a). The facts indicate that Able's order represented new business; at the time of the order the partnership had already covered its outstanding obligations to customers. Therefore, Able was acting without authority.

Under UPA §35, however, a partner can have the power to bind a dissolved partnership even if he or she lacks the authority to do so. Since Able's order constituted new business, UPA §35(1)(b) applies. (UPA §35(1)(a) is inapposite, because Able's order was not an "act appropriate for winding up partnership affairs or completing transactions unfinished at dissolution." The partnership had on hand ample cloth to finish all predissolution orders.)

Under UPA §35(1)(b)(I) a partner's postdissolution commitment binds the partnership if: (i) the commitment would have bound the partnership prior to dissolution, (ii) the third party had previously extended credit to the partnership, and (iii) the third party had no knowledge of the dissolution.

The given facts meet all three criteria. Able's issuing of the order was an act "for apparently carrying on in the usual way the business of the partnership," UPA §9(1), so the transaction would indeed have bound the partnership prior to dissolution.[108] IDO had previously extended credit to the partnership (the "net 30" term), and, as IDO's president indicated, IDO received and accepted the order unaware of the dissolution.

None of the "de-powering" exceptions of UPA §35(3) apply. The only exception remotely connected to the facts is found in UPA §35(3)(c) (partner lacks authority and creditor had notice or knowledge of the lack of authority). Able did lack authority, but IDO was totally unaware of that fact. Able's lack of authority stemmed from the dissolution, and when IDO accepted the order it had neither knowledge nor notice of the dissolution.

PROBLEM 108

John, Jacob, and Susan form an investment partnership with a term of five years. John prematurely and wrongfully dissolves the partnership, and Susan does not want to continue the business without John's participation. Jacob does want to continue, and Susan is willing to wait for her money (assuming Jacob guarantees it and she is compensated for her wait). However, John, the wrongful dissolver, demands liquidation. The partnership agreement does not address business continuation in the event of premature dissolution. Can John compel liquidation?

Explanation

Yes. Susan's desire not to participate in a successor venture costs Jacob his right to continue the partnership business under UPA §38(2)(b). That pro-

108. See section 10.2.

vision allows business continuation only if all the remaining partners agree. Since UPA §38(2)(b) does not apply, under UPA §§38(2)(c)(I) and 38(1) each of the partners (including John) has the right to insist on liquidation.

PROBLEM 109

Three law students, Charlotte, Paul, and Sophie, form a partnership to operate a used bookstore at their law school. Nearing graduation, Sophie dissolves the at-will partnership. Charlotte and Paul decide, with Sophie's consent, to continue the business. They bring Jacob into the business and with him form a successor partnership. The dissolved partnership assigns its lease with the law school to the successor partnership. The law school consents to the assignment but does not agree to release the dissolved partnership.

Always attentive to legal niceties, Charlotte decides that the students who consigned their used books to the old partnership should be informed that the successor partnership is taking over. On credit, she buys a $40 ad in the law school newspaper. The ad proclaims "A Changing of the Guard" and explains the change.

Charlotte, Paul, and Jacob decide that the bookstore should expand its "product line." They write to a supplier of the dissolved partnership, inform that supplier of their new arrangement, and buy on credit $500 worth of study aids for resale to the students.

(1) The bookstore falls on hard times and fails to pay its rent to the law school. Whom can the law school hold liable?
(2) No one pays for the study aids. Whom can the vendor hold liable?
(3) No one pays for the ad in the law school paper either. Whom can the paper hold liable?

EXPLANATION

These facially simple questions have some rather complicated answers. To keep the answers coherent, it is helpful to separate the obligors into the three groups described in section 11.3.3:

- *The Dissociated Partner* — A partner of the dissolved partnership, who is not continuing in the business as a member of the successor partnership. Sophie is a dissociated partner.
- *The Continuing Partners* — Partners of the dissolved partnership, who are continuing in the business as members of the successor partnership. Charlotte and Paul are continuing partners.
- *The New Partner* — A member of the successor partnership, who was not a member of the dissolved partnership. Jacob is a new partner.

(1) The lease. All four individuals are liable.

Liability of Sophie (Withdrawing Partner) — The lease obligation is clearly a debt of the dissolved partnership. Absent a novation, even a withdrawing partner like Sophie remains liable for such debts. UPA §36(1) and §36(2). (There has been no material alteration in the obligation, so UPA §36(3) does not apply even if the creditor was aware that the successor partnership had assumed the responsibilities of the dissolved partnership.) If the school actually pursues Sophie on this debt, then she will probably have an action against the successor partnership and its partners. Typically, the same agreement by which the old partners provide for the continuation of the business also obliges the successor partnership to hold harmless the withdrawing partner from any further liabilities related to the dissolved partnership.

Liability of Charlotte and Paul (Continuing Partners) — On three different grounds, Charlotte and Paul are liable on this debt. First, like Sophie, they are liable as members of the dissolved partnership. Second, under UPA §41(1), the debts of the dissolved partnership are also the debts of the successor partnership, and, per UPA §15, Charlotte and Paul are liable as members of the successor partnership. (UPA §41 does not limit their UPA §41 liability, because they are not new to the business.) Third, the successor partnership's assumption by contract of the dissolved partnership's obligations makes Charlotte and Paul, as members of the successor partnership, liable for this debt.

Liability of Jacob (New Partner) — Jacob is also liable on the lease to the school, but only on two grounds, not three. Unlike Charlotte and Paul, Jacob is not liable as a member of the dissolved partnership, but he *is* liable due to the operation of UPA §§41(1) and 15. However, unlike Charlotte and Paul, Jacob benefits from UPA §41(7)'s limitation on liability. Jacob is a partner new to the business. Finally, like Charlotte and Paul, Jacob is liable under contract law theory.

(2) The study aids.

Liability of Sophie (Withdrawing Partner) — This debt is exclusively a debt of the successor partnership, so Sophie, who is not a member of that partnership, is not liable. UPA §35(1)(a) does not bind the dissolved partnership, because the new purchase is not "appropriate for winding up." UPA §35(1)(b) cannot bind the dissolved partnership, because the supplier had notice of the dissolution. The only other possible theory of liability is UPA §16, but nothing in the facts supports the notion of partnership by estoppel.

Liability of Charlotte and Paul (Continuing Partners) — All three partners of the successor partnership agreed to expand the product line, so the study aids purchase binds the partnership. Under UPA §15 Charlotte and Paul are liable for the resulting debt as members of the successor partnership.

Liability of Jacob (New Partner) — Jacob is personally liable for this debt as a member of the successor partnership.

(3) The newspaper ad.

Liability of Sophie (Withdrawing Partner) — The question of Sophie's liability turns on whether this debt is part of the winding up of the dissolved partnership, or part of the business of the successor partnership. If the former, Sophie is liable. If the latter, she is not. (UPA §35(1)(b) will not apply because the ad itself provided the vendor notice of the dissolution.)

With the facts stated, it is impossible to characterize the debt. The person who placed the ad had authority to act for and power to bind both the dissolved partnership, UPA §§37 and 35(1)(a), and the successor partnership, UPA §§18(e) and 9(1). The ad's purpose was ambiguous. Was it intended to announce the demise of the dissolved partnership (hence, winding up) or to advertise the advent of the new one (hence, an act of the successor partnership)? Or both?

Liability of Charlotte and Paul (Continuing Partners) — Charlotte and Paul are liable no matter how this debt is characterized. If it is a winding up debt of the dissolved partnership, then the analysis is the same as for the lease. If instead the debt is directly a debt of the successor partnership, then Charlotte and Paul are liable because they are members of that successor partnership.

Liability of Jacob (New Partner) — Jacob is liable no matter how this debt is characterized. If it is a winding up debt of the dissolved partnership, then the analysis is the same as for the lease. If instead the debt is directly a debt of the successor partnership, then Jacob is liable because he is a member of that successor partnership.

PROBLEM 110

On January 1, 1981 Alice, Betty, and Gerald form a general partnership to invest in and manage residential rental property. They form the partnership on a handshake, agreeing to "share and share alike." They agree that the partnership will have a term of eight years. They make no other specific agreements with each other. On December 31, 1986, Alice dies of a heart attack. About a month later, on February 3, 1987, Betty and Gerald contact Alice's brother (her sole heir and, under her will, the personal representative of her estate) and ask him what he wants to do with Alice's share of the business. The brother responds, "I don't really want to think about that now. Alice always said that her money was locked in until the end of 1988. Why don't you keep hold of Alice's share until then and use it in the business." Betty and Gerald agree to do so. They make no other agreement with the grieving brother. At the date of Alice's demise, the partnership's net worth is $400,000. Alice's capital account stands at $200,000.

(1) On January 1, 1987, what is the status of the Alice-Betty-Gerald partnership? What is to be the fate of the partnership business, and why?

(2) On February 3, 1987, what is the status of the Alice-Betty-Gerald partnership? What is to be the fate of the partnership business?
(3) In 1987, Betty and Gerald's business loses $50,000. At the end of 1987 is anything due from their new partnership to Alice's brother? Does the brother have to contribute to the loss?
(4) In 1988, the business makes $120,000. How much, if anything, do Betty and Gerald owe the brother at the end of 1988?

EXPLANATION

(1) The death of a partner has dissolved the partnership. UPA §31(4). The fate of the business is up in the air. Betty and Gerald have the right to demand liquidation, and perhaps the brother does as well. UPA §38(1).

(2) The partnership has been dissolved. An agreement among the partners (including the representative of the deceased partner) has superseded UPA §38(1), and the business is to be continued rather than liquidated.

(3) Because the brother has agreed to wait until the end of 1988, nothing is due him from the new partnership. The brother does not have to contribute toward the loss. He is not a partner in the new enterprise. Nothing in the facts indicates that he agreed to join Betty and Gerald as a co-owner in the business. His relationship to the successor partnership is merely that of "an ordinary creditor." UPA §42.

(4) Alice's brother agreed to wait until the end of 1988 to be cashed out. When that time arrives, the continuing partners owe the brother the value of Alice's interest at the time of dissolution — $200,000. In addition, the partnership owes the brother compensation on account of the period during which it has had the use of his money — that is, 1987 and 1988. The amount of compensation depends on whether the brother selects interest or profits.

If Alice's brother selects the interest option, either the parties will agree on an interest rate, or a court will have to determine the rate. If Alice's brother selects the profits option, the partnership owes the brother an additional $35,000. At dissolution, Alice's capital account stood at $200,000 and the partnership's net worth was $400,000. Since at dissolution the value of Alice's interest represented 50 percent of the value of the partnership, Alice's brother — if he elects profits — will be entitled to a 50 percent share. Over the two-year period, the partnership has had a profit of $70,000, so Alice's brother's share is $35,000. (1987 — loss of $50,000; 1988 — profit of $120,000; net profit — $70,000; 50 percent share is $35,000).

PROBLEM 111

John, Jacob, and Susan form an investment partnership with a term of five years. John prematurely and wrongfully dissolves the partnership, and Susan does not want to continue the business without John's participation. Under UPA §38(2)(b) Susan's position means that the business of the partnership will not continue. Under UPA §§38(2)(a)(I), 38(2)(c)(I), and 38(1), each of the partners has the right to insist on liquidation. Jacob does. Unfortunately, one of the partnership's assets is a large certificate of deposit that will not mature until the end of the partnership's intended five-year term. Liquidation involves an "early withdrawal," and the bank assesses an early withdrawal penalty. Under the partnership agreement the partners ordinarily share losses equally. How should the early withdrawal penalty be treated?

Explanation

The penalty is not a garden-variety business loss. It is a consequence of John's wrongful dissolution. Under UPA §§38(2)(c)(I) and 38(2)(a)(II), the amount of that penalty will be deducted from John's liquidation share.

PROBLEM 112

Jacob, Paul, and Leah form a partnership at will. They do not discuss how the business will be handled after dissolution. Later, Leah dissolves the partnership. She demands that the assets be liquidated so that she can have her share. Jacob and Paul object that liquidating the assets will cause everybody to lose value. Can Leah successfully insist on a liquidation? What argument can Jacob and Paul make against liquidation? What additional facts could strengthen Jacob and Paul's position?

Explanation

Leah can most likely compel liquidation. Since the partnership was at will, under UPA §31(1)(b) Leah's express will caused a rightful dissolution. Under UPA §38(1), absent an agreement to the contrary, following a rightful dissolution each partner has the right to compel liquidation.

Jacob and Paul might argue for an in-kind division of assets, but to succeed they will have to show something beyond the general proposition that liquidations usually do not bring best value.

With some additional facts Jacob and Paul might also argue that the partnership had an implied term (not yet expired) or that Leah's dissolution somehow breached her duty of loyalty (e.g., by allowing her to appropriate an opportunity that otherwise the partnership would have enjoyed). Either showing would saddle Leah with the status of "wrongful dissolver." In that case, under UPA §38(2) Jacob and Paul could avoid liquidation by opting to continue the business.

PROBLEM 113

Last year Theodora became a partner in the law firm of Grand, Summit and St. Clair. The firm has 150 attorneys, including 85 partners. When Theodora became a partner, she signed the partnership agreement. That agreement states in part:

> Any member may be expelled from the firm by a two-thirds majority vote of the executive committee, and the committee need not have, state, or demonstrate good cause, nor need the committee afford the member being expelled any opportunity to be heard.

On May 1 of this year Theodora gave a speech, widely reported in the local media, on the abortion issue. The next day the president of one of the law firm's most important clients called the firm and complained vociferously to a senior partner about Theodora's speech. The president said, "Where did you guys get that crazy lady? We're not going to be able to entrust our business to a firm that gets publicly branded on this issue and can't keep its people in the office doing what they're supposed to be doing."

Although Theodora is an excellent lawyer, this is not the first complaint the firm has received about her outspoken public remarks. On May 3 the firm's nine-member executive committee meets and votes 7-2 to expel Theodora. Is the partnership dissolved? If so, can Theodora establish that the dissolution was wrongful?

EXPLANATION

The expulsion dissolves the partnership. Theodora is certainly "ceasing to be associated [with the other partners] in the carrying on . . . of the business." UPA §29.

But is the expulsion wrongful? Probably not. The partnership's executive committee acted under the authority of the partnership agreement. This seems to be an expulsion "bona fide in accordance with such a power conferred by the agreement between the partners." UPA §31(1)(d).

The firm's failure to state its reasons for expulsion or to accord Theodora a hearing are not likely to change the result. By signing the partnership agreement, Theodora (like the rest of the partners) agreed that no-cause, "no process" expulsion comports with the partners' reciprocal fiduciary duties.

Nor will Theodora succeed if she claims that the expulsion is wrongful because it violated the constitutional guarantee of due process. The firm is a private organization, and unlike the government, has no constitutional obligation to accord due process. For the same reason, it is likely irrelevant that the expulsion has penalized Theodora for speaking out. The First Amendment does not apply to private organizations. It is therefore not wrongful to expel a partner on account of the notoriety or even the content of his or her speech.

All is not necessarily lost for Theodora, however. Perhaps the expulsion was wrongful because it was unlawful. Was the executive committee motivated in part by the characterization of Theodora as a "crazy lady"? Would the firm have been so quick to expel a male partner? If Theodora can show that the expulsion reflected sex discrimination and that, despite her formal status as a partner, her real role was that of an employee, then she will have demonstrated not only sex discrimination but also wrongful dissolution.

PROBLEM 114

In 1979 four friends, Albert, Bernice, Carl, and Donald, form a partnership to do carpentry work in single-family residential construction. They make no written agreement, but after an evening-long discussion Bernice finally says, "So that's what we're going to do. Let's do carpentry work on houses; we'll all be in it together. Share and share alike." The other three agree, and they all shake hands on the deal.

For the five years following that agreement, their partnership operates very successfully. The partners make good livings and also put a substantial amount of the partnership's revenues toward purchasing two company trucks and state of the art carpentry equipment. The partnership's success impresses local banks, and the partnership obtains a line of credit with two of them. Each line of credit allows the partnership to borrow as it wishes up to a predetermined limit.

For its first five years the partnership decides by consensus which projects to bid on. In 1985 the partners have for the first time a serious disagreement about whether to bid on a particular project. The disagreement concerns a residential development called "The Eagan project." Albert objects to bidding on the Eagan project because he believes that both the profit margins and the developer's quality standards are too low. The other three partners disagree, perhaps in large part because recently the partnership has had difficulty finding work. The partners vote 3-1 to bid on the project, and the bid is successful. Albert grumbles, "I don't like this. This is not the way we've always made our decisions, and this project is not our kind of business." However, he does show up at the worksite, and for three weeks he works side by side with Bernice, Carl, and Donald.

Then, three weeks into what the partners expect to be a three-month project, Albert announces, "I've had it. I don't like this work; never did. I'm outta here. I'm going to Alaska. I've got a chance to get in on the ground floor of a new fishing business."

That evening Albert, Bernice, Carl, and Donald meet, and Bernice, Carl, and Donald declare that they intend to finish the Eagan project and "maybe keep going after that." Albert reiterates that he is leaving the project and the partnership. He adds that he wants the partnership to turn over his share of the money tied up in the partnership trucks and other equipment.

What is the status of the partnership?

Explanation

It is dissolved. Albert's "express will" is clearly to dissociate himself from carrying on the partnership business. Under either UPA §31(1)(b) (rightful dissolution of an at-will partnership) or UPA §31(2) (wrongful dissolution) that express will causes dissolution.

PROBLEM 115

Is Albert's decision to dissociate wrongful?

Explanation

Most likely not. The original, oral partnership agreement specified "no definite term or particular undertaking." Therefore, under UPA §31(1)(b) Albert's express will caused a rightful dissolution.

The fact that Albert may be leaving for greener pastures does not make the dissolution wrongful. According to some cases, a partner's duty of loyalty may constrain the right to dissolve at will. But these cases all involve the dissolving partner's exploitation of assets or opportunities that belong to or are closely associated with the partnership. Those cases would not apply here. There is no apparent connection between the partnership's carpentry business and Albert's fishing prospects.

It is possible to argue, however, that Albert dissolved wrongfully because he contravened an implied agreement not to dissolve with a partnership project underway. Under this analysis, each decision by the partners to undertake a project would transform their partnership at-will into a partnership for that "particular undertaking." Albert's dissolution would therefore be premature and wrongful. UPA §31(2).

If so, Albert would lose the right to wind up the partnership, UPA §37. Beyond that, however, nothing would change. Dissolution does not end even an at-will partnership; the partnership continues until it has wound up its affairs, including ongoing projects. It is possible to argue that Albert will face a loss of good will value under UPA §38(2)(c)(II). However, that provision applies only if the remaining partners decide to continue the business. Albert could forcefully argue that finishing the Eagan project constitutes winding up rather than continuing the business.

PROBLEM 116

Assume that the partners had originally agreed to a partnership term of seven years. Given this change in facts, is there any way for Albert to avoid the label of "wrongful dissolver"?

Explanation

Probably not. Albert might be able to claim that the decision to bid on the Eagan project violated implied agreements (created through the partners' course of dealing with each other) on the type of work to be done by the partners (e.g., no low budget, low quality jobs) and on the decision-making process to be used by the partners (e.g., projects selected by consensus only). That argument would allow Albert to claim that the decision to bid on the Eagan project constituted a wrongful dissolution.

That argument would probably fail, however, because Albert eventually consented to the Eagan project. By showing up to work on the project, Albert at least acquiesced in the decision. That acquiescence probably satisfies the requirement of UPA §18(h) that an "act in contravention of any agreement between the partners may be done rightfully [with] the consent of all the partners."

PROBLEM 117

Assuming that the partnership had no specific term, can Albert force the partnership to immediately give him his share of the money tied up in the trucks and equipment?

Explanation

Not at least until the Eagan project is finished. The trucks and equipment are partnership property. Regardless of whether the dissolution is rightful, Albert cannot compel liquidation until the partnership has performed or otherwise discharged its obligations on that project.

PROBLEM 118

Bernice, Carl, and Donald think that they will "maybe keep going after [the Eagan project]." If they do so, can they retain the trucks and the carpentry equipment for use in further projects?

Explanation

Only if they can show that Albert wrongfully dissolved the original partnership. If they can, then they can use UPA §38(2) to retain the assets and continue the business of the dissolved partnership. Eventually the continuing partners will have to pay Albert the value of his interest (calculated as of the time of dissolution) plus interest or a profit share for Albert's "forced loan," but the operation of UPA §38(2) will deprive Albert of his right to compel liquidation.

PROBLEM 119

Two days after his announcement, Albert leaves for Alaska. Before leaving he writes to all the companies that had previously sold materials to the partnership. In his letters he states, "The original partnership is dissolved. I am no longer associated with the business. I am not responsible for any of its debts."Bernice, Carl, and Donald continue to work on the Eagan project. As they continue the work, they make purchases necessary to finish the project. For example, they buy wood costing $10,000 from the Wabasco Wood Company, which happens to be a new supplier. Is Albert personally liable for this debt?

EXPLANATION

Yes. This purchase is clearly an "act appropriate for . . . completing transactions unfinished at dissolution." As such, the purchase binds the dissolved partnership under UPA §35(1)(a). UPA §15 makes Albert personally liable for the partnership debt.

PROBLEM 120

Bernice, Carl, and Donald also buy nails after Albert's departure. They buy from Nantucket Nail Emporium, which previously sold the partnership nails on a "net 30 date of shipment" basis (i.e., payment due within thirty days of shipment). Bernice, Carl, and Donald order and receive nails costing $600 before the Emporium receives Albert's letter, and they order and receive nails costing $1,100 after the letter arrives. Is Albert personally liable for these amounts?

EXPLANATION

Yes — under UPA §35(1)(a). The analysis is the same as for Problem 119. Albert's letter is irrelevant to the analysis under UPA §35(1)(a). Nothing in that provision concerns the third party's knowledge of the dissolution.

None of UPA §35(3)'s "depowering" provisions will help Albert. The only provision even remotely of interest is UPA §35(3)(c)(I) (partnership not bound where the acting partner lacks authority, the third party has previously extended credit, and the third party has knowledge or notice of that lack). The Emporium has previously extended credit (the "net 30" term), and Albert's letter could perhaps be stretched to imply notice that Bernice, Carl, and Donald lack authority to bind the dissolved partnership. But even with that considerable stretch, UPA §35(3)(c) would still not apply. The provision's first element — that the acting partner actually lacked authority —

would be missing. Under UPA §37, "the partners who have not wrongfully dissolved the partnership [i.e. in this case, all four partners] [have] the right to wind up partnership affairs."

Albert's letter would have made a difference if the $1,100 worth of nails ordered after the letter arrived were used for new business. In that case, under UPA §35(1)(b)(I) the nail order would not have bound the dissolved partnership.

PROBLEM 121

Bernice, Carl, and Donald fare poorly on the Eagan project. Within a month after Albert leaves, the business falls behind in its payments to both banks. One bank, the First Bank, promptly sends written notice to the partnership, complaining about the delay in payments. Prior to Albert's departure, the partnership had borrowed the full $50,000 available under the First Bank line of credit. After receiving the notice, Bernice, Carl, and Donald meet with an officer of the First Bank to explain what has been happening and to discuss some new projects they have underway. To help the continuing partners "get back on their feet," the bank agrees to a four-month moratorium on payments on the loan. Is Albert personally liable on the debt to the First Bank?

EXPLANATION

Possibly not. Under UPA §36(1), the dissolution by itself does not discharge him, but UPA §36(3) may. Under that latter provision, a discharge occurs if the continuing partners agree to assume the dissociated partner's liability, the creditor knows of that agreement, and the creditor agrees to a material alteration in the "nature or time of payment" of the obligation. If the continuing partners agreed to assume Albert's responsibility, and if the explanation and discussion with the Bank officer caused the Bank to know of the assumption agreement, then UPA §36(3) is probably satisfied. A four-month moratorium is probably a material change in the "time of payment."

PROBLEM 122

The other bank, the Second Bank, does not initially object to or even take note of the late payments. Bernice, Carl, and Donald decide to "let sleeping dogs lie." Indeed, to fund new projects they actually borrow additional money under the line of credit. Before Albert's departure, the partnership had borrowed $40,000. To fund the new projects, Bernice, Carl, and Donald draw down the final $30,000 available under the original line of credit agreement. Is Albert personally liable for any of the $70,000?

Explanation

Yes — for all of it. As to the first $40,000, Albert is liable under UPA §15, and UPA §36(3) will not save him. Even if the continuing partners agreed to assume Albert's liability and the $30,000 draw down constituted a material change in the nature of the obligation, there is no basis for finding that the Second Bank knew of the assumption agreement. Indeed, the Second Bank was not even aware of the dissolution; Albert notified only "companies which had previously sold materials to the partnership."

Albert is also liable as to the $30,000 draw-down, per UPA §35(1)(b)(I). The draw-down would have bound the partnership prior to dissolution; the Second Bank had previously extended credit to the partnership; and the Second Bank had no notice or knowledge of the dissolution.

RUPA HIGHLIGHTS

RUPA:

- establishes an elaborate, new structure for partner dissociation and partnership dissolution, although in many circumstances the RUPA structure will produce the same results as the UPA approach
- with respect to partner dissociation
  - — formally defines partner "dissociation," RUPA §601
  - — identifies certain circumstances under which a partner may be expelled by the unanimous vote of all of the other partners, RUPA §601(4)[109]
  - — provides that in a partnership for a definite term or particular undertaking, a partner's bankruptcy constitutes wrongful dissociation, RUPA §602(b)(2)(iii)
  - — provides that a dissociated partner has no further duties of loyalty to the partnership except to the extent that the dissociated partner participates in winding up, RUPA §603(b)(2) and §603(b)(3)
- with regard to dissolution
  - — provides that dissociation does not automatically cause dissolution, RUPA §801
  - — allows a partner to dissolve an at-will partnership by giving notice of "express will to withdraw as a partner," but only if that partner has not been dissociated involuntarily (e.g., by expulsion, death, bankruptcy), RUPA §801(1)
  - — provides that a partner's premature dissociation from a partnership for a definite term or undertaking does not cause dissolution unless within 90 days at least half of the remaining partners manifest an "express will" to dissolve, RUPA §801(2)(i)
  - — allows a dissolved partnership that has not completed winding up to "undo" the dissolution, upon the agreement of "all of the partners, including any dissociating partner other than a wrongfully dissociating partner," RUPA §802
  - — handles the issue of a partner's post-dissolution power to bind the dissolved partnership by:
    - — slimming down UPA §35 into two empowering rules: a partner's post-dissolution act binds the partnership if (i) the act is appropriate for winding up, or (ii) the act would have bound the partnership prior to dissolution and at the time of the act

109. RUPA also allows expulsion pursuant to the partnership agreement. RUPA §601(3).

the third party had no notice of the dissolution, RUPA §804
    - — allowing the partnership to file a Statement of Dissolution which, beginning 90 days after filing, constitutes constructive notice to all third parties that the partnership is dissolved, RUPA §805(c)

- with regard to the fate of a dissociated partner when the partnership does not dissolve[110]
  - — requires the partnership to buy out the dissociated partner; the intricate buy-out provisions resemble the corporate appraisal remedy, RUPA §701
  - — allows the partnership to withhold payment of the buy-out price from a partner who has dissociated prematurely from a partnership for a definite term or particular undertaking, unless the dissociated partner "establishes to the satisfaction of the court that earlier payment will not cause undue hardship to the business of the partnership;" requires deferred payments to bear interest and be adequately secured, RUPA §701(h)
  - — establishes a two-year period following dissociation, during which:
    - — the dissociated partner can bind the partnership to a third party who (i) reasonably believes the dissociated partner is still a partner, (ii) has neither actual nor constructive notice of the dissociation,and (iii) lacks even constructive knowledge of the dissociation, RUPA §702(a)
    - — any transactions entered into between the partnership and a third party can result in the dissociated partner being liable as a partner to that third party if at the time of the transaction the third party (i) reasonably believed the dissociated partner was still a partner, (ii) did not have either actual or constructive notice of the dissociation, and (iii) lacked even constructive knowledge of the dissociation, RUPA §703(b)
  - — allows both the partnership and the dissociated partner to file a Statement of Dissociation which, beginning 90 days after filing, constitutes constructive notice to all third parties that the partner is dissociated, RUPA §704
- with regard to claims for wrongful dissolution in the absence of breach of an express agreement
  - — appears to exclude such claims, RUPA §602(b)

110. This situation is analogous to the situation under the UPA in which a partner dissociates, the partnership perforce dissolves and some or all of the remaining partners continue the partnership business.

12

Limited Partnerships, Limited Liability Companies, and Limited Liability Partnerships

§12.1 Limited Partnerships

§12.1.1 Limited Partnerships Distinguished from General Partnerships

Limited partnerships differ from general partnerships in six fundamental ways:

1. *Creation* — Creating a limited partnership involves special formalities: namely, the filing of a "certificate of limited partnership" with an appropriate public official.
2. *Types of Partners* — A limited partnership has two types of partners: general partners and limited partners. A limited partnership must have at least one general partner and one limited partner.
3. *Personal Liability* — A limited partnership's general partners are, like the partners in a general partnership, personally liable for the part-

nership's debts. Limited partners are not personally liable except in extraordinary circumstances.

4. *Management* — In the default mode,[1] both the right to manage and the power to bind the partnership are reserved to the general partners. Limited partners are essentially passive investors.
5. *Profit and Loss Sharing* — In the default mode, partners in a limited partnership share profits and losses essentially in proportion to their respective capital contributions.
6. *Dissolution* — In the default mode, the dissociation of a limited partner does not dissolve the partnership, and the dissociation of a general partner merely threatens the partnership with dissolution.

§12.1.2 Limited Partnership Statutes

Every limited partnership is governed by some state limited partnership statute. The National Conference of Commissioners of Uniform State Laws[2] has promulgated three versions of the Uniform *Limited* Partnership Act: the original Act in 1916 ("ULPA"), the Revised Uniform Partnership Act in 1976 ("RULPA (1976)"), and the 1985 amendments to RULPA ("RULPA (1985)"). Most states now have in effect some version of RULPA.

This section's discussion of limited partnerships will focus on the provisions of RULPA, as amended in 1985. RULPA covers numerous issues peculiar to limited partnerships and then provides generally: "In any case not provided for in this [Act] the provisions of the Uniform Partnership Act govern."[3]

> ***Example:*** Rachael, Samuel, and Carolyn are the general partners in a limited partnership that owns several apartment buildings. For some time the partnership has used Joe's Maintenance for routine maintenance work. Rachael and Carolyn wish to replace Joe's with R. M. Dorothy & Co., but Samuel disagrees. RULPA provides no rules for this type of management disagreement, so the UPA governs. In particular, UPA §18(h) applies to this "ordinary matter."[4]

---

1. The "default mode" refers to circumstances in which statutory default rules remain in place. For an explanation of default rules, see section 7.1.2.

2. This is the same organization that promulgated the Uniform Partnership Act and the Revised Uniform Partnership Act. See sections 7.1.1 and 7.1.3.

3. RULPA §1105. RULPA also expresses this dependence on UPA more particularly. For example, RULPA §403 provides that a general partner in a limited partnership has the same rights, power, and liabilities as a partner in a general partnership.

4. Under UPA §18(h), differences as to ordinary matters are decided by majority vote, with each partner having one vote. See section 9.5. The rule is a default rule. See section 7.1.2.

§12.1.3 Formalities of Creating a Limited Partnership

In order to form a limited partnership the general partners[5] must first select a state of organization — that is, a state under whose limited partnership statute the limited partnership will be established and governed. Most limited partnerships are organized under the law of the state in which the partnership does all or most of its business, but it is not legally necessary to do so. Indeed, if a limited partnership does business in more than one state, the partnership will necessarily do business outside its state of organization.[6]

After choosing a state of organization, the general partners must invoke that state's limited partnership statute by filing a "certificate of limited partnership" with that state's secretary of state.[7] Each general partner must sign the certificate,[8] which must contain: (1) the limited partnership's name, (2) the name and business address of each general partner, (3) the latest date on which the limited partnership will dissolve,[9] and (4) the address of the office and the name and address of an agent designated to receive service of process on behalf of the limited partnership.[10]

The certificate may include other information, but most certificates contain only the bare minimum required by statute.[11] The certificate is a public document, and business people usually prefer to keep their business arrangements as confidential as possible. The key document for a limited partnership is therefore typically the partnership agreement. Although RULPA does not expressly require a partnership agreement, almost all limited partner-

---

5. For the sake of convenience, this section will usually refer to general partners in the plural, although a limited partnership can exist and operate having only one general partner.

6. A limited partnership that does business in states other than its state of organization must register in each of those other states as a "foreign limited partnership." RULPA §§101(4) (defining the term) and 902 (requiring registration of foreign limited partnerships). With respect to its state of organization, a limited partnership is considered a "domestic" limited partnership. RULPA §101(7). Both the nomenclature and the registration requirement parallel those applicable to corporations. See, e.g., Revised Model Business Corporation Act §§1.40(4) (defining domestic corporation), 1.40(10) (defining foreign corporation), and 15.01 (requiring foreign corporations to obtain a certificate of authority before transacting business).

7. RULPA §201(a).

8. RULPA §204(a)(1).

9. This date effectively sets the term of the partnership. Other events may dissolve the partnership prematurely. See section 12.1.7.

10. RULPA §201(a).

11. Both ULPA and the 1976 version of RULPA required greater disclosure in the certificate. See, e.g., ULPA §§2(1)(a)(VI) (requiring disclosure of each limited partner's capital contribution) and 2(1)(a)(IX) (requiring disclosure of each limited partner's profit share), and RULPA (1976) §§201(a)(5) (requiring disclosure of each partner's capital contribution) and 201(a)(9) (requiring disclosure of each partner's right to receive distributions).

ships have one. It is the partnership agreement, not the certificate of limited partnership, that details the rights, responsibilities, and relationships of the partners.

If the certificate of limited partnership substantially complies with the limited partnership statute, filing the certificate brings the partnership into existence either immediately or at a later date specified in the certificate.[12] Once formed, a limited partnership is a legal entity, distinct from its co-owners. It is not an aggregate of its partners.[13]

§12.1.4 *Personal Liability of Partners*

Each general partner in a limited partnership is personally liable for the partnership's debts, just as if the partnership were a general partnership.[14] Limited partners face no such automatic liability. They can, however, be liable in the following special circumstances:

1. *Wrongful personal conduct* — If a limited partner engages in wrongful conduct on behalf of the limited partnership and that conduct causes actionable injury, the limited partner is liable to the person injured.[15]
2. *Unfulfilled promise to contribute* — If a limited partner makes an enforceable promise to contribute to the limited partnership, the limited partner is liable to the partnership on that promise.[16]
3. *Wrongfully returned contributions* — If the limited partnership has returned all or part of a limited partner's contribution and the return violated the partnership agreement or left the partnership insolvent, then for six years afterwards the limited partner is liable to the partnership for the amount of the wrongful return.[17]
4. *Properly returned contributions* — If (a) the limited partnership has returned all or part of a limited partner's contribution without violating the partnership agreement and without leaving the partnership insolvent, and (b) the limited partnership cannot pay creditors "who extended credit to the limited partnership during the period the contribution was held by the partnership," then for one year after the return the limited partner is liable to the partnership

12. RULPA §201(b).

13. Compare the mixed entity/aggregate nature of a general partnership, discussed in section 7.2.7.

14. RULPA §403(b).

15. Compare section 4.2.3 (agent liable for tortious conduct).

16. RULPA §502(b). For an explanation of partner contributions, see section 8.6.

17. RULPA §§608(b) (stating the general rule) and 607 (prohibiting distributions that leave the limited partnership effectively insolvent).

for whatever amount of the returned contribution is necessary to pay those creditors.[18]

5. *Use of limited partner's name* — If a limited partner allows its name to be used in the name of the limited partnership and a third party extends credit to the partnership without knowing that the limited partner is not a general partner, then the limited partner is liable to that third party on the transaction as if the limited partner were a general partner.[19]
6. *Mistaken belief in limited partner status* — If (a) a person makes a contribution to an enterprise, believing in good faith that the contribution is made as a limited partner, but (b) either no limited partnership exists or the certificate of limited partnership erroneously identifies the person as a general partner, and (c) when the person learns of the problem, the person either formally withdraws from the enterprise or has the certificate corrected, then the person is not categorically liable as a general partner in the enterprise. However, if before the person takes corrective action a third party transacts business with the enterprise, believing in good faith that the person is a general partner, then the person is liable on that transaction as if a general partner.[20]
7. *Participation in control* — If (a) a limited partner "participates in the control of the business" of the limited partnership, (b) that conduct causes a third party to reasonably believe that the limited partner is a general partner, and (c) with that belief the third party transacts business with the limited partnership, then the limited partner is liable to the third party as if a general partner.

The last-mentioned rule has been the most litigated. Under both ULPA and the 1976 version of RULPA, it was impossible to draw any bright line or find any safe harbors for limited partner conduct. The current version of RULPA contains a lengthy list of activities that do not constitute participating in control. The list includes not only specific items (e.g., being an agent or employee of the partnership,[21] acting as a consultant to the general partner[22]) but also a very general provision that protects any right of control granted to the limited partners by the partnership agreement.[23]

---

18. RULPA §§608(a) (stating the general rule) and 607 (prohibiting distributions that leave the limited partnership effectively insolvent).

19. RULPA §303(d). This rule does not apply if the limited partner's name is the same as a general partner's or if the limited partnership had used the name before the limited partner became a limited partner.

20. RULPA §304(b).

21. RULPA §303(b)(1).

22. RULPA §303(b)(2).

23. RULPA §303(b)(6)(ix).

Example: Liza persuades Joel to invest $10,000 in a business. The business is supposedly a limited partnership, with Liza as the general partner and Joel as the limited partner. Joel makes the investment, but Liza does not file any certificate of limited partnership. Subsequently, Danny sells 5,000 widgets to the business, having been assured by Liza that "the company is good for it and besides both Joel and I are on the hook as general partners." When Joel later learns of Liza's misstatement, he immediately confronts her and causes her to file a proper certificate of limited partnership. Joel is nonetheless liable to Danny as a general partner. (Circumstance #6)

Example: Resa is the sole general partner of a limited partnership, but she relies heavily on the services of Neil, who is both a limited partner and the partnership's purchasing manager. In his capacity as purchasing manager Neil causes the partnership to buy 500,000 widgets from Maya. The contract price is large, and it seems to Maya that Neil has complete discretion in the matter. Maya accordingly assumes that Neil is a general partner. The limited partnership has filed a certificate of limited partnership, and Neil is not listed as a general partner. No matter how reasonable Maya's assumption, Neil is not personally liable on the widget transaction. He was acting as an employee of the partnership and is therefore within one of the safe harbors provided by RULPA. (Circumstance #7)

§12.1.5 Management

The default management structure of a limited partnership is easily described. The general partners manage the business, and only the general partners have the power *qua* partners to bind the partnership.[24] Because of their management role, general partners owe fiduciary duties of loyalty and care to the partnership.

Limited partners are essentially passive. They do have the right to information about the partnership business,[25] may have the opportunity to consent to avoid dissolution,[26] and in extraordinary circumstances can bring derivative suits to assert partnership claims against the general partners.[27]

---

24. Limited partners may have the power to bind the partnership as a matter of agency law. See Chapters Two and Three.

25. RULPA §305.

26. See section 12.1.7.

27. RULPA §§1001-1004. In a derivative suit, a limited partner asserts standing to enforce the partnership's rights. Protecting the partnership's rights — whether by litigation or otherwise — is a management matter and therefore ordinarily the province of the general partners. Derivative plaintiffs typically assert, however, that the general partners cannot be trusted to protect the partnership's interests because the general partners are or will be defendants.

They do not, however, have any say in the ordinary operations of the partnership.

The partnership agreement can enlarge the management role of the limited partners and can also shape the management prerogatives and responsibilities of the general partners. For example, some limited partnership agreements give the limited partners the right to remove the general partners.

§12.1.6 *Profit and Loss Sharing*

RULPA's default rules on profit and loss sharing differ both structurally and substantively from the UPA rule. The UPA provides simply that the partners share profits per capita and losses according to profit share.[28] RULPA addresses the *allocation* of profits and losses (which is important for bookkeeping and tax purposes) separately from the sharing of actual *distributions*. However, the default rule is the same under both rubrics. Subject to the partnership agreement, profits and losses are allocated and distributions are shared in proportion to "the value . . . of contributions made by each partner to the extent they have been received by the partnership and have not been returned."[29]

> ***Example:*** Ann, Bennett, Ken, and Roberta are partners in a limited partnership. Ann and Roberta are the general partners, each having contributed $10,000. Bennett and Ken, the limited partners, contributed $50,000 and $40,000, respectively. Ken subsequently received $10,000 as a partial return of his contribution. The partnership agreement provides that Ann and Roberta will each receive $50,000 per year as a management fee but says nothing about profits, losses, and distributions. The partnership will therefore allocate profits and losses and make distributions according to the following percentages:

Ann	10%
Bennett	50%
Ken	30%
Roberta	10%

§12.1.7 *Partner Dissociation and Partnership Dissolution*

In a general partnership, each partner has the power to dissociate at any time. Any dissociation inevitably causes dissolution and immediately puts the partnership into winding up. As part of winding up, absent a contrary agreement

28. UPA §18(a). See section 8.3.1.

29. The same language appears in RULPA §§503 (sharing of profits and losses) and 504 (sharing of distributions).

each partner has the right to be paid the value of its interest in the partnership.[30] A general partner in a limited partnership also has the power to "withdraw" at any time,[31] but that withdrawal does not necessarily cause dissolution. The limited partnership can avoid dissolution if either (1) the partnership has at least one remaining general partner, the partnership agreement allows the remaining general partners to continue the partnership, and the remaining general partners do so, or (2) within 90 days after the withdrawal, *all* the remaining partners (limited as well as general) agree in writing to continue the partnership.[32]

If a general partner's withdrawal does result in dissolution, the consequences are comparable to the dissolution of a general partnership. If the partnership avoids dissolution, the dissociated general partner has a right, subject to the partnership agreement, to be paid "within a reasonable time after withdrawal, the fair value of his [or her] interest in the limited partnership."[33] A limited partnership agreement could conceivably freeze in the interest of a general partner who withdraws in breach of the partnership agreement.[34] In any event, if the withdrawal breached the partnership agreement, the payout amount is subject to any damages caused by the breach.[35]

In contrast to general partners, limited partners have no omnipresent power to dissociate. Whether they ever have that power depends on whether the partnership agreement states in writing a particular term for the partnership and whether the agreement provides in writing for limited partner withdrawal. If the partnership agreement does neither, then a limited partner can withdraw by giving at least six months written notice to each general partner.[36] If the partnership agreement states a particular term, then a limited partner can withdraw only if allowed by the agreement. If the partnership agreement provides for limited partner withdrawal, then — regardless of whether the agreement states a particular term — a limited partner can withdraw only as provided in the agreement. In tabular form:

30. For a detailed discussion of partner dissociation and partnership dissolution in a general partnership, see Chapter Eleven.

31. RULPA §602. RULPA uses the term "withdrawal" to refer to partner dissociation. RULPA §402.

32. RULPA §801(4). If there is no remaining general partner, then the limited partners must also consent to appoint at least one new general partner. Id.

33. RULPA §604 (brackets in the original).

34. Compare UPA §38(2) (if a partner wrongfully dissolves a general partnership, the remaining partners may delay that partner's payout and use the resources in a successor partnership). For a discussion of UPA §38(2), see section 11.4.5.

35. RULPA §602.

36. RULPA §603. This situation seems unlikely to occur, since RULPA §201(a)(4) requires the certificate of limited partnership to state a definite term. In light of RULPA §603, the term will be repeated in most limited partnership agreements.

	Limited Partnership Agreement Provides for Limited Partner Withdrawal	*Limited Partnership Agreement Does Not Provide for Limited Partner Withdrawal*
Limited Partnership Agreement Provides for Particular Term for Partnership	limited partner can withdraw only as provided in partnership agreement	limited partner cannot withdraw
Limited Partnership Agreement Does Not Provide for Particular Term for Partnership	limited partner can withdraw only as provided in partnership agreement	limited partner can withdraw on six months' written notice.

The withdrawal of a limited partner does not cause or even threaten dissolution.[37] A limited partner who withdraws does have the right to be paid out within a reasonable time, unless the partnership agreement provides otherwise.[38]

§12.2 Limited Liability Companies[39]

§12.2.1 The Advent of Limited Liability Companies

The limited liability company is a new, hybrid form of business entity that combines the liability shield of a corporation with the federal tax classification of a partnership.[40] The shield protects a limited liability company's owners (called "members") from being personally liable for the business's debts,[41] and the classification provides the advantages of pass-through taxation.[42]

---

37. RULPA §801 (stating causes of dissolution and not mentioning the withdrawal of a limited partner). The partnership agreement could make a limited partner's withdrawal a cause of dissolution. See RULPA §801(2) (allowing the partnership agreement to specify additional events that cause dissolution).

38. RULPA §604.

39. This section on limited liability companies is drawn from Bishop & Kleinberger, Limited Liability Companies: Tax and Business Law ¶1.01 (1994).

40. Tax status under *state* law varies from state to state.

41. As with an other liability shield, the LLC shield relates only to liability asserted on account of ownership status, that is, to claims that merely being an LLC member makes one personally liable for the LLC's obligations. Such liability is the hallmark of being a general partner, both in an ordinary general partnership and in a limited partnership. See sections 7.3 and 12.1.4. The LLC shield does not protect partners from direct liability on account of their own, individual actions. See the discussion in section 4.2.

42. For a brief discussion of these benefits, see section 7.3.2. For a more detailed treatment, see Bishop & Kleinberger, supra note 39, ¶1.01[2].

A creature of state law, each limited liability company is organized under an "enabling" statute. The enabling statute authorizes creation of the company, gives the company a legal existence separate from its members, shields those members from personal liability, governs the company's operations, and controls how and when the company comes to an end.

Federal tax regulations account for the limited liability company's partnership tax status. Enabling statutes have been crafted to meet the "Kintner" regulations, which (1) analyze the fundamental attributes of corporations and partnerships according to state law, and (2) identify four essential corporate characteristics to be used in determining whether unincorporated business organizations are to be taxed as corporations or partnerships. The four essentially corporate characteristics are: limited liability, continuity of life, free transferability of ownership interests, and centralized management. Properly structured, a limited liability company will lack at least two of these four characteristics and will accordingly be classified as a partnership for federal tax purposes.

Wyoming enacted the first LLC enabling act in 1977, but it took the Internal Revenue Service more than ten years to formally bless the Wyoming approach. In Rev. Ruling 88-76[43] the Service announced that Wyoming LLCs would be taxed as partnerships and made clear that a business organization could have partnership tax status even though none of the business's owners faced partner-like personal liability.

Rev. Ruling 88-76 started a bandwagon. Before the ruling only Florida had followed Wyoming in enacting LLC legislation.[44] In the first three years after the ruling six states enacted statutes. In the next year, another ten states followed suit. Since then, the momentum has increased. As of September 1994, 46 states and the District of Columbia have adopted enabling statutes, and the others all have legislation pending. The American Bar Association is considering a Prototype LLC Act, and the National Conference of Commissioners of Uniform State Laws has approved a uniform Act. The Service has followed its seminal Wyoming ruling with more than 15 other revenue rulings and a myriad of private letter rulings.

§12.2.2 *The Basic Structure of a Limited Liability Company*

The allure of a limited liability company lies in its unique combination of liability shield and federal tax status. Each enabling statute can create an LLC liability shield as a matter of state law, but partnership tax status requires compliance with federal tax classification regulations. Indeed, all enabling

43. 1988-2 C.B. 360.

44. Florida enacted a statute in 1982.

statutes have been drafted with an eye on the tax classification regulations and use essentially the same approach on tax-sensitive attributes. All enabling statutes provide a corporate-like liability shield, which means that, at least in the default mode, they must negate at least two of the three remaining corporate characteristics. Virtually all enabling statutes negate the attributes of continuity of life and free transferability of ownership interests. Most also negate centralized management.

Enabling statutes also resemble each other in their approach to ownership interests; they use a capital structure modelled on partnership law. Nothing in the tax classification regulations expressly requires this approach, but a more corporate concept (i.e., stock) might cause "look and feel" worries — that is, concerns that an entity with stock looks too much like a corporation to be classified as a partnership.[45]

Under most enabling statutes the rules on entity termination, membership transfer, management, and capital structure can be reshaped by member agreement, but individual limited liability companies nonetheless exhibit similarities comparable to the pattern set by the enabling statutes themselves. The same tax classification concerns that shaped the enabling statutes limit the extent of special tailoring. Varying the default rules too much will cost a limited liability company its partnership tax classification. As a result, all limited liability companies have similarities with respect to entity termination rules and restrictions on assignment of ownership rights. To a lesser extent, they have similar approaches to management and capital structure. The similarities reflect the paradigmatic approach of enabling statutes, which in turn reflects the strictures of the Treasury's tax classification scheme.

Entity termination. To avoid the corporate characteristic of continuity of life, enabling statutes amalgamate aspects of general and limited partnership law. At least in the default mode, any member's dissociation from the entity for any reason (e.g., death, resignation, sale of complete interest) threatens the entity with dissolution. The entity can avoid dissolution only if the requisite quantum of remaining members consent to continue the business. Some statutes require unanimous consent, while others make unanimous consent the default rule. Many statutes also set a limit on the number of years a limited liability company may exist, although the trend is to the contrary.

Assignability of ownership rights. To avoid the corporate characteristic of free transferability of ownership interests, enabling statutes again follow an approach borrowed from state partnership law. LLC members may assign

---

45. A more prosaic explanation is also possible. LLC statutory provisions on transferability restrictions and management structure borrow heavily from state partnership law. Use of the partnership approach to capital structure may therefore have been a matter of convenience or "thematic coherence" or both.

their economic rights (i.e., the right to receive distributions), but must have the consent of the other members to effectively assign their entire interest (including the right to participate in management).[46] On this issue too, some statutes require unanimous consent, while others make unanimous consent the default rule.

Management structure. Most enabling statutes provide for decentralized management, that is, management by members. A few provide for management by managers. Under all but the Colorado enabling statute, the management structure is a default rule.

Capital structure. All enabling statutes follow the partnership law approach to conceptualizing capital structure. Ownership interests are not reflected in shares, but rather in membership interests. At least under the default rules, the size of an interest is not reflected in numbers of units[47] (as is the case with shares), but rather in the value of contributions the owner of the interest has made to the limited liability company. Enabling statutes typically require each limited liability company to maintain records reflecting the value of each membership interest but otherwise provide no default rules for structuring the interests. A few enabling statutes expressly bifurcate membership interests into financial rights and governance rights, and a number of statutes note that a membership interest is personal property. The enabling statutes differ as to how, in the default mode, capital contributions affect a member's voting power and right to share profits, losses, and distributions.

§12.3 Registered Limited Liability Partnerships[48]

§12.3.1 Nature of an LLP

Limited liability partnerships (often called registered limited liability partnerships or "LLPs") are the newest development inspired by the Service's tax classification regulations. Made possible by amendments to various state versions of the UPA, a limited liability partnership is a general partnership with a partial liability shield attached.[49] To erect the shield the partnership files a

46. Most enabling statutes deal with this issue under the rubric of admitting a new member.

47. Nothing in any enabling statute prevents organizers or owners from replacing the default rules and measuring membership interests in terms of units. Organizers of limited partnerships often take that approach.

48. This section on limited liability partnerships is drawn from Bishop & Kleinberger, Limited Liability Companies: Tax and Business Law ¶1.03 (1994).

49. The first generation of LLP statutes protect against liability arising in tort but not in contract. See section 12.3.2.

registration with a public official or office designated by statute and pays an annual registration fee. Despite the liability shield, the LLP is classified for federal tax purposes as a partnership.[50]

The registration discloses information about the partnership and its partners, and disclosure requirements vary from statute to statute. All statutes require disclosure of the partnership's name and principal place of business. Some statutes also require (1) the address of the registered office in the state, (2) the number of partners, (3) a brief description of the partnership business, (4) a statement that the partnership is applying for status as a limited liability partnership, (5) a statement that the specified registered agent has authority to serve in that capacity, (6) a statement that the partnership will maintain insurance, (7) the purpose for which the partnership exists, (8) the name of the registered agent, and (9) an acknowledgment that LLP status can expire.

The registration fee also varies. In Minnesota, for example, the fee is $135 per year. In Delaware, the fee is $100 *per partner* per year. In Texas, the fee is $100 *per partner* the first year and $200 *per partner* per year for each renewal.

As of September 1994, nearly 15 states had amended their version of the UPA to provide for limited liability partnerships.

§12.3.2 *Nature of the LLP Shield*

As with any other liability shield, the LLP shield relates only to liability asserted on account of ownership status, that is, to claims that merely being a partner makes one personally liable for partnership obligations. Such liability is the hallmark of being a general partner, both in an ordinary general partnership and in a limited partnership.[51]

The shield and registration requirements. The LLP shield depends on the general partnership having a proper LLP registration in effect. The shield applies only to claims that arise or accrue while the registration is in effect, which means that converting an ordinary general partnership to a limited liability partnership has no effect on claims that arose or accrued before the shield took effect. Moreover, failing to renew an LLP registration will cause the shield to lapse, leaving partners exposed to personal liability for claims that arise or accrue afterwards. No other shield faces this latter risk. The corporate shield, the LLC shield and the shield for limited partners all pre-

---

50. This result follows from the tax classification regulations discussed in section 12.2.2.

51. See sections 7.3 and 12.1.4. The LLP shield does not protect partners from direct liability on account of their own, individual actions. See the discussion in section 4.2.

suppose *initial* compliance with filing requirements. There is, however, no risk that a single failure to refile will eliminate the shield.

The shield's coverage. The first generation of LLP statutes provide only a partial shield, protecting partners from personal liability for partnership obligations arising in tort but not in contract. Viewed from a policy perspective, this is a curious approach. A shield limits the recourse of those harmed by a business and is most defensible as to victims who could have averted the shield by contract. Such contracting out occurs regularly with regard to the ordinary business debts of start up enterprises. If the enterprise is a corporation or limited liability company, major creditors often require the shareholders or members to provide personal guarantees.

This approach is hardly likely, however, for tort claims. The typical tort victim has no preexisting contractual relationship with the business, so there is no occasion to contemplate contracting out. Consider, for example, a limited liability partnership that owns an apartment building and fails to properly maintain the roof. During a windstorm, a piece of roofing materials blows off the roof and injures a passerby. Contracting out from the shield was never a possibility.[52]

The half-way shield is also curious from a practical perspective. Limited liability partnerships are of great interest to professional firms, and the tort protection seems almost targeted at protecting professionals from vicarious liability for malpractice. In some jurisdictions, however, malpractice claims sound in contract as well as tort.

One recent LLP statute has abandoned the half-way approach. The Minnesota LLP provisions establish a full, corporate-like shield.[53]

Effect of dissolution and business continuation. General partnerships are the most dissolvable of business entities. The dissociation of any partner causes dissolution.[54] However, few LLP statutes expressly contemplate the effect of dissolution on a limited liability partnership's shield. Presumably, since dissolution does not end the entity,[55] the shield remains in effect through the end of winding up.

52. There is one category of tort that does occur within the context of a preexisting relationship — professional malpractice. However, contracting out is almost as implausible in these situations as in the absence of preexisting relationships. A professional relationship by its nature induces and requires the client to repose trust and confidence in the professional. It would be extraordinary for a client to embark on such a relationship while contemplating professional misconduct and seeking to contract out of a liability shield.

53. 1994 Minn. Sess. Law Serv. ch. 539, §12 (1994), amending Minn. Stat. Ann. §323.14(2) (1994).

54. See section 11.1.1.

55. See section 11.1.1.

A more difficult problem arises if a dissolved partnership winds up its affairs by transferring its business to a successor partnership and that successor partnership fails to promptly file its own LLP registration. Such a failure seems quite likely, since many such transitions occur without the partners understanding that a new partnership has been formed. Only the Minnesota LLP statute addresses this issue, extending the dissolved partnership's shield to the successor partnership for the duration of the registration which was in effect for the dissolved partnership at the moment of dissolution.[56]

56. 1994 Minn. Sess. Law Serv. ch. 539, §12 (1994), to be codified at Minn. Stat. Ann. §323.14(4)(b).

Table of Statutes

Index

Index